A HISTORY OF THE
FLEET PRISON, LONDON

The Anatomy of the Fleet

A HISTORY OF THE
FLEET PRISON, LONDON

The Anatomy of the Fleet

Roger Lee Brown

Studies in British History
Volume 42

The Edwin Mellen Press
Lewiston/Queenston/Lampeter

Library of Congress Cataloging-in-Publication Data

Brown, Roger Lee.
    A history of the Fleet Prison, London : the anatomy of the Fleet /
Roger Lee Brown.
        p.   cm. -- (Studies in British history ; v. 42)
    Includes bibliographical references and index.
    ISBN 0-7734-8762-X (hardcover)
    1. Fleet Prison (London, England)--History.   I. Title.
II. Series.
HV9650.L72F533   1996
365'.94212--dc20
                                                                96-20614
                                                                CIP

This is volume 42 in the continuing series
Studies in British History
Volume 42 ISBN 0-7734-8762-X
SBH Series ISBN 0-88946-450-2

A CIP catalog record for this book is available from the British Library.

The Edwin Mellen Press   The Edwin Mellen Press
        Box 450   Box 67
Lewiston, New York   Queenston, Ontario
    USA 14092-0450   CANADA L0S 1L0

The Edwin Mellen Press, Ltd.
Lampeter, Dyfed, Wales
UNITED KINGDOM SA48 7DY

Printed in the United States of America

The exterior of the Fleet prison in the 1820s, by Thomas Shepherd. Collection of the author.

CONTENTS

ILLUSTRATIONS

Introduction

"The Fleet is a fair prison", *John Paston, 1465*[1]

The Fleet prison, whose site is still to be seen near the north eastern corner of Ludgate Circus, where the Congregational Memorial Hall once stood, had been regarded throughout its long history as one of the most important and substantial of the English prisons. William of Lancaster emphasised its importance by giving it to his brother Osbert in 1189, while he endeavoured to strengthen his hold on the kingdom during the absence of Richard 1.[2] Alexander Harris, warden of the prison in the 1620s, argued that the Fleet "is the king's own proper prison next in trust to his Tower of London, and as that is his fort in the east, so was this one in the west".[3] William Paget writing in 1749, described the Fleet as "the prince of prisons",[4] an assertion that few other writers of the eighteenth century cared to dispute; many agreeing with Edward Hatton that because of its amenities and "pleasantness" it was "preferred before most other prisons".[5] The prison's literary associations, from Falstaff to Mr Pickwick, testify to this assertion.

By the beginning of the sixteenth century the Fleet was recognised as the prison for the courts of Common Pleas, Chancery, Exchequer, the Curia Regis, and of the Star Chamber.[6] After the abolition of this latter court in 1641 and through the decay in conciliar government, the prison became regarded mainly as a debtors' prison, although prisoners were still sent to it by the remaining courts and it was administered by the court of Common Pleas.

Although the prison did not close until 1842, it retained to the end a form of administration which dated back to medieval times. Holdsworth has argued, for example, that "in the eighteenth century the gaols were perhaps the most medieval institutions in England".[7] Almost until the closure of the prison it was still possible to sell, lease or mortgage the prison house and the office of warden, while prisoners were permitted such privileges as the open access of their friends to the prison and facilities enabling them to lease houses just outside the confines of the prison house. Nevertheless, from the late seventeenth century onwards the prison was an institution in decline. The office of warden had always been regarded as an office of profit, for the prisoners were not only expected to maintain themselves, but also to contribute towards the cost of the prison. This, of course, was the case with all medieval institutions. Throughout the latter history of the prison much concern was expressed about the wardens' ability to extract from their investment the maximum possible profit, by legitimate or illegitimate means. The abolition of the court of Star Chamber meant that its wealthy victims no longer graced the wardens' list of prisoners. This, together with the diminution in the number of long-term prisoners from the latter half of the eighteenth century and onwards, and the tighter regulation of the prison and its sources of profit as the result of innumerable parliamentary inquiries, meant that by the end of that century the prison was no longer such a profitable source of revenue to the warden as it had been previously. It was the Office of Works, for example, which finally paid for the rebuilding of the prison house in the 1770s, rather than the warden.

The 1729 parliamentary report was the first major government report on the English gaol system as a whole, although its final statements only applied to the three great London debt prisons. Though the report on the Fleet prison revealed much that disturbed society (and guilty consciences demanded the punishment of scapegoats), the inquiry revealed that the real problem lay not so much with individuals, but with the whole system of debt imprisonment. It was not until the end of that century that the humanitarian movement, led by such men as Howard, Neale, and others, endeavoured to alleviate the condition of prisoners in general, and to obtain some reform in the laws of debt imprisonment. The attempt may be noted in the 1792 report, which was an investigation into the laws of debt imprisonment, and in the two inquiries of 1814 and 1818. These, part of a wider concern about penal reform, revealed much that was disquieting about the Fleet and other such prisons. The 1814 report suggested considerable improvements. The next report of 1818, however, found face-saving clauses to prevent any radical change, and this was accepted by a complacent public. This change of heart was undoubtedly due to the fact that the Fleet prison was a privately run affair. If this meant that the warden and his officers would have to be compensated for any change in their position (at a time when the rights of property were rigorously respected), or that the Fleet, as a national prison, should be closed and replaced by another (or even taken over), the only source of appropriate funding was the Exchequer. The thought may not have escaped some, too, that the projected reforms in the law of imprisonment for debt, which would reduce the number of debtors and diminish the length of imprisonment, would cause such a decline in the finances of the Fleet prison that the warden would have little option but to close the prison. And so it proved to be.

This study records the history of the prison, and then endeavours to study its administration, the prisoners and their day-to-day life, and in a final section, their privileges. It concentrates on the latter part of its history because it is only for this period that some of the prison books and the printed accounts of the prison are available. Whenever possible reference is made to the sister prison of the Fleet, the King's Bench in Southwark, which enjoyed a similar administration and similar privileges.

Much of what is related will seem strange to those accustomed to modern penal practices and conditions. It must be remembered, however, that many of the privileges of the Fleet and its sister prison derived from the fact that their prisoners were debtors, whose bodies had been seized instead of their estates, and their custody entrusted to a person, rather than to a particular place. That person, the warden in the case of the Fleet, was responsible for the safe keeping of prisoners, and for the payment of the debts of an escaped prisoner. The wardens diligently maintained for many centuries that their office and the prison house were two separate entities, and that the prisoners were only lodged at the prison house for their, the wardens', greater convenience. It must also be remembered that imprisonment as a punishment is a nineteenth-century notion; previous to that date prisons were used to house those awaiting trial, transportation, corporal or other physical punishment, and debtors.

It must not be assumed that debtors were without resources of their own. If a minority entered the prison in a deliberate attempt to safeguard their estates from the hands of their creditors (thus allowing themselves considerable financial resources to ease their voluntary captivity), many more had made a conscious decision to enter the most comfortable and expensive prison in the kingdom via the writ of *habeas corpus*, rather than to pay their debts and thereafter live in poverty or by their wits. Better, they agreed, to live on a small income reasonably well inside a prison, than badly on little or nothing outside! In fact a large majority of the prisoners were able to live with some degree of comfort in the Fleet, certainly by the standards of their own age, either through their own resources, or by finances allowed them by their families, friends and creditors. Others were helped by the prison economy, in which they were enabled to let their prison rooms, act as servants within the prison, or use their craft or professional skills in the prison house or the *rules*. It is not surprising, therefore, that there was always a state of tension between the prison authorities and the creditors, who felt that the expense and privileges of this prison, in addition to the greater possibilities of escape, seriously undermined their position and the repayment of their just debts.

The term *imprisonment for debt* was almost synonymous with failure: the failure or refusal of a debtor to pay what he owed; the failure of the creditor to obtain it. While debt imprisonment seemed a harsh alternative, it was regarded as a necessary coercive force by those involved in the commercial life of the nation in order to back up the system of credit. Under such circumstances debt imprisonment served to encourage people to avoid falling into debt. Yet, as was so widely noted, this attitude failed to distinguish between the fraudulent debtor and the unfortunate victim of circumstances.

We must also note that the Fleet was a self-contained society. It could prove an attractive exercise to compare the social and administrative set-up of a nineteenth-century public school with the Fleet prison. Prison life could be very congenial, even if there were restrictions of movement. Many, technically able to be discharged, preferred to remain in this society, and had to be coerced out of it by being denied the use of their rooms.

The whole structure of the prison administration, with its few officers, mainly paid by the fees of office, demanded a large measure of co-operation from the prisoners themselves. Subject, it is true, to some restrictions, and to the oversight of the court of Common Pleas, it is not surprising that a semi-official prisoners' organisation developed which generally co-operated with the warden and his officers for the good administration of the prison and the welfare of its inhabitants. It was in the interests of both sides to do so. The warden needed the co-operation of his prisoners to keep the prison in good order, or else he would have to obtain another form of security which would considerably reduce the profitability of the prison. After Bambridge's ejection the termination of the warden's patent for bad conduct was like an Achilles' heel to each occupier of that office. The prisoners, on the other hand, were well aware that many of the privileges they enjoyed were available only through the good will of the warden, such as the day *rules* and the *rules* which allowed outside access, or the entry of family and friends into the prison house. The system appears to have worked well; so well in fact that it is generally only noted when those good relationships it endeavoured to foster broke down and conflict ensued. Frequently this occurred because of a general breakdown in the prison administration, or when a small group of highly articulate prisoners (always a danger in such a prison as the Fleet) were able to mount an effective resistance against the warden's government of the prison. When both factors were combined, as during the time of warden Harris in the 1620s or during Huggins's administration of the prison a century later, the situation became explosive, particularly when a new warden endeavoured to reassert the authority of his office.

Many of the Fleet prison's records were destroyed during the Great Fire of London or during the Gordon riots. A small selection, mainly from the latter part of the eighteenth century and thereafter, now comprise part of the prison records at the Public Record Office.[8] The surviving prison commitment books run from 1686 to 1842, and other documents relate to discharges, *habeas corpus* entries, fugitive and *rule* books. The Corporation of London Record Office at the Guildhall holds the debtors' lists and papers for the Fleet from 1736 to 1820. These were required by the various Insolvent Debtor Acts of the period, and the papers include a complete list of all the prisoners in the prison at a given date, together with new entries, discharges and admission to *rules* between that and a later date. These papers have been much drawn upon to provide the statistical tables in this book.[9]   Another major source of material for the history of the prison has come from the numerous inquiries into the administration of the prison. Alexander Harris's reply to the allegations made against him by his prisoners in the 1620s was published in 1879. The long dispute relating to Tilly, the warden in the 1690s, has been traced from the State Papers Domestic and the *Journal of the House of Commons*, while the controversy of the 1720s is detailed not only in a parliamentary report, but also in an account from the prisoners' side produced by their attorney, Mackay, and the trials of Huggins and Bambridge printed in Howell's *State Trials*. The reports of parliamentary inquiries of 1792, 1814, and 1818 have been noted already. The many reports on the Fleet and other prisons produced by independent observers such as Howard, Neale, and Smith, have yielded much information, as also have the various nineteenth-century guides to prison life published for the benefit of debt prisoners. I am indebted for some of my argument to an outstanding study of the King's Bench prison during the late eighteenth century by Joanna Innes.[10]

This study of the Fleet prison arose from my work on the Fleet marriages, which I thought at first were more closely identified with the eighteenth-century prison than proved to be the case. I express my gratitude for much help and advice to the late Professor T F Reddaway, the late Professor R B Pugh, the staff of the Public Record Office, the British Library, the Guildhall Library, and the County of London Record Office, and, above all, to my wife Phyllis, who has facilitated the gradual transformation of several files of notes, over a period of numerous years, into something which I trust may be of value to all those who share with me an interest in the underworld of eighteenth-century history.

NOTES

1   *The Paston Letters*, edited by James Gardner (Edinburgh 1910), III 40.

2   M B Honeybourne, "The Fleet and its Neighbourhood in Early and Medieval Times", *London Topographical Record*, XIX (1947) 22.

3   Harris*, p 23.

4   W Paget, *The Humours of the Fleet* (London 1749), p 13.

5   Edward Hatton, *A New View of London* (London 1708), II 745; Cf Wood*, p 15; *London in Miniature* [London 1755], p 96; and Strype's edition of Stow's *Survey* (London 1720), section B3, p 210.

6   See, for example, Honeybourne, "The Fleet", p 20. The other principal court, the King's Bench, had its own prison in Southwark.

7   William Holdsworth, *History of English Law* (London 1966), X 181.

8   A single exception is the admission register of 1565-7 at BL, Harl Ms 537, fols 14, 20. There is some confusion between the Fleet and King's Bench registers at the PRO. PRIS 10/17 relates to the King's Bench Prison and not to the Fleet.

9   The prisoners' petitions under the Insolvent Debtors' Acts are also available under the class-mark DS 15 from 1755 onwards.

10   Joanna Innes, "The King's Bench Prison in the late Eighteenth Century", in J Brewer and J Styles, *An Ungovernable People* (London, 1980), pp 250-98.

*   See short-title list on pages xv-xvi.

A diagram of the Fleet prison area in 1560, drawn by Gary Llewellyn from Ralph Agas's map of London. The prison is situated above Fleet Bridge.

Short Titles and Abbreviations used in the Footnotes and an Explanation of various Technical Terms used

SHORT TITLES AND ABBREVIATIONS

Berisford: John Berisford, *An Argument that it is Impossible for the Nation to be Rid of all the Grievances occasioned by the Marshall of the King's Bench and Warden of the Fleet without an Utter Extirpation of their Present Offices* (London 1699).

BL   British Library, London.

BLO   Bodleian Library, Oxford.

Cal SPD   Calendar of State Papers Domestic.

Cal TB   Calendar of Treasury Books.

Cal TP   Calendar of Treasury Papers.

CLRO   County of London Record Office, Guildhall, London.

Coll BL   *Fleet Prison: Collection of Newspaper Cuttings and Broadsides etc* (BL, pm 11633 h2).

Dobb   Clifford Dobb, unpublished Oxford B Litt thesis, 1952, *Life and Conditions in London Prisons, 1553-1643, with special reference to Contemporary Literature.*

GLL   Guildhall Library, London.

Harris   Alexander Harris, *The Oeconomy of the Fleete*, edited by Augustus Jessop,

Camden Society, NS XXV, 1879.

Howard	John Howard, *The State of the Prisons in England and Wales* (1st edition 1777, 2nd 1780, and 3rd 1784, all published at Warrington).
Howell	T B Howell, *A Complete Collection of State Trials*, vol XVII (London 1816).
Jnl H of C	*Journal of the House of Commons.*
Mackay	John Mackay, Sen, *A True State of the Proceedings of the Prisoners of the Fleet Prison, in order to the Redressing their grievances before the Court of Common Pleas* (London 1729).
PRO	Public Record Office, London.
PP	Parliamentary Papers.
Report 1729	*A Report of the Committee Appointed to Enquire into the State of the Gaols of this Kingdom relating to the Fleet Prison* (1729).
Report 1729 (KB)	*Ibid, relating to the King's Bench Prison* (1729).
Report 1729 (M)	*Ibid, relating to the Marshalsea Prison, and further relating to the Fleet Prison* (1729).
Report 1792	*The Report of the Committee Appointed to Enquire into the Practices and Effects of Imprisonment for Debt*, in Jnl H of C, XLVII, 640-71.
Report 1814	*Report of the Committee Appointed to Enquire into the State of the King's Bench, Fleet and Marshalsea Prisons*, in PP 1814-15 [152)] 531-790.
Report 1818	*Report of the Commissioners Appointed to Enquire into the State, Conduct and Management of the Prison and Gaol of the Fleet*, in PP 1819 [109] XI 325, but paginated here according to the report.
Smith	William Smith, *State of the Gaols of London, Westminster and Southwark* (London 1776).
Sess P	Sessions Papers at CLRO.
Wood	Simon Wood, *Remarks on the Fleet Prison, or Lumber House for Men and Women* (London 1733).

AN EXPLANATION OF VARIOUS TECHNICAL TERMS USED

Common side: a more unpleasant part of the prison, where the prisoners in receipt of charity lived.

Day rules: the writ of day *rules* permitted a prisoner to leave the prison house for a whole day.

Fees had to be paid, security given for a safe return, and the prisoner, until the mid-eighteenth century, generally accompanied by a prison officer.

Execution process: this was the final process in debt imprisonment, and followed the mesne process. In it the debtor was imprisoned in his person, so that his body should satisfy his creditors as a substitute for the repayment of the debts he owed them.

Habeas corpus: this was a legal writ which required the body of a person to be brought before a judge. The more familiar use of it was to investigate the lawfulness of a person's imprisonment, but modifications of this writ enabled it to be used by prisoners who wished to transfer to the Fleet from other prisons, or vice versa. An earlier use permitted prisoners to leave the prison-house for a length of time on the giving of security for their safe imprisonment. The day *rules* was a modification of this practice.

King's (or Queen's) Bench prison, in Southwark, with the Fleet and Marshalsea prisons, was one of the three great debt prisons of the Kingdom. In many respects it was a sister prison to the Fleet. Its prisoners had very similar privileges to those enjoyed by the Fleet prisoners. Its chief officer was known as the Marshall.

Marriage, clandestine: these were irregular marriages, which, while they contravened the law of the church in one or more respects (that is, being performed without the prior publicity of banns or the obtaining of a licence, outside canonical hours, or solemnised other than within the parish church of one of the couples concerned), were still regarded as valid. During the seventeenth century various centres for their performance were established in London, including the Tower of London. After these were ended by ecclesiastical authority, the marriage trade concentrated on the Fleet prison, which was regarded as a privileged place, and outside the authority of the bishop of London. Legislation forced the clergy and others concerned in this trade to move out of the prison-house and its chapel, and into the prison *rules*. Here various houses were established as 'chapels', registers were obtained, and business commenced. At the height of their popularity, five to six thousand such marriages took place on an annual basis. Lord Hardwicke, noting the powerlessness of the ecclesiastical authorities to end this trade, with its many abuses and irregularities, introduced the Marriage Act of 1753 with the clear aim of ending these marriages. Lady day, 1754, saw the last of these Fleet marriages, but, by that date, their direct association with the prison was almost non-existent. An account of these marriages will be found in my article, "The Rise and Fall of the Fleet Marriages", in R B Outhwaite (ed), *Marriage and Society,* (London 1981), pp 117-36.

Master's side: this was the main area of the prison. Those who entered it paid a higher commitment fee than those on the common side. They were also required to pay chamber rent.

Mesne process: this was the primary process in debt imprisonment, by which the prisoner was imprisoned as a defendant in an action.

Rules: the *rules* was an area around the prison house, but outside it, in which prisoners who offered security for their safe imprisonment were permitted to reside. Allowed first as a privilege, it developed into a custom, and soon became an accepted right. For the purpose of distinguishing between this and the 'rules' noted below, this usage of the word is printed in italics.

Rules and regulations: the constitutions of the prison were revised in 1562. A further revision took place in 1729 as a result of the celebrated parliamentary inquiry into the prison of that year.

Throughout the work (save for the Appendices) the dates have been changed to new style where applicable and the quotations rendered into modern English spelling and capitalisation.

Prologue

"The most venerable of all English prisons" (Margery Bassett)

When the Fleet prison was rebuilt on its old site in 1670, after its destruction in the Great Fire of London, it had every right to claim for itself the title of the oldest prison in England, even though its origin was veiled in medieval obscurity.

Its name first occurs in a document of 1197. In that year Nathaniel de Leaveland claimed that the Fleet prison had been in the keeping of his family since the Norman conquest.[1] This claim was probably exaggerated, but it is reasonably clear that the Fleet prison was the same prison as that described by the title of "the gaol of London". This was first mentioned in 1130, and under that description the Fleet was granted to Osbert de Longchamp in 1189 by his brother William, bishop of Ely, who as Richard I's chancellor was endeavouring to strengthen his own hold on the country during his monarch's absence on crusade. Despite the subsequent fall of this scheming bishop, and the illegal nature of the grant, Osbert retained his position until 1197 when Nathaniel and his son's counter-claim to the wardenship of the prison was accepted. The use of the word *Fleet* in the title of the prison probably reflected the need to distinguish it from Newgate prison, established by 1188 as the county gaol for London.

It is noteworthy that the warden of the Fleet also had the custody of the palace of Westminster and the care of the Fleet bridge. This has led to the suggestion that the warden's main task was the safeguarding of this bridge, and thus the land route, between the palace of Westminster and the Tower of London. It is thus argued that the custody of the king's prisoners was incidental to this task, and that these prisoners were kept in a place from which the warden could also control the bridge. Although this is an attractive theory, it must be discarded in view of the fact that Nathaniel de Leaveland claimed the keepership of the palace in 1197 together with his son Robert, in the right of his paternal inheritance. His great-grandfather was probably Richard the Constable, who arrived in London with the Conqueror. However Nathaniel also claimed the prison for his son Robert, in that same year, but this time in the right of his wife, Desirea, who was presumably a member of the family of Ralph and Henry Arborarius (crossbow makers). They were former keepers of the gaol of London.[2] It appears, therefore, that these two offices came together by marriage and not by design or convenience.

These two offices were held by members of the de Leaveland family until the reign of Edward I. The Senche family held them between 1293 and 1361, and the Sapperton family from that date until 1461. In that year the *serjeanty* was disputed between Robert Worth and William Babington, both of whom had married into the Sapperton family. Worth established his claim in the right of his wife Elizabeth, but after his death the succession passed to another William Babington, and it remained in his family until 1558.[3] The line thus passed through several females. One of them was Joan, wife of Edmund le Cheyne. She is mentioned in an inquisition of 1332, taken after her death. This found that Joan had held the bailiwick of the king's palace, together with the payment of sixpence, and allowances of bread, wine, ale, kitchen dishes, and candles as one of the king's sergeants, during the time of the king's residence there, and after his departure the remaining fuel in the kitchen, litter (straw used as bedding) in the chambers, and hay in the stables. In addition Joan received eight pence yearly from every merchant with a stall in Westminster Hall, together with her own house and other tenements in the precinct of the palace. She also held the Fleet prison, with its garden and curtilege, of the king, together with a charge of sixpence per day from the sheriffs and two shillings and four pence from every prisoner committed to her safe custody.[4] These two offices of the prison and palace remained linked with each other until the abolition of the prison in 1842, when the custody of the palace was taken over by one of the commissioners of woods and works.

The majority of the keepers appear to have lived at their official residence at Westminster. The prison was governed by deputies. This applied as early as 1292.[5] One of them, William le Palmer, was concerned in a robbery at Westminster Abbey in 1303. Although he ostensibly lived with his wife at the prison, at the time of the robbery he was living at Westminster Palace with a "loose woman". Material taken in the robbery was found under his bed. William was subsequently hanged, and John Senche, warden in the right of his wife, Joan de Grandon, although not implicated in the robbery, had his office sequestrated. A year later it was restored to him and by 1311-12 one Richard Abbot was serving as his deputy at Westminster, if not at the Fleet.[6]

The building, in the words of R B Pugh, was "an altogether exceptional building". It was probably built in stone, indicating the security thought necessary for the king's prisoners. Between 1156-1207 substantial sums of money were spent on the prison, indicating a major reconstruction. One hundred and twenty-eight pounds was paid by the Exchequer between 1189 and 1209 for this work, which is a large amount compared to the cost of thirty-six pounds for the building of Newgate prison in 1188.[7] Further rebuilding took place in 1335. This time the work was undertaken by the then warden at his own cost, a precedent carefully noted by the crown, which endeavoured on further occasions to place the liability of repair onto the warden, though not always successfully. Thus in 1355, twenty years after its supposed rebuilding, the warden was required to repair the gaol buildings which were then described as fallen and wasted.[8]

The prison was surrounded by a moat. This was dug or re-dug in 1335 to a width of ten feet. The moat enclosed not only the prison but also its close. This was about an acre in extent and enclosed various buildings.[9] Twenty years later in 1355 the moat and its stream were so foul that even a medieval writer complained of "the imperfection of the air, and the abominable stench". Investigation revealed that not only had the moat been encroached upon, but that several sewers and three tanneries discharged their contents into it, and eleven latrines had been illegally built over it. The result was that those imprisoned in the Fleet were "often affected with various diseases and grievous maladies, not without serious peril unto them".[10]

A whole variety of prisoners entered this prison. At first, because it also served as the county gaol for London before Newgate was built, criminals and felons, as well as civil prisoners, would have entered it. By the thirteenth century the Fleet was used more for the king's prisoners: those who had trespassed in the king's parks and forests; those guilty of contempt or of frustrating the courts of justice, such as jurors who made false oaths, as well as for the less dangerous political prisoners. This meant that the Fleet prison was being increasingly regarded as the prison for the courts of Common Pleas and Exchequer, both based at Westminster, unlike the peripatetic King's Bench, so that from the 1230s onwards it was considered to be the prison for the king's debtors. By the late fourteenth century it was used by the king's Council and by the court of Chancery as well.[11] Thomas Asthall, one of the chamberlains for north Wales, was typical of many prisoners held at the Fleet. Failing to make up the deficiencies in his account, he was imprisoned there in 1312. He remained in the Fleet, save for one short interval, until 1331, when his arrears were pardoned.[12]

A clause in a statute enacted in 1352 placed common creditors in the same position as the crown. This allowed such men to imprison their debtors' bodies until the debt had been settled. From this statute all imprisonment for debt is derived and established.[13] Those debtors whose creditors removed their suits to the court of Exchequer, or those debtors who desired the comfort and freedom of the Fleet, and so declared themselves crown debtors by a legal fiction, also entered this gaol. It thus became known as a debtors' prison.

Much comfort was available to those who possessed the necessary money. Food and wine could be sent in from the outside, and there was the privilege of being allowed to go outside the prison "abroad". Many men found themselves able to come to terms with their gaolers, who thereby permitted them all kinds of liberties. Matthew of the Exchequer, imprisoned for misconduct in 1291, was allowed to go to a Christmas dinner at a friend's house, accompanied by a keeper. A few days later he was permitted to attend the Carmelite church and the king's court at Westminster. As a result of this freedom Matthew found himself in the Tower, the deputy warden was imprisoned in Newgate, and the warden lost the custody of the prison. The crown clearly regarded these "wanderings abroad" in the same light as escapes.[14] This was not the only such "escape". Indeed, the situation became sufficiently serious for the enactment of a statute of 1377 which endeavoured to regulate these practices.[15] Its preamble stated that prisoners had been permitted to leave the gaols for days and nights together, and even though they had provided securities for their safe return, and/or were in the custody of a keeper, they could not "be readily restored". The statute provided that prisoners could not leave the prison in future unless they had satisfied their plaintiff's demands. It also prohibited prisoners describing themselves as crown debtors in order to gain admittance to the Fleet, and thus obtain its privileges of egress. Any creditor whose prisoner was permitted such admittance and liberty by the warden, could bring an action for debt against him, while the warden was also liable to lose his office. R B Pugh suggests that this statute was probably caused by an incident of the previous year. In this a man, convicted and fined for rape, refused to pay the fine, and was outlawed. He borrowed some money from an auditor in the Exchequer, refused to repay, and was thus imprisoned in the Fleet. He then made arrangements with the warden which permitted him to be released during the daylight hours in order to continue his previous way of life, so regarding the Fleet almost as a form of sanctuary, and thus escaping the consequences of his first conviction.[16]

With open access to the prison and such privileges of egress, escapes were frequent. In 1342, for example, ninety-one indicted persons were missing from the King's Bench prison. Escapes became so frequent that later statutes for debt obliged the warden to answer to the creditors for the debts of an escaped prisoner.[17] Furthermore the prison officials were punished for allowing or condoning escapes. Richard de Flete, a deputy warden, was committed as a prisoner to his own prison for allowing an escape in 1361, while Roger Sapperton, the warden, held responsible for an escape in 1378 which had been permitted by another deputy, was required to pay a fine of forty shillings before being restored to his office as warden.[17]

****

Thomas Babington, described as of Kidlington, Oxfordshire, esquire, and his son and heir William, obtained a licence in 1558 which enabled them to grant to one John Heath of London, esquire, his heirs and assigns, the capital messuage, mansion and garden called *Le Flete,* all houses within and without the close, together with the office of keeper of the prison and of the prisoners, and the office of keeper of the palace of Westminster. Within a year John Heath conveyed these interests to Richard Tyrrell of Steventon End in Essex for a sum of four thousand pounds, calculated on the value of a lease of the prison for a period of ten to twelve years.[18] In fulfilment of this, the prison was leased at the extremely low annual rental of eighty pounds to one Henry Tyrrell, a relation of the new warden. As Richard Tyrrell died in 1566, leaving a young son, the offices were eventually sold to two brothers, Sir Henry Lello and John Eldred Lello of Ashton in Essex for the sum of eleven thousand pounds. Henry later bought his brother's share for the immense sum of eight thousand pounds. This share appears to have been the keepership of the palace.[19] Lello found the prison a profitable enterprise, and was able to lease it in the 1610s to one Anstowe for six hundred pounds per annum, though John Phillips had paid an annual charge of eight hundred pounds in 1603. In addition the warden was able to sublet the cellars of the prison, and other rents, at a sum of sixty pounds per annum. From these sums, however, the warden was expected to find the monies required to improve and repair the prison buildings.[20]

The cost of the prison to its various purchasers indicates not only its value and profit, but also the status of the prisoners sent there, in particular by the court of Star Chamber. A hint of the prison's reputation is indicated by the experience of Edward Underhill, who found himself before Queen Mary's Privy Council in 1553 charged with heretical opinions. The earl of Sussex wished him to be sent to the Fleet, but other members of the council preferred Newgate or the Marshalsea. Underhill himself requested to be sent to the Fleet, stating, "I have not offended. I am a gentleman as you know." His plea was in vain.[21] It was alleged in 1635 that the warden or his deputy was in constant attendance on this court "in order to receive their lordships' commands as there was occasion".[22]

To this prison, therefore, were committed numerous men who had defied the official religious or political policies of the court. Bishops Gardiner of Winchester and Bonner of London found themselves in the Fleet during the reign of Edward VI, while Bishop Hooper of Gloucester was admitted in 1553 for his opposition to the papal policy of Queen Mary. Fox the martyrologist allows us a considerable description of the prison and its conditions during this period. He alleged that though Bishop Hooper had paid the warden five pounds for the liberty of the prison (as opposed to strict confinement), he was confined to his chamber by the orders of Bishop Gardiner. However he was later allowed to come down to dinner and supper at the warden's table, but without speaking to any of his friends.

Warden Babington and his wife manufactured a quarrel with the bishop, particularly about the "wicked mass", and consequently Hooper was put in one of "the wards". Here he was required to sleep on a little bed of straw with a "rotting covering", placed in a vile and stinking chamber which lay between the prison midden and the ditch. The result was not only severe illness, but also the refusal of the warden to help the bishop, though he "mourned, called and cried for help", and had paid the fees required for a baron, twenty shillings per week. Hooper remained in the Fleet for eighteen months. He was later transferred to Oxford where he was burnt as a protestant heretic.[23]

Other prominent men who were imprisoned at the Fleet during this time included Lord Surrey the poet, from 1553 to 1555, who found the prison "a noisome place with a pestilent atmosphere"; William Herbert, earl of Pembroke, in 1601; Dr Donne, poet, and later dean of St Paul's,[24] and Lord Henry Howard. Sent to the archbishop of Canterbury's prison at Lambeth in 1572 from the Fleet, Howard wrote that he had more comfort in the Fleet, for the "access of my friends ... helped to pass away my weary time, but now I am restrained from all acquaintance. I rather crave open imprisonment in the Fleet than a kind of close keeping in the palace."[25] Many of the recusant gentry also found their way to this prison.[26]

The presence of these wealthy prisoners necessitated considerable improvements in the prison. New chambers were built for their reception, particularly between 1596 and 1604 when forty new chambers were built at a cost of nine hundred pounds.[27] They were needed. Alexander Harris, warden in the 1610s, reckoned that the number of lodgings in the prison had increased five-fold from the 1560s, and probably the number of prisoners in like measure.[28] The older prison appears to have been used for the common wards. Harris maintained these wards were over five hundred years old. Known as the Queen's, Baron's, and Boston's wards, each contained at least eight beds, the prisoners sleeping two to a bed. Their condition was described by Sir Arthur Ingram who had visited them in the course of a parliamentary inquiry into the prison. The prisoners "were kept so close that some of them could not in seven days receive their food. That the places are so loathsome as the committees had like to have been poisoned with the smell. That men of good fashion lay so many in a chamber that they could not spit but they must spit upon one another. That one had no bed but his head laid on a trunk, his body on a stool, and his legs on a block."[29]

Thomas Cranley was one of the prisoners who occupied these new chambers. They appear to have been built alongside Fleet Lane, where almost every house, declared Cranley, was filled with prisoners. His story is interesting. Walking on the leads of the prison, to offset "the tedious pursuit of idle time", he saw a woman below looking out of a window in Fleet Lane. With the help of a long pole, and leaning out of his own chamber window, he was able to place a letter through her window, and eventually spoke to her from the same position. Later he wrote that he was able to visit her by making use of the various privileges available to the prisoners.[30]

There were other facilities available for the prisoners, such as the prison garden, where they could play bowls, a green having been laid out for this purpose. The water poet, John Taylor, thus wrote in his *The Praise and Vertue of a Jayle and Jaylers*:

> Since Richard's reign the first, the Fleet hath been
> A prison, as upon records is seen,
> For lodgings and for bowling there's large space.[31]

On Christmas day 1523 the warden joined his prisoners in various games and festivities, while at a later date warden Babington acted as "master de misrule", during which a prisoner was killed. He received a royal pardon.[32] There is no reason to assume that these games were isolated incidents.

Many of the new prisoners were articulate and well connected. It is not surprising, therefore, that they should have obtained an agreement about the fees and rules of the prison, in order to remove any uncertainties. Neither is it surprising that the group of prisoners who assisted in this work should have included the deprived bishop of Chester and the deprived dean of St Paul's, or that the fees were graded downwards from the high dignities of dukes and archbishops.[33]

The commitment fee, as established by this table, was £21.10s. for dukes and archbishops, who also paid £3.6s.8d. for their weekly commons. Passing through the ranks of earls, lords spiritual and temporal, the table descended to knights and doctors of law and divinity, who paid £5 for their commitment fee and

18s.6d. for their more meagre commons; esquires and gentlemen who had the ordinary commons of the parlour paid £3.6s.8d. and 10s. respectively; yeomen or any other person who had half commons £1.14s.4d. and 5s., while a poor man in the wards, who shared in the prison charities but had no "diet" paid merely an entry fee of 7s. 4d. Additional fees were charged for taking prisoners to and from the courts, for the liberty of the prison, as well as for discharge. In many cases these fees served as a respectable cloak for the practice of placing a new prisoner in the worst possible accommodation in the expectation that he would more readily pay for something better.

The prisoners were expected to pay these board or commons charges, even if they obtained their food from outside the prison. In 1592 the Privy Council sent a list of the diet to be given to the recusant prisoners imprisoned at Ely and Wisbech. For this purpose it chose the parlour commons of the Fleet, the cost of which was ten shillings per week. The weekly diet consisted of a bone of meat with broth, "bone beef a piece", roasted veal or a breast of "els", one capon, as much bread as required, a quart of wine claret and small beer, together with two dishes of butter and three good fishes of fresh fish "as the market will serve".[34] In spite of such a luxurious diet many of the Fleet prisoners preferred to obtain their food from sources outside the prison, and thus frequently disputed with the warden about his claim to receive from them their weekly commons money. John Stow records one such dispute of 1586. It appears that the warden had farmed out the victualling and lodging of the prison to one John Harvey, and had let the prison to a deputy, Joachim Newport. Regarded as poor men, and thus as men "greedy of gain" who lived by bribery and extortion, complaint was made that they introduced new customs and payments in order to gain more income from the prison, and confined any prisoner who complained, "nor permitting their friends to come unto them". And, it was claimed in addition, that "to do these wrongs with the utmost secrecy, [they] made away with the book" of prison rules and constitutions. The petitioners thus requested that the council should examine Harvey and Newport separately, so that they could "have no conference together".[35]

Some redress was given at this time, but seven years later the prisoners preferred a bill in parliament for the "reformation of the Fleet". They claimed that the deputy warden, still Joachim Newport, did all he could to prevent this bill.

This was hardly surprising, for his prisoners accused him in twenty-eight articles of all kinds of misdemeanours, including murder.[36]

It was not always the prisoners who complained. In 1597-8 the deputy warden, George Reynell, complained to the court of Whitehall about the activities of a small group of his prisoners. They had brought an exhibition against him in the court of Exchequer, alleging that he had extorted money from them. This they could not prove and so the warden was exonerated from these charges. The problem lay in the interpretation of the prison rules. The court, however, having taken advice from a former deputy warden, Mr Ausley, agreed with the warden's interpretation that the prisoners were required to victual themselves upon the warden's provision, provided that these "victuals" were sold at such prices as were common within the city of London, unless they made an agreement with him. It was also agreed that those who entered the prison and were unable to meet the cost of the parlour and the hall commons, but could not take part in the charity box, were to be allowed to share a bed and a chamber, and should "agree with the warden for the same". Those who had a share in the charity box, and who required "more ease than for the same is appointed", could make similar agreements. The cost of a bed and chamber for those paying for the parlour commons was agreed to be 2s. 4d. weekly, and 14d. for those on the hall commons, "lying like prisoners two in a bed together".[37] These interpretations were later incorporated into the prison rules, but the hope that they would take away all "ambiguities" and "be a better explanation of the same" proved groundless.[38]

A further and far more serious dispute arose in the 1610s. The title of a pamphlet occasioned by it indicates its extent and the areas of dispute:

> *A brief collection of some part of the exactations, extortions, oppressions, tyrannies, and excesses... towards prisoners, done by Alexander Harris, warden of the Fleet, in his four years misgovernment, to be proved by oaths and other testimonies.*

Its writer accused Harris of murder, in so far as he allowed two prisoners of known hostility to each other to occupy the same chamber: "he kept them together till one murdered the other". A list of nineteen charges made against Harris included felony, robbery, infidelity or false imprisonment, detaining prisoners who had been discharged, close imprisonment of many without authority (often for the purpose of extortion), detaining the goods of prisoners, starving prisoners in close confinement, robbing the poor in the prison, taking the fees of his servants, and using blank warrants to seize "his majesty's subjects" and forcing them to give bonds to be his prisoners. It was also alleged, in terms soon to become familiar, that he demanded chamber fees of eight or even twenty shillings per week, without bedding, whereas the set fee was two shillings and four pence with bedding. He even required fees, it was claimed, for those lodging in the common ward. Charging far more for meat, drink and coals than the market allowed, he continued to charge for commons when men obtained theirs from other sources. Those allowed abroad "by the king's writ" were still required to pay their chamber rent and diet, and Harris demanded bribes from these men before he would allow them such liberty. The warden's "worthy instruments", namely the clerk, porter and other prison officials, were also accused of similar extortions. To stress that such matters were not only against the law of England, but also offended divine law, the theologians amongst the prisoners incorporated Proverbs 1.19 into their petition, "such is the way of every one that is greedy of gain, which taketh away the life of the owners thereof."

Similar complaints of Harris's "hard and unchristian dealings" were made to a parliamentary committee which met at the Fleet on four separate occasions. This had been appointed after various prisoners (who appear to have organised various committees for this purpose) had successfully organised their parliamentary contacts. One of the members of this parliamentary committee, a Mr Neville, must have delighted the prisoners with his comments that "the warden of the Fleet is a jailor that delighted in no other music but in the rattling of fetters and chains". Warming to his eloquence Neville informed the House of Commons that Harris was "a monster in nature, a body of a Jew without the soul of a Christian", and begged his fellow members "to tie up this cruel Achmon until he may have some deserved punishment". Harris, however, had his friends on the committee too, including the actual warden of the prison, Lello, who wisely asked the question, should the deputy warden be removed, who then would be responsible for the prisoners? Harris, this "'cunning and intelligent fellow" to use Lord Chief Justice Coke's phrase, replied to these and to all other accusations, that the fees he had taken were in accordance with his predecessor's scale.[39]

Harris, obviously regarding such writings and commissions as a serious challenge, replied not with a mere pamphlet, but with a substantial book. He called it *The Oeconomy of the Fleet, or an Apologetical Answer of Alexander Harris unto Nineteen Articles set forth against him by the Prisoners.* This work was later edited by Augustus Jessop and published by the Camden Society in 1879. Jessop regarded it as giving a picture of a London prison of the seventeenth century "such as can, possibly, be found nowhere else". In fact Harris would not have found it too difficult to refute the charges made by the prisoners, for they had been made beforehand, and were almost identical to those laid against a much later warden, Thomas Bambridge, in the more celebrated case of 1729.

Harris commenced his counter-attack by alleging that some of his prisoners had a conspiracy against him, particularly as they were the defendants in a Star Chamber suit he had brought against them. These men had successfully driven away the previous deputy warden, and were now spending their money in an attempt to undo him. One of the conspirators, Sir John Whitbrooke, had even attacked him, having entered his study on the pretext of illness, and while there stabbing him and two others. After this incident Whitbrooke and another prisoner, Bowden or Broughton, together with six others, had fortified their chamber and prevented the warden's entry. As Harris petitioned the Lord Chancellor to remove them from the Fleet, the two principals had quarrelled, and one had murdered the other. This, at least, was Harris's reply to the first allegation made against him.

Harris continued with a vivid description of his difficulties as warden. He was responsible for a prison which was "the receptacle of all the scum of the kingdom". It was "no novel thing for prisoners to contend and oppose their guardians", or to be prejudiced against their keepers, or to claim the slightest departure from the rules as immemorial custom: "Whatsoever they do they can but be in prison" (we can almost hear his sigh), "it is a grievous thing to have to do with them who, having practised all shifts abroad in the world, do now come and exercise their shifts and practices upon their keeper ..." And there were some prisoners, he added for good measure, whom "nothing can command, nothing persuade or induce them, nothing rule them, they are men sold and brought so to their wills, as *stat pro ratione voluntas*...".

There were still more complaints. Harris could not prevent his prisoners obtaining weapons. One of them, William Rookwood, whom he called "the vicar-general of the Romish" in the Fleet, together with his son Nicholas, had managed to smuggle into his chamber such items as food, fuel and weapons, by means of a cord suspended from his window into the street below. Thraske, a protestant prisoner, to show no religious bias on the part of the warden, used the same method to lower seditious letters to friends outside. Neither could he prevent his charges planning robberies in the prison. Some prisoners, he claimed, continued in the Fleet after their discharge, plotting robberies therein, or went outside and cut purses in town, but no constable could follow them into the prison as it was a privileged place. Drunkenness and disorder were commonplace, while the porter's wife was seized by several prisoners in an attempt to force the keeper to allow their own wives to stay with them.

The recusant prisoners, in particular, caused Harris a great deal of trouble. Rookwood, pressed to come to chapel, came and there "deloused himself" to the offence of all, and later shouted from a window that he was starved, although his chamber "abounded with meat to the warden's charge". George Lee was another such prisoner. He complained that he had been placed into a "loathsome dungeon" through which the prison sewers ran, "a place of frogs and toads". The warden explained, however, that this was a strong room with a "necessary place", in which Lee had been placed for such offences as mutiny, drunkenness, breaking windows and walls, and for drumming on the chapel door so that the service could not proceed. Further examples of trouble caused by these "Romish affected persons, with which the place doth continually abound", were specified by Harris. Several refused to pay their fees thus owing him two hundred pounds or more in rent; others sold his bedding; declined to vacate their chamber, or obtained by devious means far "greater ease" than they paid for. Another boasted that he had cost the warden three hundred pounds in suits but had never paid a penny in fees.

Other prisoners, having been discharged, keeping matters quiet, removed themselves to the common side and claimed the use of the prison charities. They then produced their discharge papers, claiming as beggars that there was nothing to pay but the discharge fee of seven shillings and four pence. Various other prisoners forged false writs in order to escape, and others again remained inside the prison to cheat their creditors, and were thus able to keep up "'large hospitality" therein. It was a common practice, according to Harris, for prisoners to draw up a great number of fictitious charges against themselves. This had the effect of preventing their creditors removing them to another and less hospitable prison, by reason of the expense of the process, the cost of which was governed by the amount of debts laid against them.   One of these men was Edmund Chambelayne, who had removed himself to the Fleet from the King's Bench for his "own ease", and had accumulated sixty processes against him of a total value of thirteen to fourteen thousand pounds.   It was a rare occasion, suggested Harris, when a poor man came to the Fleet "by accident".

To establish his claims about the misconduct of his prisoners, Harris went on to describe the mutiny of July 1619.   This appears to have been caused by Harris's attempt to enforce his monopoly in the provision of food and fuel by insisting on additional fees from the prisoners for the liberty of finding their own food and for the use of the kitchen.   The mutiny was rather an anti-climax.   A few prisoners barricaded themselves into a ward for several days.   There was the rather unedifying spectacle of various members of the Privy Council attending the prison and pleading with them to open the door, after an order of that council and of the Lord Chancellor had failed to dislodge them.   This occasion appears to be the same one as that mentioned earlier by Harris in his defence of the murder charge. As a result of this mutiny an open warrant had been issued to Sir Clement Edmonds on 2 August 1619.   It read:

> Whereas information is made unto us that Sir John Whitbrooke, knight, Nicholas Rookwood, Ashburham Peake, Esq. prisoners in the Fleet, have shut themselves up in a strong prison and by strong hand kept the same against the said warden and his servants to the disturbance of his majesty's peace, now in his majesty's absence and in time of his progress and to the scandal of the government.   These shall be to will and command you to repair unto the Fleet to let them know you are sent unto them from us to require them in his majesty's name to open these doors, to come forth and submit themselves, as in duty they ought, to the order and government of the said warden, who is required to yield to each of them such civil usage as to their quality and condition appertaineth.[40]

When the Lord Chancellor ordered that the mutinying prisoners should have no food until they surrendered, Harris wrote that they then accused him of starving them.   On another occasion the prisoners in the Tower chamber cut away the stonework of the door so that it could not be shut.   Similar incidents happened at the King's Bench prison at the same time.

The deputy warden had much to contend with, and was probably right in claiming that as a result "he was more a prisoner than the prisoners". The prison was crowded, not simply with prisoners, but with their wives, children and servants. Harris complained that the number of children was so great they infected the place with "the diseases incident of youth and fill it with stink and noisomness not to be named". Visitors could freely enter the prison, so that Sir Francis Inglefield, kept in close confinement for mutiny, could nevertheless receive sixty visitors in a single day. And when Harris blocked up the lower part of a window in Bolton's ward, through which outsiders could speak to the prisoners, one of them, Kennett, made a formal complaint against the warden.[41]

The remedies available to the warden against unruly prisoners were limited. They could be taken to the common side, but this meant the warden lost all the monies a prisoner owed for his chamber and commons. Alternatively the warden could distrain the goods of an offender or debtor, but this only led to complaints and accusation of theft being made against him. One other course was open, to have the prisoner transferred to Newgate, but this required an order from the court which committed that prisoner to the Fleet, and was not readily granted.

As deputy warden Harris's task was to keep the prison in order and the prisoners in secure custody. He thus claimed that many of the allegations made against him had been occasioned by his efforts in this direction, in which he had been supported by many of the prisoners. But as deputy warden he also had an obligation to the warden, namely to make the prison pay, so that not only would it pay his rental but also produce a profit for himself. It is not certain what rental Harris was required to pay, but his predecessor, Anstowe, paid six hundred pounds per annum. It was this factor which probably lay behind this and many other disputes. Harris, like all the wardens of the prison, endeavoured to interpret the table of fees and rules in a way which ensured the maximum profit to himself. The areas of dispute in this respect are easily identifiable. One, from the warden's side, was that the prisoners had torn down the copy of the 1562 table of fees in order to insist on an earlier and cheaper one. Another, from the prisoners' side, was that the warden claimed that those residing in his own home were not governed by the prison fees. Chamberlayne, for example, had two rooms in the warden's house. Here his wife, children and servants kept such "continual hospitality ..., gaming and talking", that they prevented the warden, whose bed chamber was below, from taking his "rest in private". Chamberlayne claimed, however, that the warden had no right to charge more for their accommodation than if he had any other prison chamber, and he also argued that as he laid on his own bed, he was under no requirement to pay the warden any dues at all. No wonder that an exasperated Harris wrote that prisoners with their families wanted chambers with "gardens, yards, places of pleasure", at a "third or less" of what it would cost abroad. Furthermore, the warden maintained that all those who requested better commons than their station in life warranted, or wished to have their own chambers, were required to make individual arrangements with him, and inferred that not only were the majority of prisoners content with this position, but that this was a sufficient answer to many of the charges laid against him.

Although Harris rigorously maintained that he only took what other wardens had taken before, he went on to assert that the cost of provisioning the prison was three to four hundred pounds more each year than the amount of the fees. If this was partly due to the cost of inflation since the date of the fees table, it was also because of competition from others, including a prisoner who had established an "ordinary" in his own chamber. The warden also lost heavily through the refusal of prisoners to pay their fees, and when he opened the trunks of one prisoner, Peck, in the presence of others, and removed forty pounds out of a hundred pounds he found there, it was little return for the debts owed him for eight years' imprisonment. The warden also had to bear the cost of the debts of an escaped prisoner, and the king's debtors alone, for whom he was also responsible, had a collective debt of two hundred thousand pounds. If a prisoner died he would be unable to claim any debts due to him, although it was argued by others that Harris was not adverse to retaining a prisoner's corpse until his relatives had paid the outstanding fees. Perhaps it was an afterthought which prompted Harris to mention that the profits of the prison could amount to two thousand pounds per annum. Its appearance in print rather destroyed his case.

Harris's final and decisive answer was to claim that as most of the prisoners entered the prison from other prisons, in order to obtain "more liberty and less payment" than anywhere else, then those who did not like their usage in the Fleet could remove themselves elsewhere. If a warden should endeavour to oppose the prisoners and their practices they could "touch him with murder, felony, robbery and infinite enormities". The warden, he continued, is "between Silla and Caribdis, [*sic*] so that either he must through that gulf of averice run upon the rock of Turpe lucrum, or through the Syrens' allurements of charity, pity and remorse make shipwreck of his own estate".

These were prophetic words, for one who, when he became warden, "besought of God to give him an heart answerable to serve the commonwealth and do poor men good". In the end the faults of Harris were more those of his office than of himself, a fact recognised by his acquittal in two cases brought against him by the prisoners, and after six "examinations" before the council.[42]

****

Sir Henry Lello, for whom Harris had served as deputy warden, died at a great age in January 1630, and was buried with many of his predecessors in the office of warden at St Bride's church. His nephew Henry or Harry Hopkins was bequeathed his manor or capital messuage called the Fleet together with those offices of warden of the Fleet and keeper of the palaces of Westminster. Twenty-four years later he too was gathered to his "fathers in office" at St Brides.[43] The earlier years of his wardenship marked the high water level of the prison's finances, for in 1641-2 the abolition of the court of Star Chamber meant that the "political" category of prisoner was lost to the prison. It was these prisoners, who were often wealthy men, who were prepared to pay for those extra privileges which made life in prison more bearable. Until that date the prison was a prosperous undertaking, and sufficiently attractive for James, earl of Buchan, Sir Garret Rainsford, and others to enter into a conspiracy "to draw the prison of the Fleet to be forfeited". Their aim was to charge the warden and his deputy with such offences that they would be fined and their offices forfeited. Buchan was said to have offered a privy councillor five thousand pounds to beg the king to grant the forfeited office to himself.[44] This at least was alleged by Hopkins and his deputy, James Ingram, but it may well have been part of their counter-suit to offset the charges laid against them. These charges were that they had extracted money under the colour of fees; permitted escapes; abused the processes of *habeas corpus* (the day *rules*) under which the prisoners were allowed to leave the prison; possessed blank writs into which were written the names of escaped prisoners, thus protecting the warden from legal proceedings; refused Thomas Browne, a prisoner, any victuals, hearing he was about to petition the king "for his intolerable abuses" (presumably of the warden rather than regality); and also taken the charity money of the prisoners, so allowing some to starve to death. Sir Nicholas Stodderd, one of the defendants, along with the warden and his deputy, was also accused of seditious words against the Scottish nation, saying that "The kingdom of England never prospered since a Scot governed the same", and that "the basest of English men ... was better than the best Scottish man." They must have been exasperated by some of their Scots prisoners.

A commission of the Privy Council was appointed to inquire into these matters, and in particular the uses made of the writ of *habeas corpus*. Arrangements were made for the prison's books to be inspected, while Mr Philip Smith, a solicitor acting for the council, was to be allowed to speak freely to any prisoner who wished to see him. If some made complaints, others petitioned in the warden's favour. Some alleged that one of the main complainants, Thomas Gray, was a troublesome prisoner who had been removed to the poor ward for a month in accordance with the prison rules, and then, released, had continued with his "wicked purposes" by presenting "a most scandalous petition" against the warden.[45] Another claimed that Hopkins was "free and faultless in all ... and that he hath carefully, discreetly and orderly managed the [prison], without the least offence or damage to the laws, creditors, or prisoners, that in so great a charge might happen". Others wrote that they believed that the complaints were occasioned by those who, having been denied various privileges, "did attempt to satisfy their private malice"; and another suggested that the commission was biased, being comprised of many of the earl's confederates.[46]

As a result of this controversy various liberties which had been allowed the prisoners were curtailed. Among them were the right of dwelling without the gate, and the free use of the yard and house, the former permitting them to meet their families, "who will not come to the house".[47] As all the petitions in favour of the warden were also accompanied by requests for the restoration of these privileges, it may be suggested that the prisoners had other ulterior reasons for their support of the warden. Hopkins was able to show that the 1562 rules established some of the disputed matters in his own favour. The result was that this commission, chaired by Francis, Lord Cottington, reported in May 1635 that those who had made the allegations were "men notoriously infamous and of no credit"; their complaints were unsubstantiated by the other prisoners, and there was nothing on which they could ground a charge against the warden or his deputy. The commission concluded with words which must have gratified the warden, for they held that "the warden being an officer of great trust, and bound to daily attendance on the king's courts, ought not to be further distracted with the groundless clamour of the prosecutors, but that they be left to proceed in the ordinary courts of justice."[48] Nothing further is known of this matter or of the earl's attempt to gain the prison for himself.[49]

Hopkins continued as warden until his death in 1654. He survived the plague of 1636, during which those prisoners who could afford the cost and the securities required were permitted to obtain writs of *habeas corpus* allowing them to leave the prison. They wrote in favour of their petition: "the destroying angel ... has begun to stretch his hand over the city, and this close prison is in greatest danger." And they added, by way of special pleading to the commercial interests of the nation, that their "death would deprive their creditors of all hopes of satisfaction, and his majesty of dutiful and hereafter useful subjects".[50] One wonders if they noted the irony of their petition, that the courts should have mercy on them for the sake of their creditors?

Hopkins also survived a taste of his own medicine. In 1640 the speaker of the House of Commons was committed to his custody at the Fleet. The next meeting of the house required the warden to deliver his prisoner. He refused, and was committed by the house to the Tower where, still obstinate, he was placed in "little ease". Unable to bear its confinement, he released the speaker and gained his own discharge.[51]

He also survived John Lilburn, which was no mean feat. Lilburn, one of the most noteworthy of the Fleet prisoners, was imprisoned there because of his libels on the royal family and his verbal assaults on tender episcopal consciences. Fined and imprisoned by order of the court of Star Chamber in 1637, he was also whipped and placed in the pillory. This he promptly converted into a political platform by distributing leaflets he had concealed in his pockets. He was ordered, as a result, to be removed from a private chamber in the prison to the "common gaol", there to be kept close prisoner, "ironed on hands and feet", amongst the "meanest and most degraded prisoners". None were allowed to visit him, and those who endeavoured to do so were allegedly beaten at the prison gate. Yet while his friends were unable to smuggle food into him, Lilburn managed to obtain writing materials, and send out various manuscripts which he had had printed in Holland. When fire broke out in the prison, the prisoners as well as the local population insisted that it was the desperate Lilburn who had set the place on fire, and demanded that he be allowed the liberty of the prison. This he enjoyed until his release by parliament in 1640.

As a result of his experiences in the Fleet, Lilburn wrote his pamphlet, *Liberty Vindicated against Slavery*, in 1646. In it he argued that imprisonment should never be a punishment. As the prisons belonged to the king, the king himself ought to provide the necessary accommodation and furnishings, while any man who demanded fees or chamber rent was guilty of extortion. Was he thinking of the Fleet when he wrote that "the gaolers ... rore like lions, devour like tigers, ravine like wolves, and like beasts crush the prisoner under their feet ... [We] looked for prosperity and justice, but behold misery and oppression, for liberty, but, behold thraldom, vayled by fair promises"? Lilburn even considered that it would be "less grievous to die at once by the hand of the cruel executioner, that to thus mourn, live, waste and consume, in these soul destroying prisons", in which one could only be freed from misery and want by kindly death.[52]

Another prisoner, however, had a different report to make about the warden. James Howell claimed that he was imprisoned for his royalist sympathies, although Anthony à Wood maliciously suggested that he was in the Fleet as a straightforward debtor. Entering the prison in 1643, three years after Lilburn's release, he wrote in one of his now celebrated letters: "as far as I can see, I must lie at dead anchor in this Fleet a long time, unless some gentle gale blow thence to make me launch out." He found the warden, Harry Hopkins, one of "the most knowingest and most civil gentlemen that I have convers'd withal". But even if the warden was civil, and some of his "co-martyrs" "choice gentlemen", imprisonment to this most travelled and urbane of men became as irksome as it was to Lilburn. A mood of deep melancholy replaced that earlier mood of buoyancy: "finding my soul weary of this muddy mansion, and methought, more weary of this prison of flesh, than this flesh was of the prison of the Fleet". Three years later, not having been over the threshold of "this house this four years", he longed to be able to breathe free air: "I converse sometimes with dead men, and

what fitter associates can there be for one buried alive (as I am) than dead men."
Yet, "while still underhold in this fatal Fleet", he was able to thank God that
"notwithstanding this outward captivity, I have inward liberty still". Such qualities
were needed, for his release did not come until 1651.[53]

Little is known of the prison during the commonwealth. A schedule of 1653
gives a list of prisoners in the Fleet. Its title page states that it was "delivered by
Mr Henry Hopkins, warden of the Fleet, to the committee appointed by the
Council of State for examining the state of the said prison". Regrettably this
appears to be the only surviving evidence for such an investigation. Amongst its
230 prisoners were Sir John Tompson, Sir Edmund Plowden, Sir Miles Sandys,
and Sir Thomas Dacre. One prisoner had entered the prison in 1624 charged with
a debt of seven hundred pounds; another in 1627; eight between 1630 and 1640;
five between 1641 and 1645; fifty-six between 1646 and 1650, and one hundred
and fifty-nine between 1651 and 1653. It is clear that even at this early date most
prisoners had a shorter length of imprisonment than has often been alleged. Harris
found the prison full in the 1610s with two hundred prisoners, so that the two
hundred and thirty confined in 1653 must have found the place unbearably
crammed.[54]

There is much uncertainty as to who followed Hopkins as warden. Sir
Jeremy Whitcott, who was clearly warden in the late 1660s, allowed a tradition to
develop that he had been persuaded by the exiled Charles II to purchase the prison
in order to shelter the king's agents within it, and for which service he had
received the honour of a baronetcy in 1660. Apart from the baronetcy, the
remainder of his claim rests on very poor evidence, for in 1661 it was one Bold
Boughey, and not Sir Jeremy, who was described as the keeper of the prison and
of the two palaces at Westminster, when he unsuccessfully claimed the right to
attend the king when he came to the palaces during his coronation festivities.[55]
Bold Boughey was also mentioned in other documents as warden of the Fleet in
January 1665, and in May 1666 he claimed the right to erect scaffolding in
Westminster Hall for the trial of Lord Morley as some recompense for his work in
keeping the courts therein.[56] One would hardly have expected a deputy warden to
have pursued these claims.

Bold Boughey appears to have died or to have surrendered his wardenship
in that year, for a dispute then arose between Sir Jeremy Whitcott and Sir Edward

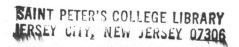

Savage about the office of warden. Whitcott appears to have initially gained the advantage by transferring the prison, and its prisoners, to his own property in Southwark, called Caron or Caroon House, when the prison house was destroyed in the Great Fire of London. This initiative was rewarded in July 1667 by letters patent which gave Sir Jeremy the office of warden of the Fleet and keeper of the old and new palaces of Westminster for the term of four lives. It also confirmed the rules of 1562, and permitted the prison to continue at Caroon House as "the King's prison of the Fleet".[57]

Two days after this grant, Sir Edward Savage's petition for the wardenship of the Fleet was ordered to be considered by the attorney and solicitor generals. It was mentioned that the king also wished to gratify the petitioner's "ancient loyalty and services" to the crown. As a result Sir Jeremy was required, in the following year, to attend the lord commissioners of the Treasury, together with the documents and patents by which he claimed the inheritance of warden of the Fleet. These were obviously sufficient to prove his title.[58]

Sir Edward remained unsatisfied, as did the Fleet prisoners in their new surroundings at Southwark. In July 1668 they petitioned the king and council asking that the warden should be ordered to rebuild the old prison, and meanwhile to obtain a more convenient one for them, "as their distance prevents their having the comforts of friends and counsel". They also requested the continuance of those writs of *habeas corpus* which enabled them to leave the prison, "for lack whereof many of them are unable to satisfy their creditors, and perish for want".[59]

Their petition was partly successful. The prison was rebuilt on its former site, at the expense of the warden. The prisoners returned to it in January 1671, in the care of the deputy warden, Edmund Pierce.[60] The *London Gazette* thus reported in its issue number 541:

> For the information of clerks, attorneys, sheriffs and bailiffs, and all other officers and persons concerned, these are to let them know, that the prison of the Fleet, being very fairly rebuilt in the place where it anciently stood at Fleet bridge, London, containing about one hundred and fifty rooms new furnished and well fitted, with all manner of necessaries for prisoners, upon Saturday last [21 January 1671], were all removed from Caroon house at Lambeth into this new prison, and the said house at Lambeth is no longer to be a prison. [61]

A further grant of office was given to Whitcott in February 1672. This repeated the terms of the previous grant but related it to the new prison house at the Fleet.[62]

The new prison brought about many desirable features. The old wards, providing one hundred and sixty "lodgings" (which meant that up to sixteen people were required to live in some chambers), were replaced by individual chambers, in theory at least. Other new facilities were provided. But these new buildings could not sweep aside the anachronisms of the prison's administration: its status as a profit-making concern, the requirement that prisoners had to pay for their own upkeep, and the various privileges given to debt prisoners. The constant complaints that these matters caused led to many further inquiries into the working of the prison, and to another long dispute as to the ownership of this apparently profitable institution. Its subsequent history, however, was to show that not only was it an institution in decline, but that its prisoners lacked the eloquence and status that they had once possessed.

NOTES

1   C T Clay, "The Keepership of the Old Palace of Westminster", *English Historical Review*, LIX (1944) 2f.

2   Clay, "The Keepership", pp 3ff; M B Honeybourne, "The Fleet and its Neighbourhood in Early and Medieval Times", *London Topographical Record,* XIX (1947) 20ff; and R B Pugh, *Imprisonment in Medieval England* (Cambridge 1970), pp 156f. Pugh notes that the dispute which culminated in 1197 may have been caused by the Crown's attempt to break the continuity of a gaolership in fee, as it was difficult to keep such hereditary appointments under royal control.

3   For the succession of wardens see Honeybourne, "The Fleet", pp 24ff. The result of a prisoner marrying his female warden is noted in John Vaughan's *Reports and Arguments* (1706), p 243, in which he cites a medieval precedent: "for the husband cannot be prisoner to his wife, it being repugnant that she, as jailor, should have custody of him; he as husband, the custody of her." He was ordered to be set at liberty.

4   Clay, "The Keepership", pp 13f. These rights were repeated at Edward VI's coronation (BLO, MS Tanner 301, fol 90).

5   Pugh, *Imprisonment*, p 161.

6   Clay, "The Keepership", p 13. Joan de Grandon later married Edmund le Cheyne.

7   R B Pugh, "The King's Prisons before 1250", *The Transactions of the Royal Historical Society,* 5th series, V (1955) 12ff. He suggests the building was of stone, whereas the common gaols were "usually wooden, flimsy".

8   Pugh, *Imprisonment*, p 340; Honeybourne, "The Fleet", pp 28f; Margery Bassett, "The Fleet Prison in the Middle Ages", *The University of Toronto Law Journal,* V (1944) 389f.

9   Honeybourne, "The Fleet", pp 36-8. She suggests that although the moat had disappeared by Stow's time, a plan of 1613 still indicated its outline.

10   H Riley, *Memorials of London Life* (London 1868); Pugh, *Imprisonment*, p 332: Honeybourne, "The Fleet", p 39.

11   Pugh, *Imprisonment*, pp 115f.

12   W H Waters, *The Edwardian Settlement of North Wales* (Cardiff 1935), pp 66f.

13   Pugh, *Imprisonment*, p 46. The statute is 25 Edward III s V c 17.

14   Pugh, *Imprisonment*, p 241.

15   Richard II c 12.

16   Pugh, *Imprisonment*, pp 118, 243f. In order to counteract the 1377 act, the wardens

purchased letters of protection from the crown. Though this was forbidden in 1406 it was probably without success. By 1561 the right of exit had become an accepted and unchallenged custom.

17   Pugh, *Imprisonment*, pp 242f.

18   Honeybourne, "The Fleet", pp 27, 29.

19   Clay, "The Keepership", p 15; Bassett, *The Fleet*, p 386; cf Harris, pp 16f.

20   BL, MS Addit 38170, fol 261.

21   Dobb, thesis, p 98, quoting BL, MS Harl 425, fols 85ff.

22   Quoted by J S Burn, *The Star Chamber* (London 1870), p 7.

23   *The Acts and Monuments of John Foxe*, edited by S R Cattley (London 1838), VI 647f.

24   H B Wheatley and P Cunningham, *London Past and Present* (London 1891), II 59.

25   Dobb, thesis, p 36, quoting SPD, Eliz, LXXXVI, no 25.

26   Their number included Anthony Throgmorton, Dr Andrew Oxenbridge and his wife Marie, and at least two Welshmen committed by the bishop of London, Edward Ellis, yeoman, and Gryffith Apparry, yeoman. Between 1577 and 1580 the warden certified 26 such prisoners [J H Pollen, "Prisoners in the Fleet, 1577-80", *Catholic Record Society*, XXII (1921) 130f].

27   BL, MS Addit 38170, fol 261.

28   Harris, p 17.

29   Wallace Notestein, *Commons Debates, 1621* (New Haven 1935), I 105.

30   Thomas Cranley, *Amanda or the Reformed Whore*,(London 1869), pp 9f, 21, 28ff.

31   quoted by Clifford Dobb, "London's Prisons", *Shakespeare Survey*, XVII (1964) 87.

32   *Letters and Papers, Henry VIII*, IV (1) no 390, item 30.

33   The rules are printed in Harris, pp 111ff. A more accurate version is found in BLO, MS Rawlinson D1123, fols 28v and 29a; cf Bassett, *The Fleet*, p 394n. See also Appendix 4.

34   *Acts of the Privy Council*, 1592, pp 109f, quoted by Dobb, "London's Prisons", p 97.

35   John Stow, *Survey of the Cities of London and Westminster*, edited by John Strype, (London 1720), III 256. No record of this case has been found in the papers of the Privy Council.

36   Stow's *Survey*, III 256.

37   BLO, MS Rawlinson D1123, fol 27. This is a copy of the original, and signed by Henry Lello.

38   A great mutiny occurred at the King's Bench prison in 1620, when the prisoners kept the prison against its officers. This may have been inspired by the troubles at the Fleet, or was part of the same movement. Significantly, riots also took place in the Marshalsea in 1639 and in the King's Bench in 1640 [Dobb, thesis, pp 395-402].

39   Notestein, *Commons Debates*, I 102n, 157f, 373, 375, IV 277, V 510. Similar complaints had been exhibited against Harris in 1619 which had been heard by a commission consisting of the Lord Chancellor, the Chief Justices and Baron, and others, including Coke. The chronology of the dispute remains uncertain.

40   Quoted by Harris, p 167.

41   Notestein, *Commons Debates*, V 510.

42   The various references to Harris are to pp 2ff, 8f, 12, 17, 25, 28, 32ff, 37, 43, 47ff, 59, 61, 63ff, 68f, 73f, 86, 98f, 105, 120, 128ff, 134ff and 167.

43   William Brown, *The Fleet. A Brief Account* (London 1843), p 8.

44   Cal SPD, 1633-4, p 525; 1635-6, pp 255f, 268.

45   Cal SPD, 1635, p 58.

46   BL, MS Harl 2107, fols 149f; Cal SPD, 1633-4, p 525.

47   BL, MS Harl 2107, fols 149f; Cal SPD, 1635, p 25.

48   Cal SPD, 1635, pp 80f.

49   BL, MS Harl 2107, fols 149f; Cal SPD, 1633-4, p 525; 1634-5, pp 426, 465f, 566f, 588f, 594f; 1635, pp 24f, 80f; 1635-6, p 260.

50   Cal SPD, 1635-6, pp 460, 528. An earlier precedent was noted, but these precedents do not appear to have been allowed in 1665.

51   Quoted in PRO, SP35/68, fol 80, endorsed, "copy of a paper found among several old writings relating to the Fleet prison".

52   John Lilburn, *Liberty Vindicated against Slavery* (1646), pp 8f, 29. See also Pauline Gregg, *Free Born John* (1961), pp 62ff, and cf Dekker in *The Divel's Last Will and Testament* [quoted by Dobb, thesis, p 423], "I give to all jailors and keepers of prisons ... the soul of a bear (to be ravenous), the body of a wolf (to be cruel), the speech of a dog (to be churlish), and the talents of a vulture (to be griping) ...".

53   James Howell, *The Familiar Letters*, edited by Joseph Jacobs (1892), I 356f, 369, II 421, 431, 540.

54   *A Schedule, or List of Prisoners in the Fleet*, BL, pm E698/13.

55   Cal SPD, 1660-1, p 585.

56   Cal SPD, 1664-5, p 174; 1665-6, p 386.

57   Cal SPD, 1667, p 496; Brown, *The Fleet*, p 8.

58   Cal SPD, Add 1660-70, p 726; 1667, p 462: PRO, T27/1, fol 254.

59   Cal SPD, 1667-8, p 510.

60   He is described as *warden*: see Cal SPD, Add 1661-85, p 302.

61   Wheatley and Cunningham, *London Past and Present*, II 57.

62   Notestein, *Commons Debates*, V 512.

The Fleet prison gateway in 1691. An illustration taken from Moses Pitt's
The Cry of the Oppressed. Collection of the author.

Part One: The History of the Prison

Chapter One: As Bad as a Standing Army

"The mischiefs and distractions, which daily arise from these infernal offices, are not less dangerous to our constitution, than a standing army."
John Berisford, writing in 1699.[1]

The Cry of the Oppressed, an account of the sufferings of debtors, including the sad case of the author and publisher, Moses Pitt, was written in 1691. His preface gives the flavour of his thoughts:

> That men and women should be imprisoned all the days of their lives, by bribers, oppressors, extortioners, perjured persons, etc, and there lie starving, rotting with sores and carbuncles, devoured with vermin, poisoned with nasty stinks, knocked on the head, and that for no crimes, but for their misfortunes.

The debtor was in a far worse plight than the criminal, for he was "kept a prisoner as long as it shall please God to lengthen out his life". And why should this be? Moses Pitt asked, to answer himself, because his "oppressor has taken away all the estate he has ... and knows that his imprisonment is no advantage to him, yet his cruelty is so great, knowing that our laws do not check his revenge ...

that he will keep him in to starve him to death ...."

Pitt added the details of his own case to this powerful plea against the whole concept of imprisonment for debt. He had entered the Fleet in April 1689, having spent some time before in a spunging house. As a result of being involved in a petition requesting an act of insolvency, which permitted the release of debtors on certain terms, the deputy warden, under the false pretence of non-payment of chamber rent, threw him "into the ward of the prison". Here he lodged with twenty-seven other prisoners, "most of whom lived on the basket and begged at the grate". Pitt gave a vivid description of what this meant in order to obtain the sympathy of his readers. It was impossible to keep himself free from vermin, even though "he was forced to louse himself most commonly twice a day, either in open yard, or in the house of office", while his fellow prisoners were "so lousie, that as they either walked, or sat down, you might have picked lice off from their outer garments; but enough of this, lest my reader scrubs or scratches at the reading of it".

Pitt's main complaint concerned the fees charged at the prison. He claimed, for example, that he was charged eight shillings a week for his chamber rent, instead of the two shillings and four pence given by the prison rules. By such practices the prison officers became "those wicked oppressors ... [who] oppress even we the oppressed". The problem to Pitt was a simple one, and he spelt it out in such words as these:

> If any man buys or sells any place or office for which he is not empowered by law to do, its plain bribery. If it be the prison keeper's place, the crime is the greater because the buyer is under a strong temptation of oppression and extortion, and he thinks himself put upon a necessity of grinding the face of the poor, to get up his principal monies again.

It was not an inaccurate assessment of the problem.

In order to clarify his allegations, Pitt itemised the charges he laid against the then deputy warden, Richard Manlove. A jury had found him guilty of oppression and extortion. He had locked up men in the wards for non-payment of his excessive chamber rent and refused them beds. He even kept "the dead" among them, until "they affected others", in the hope of persuading their families to pay his pretended charges so that their bodies could be released for burial. One of these dead bodies, "kept many days above ground", was that of Sir John Pettus, baronet, of Suffolk. By connivance with the coroner Manlove had managed to have dismissed a verdict that the death of one of his prisoners, Richard Brockas, had been occasioned by his cruelty, Brockas having been deprived of "victuals, rum and physick". Another baronet, Sir William Ducy, had been kept in the warden's coach-house, and had had to be drawn out with ropes as he was "so offensive, none could come near him". Moreover, Pitt claimed, the warden kept the common side or the wards of the prison in a deplorable condition so that it might be "a curb upon the rest to pay those great fees the gaoler exacts, he unmercifully threatening all for non-payment with dungeons and irons".[2]

Moses Pitt makes it clear that some commission of inquiry into the prison took place, but whether this was the one which Colonel Baldwin Leighton claimed had declared the prison forfeited to the crown is not known. Leighton claimed that he was one of the first commissioned officers who had "appeared in the interests of the present government", that is, who had declared for the protestant succession in 1689. He had taken part in some Irish mission in which the King had "owed his fidelity and service". To such slight royal praise Leighton added his own superscription: "to the hazard both of his life and fortune", having spent two thousand four hundred pounds in chartering three ships and a company of one thousand men. Indeed, he added, he had been entrusted by "the nobility and gentry" of Ireland with bringing their address to "His Majesty".[3] Leighton's efforts in the Irish wars were rewarded by a pension of two hundred pounds, secured on lottery money, and thus indifferently paid.[4] But he was not satisfied, and obviously considered that the apparently lucrative office of warden of the Fleet would offer him that compensation he believed himself entitled to for his distinguished services to the crown. He started, therefore, his long pursuit of that office by claiming that the previous warden, Bromhall, had been found guilty not only by the commission but also upon a trial "at bar" of "several abuses and extortions". As the prison had been granted to Bromhall only "for so long as he should well demean himself in the said office", Leighton consequently argued that the prison was thereby forfeited, and therefore petitioned that "your majesty [should] grant the said office to him for life".[5] A commission was accordingly appointed to check whether the office of warden of the Fleet, formerly granted to Sir Jeremy Whitcott, "is not forfeited or otherwise become void",[6] and the

Solicitor General was required to report "as to what the petitioner has to offer as to the forfeiture of the office ... and his opinion of what may be done for the petitioner's gratification, the King having a gratuitous sense of the petitioner's early services in Ireland".[7]

The result was that a grant of the office was prepared for Leighton. The attorney general was informed:

> Whereas by an inquisition lately taken at Westminster within our county of Middlesex by virtue of a commission under our great seal in that behalf issued it is found that the office of warden of the Fleet is forfeited and in our dispose. Our will and pleasure is that you prepare a bill for our royal signature to pass our great seal containing our grant of the said office unto our etc. Baldwin Leighton, esquire, to have hold and enjoy the same by himself or his sufficient deputy or deputies *quam diu se bene gesserit* together with all rights fees profits perquisites and advantages thereunto belonging in as full and ample manner to all intents and purposes whatsoever as any other person or persons hath or might lawfully have enjoyed the same ...

This was dated 6 April 1690.[8] For eighteen years, until he was finally successful, Leighton repeatedly based his claim to the prison on this grant. However others had to remind him of some facts that he had conveniently forgotten, namely, that while this grant had passed the privy seal, it had been stopped at the great seal, as "the inquisition by which the office had been found to be forfeited" had been squashed.[9] But such matters as these did not deter this intrepid adventurer of the Irish wars.

****

A private act of parliament was passed in 1692: *An act for the sale of such interest as Thomas Bromhall, infant, hath in the office of warden of the Fleet and in thirteen houses adjoining, and in an office of the custody and keeping of the palace of Westminster for the more effectual payment of debts.*[10] Thomas Bromhall's father, another Thomas, had either succeeded to, or had purchased, the office of warden of the Fleet, on the death of Whitcott in 1677. The chaplain of the prison, William Hill, complained "by hearsay" that Thomas senior was an anabaptist, belonging to Goznell's congregation, and wrote to the council regarding his suspicion that he had also a private printing press in his lodgings at the prison, on which "'seditious libels" were printed.[11] But, more decisively, in the same year of 1678, Bromhall had mortgaged the prison for five hundred years, for the "valuable consideration" of two thousand, two hundred and ninety-nine pounds.[12] His son, a minor, had inherited the office, but his trustees decided to sell the prison in order to repay the capital sum and the interest arising on that mortgage, and obtained an act of parliament to enable them to do so. One Mr Tilly was the purchaser, and thus he became the last warden under the terms of the 1667 grant of the prison to Whitcott for four lives.

It was later alleged that Tilly had obtained this enabling act by means of bribery and corruption, and had entertained various members of the House of Commons after the bill had been passed.[13] The truth of this is not known, but Mason, his solicitor and trustee, had revealed to an inquiry of 1696 that Tilly had given various bonds to particular people who had petitioned against the granting of this bill. One of these bonds, for five hundred pounds, was given to one Richardson, on condition that he withdrew his opposition, which was based on various debts owed him by the warden. Tilly later had this bond set aside on the ground that Richardson had petitioned in the names of others but without their authority.[14] Such action on Tilly's part could only inflame the allegations made against him.

Revelations of a more serious nature followed. The main reason why the prison was sold, and why the bill was acceptable to parliament, was because the mortgages of the prison would be redeemed by it. The principal mortgage had been made in 1678 to John Clements in a sum of over two thousand pounds. It appears he acted as trustee for the five sisters of one Sir Edward Low. In 1693 they adjusted their claim to the interest on this sum, amounting with the principal sum to over five thousand pounds, upon condition that this bill was presented and passed, and the principal sum paid thereafter. Tilly, however, refused to honour this agreement, and immediately re-mortgaged the prison. This meant that not only was the requirement that the original mortgages be redeemed ignored, but also that with the prison mortgaged to others again the original mortgagees would find it almost impossible to sequestrate the prison and its profits in order to regain their lost investment. At least this was the claim they made. Tilly also appointed trustees to act for him, one, as noted above, being his solicitor Mason.[15]

These moves were certainly interpreted as a device to protect the profits of the prison from the claims of creditors whose debtors had escaped, for the prison keeper was responsible at law for the debts of any prisoner who had escaped from his custody. The liberties of the prison were such that escape was not difficult. Thus to safeguard his purchase and still retain the full profits of his office, Tilly mortgaged the prison so that his mortgagees, rather than the aggravated creditors or the original mortgagees, always had the prior claim upon its profits. Thus if a creditor obtained judgment against the warden for an escape, the mortgagees would enter in with pleas that their own interests should be respected, and that no claims should be allowed which would affect the security of their mortgage. This meant, in effect, that Tilly had the best of both worlds. The mortgagees protected his interests, ensuring that no claim against him would succeed, whether for an escape or for the forfeiture of his office for bad conduct, while he could turn a "blind eye" to the liberties he permitted his prisoners to purchase, and so increase his profits. If Bromhall had devised this escape route from his responsibilities as warden, it was Tilly who utilised to the full the possibilities it offered.

That such suspicions were not untrue is shown by Tilly's use of a rather shadowy trustee, and by various allegations made and proved in an Exchequer case of 1712.[16] This court discovered that Tilly used yet another device to protect himself against the claims of creditors. This was by the employment of deputy wardens in a way which clearly violated the understanding of the patent of office which permitted their use. Between 1693 and 1696 the deputy warden was one Fox, a prisoner in the Fleet, "who was made use of [as warden] for the benefit of the said Tilly", to whom he was accountable. A committee of the House of Commons discovered that Fox left the wardenship when twelve judgements for escapes had been made against him of a total value of between two to three thousand pounds.[17] Another deputy, Church, had also absconded under similar circumstances,[18] while a third, Ford, had been appointed not by Tilly, but by his trustee Mason.[19] The purpose of employing such deputy wardens was to cause confusion in the minds of creditors as to who was responsible for the security of their prisoners, and thus as to whom they should charge with an action of escape. More detailed revelations of this practice were to be made later.[20] It also meant that any judgments made against such deputy wardens in their capacity of "warden" would simply be added to the number of the other writs against them when they reverted back to their former status as prisoners. This device was an alternative to the use of mortgages, and was superseded by their use, particularly from the 1690s onwards when the various acts passed to remedy this position always had saving clauses added to them which effectively barred all proceedings and judgments against the warden until the mortgages had been paid. With such devices as these to back him up, Tilly could readily maintain that he was "in his castle" and could not be sued.[21]

The whole position was exacerbated by the fact that almost identical conditions prevailed at the King's Bench prison in Southwark, so that the various acts passed to remedy these abuses endeavoured to deal with both prisons. There Lentall, the marshall or keeper, had leased the prison in 1696 to one Blower at a rate of one and a half thousand pounds per annum. Taylor, who acted for Blower, was "only sworn in to take him off from escapes". Joseph Dell reported that when any deputy marshall discovered that he could hold out no longer against the writs against him, "he quitted the office and another was sworn in, after that several others ....". He added, "he turns himself into his own gaol, which is accompanied by a kind of gaol delivery...". There were also several "incumbrances" on the prison. Thomas Sevear successfully claimed that he was owed over two thousand pounds by Lentall, who had failed to implement an agreement which had appointed him, Sevear, marshall of the King's Bench. Sevear thereupon claimed that he was in the same position as the prison's mortgagees, and consequently obtained the same saving clauses in the various acts in order to safeguard his claim. One is led to wonder whether this was a genuine claim, or one deliberately designed to protect the marshall. The main "incumbrance" on the prison, however, was a mortgage of 1684 on the office and prison house, together with lands in Oxfordshire, to Sir John Cutler for the sum of ten thousand pounds. His assignees obtained the same saving clauses as Sevear, but in their case their claim was not satisfied until an act of 1754,[22] when the amount outstanding had reached the immense sum of thirty thousand pounds. By this act the crown settled with the creditors for a third of the amount outstanding, and took possession of the prison. Thus for over seventy years the creditors of prisoners who had escaped from the King's Bench prison, and who had not given security for their safe imprisonment, were unable to obtain the redress the law provided for them.[23]

There were equal difficulties about what constituted an escape in law.

Opinions varied as to whether a prisoner who had strayed outside the limits of the prison *rules* but had returned, or who had clearly escaped but had not been charged in the final process of debt imprisonment, or who had been allowed abroad outside the prison *rules*, having given security for his safe imprisonment, but without the escort of a prison keeper, had legally escaped. The warden claimed, as was to be expected, that these were not escapes, while the creditors, and Leighton, argued otherwise.

Leighton was not slow to make use of these matters, and, in all probability joined by aggravated creditors and others, continued to prosecute his case. He was undoubtedly helped by his original loyalty to the protestant succession, while Tilly, described as a barrister of Hatton Gardens, was accused in 1695 with one Matthew Goodyear, a Fleet prisoner, of sedition. It could not have helped his defence.[24]

Leighton's first move took place immediately after Tilly had obtained the wardenship. He presented a petition against the bill selling the office to Tilly, on the grounds that he had a prior claim and a just title.[25] He was obviously unsuccessful. Nevertheless he obtained a parliamentary inquiry in 1696-7, possibly utilising his loyalist sentiments and revealing some of the abuses already mentioned. One clearly has the impression that Leighton, for all his faults, had done his homework. This inquiry called before it the warden of the Fleet and the marshall of the King's Bench, and eventually placed them both in the custody of the house.

The report of this enquiry revealed a whole series of abuses and malpractices confirming many of the allegations already made. It is not surprising that certain matters were revealed about the leasing of the prison, and the number of escapes the warden was alleged to have permitted. Francis Geary stated that in 1695 Tilly with his trustees, Francis Church, Harrison, and Guy, encouraged him to take the Fleet on a seven-year lease, after Fox's departure, by informing him there were two thousand prisoners, all of whom had given securities and paid chamber rent. He was told that these charges and other fees would bring in twice the money required for the annual rental of one and a half thousand pounds, together with the one thousand pound entry fine. Upon this encouragement he joined with Church, and together they leased the Fleet, only to discover, according to Geary, that no more than sixty-eight prisoners on the master's side and twenty-eight on the common side were handed over to them. He was told that Tilly reserved "the rest" for himself. Church stated that the number turned over was one hundred and fifty out of a thousand prisoners, and alleged that the warden considered himself chargeable in cases of escapes only for those whose names had been "turned over". Hence the frequent defence in escape actions, that prisoners had not been "handed over" to the new deputy warden. As deputies they could do nothing without Tilly's leave. Church failed to pay his share of the entry fine with the result that Tilly cancelled their lease, handing the prison over to Ford, and refused to repay Geary the six hundred pounds he had already paid as his share of the fine. Church clearly acted for some time as deputy warden.

Many creditors came forward to allege that the warden had permitted their debt prisoners to escape. One case specified was that of Barkstead, a prisoner in the King's Bench prison whose debts amounted to over ten thousand pounds. Wishing to "transport himself to Pennsylvania", he regarded the five hundred pounds demanded by the marshall for his liberty as exorbitant, and therefore removed himself to the Fleet in the hope that Tilly's charges might be more suitable to his pocket. They were, and Tilly not only suggested a fee of fifty pounds, but included in that price his willingness to accompany Barkstead "to the buoy in the Nore, and see [him] on shipboard, before he received the money". Tilly replied that he had not received any money, and that Barkstead had been discharged by his creditors.

Another complaint concerned a merchant, James Fade, who turned himself over to the custody of the warden charged with debts of just under ten thousand pounds. Tilly was requested by Fade's creditors to take care of him, "yet, nevertheless, they never put him into the prison, but went to a tavern the same night, let him go from thence, without even a keeper, or giving security". His creditors were now informed that Fade was in Holland. Tilly replied that he was a prisoner on mesne process only, and "that he doubts not to satisfy the creditors as to the recovery of his prisoner". More complaints followed. Some alleged that Tilly had claimed that the *rules* of his prison extended to the East and the West Indies, and that when any prisoner was sued to an execution (the final process of debt imprisonment), Tilly "could but look over the bar, and have two witnesses to swear he was then actually in prison, though he was forty miles off". Others complained that while "one goes out, by virtue of a day writ, forty go abroad without it", and that the warden or his agents charged between ten and thirty guineas for such liberty. An example was given in the case of a player, Hudson, who though committed as a prisoner had paid one hundred pounds to receive his liberty, and, to the consternation of his creditors, frequently acted in the Playhouse. There were at least two hundred prisoners "at large", charged in execution, whose debts amounted to "more than the inheritance of the Fleet is worth". Tilly meekly replied that he was satisfied that most of these examples referred to the time when Fox was warden. Clearly, there were conflicting ideas as to what constituted a prison.

These were not the only complaints which were substantiated. It was alleged that Tilly had allowed between two and three hundred people into the shelter of the Fleet, who had never been committed as prisoners. One of them was John Scoltock, an ironmonger, who was allowed to carry his goods into the Fleet, "where his body and goods should be protected" against arrest for debt. Fox permitted him to rent a room at six shillings a week, allowed him a warrant of protection, and arranged that Scoltock's two sons should act as his keepers. Fox, it was said, even travelled into Yorkshire to look after his "outlying deer", these being men to whom he had given warrants of protection, which were lodged with the local sheriff. These meant that if such a person was arrested for debt he would be looked upon as a Fleet prisoner, with the expectation that any new creditors would probably drop proceedings as soon as they realised it would involve taking matters to the court of Common Pleas at Westminster. Church had allowed an equally serious abuse. He had sworn a man a prisoner, who had never been committed to the prison, to enable him to take advantage of an act for the relief of poor debtors. For this he had been bound over by the recorder of London. Tilly had also sold prison offices, charging one Duncomb three hundred and fifty pounds for a place as a tipstaff. However, there was nothing illegal about this transaction for it was sanctioned by immemorial usage. Tilly was also accused of having torn out various pages in the prison books in order to conceal evidence.

Equally serious allegations were made against Tilly as an individual. Evidence was given of his Jacobite tendencies, while he was accused of permitting one White, a counterfeiter, to enter the prison from the Gatehouse prison, and to continue his activities in the two chambers he rented at the Fleet. One Hobson said that he had heard Tilly on several occasions, when he needed to change a guinea, call to White to change it, but "bid him not to give him any of his own making". When a warrant was issued for White's arrest, another was issued for Tilly's, so that Tilly was forced to shelter at Holland's house, where "many people came to him there daily, about business concerning the Fleet", although sometimes Tilly would "go over the water to bowls". Tilly denied that he had secured White's reprieve from a charge of clipping, and argued that he did not believe that White could have practised such coining at the Fleet.

Tilly was further accused of having prevented a bill of 1694, whose aim was to better regulate the Fleet and the King's Bench prisons, and to provide effective remedies for the creditors of escaped prisoners. Evidence was given that he had sent a servant with two to three hundred pounds to one of the committees of the house, given a clock to its chairman, and forced his prisoners to contribute to the costs of his defence against this bill. It was claimed that Tilly had paid three hundred pounds towards his share of the "bribes", and the same amount for the "other shop meaning the King's Bench", while he had added for good measure that the House of Commons was a company of bribed villains, a great many being "members of his house", and the judges, if a complaint was made, "would swallow his gold faster than he could give it them". Tilly argued in his defence against these charges that it was in his interest to oppose the bill; he had paid the appropriate fees, and the purpose of the money collected from the prisoners was to obtain a bill for the relief of poor prisoners.

Many of these allegations were made by a Mrs Hancock. She declared that Tilly had endeavoured to bribe her to remain silent by the promise of a hundred pounds and the payment of her assumed husband's debts, his agent informing her that "Tilly's money flew about like feathers out of an opened feather bed in a windy day". Tilly argued, however, that she was one of the leading members in a conspiracy whose aim was to obtain the forfeiture of the prison. Its members also included two former officers of the Fleet, who had been turned out of their offices, and were thereby prejudiced persons. Madam Hancock, alias Gilbert, was but "a peddling lady" with "a very good tongue", who had "robbed her husband on the road in man's clothes, and lives in adultery". Tilly alleged he could "bring a hundred witnesses to invalidate her testimony", and added that it had been stated by this group that "if they missed of the business in the House of Commons, yet White's business would do Tilly's work". And finally Tilly produced evidence that

Leighton had endeavoured to persuade various men to prosecute matters against him, as well as "to carry on a complaint" about him to the House of Commons at their own expense, promising them the lease of the prison, with half the profits and no rent, if they were successful.[26]

Whatever the truth of these matters may have been, and much was based on hearsay evidence and gossip, Tilly's defence did not convince the House of Commons. The recommendations made by the committee of investigation were incorporated into an act of May 1697, *An Act for the more Effectual Relief of Creditors, in Cases of Escapes, and for Preventing Abuses in Prisons.*[27] Its preamble stated that it had been occasioned "by many grevious extortions and ill practices". By this act the warden of the Fleet and the marshall of the King's Bench were held responsible for their deputy's actions. The deeds of the various mortgages, conveyances, grants and leases of the prisons were to be enrolled in the court of Common Pleas, in the case of the Fleet, and that any deeds which were not enrolled would be rendered void. This act also defined an escape. Any prisoner allowed out into the *rules* without having given security, or seen outside the limits of those *rules*, would be deemed to have escaped, and no retaking of a prisoner could be pleaded in mitigation by the warden unless oath was made that the prisoner had escaped without consent. If the keeper was unable to produce a prisoner held in execution to his creditor or his attorney, after one day's written notice, it would be deemed an escape, while the warden or marshall was required to give a note, on pain of a fifty pound penalty, that any prisoner about to be charged in execution of his debt was in his actual custody. After stating that "notorious great sums and other rewards" had been "given and received to assist escapes", the act provided that if the warden continued this practice, and allowed escapes, he should forfeit five hundred pounds and his office be confiscated. Upon any such conviction of a prison officer for the escape of a prisoner the fees and profits of the office would be sequestrated, in order that satisfaction could be made to the creditor or creditors of the escaped prisoner in those actions which had been charged against him.

The bill was passed only after a vigorous opposition. Much was made by some of the bill's provision to regulate the *rules* of the prison, in so far as escapes were concerned. They argued that because of the difficulties of obtaining effective securities for safe imprisonment the warden would be unable to allow his prisoners the use of such privileges. Thus all the prisoners would have to be accommodated in the prison house, with the consequent dangers of misery and disease always evident in an overcrowded prison. There would be "so many unfortunate people, so closely huddled together, wanting the conveniences perhaps even the necessities of life", he wrote, who rather than endure such "perpetual doom to poverty, confinement, stench and vermin", would be prepared to take desperate measures against the prison's government.[28] Another argument was offered by an unknown writer. After mentioning the vast number of prisoners who would need to be confined in a small area, the inability of the warden to obtain fees for the use of the *rules* and other such liberties, the difficulties of confining such prisoners safely, he suggested, in delightful anticipation, that this could only lead to a position where there was neither gaoler for a prison such as the Fleet, nor any prisoners for debt within it.[29]

It is hardly surprising that the most powerful opposition to the bill was mounted by the mortgagees of both prisons. The Fleet morgagees pointed out that the outstanding interest on their mortgage now amounted to more than the original sum mortgaged. They managed, therefore, to have saving clauses inserted into the bill which defended their rights, and in effect rendered that part of it which related to the confiscation of the office of warden or the sequestration of its profits ineffectual until their mortgages had been redeemed. Thus though the bill passed, it made but little difference to the situation caused by such escapes due to these "saving clauses".

****

Leighton obtained no profit from this enquiry, but he managed to obtain a further inquiry in the following year of 1698. He also alleged that as the office had been granted to Tilly for as long as he exercised "good conduct" in it, it was now forfeited because of the abuses discovered in the previous inquiry. He accordingly prayed for a further grant of the office to himself, particularly as he had spent several thousand pounds, almost to the value of the office, to maintain, as he put it rather nobly, the royal title to it.[30]

Thus another committee of the House of Commons met during May 1699 to concern itself with various abuses in the Fleet and King's Bench prisons. This committee received a considerable number of petitions from various merchants and traders who argued that the prison was no better than "a licensing office for cheats".[31] One of these petitions was probably redrafted into a pamphlet under the title:

> *An Argument that tis Impossible for the Nation to be Rid of the Grievances Occasioned by the Marshall of the King's Bench and the Warden of the Fleet without an Utter Extirpation of their Present Offices.*

Its author was John Berisford, who clearly had substantial experiences of these grievances. After arguing that the *rules* made imprisonment "a tease", and were contrary to law, he saved his considerable store of venom for a bitter complaint that because the prisons were legal inheritances and thus subject to mortgages, all the advantages the former act was thought to produce had proved to be "imperfect and abortive, and our great expectations are dwindled into air". He complained that the mortgages and securities were secretly shifted from one person to another, so that it became "impossible to know against whom to bring an action or have their remedy; the person who is the superior marshall or warden, or the person who had their interest, and the temporary marshall or warden who did actually officiate". He continued: "These underlings have all along been only servants, and mere tools, nothing but statues set up to receive the shot of the creditors and to screen their masters from any harm; and when one is pierced through and through, down he tumbles, and another such legg is advanced in his room..." Even if the responsible person was found, the profits were "excused as pre-engaged" to the mortgagees, for "their demands must first be satisfied". Thus the unfortunate act had received a "mortal wound".[32] The truth of his remarks was more than substantiated by the committee's examination of the deputy warden, Ford, and by the evidence of various creditors.

In his evidence Ford stated the now familiar story that when he was admitted to his charge in September 1697 only one hundred prisoners had been handed over to his custody. Several creditors appeared to testify that their prisoners were not amongst this number, and appeared to have escaped. Others came to complain about the futility of the previous legislation. Amongst them were the creditors of another escaped prisoner, Sir John James, who with debts of forty thousand pounds, had been discovered in Gerrard street, by St Anne's church. They had endeavoured to test the efficiency of the previous act, and had moved the court of Common Pleas for a sequestration of the prison, as the act allowed. It had not been granted, because the judges had argued that the petitioner could "have no advantage thereby ... by reason of the many incumbrances that were upon the office of the Fleet". Church, then deputy, admitted that James had been handed over to him, but as he had returned the same day as his "escape" hoped that this would not be held against him. In case it did, however, he absconded. James had subsequently removed himself to the King's Bench prison by a writ of *habeas corpus*, but Gimbart, the then deputy marshall, stated that he had only become marshall in the previous December, when only thirty prisoners had been handed over to him. Sir John James was not one of these, and he had heard that he had been a prisoner to the late marshall, Mr Taylor, who had "suffered him to escape". Another similar petition was presented by Sir William Duncomb. He had obtained a judgment of four hundred pounds because of the escape of his debtor, one Killigrew, from the Fleet. But he could obtain no relief, even though he had obtained a sequestration of the profits of the prison "pursuant to the late act". He had finally agreed to accept two hundred and fifty pounds in satisfaction, made up of an assignment of a former mortgage on the Fleet, "but looking upon this as a sham security", he afterwards refused to accept it. John Praed, in a similar petition, alleged that Church had said to his prisoner, William Warr, who owed well over six thousand pounds, that as long as he could feed Mr Tilly with money, he would have liberty to go where he pleased.[33]

The committee also received petitions from the prisoners. One claimed that the "pretended" warden of the Fleet, Ford, was demanding excessive fees for chamber rent, commitment charges, and gratuities for the liberty of the prisoners. Another complained that the warden and marshall had brought into their prisons, as a result of the recent legislation and this inquiry, many who had formerly enjoyed the *rules*. This meant that five or six were now confined in a narrow room "whereof two only had the benefit of a poor bed and the rest were compelled to lie on the ground". Several who had settled in the *rules* had managed to support themselves by their own labour, but were now so strictly confined that some had died for want, and others were starving and their families reduced to begging. They added, "all promiscuously are clapt up close without liberty of even discharging even the offices of nature with convenience."[34]

Its examination completed, the committee made the following resolutions which were faithfully recorded in the *Journal of the House of Commons*. They read as follows:

> *Resolved*, that it is the opinion of this committee, that the present offices of the marshall of the King's Bench and warden of the Fleet prisons, in respect of their management, have been very prejudicial to personal credit, and a great grievance to the whole kingdom.
>
> *Resolved*, that it is the opinion of this committee, that the many incumbrances of the said offices do cover those prisons against judgments, in cases of escapes; whereby the good intention of the late act of parliament for relief of creditors is eluded; the keepers of the said prisons, for bribes, continuing to suffer escapes; and the creditors left without remedy for the same.
>
> *Resolved*, that it is the opinion of this committee, that no *habeas corpus* shall be hereafter granted for removing of prisoners in personal actions to any of the courts at Westminster hall, in order to be turned over to the King's Bench or Fleet prisons, but upon sufficient cause shewn by the defendant, or some person for him, in open court, in the presence of the plaintiff, or some person authorised by him.
>
> *Resolved*, that it is the opinion of this committee, that the way for preventing the abuses of the King's Bench and Fleet prisons is, by discharging the incumbrances that are upon the same prisons, by sale of the said offices, or otherwise; and that, for the future, neither of the said offices should be liable to any incumbrances, except upon escapes.

These resolutions were passed by the house by a vote of ninety-six to fifty-four, with one qualification, that if any person "so removed" by *habeas corpus* was not bailed or totally discharged, then that person should be returned to the prison from which he was brought. This would mean that a debtor could not easily transfer himself to the Fleet or the King's Bench prisons, and that these prisons would be reserved for those imprisoned as the result of crown actions or state trials. The house resolved that a bill, incorporating these recommendations, should be brought in.[35] *A Bill for the Further Relief of Creditors in the Cases of Escapes*, which received its third reading in the House of Commons in June 1698, provided that the two prisons should accordingly be sold and the mortgages ended.[36] It appears to have gone no further, mainly because of the opposition of the mortgagees, rather than because of the warden's prayer that a clause may be received, empowering him to surrender his said office to the crown; reserving such right as he hath by law to the house where the said prison is now kept; as being distinct from and not annext to the said office, which is an incorporeal inheritance, and not local, having been formerly been kept in St Margaret's lane, Westminster, afterwards at Caroon house. and may be kept in any other place. It being humbly conceived a thing unreasonable, that the warden should (contrary to the course of other prisons), provide a house of his own, subject to the aforesaid penalties and forfeitures, for the execution of the said office, when rendered worse than nothing, and hardly (if at all) practicable.[37]

Instead a bill was passed in 1702, *An Act for the Better Preventing Escapes out of the Queen's Bench and Fleet Prisons.*[38] Mentioning in its preamble the substance of the resolutions of 1698, it ordered that any prisoner who escaped should, if recaptured, be confined to the gaol of the county in which he was seized. In the case of London, this gaol would have been Newgate. The prisoner was to remain there without bail or *mainprize* until he had satisfied his creditors. It also repeated the earlier proposal forbidding the writ of *habeas corpus* to be used to transfer prisoners to other prisons. Substantial opposition was again made to this bill as it proceeded through parliament. Many disliked the idea that debtors would mingle with felons in the county gaols, though there was nothing novel in this practice. Others argued that it was better to keep debtors in the two great London prisons whose keepers were still "under the judges' eyes" and required to give good security for their office. Bail would be too difficult to obtain, and few would dare to borrow any money, contract trade or receive credit as they would be absolutely in the power of the person they dealt with. Another argued that there were some remedies worse than diseases, holding that under this legislation debtors would escape abroad, and creditors would have considerable problems in taking out further processes against their prisoners now confined "in remote places". A Westminster Hall would be needed in every county.[39] The arguments were in vain.

During the intervening period between the bill of 1698 and the act of 1702, as thereafter, Leighton continued to prosecute his own claim to the prison. Upon the evidence presented of escapes to the 1699 committee, Leighton prosecuted Ford, the deputy warden. "A special jury, of some of the best of the county of Middlesex", found that he was guilty of permitting five escapes, and of extorting twenty-five guineas to allow one Spencer to escape. The office of warden was accordingly forfeited as a result of the 1697 act, which made the warden responsible for his deputy's acts, and the office was ordered to be vested in the crown.[40] But the battle was by no means over. Tilly counter-attacked, although Leighton impatiently accused him of using Ford in order to make "frivolous allegations of delay".[41] Arguing that Leighton was hoping "by fresh trouble to bring them to some unreasonable compliance without any just ground", Tilly obtained a further hearing at the court of Queen's Bench, when Ford was acquitted of all save one escape, that of Richard Spencer. This, however, was sufficient for the forfeiture to hold good. Even worse, the jury had found that "the messuage ... was pertinent to the office". This meant that Tilly's claim that the office of warden was entirely separate from the ownership of the prison house was disallowed, and Tilly's expectation that if he lost the office he could still partly recoup his loss by the sale of the house was stifled.[42] Yet Leighton still had grounds for consternation, writing that Tilly "seemeth now to apply to your majesty for a pardon", and had not even bothered to answer the attorney general's recommendation that he either "quit his pretensions at law, or rely on the king's mercy". Leighton was clearly becoming worried about his chances of securing the office, and hence continued to petition that a grant of it for the term of his life be passed anew.[43]

It is clear that Leighton, in spite of his fears, seriously underestimated Tilly's tenacity. Tilly now claimed in several petitions to the crown that Ford had been found guilty on the evidence of one person, Emmerson, a bailiff. Not only did Emmerson possess an unsavoury reputation, having been burnt in the hand twice (once for the theft of a silver tankard), he had been convicted of perjury at that very trial, having given false evidence against Ford. On every petition stating Tilly's case it was emphasised that Ford had been found guilty on the single evidence of a person convicted of perjury. Even more to the point, Emmerson had a vested interest in the case going against Tilly, for he had stood security for Spencer's safe imprisonment to the tune of six thousand pounds. Unless he could prove that Spencer's escape had been assisted by the warden or his officers he would forfeit that sum. Tilly continued to press home other facts as well. Spencer's creditors had been satisfied, and they had "in no respect been prejudiced by reason of the said escape, nor did they ever prosecute or complain of the warden for .... the same". This assertion seems a little contrary, however, to the previous one regarding Emmerson's position as a security for Spencer. Possibly everything was being thrown into the arena A voluntary escape could not lead to a forfeiture, argued Tilly, while Ford was merely his trustee, and did not have "the real interest of the office in him". Furthermore, he claimed, Leighton had "ventured to join in errors" in the name of the attorney general, without his leave.[44] Although Tilly's petition to the Queen asking for the whole matter to be transferred from the courts to the royal council, for "the gracious determination of her unparalleled justice and goodness", was declined by the attorney general,[45] Tilly pressed matters further in yet another petition. In this he once more declared the unfairness of Leighton's actions, and hinted again that the forfeiture of the prison applied only to the office of warden and not to the prison house. This petition read:

> That the said prosecution was carried on by Mr Leighton without any authority from your majesty or any of your predecessors in order to obtain a grant to himself not withstanding the supposed offence was not committed by your petitioner who purchased the inheritance under an act of parliament, and that several other persons are interested in the said office as mortgagees thereof, and that the late act of parliament have in a good measure prevented the inconveniences that happened to creditors by escapes; wherefore, and for as much as that the house wherein the prisoners are kept ... is now your petitioner's separate inheritance by conveyance under him [Whitcott] and the court of Queen's Bench have given no judgment touching the same, ... yet your petitioner doth hereby humbly offer to your majesty to annex and unite the said house to the said office for ever which will be a much greater security to answer for any escape than merely the office itself and is much more convenient both for the confinement and accommodation of prisoners than any other place ... and thereupon your petitioner humbly prays your majesty will graciously please to restore him to his inheritance of the said office.[46]

One wonders if Tilly was losing his nerve, particularly by reason of his mention of that most emotive subject of the prison mortgages, and by his veiled threat that he might prevent the prison house being used by any new warden. Although the judge at the Queen's Bench court may not have said anything about a link between the office and the prison house, the jury had certainly done so. This had been conveniently forgotten by Tilly in his petition. But there was still a glimmer of hope for Tilly, and he was sufficiently heartened by a report of Sir Edward Northey, a former attorney general, to publish it in 1704 under the title of *The Present Lord Keeper's ... Report to Her Majesty, upon the Petition of Mr Tilly and Mr Leighton*. In this report Sir Edward argued that Tilly should be delivered from this prosecution either by a pardon or a discharge, in the "light of the unsatisfactory evidence on which the forfeiture is based".

Though these matters must have provided some satisfaction for Tilly, this could not have lasted for long, as in late 1704 Leighton presented a further petition. In this he claimed that the prison had been forfeited as a result of the Queen's Bench case against Ford, and although he agreed that the case for forfeiture was still undetermined, he maintained this was because the record was long and he could not afford the expense of having it transcribed. Both Tilly and Ford petitioned against this claim, reciting the facts already mentioned. They were not alone in such petitioning activities, for various prisoners in the Fleet, led by one Thomas Fitz Richard Ashon, esquire, made use of the opportunity to make complaints about the arbitrary power and ill practices of the warden and his officers, and their assaults on those prisoners who endeavoured to obtain some relief. They requested an examination of these complaints by the House of Commons.[47] A pamphlet, *A Short View of Some Complaints against the Warden of the Fleet*, alleging that the warden permitted escapes, defied the laws of debt by permitting debtors to be set at liberty, protected criminals from justice, refused to pay his own debts as "he was in his castle", and allowed the prison to be "a mere licensing office for fraudulent dealers", was also published in 1705, possibly to bring pressure on the house to appoint yet another committee of inquiry, or to finally reduce Tilly to surrender.[48]

The resulting "committee" comprised the lord chief justice of the Common Pleas, the lord baron of the Exchequer, the attorney general and the solicitor general. They were requested to give their opinion on the following points, each one of them being highly prejudicial to Tilly's position:

> 1 What is the best method to prevent the present warden (till a settlement can be made) from committing further abuses in any kind, particularly from letting his prisoners go?
> 2 The judgment given below being affirmed by the House of Lords, what right the Queen hath to the disposal of that office?

3 What regulations are necessary to prevent for the future abuses in the management of the office of warden?

Your lordships will please that the report may be as full as possible, and be as quickly dispatched as the weight of the affair requires. My Lord, etc R.H. [Robert Harley].[49]

After insisting that Leighton and Grindall, "who at present officiates as warden of the Fleet", should appear before them at Powys house, "with the writings regarding the title and other documents", the commission confirmed Grindall in his office as deputy warden until the whole matter had been settled. The final result was that the attorney general was directed to bring in a bill against several persons who pretended to have an interest in the prison, as soon as the Queen's title had been allowed at common law, and her right to dispose of the office if it was forfeited established.[50]

These matters appeared to have depended on the outcome of Tilly's appeal to the House of Lords, but the position was still sufficiently precarious for the mortgagees of the prison to enter counter-petitions for their rights to be once more respected. Bromhall thus claimed a debt based on the 1692 agreement for the sale of the prison to Tilly, hearing that "the said office had been forfeited by reason of some misdemeanours of the said John Tilly or of those that hath acted under him. And that her majesty is about to make some grant or dispensation of the said office to Baldwin Leighton, the prosecutor of the said suit." The family of Sir Edward Low also petitioned that any grant should be suspended until the mortgage due to them had been paid, which with the principal money and interest combined now amounted to over five thousand pounds. They were joined by the administrators of Anthony Smith, deceased, who claimed nine hundred and seventy three pounds awarded for escapes by two decrees in chancery secured on the mortgages of the prison.[51]

Parliament's respect for property appears to have gratified the mortgagees, for the bill that was eventually passed in 1706, *An Act for Rendering More Effectual an Act Passed in the First Year of Her Majesty's Reign, Intitled an Act for the Better Preventing of Escapes out of the Queen's Bench and Fleet Prisons,*[52] merely provided that escaped prisoners could be taken up by warrant on the Lord's day, and closed some of the other loopholes in the earlier legislation which related to the holding of such prisoners in the county gaol. No mention was made of the mortgagees or of their interests whatsoever. Tilly had gained yet another round of the continuous conflict.

But Mr Leighton continued his long battle. He presented a further petition in 1708, and another commission was set up, similar in composition to that of 1705. Having already established the Queen's title to the prison (by what means it is not known) it reported that a prosecution at her majesty's charge should be made "upon the discovery of the several incumbrances on the said office". What these were is not known, but it is probable that they were additional mortgages which had not been enrolled under the 1697 legislation, although the penalty that provided was not the forfeiture of the prison but the voiding of the deeds concerned. On the other hand it is possible that a clerk simply copied out the previous precedent. The cost of this action was estimated to be at least three hundred pounds, for Sydney Godolphin, the lord treasurer, surveying the previous history of Leighton's claims and Tilly's defence, argued that it was "impossible to foresee what delays and obstructions may be met with in such a suit as this". However it was arranged that Leighton should give security to pay these costs back to the crown from the profits of the prison when he obtained the wardenship. The result was hardly unexpected. The office passed into the hands of the crown and Leighton was appointed warden. Tilly and his mortgagees, recorded and unrecorded, were the obvious losers, and Tilly's contention that the office and the prison house were separate entities was clearly disallowed.[53]

That both sides were able to continue this legal battle for the possession or retention of the prison for over fifteen years indicates that not only had each party powerful backing, possibly on political lines, but that both had some element of truth in their assertions or denials. Clearly escapes did occur, but it was a matter of interpretation as to how far the warden could be held responsible for each one. Equally clearly Tilly sheltered himself and the profits of the prison behind trustees, deputy wardens and mortgagees. Many of the other complaints made against him may well have been justified. One is also led to wonder if at the end of the day the pressure of public and commercial opinion forced the hands of the government and made them find some means whereby the prison could be forfeited, instead of allowing the two disputants to fight it out between themselves through the courts. The essential problem was that the prison was a place of profit, whose officers desired to obtain the maximum amount possible from it, the warden insisting on a high rent, and the deputy wardens not only being required to find it, but also to make a profit for themselves.

Tilly claimed that Leighton had put him to great expense, Ford estimating that by 1701 alone Tilly's defence had cost him above two thousand pounds, for which he could obtain no redress in the courts as Leighton had prosecuted in the name of the crown.[54] Neither is it hard to believe Tilly's other major assertion that Leighton had established a conspiracy against him in order to secure the wardenship for himself. Leighton's claim that he had received a grant of the wardenship of the prison in 1690 was a dangerous half-truth. His assertion that the House of Lords had stated that he had been severely used, and had urged him to obtain another inquiry into the warden's extortions and abuses, was denied by no less an authority than the lord keeper. He had carried out his prosecutions in the name of the attorney general, but without his leave, and offered various people the post of deputy warden in return for their help in prosecuting Tilly.[55] Even more revealing is a petition of the then deputy warden, Anthony Grindall, dated 1705:

> That your petitioner being legally constituted warden of her majesty's prison of the Fleet and seized of the house where the prisoners are kept, and being so possessed and charged with the custody of a very great number of persons committed for great sums of money, one Mr Baldwin Leighton with divers other accomplices did on the 23 instant at two of the clock in the morning in a violent and tumultuous manner surprise the turnkey of the said prison, took from him the keys thereof, and has ever since by force of arms kept the possession [thereof] and imprisoned your petitioner and his family in his own rooms, and neither have nor can have any legal process for such actings but pretends some direction from your majesty for so doing notwithstanding the several acts against forcible entries ...

Grindall was unable to obtain any legal redress from the magistrates, because of their uncertainty as to who was warden of the prison, Tilly, Grindall or Leighton.[56] Nevertheless as a result several of Baldwin's accomplices found themselves in the custody of the keeper of the Wood Street compter, by order of the lord mayor, though Baldwin appears to have evaded such a misfortune.[57] Both sides in the controversy were equally unscrupulous, but however just one tries to be regarding Tilly, given the difficulties of his office and the provocations of his opponents, it must be admitted that the 1729 report on the prison was entirely honest when it stated that the prison, "'falling by descent or purchase into the hands of persons incapable of executing the office of warden, was the occasion of great abuses and frequent complaints to parliament, till at length the patent was set aside".[58]   But it can hardly be believed that Colonel Baldwin Leighton served it any better.

NOTES

1   Berisford, p 29.

2   Moses Pitt, *The Cry of the Oppressed* (London 1699), pp 1f, 84-91, 93. His wife Mary was equally eloquent about the Gatehouse prison where she was a debt prisoner in 1711 [BL, MS Addit (Hodgkin papers) 38856, fol 150].

3   Cal SPD, 1691-2, pp 314f; Cal TP, 1697-1702, p 109; PRO, T1/124, fols 120ff. Leighton was appointed a captain in Sir Thomas Newcomen's regiment in 1686 to serve in Ireland [PRO, SP63/340, fols 151ff; Cal SPD, 1694-5, p 344].

4   Cal TP, 1708-14, p 211; PRO, T1/124, fols 120ff.

5   Cal SPD, 1689-90, p 431; PRO, SP44/236, fol 172; *The Present Lord Keeper his Report to her Majesty, upon the Petition of Mr Tilly and Mr Leighton, referr'd to the then Attorney and Solicitor General.*

6   PRO, SP44/97, fol 285.

7   PRO, SP44/236, fol 172.

8   PRO, SP/340.,fol 129.

9   PRO, SP44/238, fols 480f; *The Lord Keeper's Report.*

10   4 William and Mary, private act 28.

11   Cal SPD, Add 1660-85, pp 469f.

12   PRO, SP34/6 fol 110.

13   Jnl H of C, XI 676: Chandler's *Debates of the House of Commons* (London 1742), III 70.

14   Jnl H of C, XI 676. Tilly also refused to comply with several bonds he entered into as part of the sale of the prison. One of these was to maintain the infant Thomas Bromhall until he reached the age of twenty-one. By 1669 a sum of £1450 was owed [PRO, SP34/6, fol 113].

15   Jnl H of C, XI 676; PRO: SP34/6, fol 110; *The Case of John Clements* (1693). The same situation applied at the King's Bench, where the marshall in the 1720s sheltered behind two trustees. One was his illiterate footman, the other, a scrivener, was completely unaware of his appointment.

16   PRO, E134, 11 Anne, Mich 37.

17   Jnl H of C, XI 643. It was also alleged that Tilly had men available who would commit perjury in order to swear writs of error on his behalf against such claims.

18   Jnl H of C, XII 684.

19   PRO, Pris 10/157 (for 28 Sept 1697).

20   Thus in the Exchequer case quoted above of 1712 it was said that Tilly was only warden from 1693-4, while in 1699 Ford was thought to be warden [Jnl H of C, XII 685]. An inquiry of 1702 was told it was thought that various escapes had been "contrived by one Tilly", but it is clear from the evidence that he was not considered to be the warden [Jnl H of C, XIII 823]. In another case, however, it was claimed that Tilly was the "real and not the nominal warden". [BL, pm 816 m15/16].

21   Jnl H of C, XII 685.

22   27 George II, c 17: Jnl H of C, XII 685.

23   Jnl H of C, XI 645, XII 185, 251, 186, 686f; *The Case of John Taylor, Marshall of the King's Bench.* The Report 1729 (KB) shows how the devices used by Tilly at the Fleet in the 1690s still continued at the King's Bench in the late 1720s. See also *The Case of the Mortgagees of the Office of Marshall of the King's Bench* [BL, pm BS fol bills 359 d9-12/45], and *The State of the King's Bench Prison* (London 1765).

24   PRO, SP44/274, fols 46f.

25   Jnl H of C, X 823.

26   Jnl H of C, XI 641-4, 678-80; Chandler's *Commons Debates*, III 70f.

27   8 & 9 William III c 27.

28   *General Considerations relating to a Bill for Regulating the Abuses of Prisons* (London 1697).

29   *Reasons against the read Bill supposed, for Relief of Creditors, and Preventing Escapes* (London 1698).

30   PRO, SP44/237, fols 266-8; SP44/238, fol 274; Cal SPD, 1698, p 436.

31   J P Malcolm, *Londinium Redivivum*, (London 1802), I 374f.

32   Berisford, pp 2, 18, 21.

33   Jnl H of C, XII 684-7.

34   Jnl H of C, XII 201, 207. Three Fleet prisoners, Cudmore, Finch, and Francis Jones, alleged that having petitioned the house complaining about Ford, Finch and Jones were transferred to the common side, and a prison officer, Thomas Shore, came into Cudmore's chamber and broke his head [Jnl H of C, XII 235f].

35   Jnl H of C, XII 687, XIII 542. It was argued in the house that such proposals would deprive the prisons of their prisoners, so that their profits would not be sufficient recompense for their officers to attend the courts, with the result that the king's courts at Westminster would be without prisons and officers to assist them, and would be reduced to a "more mean condition than the most inferior courts of record in the kingdom". Someone had clearly mastered the

contents of the pamphlet mentioned above.

36   Jnl H of C, XII 270, 280, 299; *Reasons why the Bill should Pass, without the Clause Proposed by Edmund Boulter*; cf Malcolm, *Londinium Redivivum*, I 375. Berisford had made similar proposals, although he added that a new prison should be built in place of the other two, vested in the crown, and under the control of, and with an annual inspection by, the sheriffs. He argued that the warden's appointment should be for one year only, as "no man can pretend to conduct and [have] integrity enough to be entrusted with such a treasure for life." His first proposal was implemented in 1842.

37   *Some Considerations Humbly Offered in relation to the Bill now depending in Parliament for the Further Relief of Creditors in Cases of Escapes* (London 1698). He also argued that the officers responsible "may even expect some other security and recompense form the public for the hazard and care" of their office.

38   1 Anne s 2 c 6. A bill of the same year which endeavoured to void all the securities given by prisoners for their safe imprisonment failed to pass [Jnl H of C, XIV 43, 45].

39   *Remarks upon the Bill for Preventing Escapes out of the Queen's Bench and Fleet Prisons*; *Some Considerations relating to the Bill for Regulating the King's Bench and Fleet Prisons*; *Some Considerations about the Regulating of the King's Bench and Fleet Prisons*; and *Some Considerations for Regulating the King's Bench Prison*. These last three pamphlets appear to relate to this controversy, although their titles might suggest an earlier date.

40   PRO, SP 44/239, fols 130-2 (Leighton's petition). A pamphlet, *The Warden of the Fleet's Case in relation to Mr Baldwin Leighton's Petition to the Honourable House of Commons, wherein he suggests the Forfeiture of the Office of the Fleet to the King and a Grant thereof to Himself*, probably relates to this stage of the controversy. In it Tilly asserted that of the four prisoners who had voluntarily escaped during Ford's wardenship, whose case was to be tried by a Middlesex jury, the securities of one had paid the debt for which he had been committed, another had paid his own debts, and the other two were still his prisoners "so there is no damage done to the king or his subjects". He also argued from the *Bill of Rights* that no forfeiture should be allowed before a conviction had been secured.

41   PRO, SP54/1, fol 79.

42   BL, MS Hargrave 125, fols 7-11; PRO, SP Scotland Series II 1, 7; SP44/238, fol 480f; *The Lord Keeper's Report*; Cal SPD, 1702-3, p 143.

43   PRO, SP44/237, fols 266-8.

44   PRO, SP34/5, fols 29ff, 124; SP44/240, fol 11; *The Lord Keeper's Report*.

45   PRO, SP44/5, fol 30.

46 PRO, SP35/5, fols 29ff, 124.

47 Jnl H of C, XV 108, 169, 188. This inquiry took place, but was almost entirely concerned with the Fleet marriages.

48 GLL, broadside 29.86.

49 PRO, SP34/5, fol 121.

50 PRO, SP34/5, fols 121, 125.

51 PRO, SP34/6, fols 110, 113.

52 5 & 6 Anne c 9, otherwise known as 6 Anne c 12.

53 PRO, T1/107, fols 163ff, 167; T27/18, fols 461ff; Cal TP, 1708-14, p 45.

54 PRO, SP44/238, fols 480f.

55 PRO, SP44/5, fols 29ff, 124; SP44/237, fols 266-8; SP44/239. fols 130-2; Jnl H of C, XI 678; *The Lord Keeper's Report.*

56 PRO, SP35/5, fol 225.

57 CLRO, Misc Ms 8.16.

58 Report 1729, p 2.

Part One. Chapter Two:

"Worse than if the Star Chamber was still subsisting."[1]

"Were your lordships to visit and inspect this place, you would conclude the
unhappiness your petitioners labour under for want of necessary accommodations
[is] far greater than your petitioners have been, or are able in words to
represent."[2]

Colonel Baldwin Leighton died in 1713, and John Huggins succeeded him as
warden of the Fleet prison. Baldwin's long struggle to secure the wardenship had
been successful, but he had little time in which to reap the financial rewards of that
office and to enjoy his new-found status. It must be said for him, however, that
his tenure of the office was uneventful and his conduct gave rise to no enquiry or
scandal.

The same could not be said of his successor, John Huggins. As the patent to
Leighton had been for his life only, the office reverted to the crown. Huggins
secured it for the lifetime of himself and his son by a payment of five thousand
pounds to Lord Clarendon. The 1729 report into the prison was probably correct
in describing this payment as a bribe for the office. An attorney, Huggins had
acted as chief solicitor for Dr Sacheverell in that celebrated ecclesiastical-cum-
political scandal of 1710,[3] and by 1713 he was acting as high bailiff of
Westminster.[4] Although he claimed to have exercised the office of warden in

person until the early 1720s, it is more likely he administered the prison through the use of deputy wardens.[5] Certainly after 1720 or thereabouts his appearances in the prison house became infrequent, his residence being at St Margaret's lane.[6]

The first years of his wardenship were uneventful, but from 1723 a substantial number of charges were made against his administration of the prison. It is hardly surprising that these charges mainly related to the continuing dispute about the amount and the extent of the prison fees, although this was aggravated by other issues. At least three of these other issues need to be recorded. Huggins's deputy during this period was one Guybon, and although Huggins claimed he had the fullest confidence in him,[7] it is clear he was incompetent. The prisoners regarded him as a "silly old man" who was unable to distinguish a *habeas corpus* writ from any other, and who was governed by a prison official by the name of Welland.[8] His inability to govern the prison is noted more fully below. Secondly, Huggins was equally ill-served by the officers appointed by Guybon. One of these was Barnes, who although a prisoner had been appointed a watchman, a not unusual occurrence. Barnes was involved in several altercations with prisoners, and was accused of stabbing one Jennings with a penknife, and threatening Thomas Paine with having "his neck rung". Thirdly, Guybon's attempts to quieten the prison and the prisoners by placing the offenders in some form of restraint, and by permitting legally dubious methods of obtaining his fees, added to the aggravation. The controversy indicated that the normal and reasonable relationships between the prison authorities and the prisoners, necessary for the well-being and good order of the prison, had broken down. It is significant that Mackay, who recorded these disputes, claimed that he acted as legal advisor or solicitor to a committee of prisoners who called themselves the "court of inspectors". Although on one occasion its members claimed to have secured the support of a hundred prisoners, out of a total of five or six hundred, this "court" was actually a pressure group, perhaps unrepresentative, and yet which exerted an influence out of all proportion to its membership.

The main controversy between the warden and this group concerned the prison fees, and may be summarised briefly. It will be discussed more fully in a later chapter. It was claimed that the 1567 constitutions of the prison required the warden to keep two classes of prisoners on the master's side, the gentleman's and the yeoman's, the latter having a reduced scale of fees. This alternative, they said, was never offered to them. The composition of the commitment and discharge fees was challenged, while it was argued that only one commitment or discharge fee was required, rather than a separate fee for every action charged against a prisoner. The warden's failure to provide a public table of fees was frequently noted, as was his reply to this allegation that the prisoners continually tore it down so as to better maintain their case for reduced fees.

Further controversy was caused by disputes about the amount of the chamber rent. The warden demanded a weekly rent of half-a-crown from every prisoner occupying a chamber, and in addition a charge for its furnishing. The prisoners claimed that this chamber rent was for a fully furnished room, and that the charge of half-a-crown should be shared between those occupying it. Until the warden supplied reasonably suitable furniture they could not be expected to pay any rent whatsoever. It was the outcome of this controversy which led to claims of violence as the warden endeavoured to eject those who declined to pay the fees he demanded, and as they in turn attempted to retain their rooms by force.

Other complaints were that the warden's charges for the use of the day *rules* and the *rules* were prohibitive, and that the warden often required additional securities for which a further fee was demanded. This, it was said, meant that some prisoners were unable to give evidence in cases which concerned them as they could not provide these additional securities. Major Wilson alleged he lost a case by such default. The warden however retaliated by pointing out the ease by which escapes could be made through the use of these liberties, and their cost to him. It was further alleged by the prisoners that the warden also demanded "Christmas boxes" from those in the *rules*. Other matters concerned the use of spunging houses, where prisoners were alleged to have been confined against their wishes and to the distress of their pockets; the four pence per week prisoners were required to pay to the chaplain; and the poor repair of the prison house.

In their answers to these allegations both Guybon and Huggins claimed that the prisoners, or a small number of them, had formed a conspiracy against the warden in an endeavour to cause trouble and to have the prison fees reduced. Some were two years in arrears of their rent to the warden, and refused to pay him any part thereof, "and will by force and defiance of the warden and his officers keep in possession of their rooms and furniture, swearing to stand by each other". It was later added that those who were making these complaints owed over one thousand pounds to the warden in such fees. Huggins also claimed that these people:

> to the great terror and danger of the wardens and in contempt of ... the rules and orders for governing of the prisoners, [they] have assumed for themselves the *absolute* government and disposal of the house ... [they] withhold and keep the apartments therein ... and ... the better to support their turbulent behaviour and effect their conspiracy and design, are formed into a body, under the style and title of a steward and court of inspectors, carrying their orders and resolutions into execution, ever so far as inflicting corporal punishment on their fellow prisoners, that such as abhor and would not otherwise conform to their sentiments, are terrified into a seeming compliance, with the new mock court, from whence only springs all the confusion and disorders ...

Huggins found himself so powerless in this situation that he even informed the judges of the court of Common Pleas that "nothing less than your lordships' powerful interposition" could constrain or put an end to such proceedings.[9]

The position became equally difficult for Guybon, who was still required to obtain the fees and to pay his own rental for the prison. Clearly desperate, the measures he took to control the situation only exacerbated the dispute. He thus refused to release prisoners until they had paid their disputed fees, even though their creditors had discharged them from their debts. This occurred in the case of Joseph Hands. The body of James Richard, who lodged in the cellar and had died there, was not released until his executors had paid Guybon his alleged fees. Those who complained were frequently transferred to other prisons, so that in order to return to the Fleet they were required to pay a new set of commitment fees. Thus one Mrs Crisp, although discharged from her debts through the charity of Barbara Rush, was still detained for her outstanding fees to the warden, and later sent to the Wood street compter, "where she remains a close prisoner". A person by the name of Pugh who came to check the gifts and bequests allowed to the charity prisoners was denied access and later arrested. Guybon claimed he was a troublesome man and had caused disturbances in other prisons.

The tone of the whole dispute may be noted by an affidavit sworn by Major Wilson, Charles Relfe, and Henry Cowper, gentleman, as recorded by Mackay. It reads:

Major Wilson, for himself makes oath, that about the 28th of October 1723, he was sent for into the lodge by Mr Guybon the warden of the Fleet, and from thence removed with a *habeas corpus*, through malice, as this deponent verily believes and was informed, because he was endeavouring to have justice done him and other fellow prisoners from the warden; and this deponent says, he brought his *habeas* to remove himself back again into the Fleet, it being allowed by Mr Justice Tracey, but was no sooner brought into the lodge belonging to the said prison, but they locked too the inner door, and would not suffer this deponent to go into the inside of the said prison, there being then in the lodge some of the warden's servants, viz. John Head turnkey, Mr Pindar turnkey, Richard Bishop tipstaff, and Samuel his servant, whom they sent for, and there in the lodge Richard Bishop took this deponent by the breast and punched him several times against the wainscot, and afterwards pulled him from thence, and there the said Bishop, and others, struck at this deponent, and threw him on the ground, and this deponent says, he gave them no manner of provocation, but desired to be let into the prison, and hoped they would not murder him; but this deponent says, they still denied him entrance into the prison; and Bishop, swore would be revenged on him, and immediately pushed him into another room in the lodge, and Richard Bishop with his cane pushed at this deponent's breast, and also, at his face, and swore, damn him if he had a sword he would run it into this deponent's hearts blood, or words to that effect. And this deponent further says, and verily believes, had not one Mr Townshend and Mr Bigsby been there, who cried out, and bid them forbear, that they would have murdered this deponent.

And this deponent Charles Relfe for himself maketh oath, that having agreed with the said Mr Guybon for the rules of the said prison, and paid him his dues and demands for the same, he, this deponent, had not long enjoyed such liberty before he was again locked up, and soon after put into chains and caused to be carried into a dark room, or dungeon, belonging to the common side of the said prison, called the lion's den, where this deponent was stapled down to the floor in his chains; after which, one Thomas Pitt, nephew to the said Mr Guybon, as this deponent hath been since informed, came to the said dungeon, with John Head, a turnkey, and assaulted this deponent with a stick or cane, and broke this deponent's head; and this deponent was also, for want of length of chains to retire from such insult, pushed, or thrown, with his back against some boards like those in barrels, whereby this deponent was very much bruised in the small of the back and loins, and for preservation of health was let blood immediately in his chains. And this deponent further saith, that, notwithstanding he is an infirm person, having but one arm, and had been treated with the barbarity aforesaid, yet he the said Mr Guybon, although due application was made to him for that purpose, not only denied this deponent to be permitted the liberty of easing nature, but also caused him to be so, as aforesaid, confined for about the space of twenty six hours, on purpose, and with intent, as this deponent then conceived, and hath great reason to believe, to impose on and extort money from him this deponent.

And this deponent Henry Cowper, maketh oath, that he was actually present, and did see the said Charles Relfe assaulted and beaten in manner as aforesaid, and that he was blooded for the preservation of health, and confined in chains for the space aforesaid.[10]

As may be expected, Guybon gave a different interpretation of these incidents. Charles Relfe had been brought into the prison from the *rules* because his securities refused to act further for him. He expressed his annoyance at this proceeding by threatening to fire the prison, and by acting in the chapel "more like a madman than [one who] ... should be at his prayers", and was consequently transferred to a spunging house. Mrs Corbett, however, requested that he be removed from her house as he was so violent, and he was therefore put into a place of restraint until he was sober. Indeed, added Guybon, his prisoners had taken occasion to impute to him "all kinds of cruelties and oppressions", although he "ever held the greatest abhorrence to exercise cruelty and oppression, or to permit or connive it". Consequently he denied that he had ever allowed anything that "might cause such scurrilous and virulent aspirations from the complainants".

Such complaints were first made to the court of Common Pleas in 1723, after Huggins, as warden, had apologised to the prisoners and requested them to forbear a prosecution as he would give them the redress they required. The prisoners stated that they first trusted his integrity, but their faith in him was soon destroyed by his unwillingness to implement his promises.[11] The warden however noted in his reply to these complaints that only three prisoners were involved in them, although the house was full. Two petitions followed against Guybon, one signed by twenty-eight prisoners. This stated that he had imposed great hardships on his prisoners, and had proved harsh and unrelenting in the governing of the prison. This was, one assumes, in relation to the prison fees, for the petition mentioned his avarice and his insensibility to justice and candour. It continued with the request that "they may no longer have the illegal severities and oppressions of the warden and his officers, added to the misfortunes they already suffer from their imprisonment."[12] Although the prothonotaries of the court reported in the Michaelmas term, and the warden replied in the Hilary term, the prisoners found little relief. Their "great friend and patron", the lord chief justice of the Common Pleas, King, was made lord chancellor, and his replacement, Eyre, gave them little help. An insolvency act emptied the prison, so that the matter rested "until the prison filled again, and the grievances increased in proportion". In January 1726 a further petition was sent to Eyre signed by a hundred prisoners, and in it they accused the warden of not only continuing with the old fees but also of demanding new ones. The petition attributed most of the prisoners' "misfortunes to Guybon's avarice, inhumanity, and want of judgement", and, describing him as unfit for the office he held, demanded his replacement.[13]

In December 1726 Eyre heard these complaints. The warden produced evidence that his fees agreed with the tables determined by the same court of Common Pleas in 1686-7 and 1716. The prisoners complained that the court had only heard one side of the evidence. This was because Huggins had refused to allow them to attend the court and give evidence, even though they alleged that the lord mayor and the two sheriffs had offered to provide security for their safe imprisonment, and their solicitor, Mackay, to provide and pay for guards. Claiming that Huggins had emerged from that one-sided affair with new rules of court which not only introduced new charges but also increased the old,[14] and which were "so much to his advantage", they went on to allege that he had placed some of their leaders onto the common side, and put two, Smith and Farrington, into the dungeon for three days. And then "flushed with success" he committed his greatest crime, by placing Thomas Bambridge "in power as [one] very fitly qualified to the execution of his diabolical rage".[15]

Thus for four or five years before the celebrated inquiry of 1729 into this and other prisons took place, the Fleet prison and its warden had been subjected to repeated inquiries and reports made by the prothonotaries of the court of Common Pleas.[16] Yet the real problem hardly surfaced in any of these reports, this being, of course, the fiscal nature of the office of warden, and the requirement that the deputy warden not only had to pay his way and find some return for his outlay, but that he also had to pay a substantial rent to the warden. It is perhaps significant that these complaints were made during the time when Huggins was leasing the prison to a deputy, so that Mackay was able to claim that Huggins had allowed Guybon to increase his charges to enable him "to make up the high rent he pays for the said office".[17] Consequently as fees were demanded which few prisoners were able or willing to afford, and as the warden and his deputies endeavoured to interpret the fee tables in their own favour, it is hardly surprising that opposition developed, particularly from men who had little to lose thereby. The several cases of violence which resulted all seem to be connected with this agitation. They cannot be as readily dismissed as Guybon would have wished, although it must be admitted that the recorded cases are few and far between when spread over a period of some years and the thousand and more prisoners of that period.

The documentation of this long dispute is important, because it helps us to set the 1729 inquiry into perspective. The alleged inactivity of Eyre led him to be accused later of conspiring with Bambridge against the interests of justice.[18] It certainly might be said that had a fair trial been made of the issues involved, and the prisoners been permitted to attend the court, that inquiry of 1729 might never have materialised, although it is doubtful if the prisoners would have been successful in all their claims, for many of the fees they regarded as impositions were well grounded in the rules of the prison. Their real complaint, had they but known it, was about the very nature of imprisonment for debt in a franchise prison. It took another hundred years and more before this could be remedied.

Thomas Bambridge, the one mentioned by Mackay as "very fitly qualified to execute his [Huggins's] diabolical rage",[19] is perhaps the best known name in the history of the Fleet prison. Appointed deputy warden by Huggins in June 1727, he purchased the prison from him in the following year. Huggins had searched for a purchaser for several years, mainly because of his inability to control the prison through his ill health, which "required him to go into the country", while, on the other hand, he found it difficult to govern the prison through the use of deputy wardens, "whose power the prisoners have been apt to despise".[20] Huggins petitioned the Privy Council for a grant of the prison to Bambridge, and this was allowed for the lifetime of George II. However the reversion of the office was granted to Dougal Cuthbert.[21] The parliamentary committee of 1729, in their *Memorial*, suggested that Cuthbert had been granted the office of warden of the Fleet and keeper of the palaces of Westminster by Huggins for a payment of two and a half thousand pounds, but was double-crossed by Huggins obtaining the grant for Bambridge instead. This appears to be one of the many errors made by this committee. It is possible that Cuthbert may have misled it on this point in an effort to dissociate himself from Bambridge, for he held the reversion of the office through having paid half the purchase cost of five thousand pounds, and therefore he received half the profits of the prison from Bambridge. Cuthbert had a saving clause inserted into the act which deprived Bambridge of his office and required the prison to be sold. This ensured that his half-share should be returned to him by the new purchaser.[22] Bambridge gave land and other security for his moiety of the prison, but after his deprivation he was unable to make good this security, and found himself imprisoned for debt at the suit of John Huggins.[23]

But who was Thomas Bambridge? Little is known of him apart from the few years during which he was associated with the Fleet. Huggins described him as a person educated in the law and well qualified for the office of warden, but this may have been a biased statement as it was stated in Huggins's application for the grant of the prison to be given to Bambridge. Other descriptions., less flattering, are given by Mackay, such as a Newgate attorney, "a person of abandoned credit", or one who did not bear the "best of characters".[24] Others regarded him as vain, rash, and high-handed.[25] An even more prejudiced account is found in *Lieutenant Bird's Letter from the Shades to Thomas Bambridge in Newgate*, published when Bambridge was a prisoner there, awaiting trial on charges resulting from the inquiry. This polemical work alleges that Bambridge was the son of an Irish papist who had served as a soldier in King James II's army. After some training to be a Roman priest in Germany, Bambridge came to England supported by a roman catholic charity, studied at Oxford, and became a clerk to an attorney there. From here he ran away to London, changed his name in order to avoid detection, and cohabited with a woman of ill-repute. In order to obtain a living he became a bailiff, where he followed the well-known practice of causing writs to be made out, arresting the persons he had named, and not releasing them until he had received some financial consideration. Having abandoned two wives by forcing them into transportation, Bambridge, the writer claimed, became deputy to Huggins as solicitor of the leather office, but he lost this lucrative job by accepting a bribe of three thousand pounds from a merchant in order to prevent his prosecution for counterfeiting the office's stamp. Marrying by trickery a wealthy woman (the details are elaborate), he was enabled to set up his chambers in the Temple, and to purchase Dorney House in Weybridge.

It was during this period that Bird claimed a notice was placed on a tree in

Wimbledon churchyard, which he said gave a good description of Bambridge. This was said to have been recorded in the *Post Boy* of 25-27 November 1725, no copies of which appear to have survived. The notice read:

> Whereas a fellow, who practices in the law as an attorney, and has, or lately had, chambers up more than one pair of steps, near the bog-house in the King's Bench walks in the Temple; generally wearing a blue camlet coat, and a fair wig, twisted with black ribbon; swaybacked, bow-legged, middle or rather low of stature, and affected strutting gait, long visage, a pale pocked fretten complexion, grey eyes, a low broken unpleasant voice, a debauched rotten carcass, between forty and fifty years of age; excelling the late famous Wilde, Blueskin and Sheppard, in villainies, impudence, and bilking of jailors and bailiffs; He made his escape out of the Fleet prison in London, and has since been seen sculking about Wimbledon in Surrey, and at Wandsworth, in the same county; till such time as it was discovered in those places, who and what he was. If any person will give information of the above described fellow to the keepers of the said prison, or to the keeper of the prison of Newgate in London, ... and he be apprehended ... he shall be well rewarded for his pains.[26]

The Post Boy went on to add that "whoever will discover the author of the said writing ... shall receive one guinea reward." It is signed by T Bird. *The Post Boy* for 25-28 December contained a further note signed by Bambridge. He claimed that the notice was a forgery, and "that the person therein hinted at and designed to be calumniated and traduced was never a prisoner in the Fleet prison or Newgate or any other prison", and described it as a "false, scandalous and malicious notice". Lieutenant Bird, whose relationship to the Bird of the notice is not known, suggested that Bambridge had written the notice himself for some reason or another. He was clearly in financial difficulties, and Bird may well have been right in claiming that he had fled to Wandsworth for safety. Here he was helped by one Savage, who was later allowed to shelter himself in the Fleet under Bambridge's protection. A long list of Bambridge's other trickeries and villainies as a lawyer were catalogued by Bird, and he adds that although he had promised, in accepting the job of deputy warden, to rectify the abuses in the prison, in reality he had sought the office as he assumed his creditors would fear to meddle with a man in his position. However he was arrested, claims Bird, during this period, when attending his wife's funeral to which he had travelled incognito for fear of arrest. He was imprisoned for a few days at Sandwich jail until money was sent to him which procured his release.

Bird obviously elaborated, but he must had had some justification for making these allegations. Bambridge certainly appears to have been a person who had a dubious reputation, "a man with a past", as writers of a later age would describe it. To show the kind of man he was, Bird informs us, in a delightful aside, that, accompanied by his liveried servants, travelling in his coach, and dressed in rich clothes, he went and ordered a rich bed painted with classical scenes.[27] While this is meant to contrast with the plight of his prisoners who had to pay for these luxurious pretensions, it also reveals a man who had determined to rise above the station in life which would otherwise be his.

****

The celebrated inquiry into the prison took place in 1729. It was initiated by General Oglethorpe, a fellow soldier of prince Eugune in his Turkish campaigns, and at that time a member of parliament. He later went on to establish Georgia as one of the American colonies. One of the aims of this venture was to provide a sanctuary for the debtors who were released from the prisons as a result of this inquiry (the number was extremely few), and for those who had returned from the continent whither they had fled to escape imprisonment. Lecky in his history of England describes him as a person of indomitable energy but impulsive and hot-tempered. The actual cause of the inquiry was the death of Oglethorpe's friend, the architect and translator, Castell, in the Fleet prison.[28] The circumstances of his death so disquieted Oglethorpe that after some preliminary investigations, he demanded and obtained a parliamentary inquiry into all the prisons of England.

The committee, though it worked with great diligence, only examined three of these prisons, the Fleet, the King's Bench, and the Marshalsea. It was then allowed to sink into oblivion, for reasons which have never been adequately explained, even though it was clear that the conditions in the other prisons were equally deserving of investigation. These matters were certainly known to the committee, for there had been much publicity given to the corruptions and assaults occasioned by the deputy keeper of Ludgate prison in 1727,[29] and news of the parliamentary inquiry prompted the prisoners in many of the suburban gaols to "draw up depositions against their keepers regarding impositions and extortions" which they presented to this committee.[30] The one tangible result of the inquiry, apart from the changes at the Fleet, was an act of 1729 which regulated spunging houses, permitted prisoners to obtain their own food and bedding, fixed gaolers' fees, ordered a table of these fees to be set up in each prison, and empowered the judges to hear complaints against gaolers.[31] But this act only papered over the cracks in the system, and had no effective system of enforcement.

Huggins and Bambridge both committed a major error in treating the committee with contempt, refusing even to give it a list of prisoners in the prison and the *rules*. It was even alleged that Bambridge prepared for the committee by discharging one hundred and nineteen prisoners whose debts amounted to over seventeen thousand pounds, some of whom should have been discharged as far back as 1718. The committee accepted this allegation, which in effect accused the two wardens of retaining discharged prisoners in the prison for the sake of their unpaid prison fees, when they had been officially released by their creditors. A more simple explanation might be that many of these prisoners had been discharged by the insolvent debtors' act of 1728, or that the prison books had been brought up to date.[32]

This lack of co-operation by the two wardens meant that the committee became prejudiced against them, and took little note of what was said in their defence. *The Committee's Memorial*, a pamphlet which purported to contain their initial findings, but was probably written as an anti-Bambridge tract, stated:

> upon the whole ... Mr Bambridge expected his creatures, who were always at his service while under his wand, would have continued their former cant, and even those whom he most trusted too, would be favourable in their examinations he found himself disappointed: For as they were before under his immediate command, and must either starve or be obedient to his arbitrary will, he found now had their consciences at liberty... Thus is that mighty and wonderful oppressor oppressed himself only with this difference, that, as he himself oppressed others contrary to law, he himself is oppressed by a just and due course of law.

The memorial continued by suggesting that Bambridge's eventual defence to the committee merely showed "an aggravation of his guilt, which appeared to be of the blackest crimes imaginable".[33] Popular opinion endorsed these feelings, the

Craftsman writing that if Sir John Falstaff were alive now, instead of going to the Fleet, "he would choose rather to die in the ditch, than to linger in the prison".[34]

At the end of its inquiry into the Fleet prison, the committee made the following resolutions, which were incorporated into the *Journal* of the House of Commons, the house having agreed with them *nem con*:

> Resolved, that Thomas Bambridge, the acting warden of the prison of the Fleet, hath wilfully permitted several debtors to the crown in great sums of money, as well as debtors to divers of his majesty's subjects, to escape; hath been guilty of the most notorious breaches of his trust, great extortions, and the highest crimes and misdemeanours in the execution of his said office, and hath arbitrarily and unlawfully loaded with irons, put into dungeons, and destroyed prisoners for debt under his charge, treating them in the most barbarous and cruel manner, in high violation and contempt of the laws of this kingdom.
>
> Resolved, that John Huggins, esquire, late warden of the prison of the Fleet, did during the time of his wardenship, wilfully permit many considerable debtors, in his custody, to escape; and was notoriously guilty of great breaches of his trust, extortions, cruelties, and other high crimes and misdemeanours, in the execution of his said office, to the great oppression and ruin of many of the subjects of this kingdom.

In addition four of the prison officers, Barnes, Pindar, King, and Everett were associated with these charges, and together with Huggins and Bambridge they were ordered to be confined as close prisoners in Newgate prison to await trial. There, it is said, Bambridge persuaded the prison tapster, Anne Jones, to move in with him as his mistress, an association soon dropped after his eventual release.[35] It was also ordered that a bill be brought in to dispossess Bambridge of his office and to more effectively regulate the Fleet.[36]

On the same day Cuthbert was given the temporary care of the prison, and one Frazer, a debtor in the Fleet, assembling the other prisoners, "exerted them to a dutiful and peaceable behaviour in the present conjecture of affairs which they all promised to adhere to".[37]

These trials took place. Huggins was tried for the murder of Edward Arne. A special verdict was brought in which was then tried before the lord chief justice, Raymond. Bambridge was tried for the murder of Castell, and then on the same charge with Corbett, a turnkey, on appeal. Bambridge was also tried for felony in stealing the goods of a prisoner, Mrs Berkley, during which an attempt was made to empanel on the jury several former Fleet prisoners.[38]

Although these prosecutions were ordered by the House of Commons, and conducted by some of the most able lawyers of the day, all the defendants were found not guilty.[39] The suggestion that this was because of the impossibility of obtaining the necessary evidence from their subordinates, several of whom had fled, is hardly sufficient, as Bambridge was acquitted without having to produce any witnesses at all on his behalf. Another suggestion that bribes to the jury had settled the matter is probably equally untrue, for it seems that, as Sean McConville has pointed out, the public felt far less outrage about the committee's revelations than the committee did,[40] and this may well have been reflected by the juries concerned. In order to offer some explanation for this remarkable turn of events it is necessary to look at the allegations brought against the two wardens, and the circumstances of their trials.

****

Huggins was charged with aiding and abetting James Barnes, a watchman and prisoner in the Fleet, in the murder of Edward Arne. Barnes had subsequently fled. Arne had showed all the symptoms of insanity, and Huggins's application for him to be moved into Bethlehem hospital had failed. As he grew more disordered, running about the prison naked in the presence of women, and his behaviour making him "not fit to be a bed-fellow", it was thought necessary to confine him in a strong room. This was done at the request of the prisoners' court of inspectors. Thomas Paine, who appeared for the prisoners, significantly evaded Huggins's allegation that the "court" had put Arne there, by stating that the prisoners did not so much as visit this strong room. The strong room, in reality a dungeon, eight by seven feet, with walls of brick and lime, had been built by Guybon. It was near the prison midden and thus a place "nauseous and unwholesome", without comfort, fire, a close stool or other utensil, damp and filthy. Welland, who acted for Guybon, unconvincingly claimed that Julius Caesar's ward on the common side was an even worse place. Although Arne had been provided with a bed and food by the prison authorities as well as by "the company of upholders" to whom he belonged, his condition became deplorable. He crept into his feather bed, and having temporarily escaped from that room, entered a parlour adjoining to the chapel with the feathers of his bed and excrement "sticking about him like a magpie". He eventually died. It was established that Arne was a prisoner on mesne process only, so that the warden was not liable for his debts if he escaped, and so there was no need for him to have been placed in such strict confinement, particularly when there were other chambers available. Many of the prosecution witnesses agreed that a confinement of six weeks in that dungeon could only have a fatal outcome. On these grounds Huggins was accused of being an accessory to his murder.

In the course of Huggins's trial it was noted that Arne's case had not been entered into any affidavit made for the court of Common Pleas, and which had been published by Mackay. This seems a strange omission if the facts alleged were true. However Huggins's defence proceeded on the assumption that the facts as reported were correct, and rested on the grounds that he could not be made responsible for the criminal acts of officers of the prison, who were in any case responsible to Guybon, the then deputy warden, who had subsequently died, rather than to him. Although several endeavoured to prove that Huggins had visited the prison, seen Arne in the dungeon, and refused to allow an application for his release, Huggins produced witnesses to prove he was elsewhere, in the country or at Sir George Oxenden's, on the dates in question. Sir George, Sir John Hinde Cotton, Bart, Dr Pearce, later bishop of Rochester, and (a telling point) Sir James Thornhill, all gave evidence of Huggins's good character, Sir James stating, "I have never seen or heard of the least cruel act that he has done by anyone." Sir James was a member of the committee of the House of Commons which had brought forward that resolution to the house about Huggins's cruelties and oppressions!

A special verdict was brought in by the jury, in spite of a most adverse summing up by Mr Justice Page. Although the jury found that Huggins had visited the prison during the period of Arne's imprisonment, it agreed that while he was guilty of being an accessory to Arne's murder in so far as he could have prevented it, his offence was without malice or aforethought. This was not sufficient for the court to either acquit or convict Huggins, and so the case was pleaded before Raymond, the lord chief justice. He found that Huggins could only answer in civil law, but not in criminal law, for the acts of his officers; that Arne was not sent to the dungeon by Huggins, nor was he aware that the room was dangerous to Arne's life. The jury's verdict was regarded as insufficient for Huggins to be convicted, although it was hinted that if the special verdict had been made more specific then a different decision might have been reached.[41]

The only other case of cruelty alleged against Huggins by the committee's report concerned one Oliver Reed, who had been recaptured after an escape bid. Huggins confessed to the committee that in order to confine him securely he sent to Newgate for irons, and placed Reed in a dungeon. There he was forced to lie on a small bed, with chains of forty pounds weight on him, which even Bambridge thought too heavy. The stench from an adjacent "necessary house" and a store room where were kept "the most noisom offals to feed the dogs there kennelled" was so intolerable that the committee was unable to remain there for more than six minutes.[42]

The *Report* also accused Huggins of permitting prisoners to escape, and of utilising writs of *habeas corpus* to protect the prisoners he allowed abroad. The case of Thomas Perrin, a merchant, was mentioned. A crown debtor with debts of over forty-two thousand pounds, he was given the liberty of the *rules* with securities "of no account of substance", and in 1714 he was permitted to go to Holland for the purposes of settling his affairs, for which he appears to have given no better security than his word for his safe return. Though he returned then, he left for Holland again in 1716, as part of a joint business venture (or so it was claimed) between himself and Huggins, which resulted in a thousand pound profit for Huggins. Both these exits from the prison were technically escapes and when questioned about them Huggins claimed that he had obtained a *quietus* regarding the matter, and had purchased Perrin's securities (that is, the crown title to the debts) from the commissioners of the customs for two thousand pounds. If this was so then it was a good bargain on the part of Huggins, for this purchase prevented any escape writs being issued against him, for what was clearly an illegal offence since the legislation of the 1690s and 1700s.[43] It was further alleged that Huggins permitted one of his tipstaffs, Richard Bishop, to take prisoners "abroad", and allowed them sham credit. Bishop later took out commissions of bankruptcy against these prisoners, and in this way they managed to defraud their creditors, who instead of obtaining the totality of their debts, had to settle for a composition at so much in the pound.[44]

In reply to these allegations Huggins admitted that so many prisoners had escaped during the years of his wardenship that he found it impossible to enumerate them, but he was probably able to point out that the law required him to satisfy their creditors from his own resources. As an illustration of this he could point to the case of Boys. Huggins had been accused of permitting Boys to escape from the prison *rules* even though he had been given notice to keep him in strict confinement. Boys was charged with debts of over twenty-five thousand pounds. For this, and two other escapes, Huggins was prosecuted, but judgment was found for him by the barons of the court of Exchequer, probably because the various debts had been paid through the warden calling in the securities given him by these prisoners for their safe imprisonment.[45]

****

Huggins appears to have emerged from these investigations and trials with his honour and character reasonably intact. His friends clearly stood by him, accepting that his alleged offences were either committed by his deputy warden and his officers, for which he could not be held responsible in law, or by him in order to quieten the prison. The morality of leasing the prison for a high rental, leading to all kinds of abuses and extortions, did not concern them.

The first line of argument could not apply to Bambridge, for he was the acting deputy warden and then warden. His character has already been noted. It was not attractive. In his office he was a martinet and acted in a dictatorial and authoritarian manner. He probably owed his office to these abilities and qualities, for the one thing the prison needed at the date of his appointment was order and discipline. It could be suggested that Bambridge's real offence was the enforcing of the warden's authority within the prison, and the introduction of order and quietness amongst the prisoners. In pursuit of this aim, however, he clearly went beyond the limits of the working balance of power between the prison authorities and the prisoners necessary for the good order of the prison, and he also allowed his zeal and ruthlessness to exceed even the strict boundaries of legal restraint.

The prison to which Bambridge was appointed as deputy warden in 1727 was effectively controlled by the prisoners rather than by the prison officials. The balance of power between the two had broken down completely in favour of the prisoners, and clearly Bambridge was brought in to reverse the position. A group of prisoners, the "court of inspectors", mentioned at the trial of Huggins, had formed themselves into a jurisdiction. They made their own rules and orders, allocated the prison chambers to prisoners, established a mock court, punished those who offended them by placing them in the stocks, and required each new prisoner to pay a fine of five shillings. This money was used by the "court of inspectors" to pay for their applications to the court of Common Pleas for the regulation of the prison fees. This "court" was so troublesome that Guybon declined to enter the prison house for fear of its authority, and thus removed his office to the home of one of his turnkeys, Pindar, within the prison *rules*.[46]

Bambridge was required, therefore, to take various strong measures in order to subdue and control his prisoners. He armed several of the prison watchmen with bayonets and muskets (previously they had pikes and halberds), as he was allowed to do by the prison rules.[47] A watch-house was built in the prison courtyard. The back windows of the Vine tavern, a spunging house next to the prison whose windows overlooked the prison yard, were blocked up. All communication with the prisoners, and possibly their exits and entrances, now had to pass through the prison gate and could be controlled by the warden and his officers. Mackay complained however that he was unable to attend the prisoners as Bambridge refused him entry through the gate, and added that "nobody could come to any prisoner" without the warden's knowledge.[48]

A more controversial matter followed. "In order to quell a riot and disorder the prisoners had committed", or "to keep rioters in awe", as the contemporary newspapers noted, Bambridge requested and obtained a military force of a sergeant and twelve men of the foot guards. The *Weekly Journal* even suggested that this guard had been ordered by the government to assist the warden.[49] Lieutenant Bird satirically wrote of the prison having the appearance of a garrison, with sentry boxes at every corner, and Bambridge "affecting to exercise and march" as one "no less than a monarch" at the head of his troops.[50] There was an earlier precedent for this action. In 1717 a group of smugglers who had been committed to the prison threatened to break gaol. The deputy warden, Stone, thus requested and obtained a corporal and six men in order to keep the prison quiet.[51]

Such a precedent was unknown to the prisoners, particularly to those of the court of inspectors, who made clear to the world their own version of the events which led to the introduction of this military force.   On 7 July the prisoners "on the master's side" petitioned that by this display of force they had "'been lately publicly and falsely scandalised".   Declaring their abhorrence of all disloyalty, riot, and disorder, they expressed their concern that the "higher powers" might consider them to be unworthy of an act of clemency by the granting of an insolvency act.   This may well have been a genuine petition, expressing a real concern, but what followed was probably more representative of the "court of inspectors" than the whole body of the prisoners.   Application was made to the court of Common Pleas that the presence of this body of soldiers had put them in fear of murder.   An illustration was given of an incident in which a sentry "had fired off his piece with a brace of bullets" at a young man who was looking out of a window.   This application failed as the court refused to take cognisance of an unsigned petition.   A further application was made to General Wills, whom Bambridge alleged had sent the guard to him.

This petition, signed by Major Wilson, T Farringdon, and N Senior, and a few other prisoners, claimed that they were subject only to the civil power.   It mentioned their long controversy with the warden, whose demand for fees had become as burdensome as their debts, and argued that the military force gave more power to Bambridge to enable him to continue his tyranny.   The petition recorded the events which led to a military force being placed in the prison.   A prisoner by the name of Mackpheadris and about four-score others had been removed to a ward on the common side for their refusal to pay the warden's extortionate demands.   Here they were so closely confined that "in this hot weather" they were in danger of catching "contagion".   Their intolerable situation had resulted in some fray, in which Bambridge was the aggressor.   Even a petty constable would have considered it "a dishonour to the dignity of his staff" to have taken part in the quelling of this riot.   But this was the pretext Bambridge used in order to bring in the guards.   This "imaginary insurrection" was simply "the windmill of his own brain ... an exploit for Don Quixote ... which might furnish matter for the annals".[52]

Two things stand out.   The first is that the original controversy appears to have been a continuation of the long saga about the prison fees.   This was accentuated by the weakness of the prison's administration which permitted a small group of prisoners to virtually change the balance of power in their own favour. The second is Bambridge's over-reaction, for he used this controversy as a pretext to obtain additional help to break the power of this "court of inspectors", and thus control the prison himself. Incidentally, as Mackay records, the prisoners had no help from General Wills, but after several more weeks "in the broiling heat of summer" confined to their ward, they were released by an insolvent debtors' act. We turn now to consider the charges made against Bambridge.

The inquiry had been occasioned by the death of Castell, and Bambridge was tried on two occasions for his murder. It was claimed that Castell had given security to live in the *rules*, but when Bambridge became aware that he had received a sum of one hundred and twenty-five pounds he determined to extort this from him, and consequently sent him into Corbett's spunging house. Here there was an epidemic of smallpox. Castell, with a morbid fear of this disease, pleaded to go elsewhere. This was refused, and he caught smallpox, which was the cause of his death. However, it became clear during the trials that there was a far more satisfactory version than the prejudiced one of the *Report*. One of Castell's securities for the *rules*, Chambers, had declined to act further as Castell had made two mortgages on his estate. Chambers denied that he had surrendered the security because he heard that Castell was planning to go "abroad", that is, escape from the *rules*, but admitted that Bambridge had persuaded him to act as one of Castell's securities for his safe imprisonment. Bambridge, who was Castell's attorney, had lent him money, and was on terms of personal friendship with him (both being members of a club which met at Corbett's house), endeavoured to persuade Chambers to continue his securities for a further eight days thus allowing Castell time to find additional securities, but was unsuccessful. Unable to remain in the *rules* because of the extent of his debts, nine hundred pounds, and unwilling to enter the prison house, Castell requested that a bed be prepared for him at Corbett's spunging house. There, Thomas White, the one case of smallpox in the house, was out of danger and recovering from that disease. White was kept in a garret in the "old house", while Castell had a room on the first floor in the new house "newly taken in". Corbett even testified that he was unaware that there was a case of smallpox in his house, and it was agreed he had treated Castell with the greatest civility.

Bambridge was honourably acquitted, and although charged with Corbett when Mrs Castell appealed against the first verdict, he was permitted bail as the judge was "well satisfied" with that verdict. Although Bambridge claimed that Corbett was charged with him in the appeal in order to prejudice the evidence he would give in Bambridge's favour, both were acquitted, a fact which suggests that several of the Fleet prisoners who gave evidence at these trials committed perjury. Indeed Mr Justice Page noted at the first trial that there was "much conflict of evidence".[53]

Although the *Report* claimed that Bambridge had committed felony in taking goods from one Horder, this matter never came to trial, and instead Bambridge was tried on a similar charge relating to theft from a Mrs Berkley, although this particular charge was never mentioned in the *Report*. Holder, a rich "spanish" merchant, with property reputed to be worth thirty thousand pounds, had been sent to the common side. It was suggested that this was to better enable Bambridge to embezzle his goods, which, it was alleged, he was able to do even more freely when Holder died, reputedly, as a result of his sufferings. Horder's dying words were remembered: "the villain Bambridge would be the occasion of his death". Bambridge also removed two prisoners who acted as Holder's trustees for his thirteen-year-old son, one to a dungeon and the other outside the prison, in order, it was again alleged, to further his scheme. As nothing more was heard of this case, it appears that Bambridge's defence was accepted. This was that Holder was so poor that his family had had to support him in prison, and that he had been dispossessed of his room for non-payment of rent (though restored to it when ill), while the two "trustees" had endeavoured to remove his small effects for their own purposes. This led to one of the trustees, Major Wilson, being imprisoned in a dungeon, while the other, Piggott, left the prison as he had been discharged.[54]

Instead of Holder's case, that of Mrs Berkley was presented for trial. Bambridge's protest was fairly made, that although the matters complained of took place in October 1727, they had not been reported to the committee, and that the complainants had not only waited six months to bring it forward, but had only done so after his acquittal for the murder of Castell. He had a further complaint, namely that several members of the jury presented to the court were successfully challenged as being former Fleet prisoners. He also argued that one of his key witnesses, Douglas, a turnkey of the prison, had been "put on the indictment to take off his evidence". The case was similar to Holder's. Mrs Berkley was distressed for fifty-six pounds, being the arrears in her chamber rent. Thereupon she was evicted from her room, and later on, in her presence and that of a constable, Bambridge accompanied by other prison officers had her trunks broken open, and an inventory of her goods made. These included several valuable rings and diamonds. Although an attempt was made to prove that Bambridge had taken articles of wearing apparel, forbidden by law, having them written down in the inventory as "material sufficient for clothing", he was acquitted.[55]

The *Report* itemised other "cruelties" of Bambridge, of which no subsequent indictment was made. Jacob Mendez-Solas, a Portuguese Jew and merchant, was one of these alleged victims of Bambridge's cruelties. His examination by the committee was painted by Hogarth in vivid detail.[56] The committee wrote of him in their *Report* that after being sent back to Corbett's spunging house, he was brought back into the prison, and placed in the strong room on the master's side:

> This place is a vault like those in which the dead are interred, and wherein the bodies of persons dying in the said prison are usually deposited, till the coroner's inquest hath passed upon them; it has no chimney nor fireplace, nor any light but what comes over the door, or through a hole of about eight inches square. it is neither paved nor boarded; and the rough bricks appear both on the sides and the top, being neither wainscoted nor plastered: what adds to the dampness and stench of the place is, its being built over the common-shore, and adjoining to the sink and dung-hill where all the nastiness of the prison is cast. In this miserable place the poor wretch was kept by the said Bambridge, manacled and shackled for near two months. At length, on receiving five guineas from Mr Kemp, a friend of Solas's, Bambridge released the prisoner from his cruel confinement. But though his chains were taken off, his terror still remained, and the unhappy man was prevailed upon by that terror, not only to labour *gratis* for the said Bambridge, but to swear also at random all that he hath required of him: And the committee themselves saw an instance of the deep impression his sufferings had made upon him; for on his surmising, from something said, that Bambridge was to return again, as warden of the Fleet, he fainted, and the blood started out of his mouth and nose.

Bambridge, in his reply to these allegations, asserted that Mendez-Solas had been placed by Guybon in a strong room because he was utterly ungovernable, having endeavoured to repossess by force the room from which he had been ejected for non-payment. He was only released from the strong room after his friends had guaranteed his good behaviour.[57] The man had sufficiently recovered

The committee of the House of Commons examining Bambridge in 1729. An engraving of the picture by Hogarth. Oglethorpe (seated on left) id shown addressing Bambridge, whilst a prisoner, possibly Mendez-Solas, is exhibiting various devices used to restrain prisoners. Collection of the author.

to give evidence in Bambridge's trial for felony, during which nothing was said about his sufferings.[58]

Another case taken up by the court concerned Captain Mackpheadris, whose name has already been mentioned. He had been ruined by over-speculation in the South Sea Bubble. Having been ejected from his room, whose rent he disputed, he built a hut in the prison yard. Removed from this he fled into the prison house, from which he was taken by a detachment of soldiers, and placed in a dungeon. Here he remained in spite of a court order requiring his release, which Bambridge refused to implement because it had been made outside the legal term. Bambridge then added insult to injury by indicting Mackpheadris at the Old Bailey on a charge of assault, and, it was claimed, turning out two of his servants who refused to sign false affidavits. The prisoners claimed that the lord mayor had ordered the grand jury to the Fleet where it found that Bambridge was the aggressor, but as the bill against the prisoners had been found, this action was too late to be effectual. Eventually Mackpheadris, terrified by threats and softened by promises, pleaded guilty to various charges such as striking Bambridge and was fined one shilling. Since then he and the other prisoners had been continually harassed, and he had been tortured through the use of leg-irons. Bambridge pointed out in a defence which the *Committee's Memorial* regarded as "sorry and frivolous" that the captain had led a riot of between eighty and one hundred prisoners. They had threatened to tear down several partitions in the prison, and refused to allow any of the "servants of the prison" to interrupt them or to come within the prison house. At Huggins's request Bambridge, who was dining with him preparatory to taking over as his deputy, entered the prison with an armed guard and had Mackpheadris ironed and placed in confinement. He was later released. It would appear that this was the occasion during which the armed guard was introduced into the prison. If this was the little "fray", as described by the prisoners, then Bambridge's own version of events appears to have been equally one-sided.[59]

Two similar cases were also noted by the committee, these being those of David Sinclair and Sir William Rich, both of whom were placed in a dungeon and ironed. The *Report* stated that in the case of Sinclair:

Bambridge declared to the said James Barnes, one of the agents of his cruelties, "that he would have Sinclair's blood"; and he took the opportunity of the first festival day, which was on the first of August following, when he thought Captain Sinclair might, by celebrating the memory of the late king, be warmed with liquor so far as to give him some excuse for the cruelties which he intended to inflict upon him. But in some measure he was disappointed; for Captain Sinclair was perfectly sober, when the said Bambridge rushed into his room with a dark lantern in his hand, assisted by his accomplices James Barnes and William Pindar, and supported by his usual guard, armed with muskets and bayonets, and without any provocation given, run his lantern into Captain Sinclair's face, seized him by the collar, and told him he must come along with him: Captain Sinclair, although surprised, asked for what, and by what authority he so treated him? Upon which Barnes and the rest seized Captain Sinclair, who still desiring to know by what authority they so abused him, Bambridge grossly insulted him, and struck him with his cane on the head and shoulders, while he was held fast by Pindar and Barnes. Such base and scandalous usage of this gentleman, who had in the late wars always signalised himself with the greatest courage, gallantry and honour, in the service of his country upon many of the most brave and desperate occasions, must be most shocking and intolerable; yet Captain Sinclair bore it with patience, refusing only to go out of his room unless he was forced; whereupon the said Bambridge threatened to run his cane down his throat, and ordered his guard to stab him with their bayonets, or drag him down to the said dungeon, called the strong room; the latter of which they did, and Bambridge kept him confined in that damp and loathsome place, till he had lost the use of his limbs and memory, neither of which he has perfectly recovered to this day. Many aggravating cruelties were used to make his confinement more terrible; and when Bambridge found he was in danger of immediate death, he removed him for fear of his dying in duress, and caused him to be carried in a dying condition from that dungeon to a room where there was no bed or furniture; and so unmercifully prevented his friends from having any access to him, that he was four days without the least sustenance.

It appeared to the committee by the evidence of a surgeon and others, who were prisoners in the house, that when Captain Sinclair was forced into that loathsome dungeon he was in perfect health.

Captain Sinclair applied for remedy at law against the said cruelties of Bambridge, and had procured a *habeas corpus* for his witnesses to be brought before the *sessions of eyre* and *terminer* when the said Bambridge, by colour of his assumed authority as warden, took the said writs of *habeas corpus* from the officer whose duty was to make a return of them, and commanded him to keep out of the way, whilst he himself went to the Old Bailey, and immediately indicted Captain Sinclair and such of his witnesses he knew he could not deter by threats, or prevail with by promises to go from the truth.

Captain Sinclair had temper enough to bear patiently almost insupportable injuries, and to reserve himself for a proper occasion, when justice should be done him by the laws of the realm.[60]

Bambridge's defence amounted to this: it was assumed that Sinclair, who was confined in the prison with debts of ten thousand pounds, was planning an escape, and that so far from the warden being the aggressor, he had been the victim of his prisoner's rage when he and his officers had attempted to restrain him and his companions. He had remained intoxicated in the dungeon for several days, after which he had been taken to a room on the master's side.[61] The captain was sufficiently recovered from his ordeal, however, to give an "entertainment" to his fellow prisoners on the news that Bambridge had been removed from office.[62]

Sir William Rich had been sent to the King's Bench prison by Bambridge in the hope of quieting the prison. However he returned, claimed the warden, simply to cause trouble. He remained in dispute about his prison fees, and so far from being forced into a spunging house in order extort more fees from him, he voluntarily remained in one until Corbett refused to keep him there any longer as he was so troublesome. An incident then occurred in the prison after Rich had been ejected from his room on the master's side: each side claimed the other to be the aggressor, although the one certain fact is that Rich had a cobbler's knife in his hand. As may be expected there were two interpretations of this incident which led to Rich being placed in a dungeon. Bambridge claimed that the judges of the court of Common Pleas had decided that his actions in this case were lawful and justified and refused to relieve Rich.[63]

There were other accusations made against Bambridge by the committee. It claimed that he kept the books of the prison in such a negligent state that he could not be said to have exercised his trust as warden. This, they said, was done on purpose, for this practice allowed him to keep names of discharged prisoners on the prison books, so that either he could issue an escape warrant to retake such persons, and thereby "squeeze" from them "all the money that can possibly be got", or he would allow the others to contract new debts, and then return in order to take advantage of an act for the relief of insolvent debtors, thus defrauding their creditors. Only one instance of the former was noted. This was the case of Thomas Hogg. Having been officially discharged, Hogg claimed that he was forced into the prison house after he was seen to have given charity to the prisoners at the prison "grate". No instance of the latter was recorded. Another accusation was that Bambridge accepted money from charitably inclined people to discharge prisoners who were confined only for their prison fees, but then refused to discharge any such prisoners. It was alleged he received illicit "Christmas gifts" from those in the *rules*, collecting in one year over two thousand eight hundred pounds, while in addition he required these rulers to pay him two guineas each in order to have their names inserted into the schedule for the insolvent debtors' act. The refusal of several to pay this amount meant that they were unable to obtain its benefit.[64] Furthermore the committee considered that spunging houses were not the convenience Bambridge claimed them to be, in acting as a halfway house between the prison and outside, but rather a device used to terrorise the prisoners.

In response to these allegations Bambridge merely claimed that he had done his duty in attempting to govern his charge peacefully, and it is surely significant that no charges were made against him regarding the above allegations. However one charge appears to have been proven against him, although it was not mentioned in the *Report*.

This related to one Bygrave. After the bill to deprive Bambridge of his office and to sell the prison had been presented, Bygrave petitioned for a saving clause to protect his own interests. He had purchased the office of clerk of the papers at the Fleet from Huggins for the lives of himself and his son. This had been allowed by the court of Common Pleas, the previous holder, Adams, having absconded when that court determined to proceed against him for neglect of his office. Adams' grant had been extended to permit him to appoint his successor, but his appointment of Richard Bishop, a tipstaff, for a sum of seven hundred pounds was not acceptable to the court, who considered Bishop incapable of exercising that office. Bygrave paid an equal sum for that office to Huggins, who was then required to pay off Bishop and other incumbrances. This Huggins only did in part, retaining in his own hands another portion of the payment until various matters had been settled. Whereupon Bishop, who claimed more than had been agreed, said Bygrave, took the case into Chancery, with the result that until that was determined, Bygrave's grant of office could not be approved. Bambridge, who Bygrave claimed was offended with him for reporting one of his abuses regarding a writ of *habeas corpus* to the court, used this as his opportunity to dismiss him, selling his office to John Cotton for seven hundred pounds, but promising to reimburse Bygrave if he delivered up his receipt. Fearful of Bambridge, and now being his prisoner as he had become indebted to several people through being "an adventurer in some mines" (who had arrested him assuming that he had sold his office and thus had ready money), he accepted this arrangement, even though he had been offered twelve hundred pounds for the office which was worth three hundred and fifty pounds per annum. He then discovered that the office had in fact been sold for fifteen hundred pounds, and that the remaining eight hundred pounds had been split between Bambridge and Cuthbert. Bygrave consequently claimed that this money should be returned to him. In this he was unsuccessful, for however revealing the matter may have been of Bambridge's character, it could not be regarded as an illegal transaction as no grant of office had been made to him.[65]

****

It has been suggested more than once in passing that the committee's *Report* was highly inaccurate. When it is laid alongside Mackay's work, which, be it remembered, contained the prisoners' case against the warden, and the reports of the trials of Huggins and Bambridge, it is seen to be seriously defective. And yet it was this *Report* that was instrumental in debarring Bambridge from his wardenship, and in promoting his and Huggins's trials. It must be admitted, however, that one reason for its defectiveness was because both Huggins and Bambridge refused to co-operate with the committee, perhaps considering it was simply another stage in the long-drawn-out dispute between the administration of the prison and the prisoners' "court of inspectors" about the prison fees. The committee, therefore, was forced to accept much of the evidence presented to it by these prisoners, in the want of any defence, and these men, as Huggins maintained as his trial, were like all prisoners "natural haters of their keepers". By the time that the two wardens realised their mistake, and were summoned to appear before the committee, it was seriously prejudiced against them. In addition to the conflict of evidence already mentioned between the court cases and the statements of the *Report,* other examples of its one-sidedness may be quoted.

One example relates to the prison fees, which was one of the major areas of dispute. Because of the refusal of the "court of inspectors'" to pay their fees several of the ringleaders found themselves ejected from their rooms. The resulting trouble caused by these ejections often meant that these men ended up ironed in the prison strong room or dungeon. It is hardly to be wondered at, therefore, that the *Report* should have accused Bambridge of extorting false commitment fees and demanding excessive chamber rent, or that it should have suggested that he had maliciously persuaded the court of Common Pleas in the Trinity term of 1727 to accept that the fees he charged were the legal fees of the prison. The prisoners, for example, alleged that Bambridge had added to the commitment fee the several items which, they claimed, were already included in it, such as the clerk's fee of two shillings and four pence, or the chamberlain's and porter's fees of one shilling each. Likewise they claimed that Bambridge had demanded a separate fee for each commitment charge. But, as will be shown later, Bambridge's fees were not only the fees that had been charged in the prison in 1724, before his time, they had also been accepted by Lord Chief Justice King as the legal fees established during the 1680s. As Bambridge had only been appointed to the prison a matter of weeks before this hearing of 1727, it is hardly to be wondered at that he simply recorded the fees he had found charged in the prison at his entry.[66] There was also a major discrepancy in the report itself regarding the "Christmas gifts" which Bambridge allegedly demanded from the rulers. In the text the sum is stated to be twenty-eight hundred pounds, but in the appendix a mere fifteen hundred pounds.[67]

The *Report* also alleged that Bambridge had permitted many escapes, and the act which deprived him of his office did so for this particular reason. Yet the committee was only able to find evidence for six "escapes". Bambridge made it clear that he only had the custody of three of these men, and alleged that those who had escaped during his period of office had done so without his consent. The most telling point, however, is that no prosecution was ever made against him for an escape.[68]

It was further alleged that the ironing of prisoners and placing them in dungeons was unknown in the prison before the wardenship of Guybon. This was simply not true. Even the *Report* itself established the falsity of these allegations by inference, for by indicating that the letters patent granting the office to Whitcott in 1667 permitted him the right to exact fees for the liberty of the house and irons, it made clear that if the warden was permitted to exempt prisoners from such ironing, then he also possessed the right to iron them. The committee went on to commit an even more glaring blunder. It actually stated that the safety and peace of the prison were well preserved without the use of such expedients during the time Guybon and Bambridge were deputy wardens.[69] It was Guybon, in fact, who had built the dungeons in the prison, in spite of the observation made to him by Lord Chief Justice King that there should be no prison within a prison. As Bambridge pointed out in his defence:

> [He] apprehends it is the duty of every keeper to preserve the peace within his prison; because every breach thereof, or other disorder there, tends to promote escapes, which are highly penal to him; and that in cases of riots, mutinies, or other gross misbehaviour, he may by law justify putting the ringleaders into strong holds, and even into irons; but when he does so, it is always at his peril; and if it be without sufficient cause, he is not only punishable in the usual course of law, as all other wrong doers are, but he is punishable in a summary way, at the discretion of the court to which he belongs.
>
> That prisoners in the Fleet prison, for the most part, come thither not by compulsion, but by a voluntary surrender in discharge of bail, and thereby they in some measure stipulate to become true prisoners to the warden; and when he furnishes them with rooms, for which rent is fixed by act of parliament, if it should not be in his power to dispossess them for non-payment, he would be in a worse condition than any other of the king's subjects, as having his property detained from him, and no possibility of any satisfaction for the injury.
>
> That in a prison where there are such great numbers of prisoners, of whom the greatest part come thither for their extravagances, it would be impossible to prevent escapes, mutinies, riots, tumults, and other disorders, if the warden was not intrusted with a power to restrain the ringleaders, especially since he is in so penal a manner answerable for the consequences of them, and so frequently suffers by them; and it has been no new thing to put prisoners of disorderly behaviour into irons.[70]

These are weighty arguments.

It is not surprising, consequently, that Huggins and Bambridge should have been acquitted of the indictments laid against them, in spite of the fact that these prosecutions were ordered by the House of Commons and carried on with a great deal of public vilification, especially of Bambridge. Neither is it surprising that the committee was allowed to lapse, so that Thomson's sentiment in his poem *Winter* failed to materialise:

> Ye sons of mercy! yet resume the search;
> Drag forth the legal monsters into light,
> Wrench from their hands oppression's iron rod,
> And bid the cruel feel the pains they give.

Bambridge undoubtedly was correct in his allegation that there was a "conspiracy" against him. The "court of inspectors" has already been mentioned, and as only a few names out of the many hundreds of prisoners are mentioned in the *Report* or Mackay's account, one is led to wonder if these were the men who were the "ringleaders" who wished to control the prison in their own interests, endeavouring to secure a reduction in its fees, and who consequently resented any strong assertion of authority by the warden. These were probably the men who gave their version of these events to the committee, forced the further trial of Bambridge for felony, and endeavoured to link Lord Chief Justice Eyre with Bambridge, claiming that for Bambridge to have escaped the charges laid against him he must have received his protection.[71]

These charges are worth noting. Several anonymous letters had been sent to Edward Hughes, a member of parliament, who was a member of the committee. One read, in part:

> The late warden, Mr Bambridge, notwithstanding all his vanity and rashness, could never have been capable of so much folly, as to have committed so many notorious offences in his office, if he had not presumed on the interest of some superior power, which (at least as he fancied), might be able to prevent any enquiry into his conduct; or if that by no arts were to be evaded, would at least screen him from punishment. That this presumption of his was but too well founded, I am apt to believe is pretty apparent; the behaviour of a certain court when complaints were made against him; the difficulties there were in procuring rules, or the plainest proofs of the most flagrant oppressions; the ambiguous terms in which such rules were generally drawn up; the little regard he paid to these orders, when served upon him, and his impunity, notwithstanding such disrespect, are arguments which amount almost to a demonstration of his being in confederacy with a certain person, who, no doubt, took care to receive from him an adequate satisfaction for such favours.

Other letters accused Eyre of assisting Bambridge with his defence. The "lowness of his [Bambridge's] fortune at the time of his coming to his office at the Fleet is notorious to the world", one stated, and then continued, "he can by no means be charged with being idle ... [in the getting of money] ... the shortness of his stay there could not but prevent his acquiring half that sum of money, which has already been expended in defence of these prosecutions."

Another committee of the House of Commons was convened to examine "an affair of so extraordinary a nature". This resolved that one Roger Johnson and other "vile and infamous characters" in the Fleet and Newgate prisons had carried on this "wicked conspiracy". Johnson is not otherwise known, but he could have been a cover man for others.[72]

It seems clear that there was a pressure group or "conspiracy" amongst some of the Fleet prisoners, relating to the prison fees, and that the violence complained of was a sequel to these disputes. Is it not known what support this group had from the other prisoners, although all indications suggest it had their passive support because of Bambridge's over-reaction to the conditions within the prison. These men had carried on a running battle with the prison administration from 1724 onwards until matters culminated in the 1729 inquiry. Both Guybon's weakness and Bambridge's ruthlessness contributed to the success of their endeavours, by breaking down the unwritten agreement between gaoler and prisoners to co-operate in the good government of the prison. The fact that five of the prison turnkeys, Barnes, Douglas, Pindar, King, and Everett had fled rather than face prosecution was regarded as an admission of their guilt, although surprisingly little note was made of this in the various trials.[73] On the other hand it could equally well indicate their fear of a prejudiced parliamentary inquiry. Nevertheless the acquittals were just, for although Bambridge was rash and impulsive, he did not deserve the severe strictures made against him in the *Report* or the resolutions of the committee. Indeed even they appear to have made some allowance for his conduct when they considered that many of the problems of the prison could be imputed to the venality of the warden's office: "for the warden who buys the privilege of punishing others, does consequently sell his forbearance at high rates, and repair his own charge and loss at the wretched expense of the ease and quiet of the miserable objects in his custody."[74] To this it might be added that if Bambridge was guilty of exceeding in some instances the due proprieties of justice, it was in part because his task was to control a difficult prison. And we should not forget he had entered a prison in which good order had already broken down.

Although Bambridge was found not guilty by the courts and no escapes were charged against his wardenship, the act of 1729 debarred him not only from acting as warden, allowing the office to be granted to another "to be appointed by his majesty", but also from holding any other office of profit. The act stated that this was because he had permitted escapes, and been guilty of those charges and "enormities" laid against him by the committee, and added that the passing of such an act was not to debar any prosecutions from being made against him. This act was passed before Bambridge was aware of its implications.[75] His statement in his defence, entitled *Mr Bambridge's Case against the Bill now Depending*, argued:

> That he humbly hopes, that no invidious reports of a few facts tending to the preservation of the publick peace of the prison, and the prevention of escapes and riots, by restraining of two or three of the principal ringleaders, amongst so many hundred desperate persons (especially when not positively or particularly charged) shall be thought a sufficient foundation to turn him out of his freehold ...

This petition had more truth in it than many of the allegations made against him of cruelty and violence. Furthermore he was able to add that the facts and suggestions on which the act had been granted, had been "directly falsified by the verdicts of acquittal upon the several trials ... in the most solemn manner". He complained, therefore, that as a "free born subject", he had been deprived of his liberty, ousted of his freehold, and had had penalties and disabilities inflicted on him before any conviction had been made. This he held was contrary to the ordinary course of justice.[76]

The same act permitted the appointment of a new warden, introduced new regulations which forbade the selling or farming out of the prison offices, and required Bambridge, on pain of felony, to deliver up to the new warden a list of the prisoners and their securities. It provided that the five hundred pounds paid to Cuthbert by James Gambier as part payment for his interest in the office of warden (Cuthbert having its reversion), should be reimbursed to Gambier out of the two and a half thousand pounds granted by parliament for Cuthbert's interest.[77]

Bambridge, therefore, lost his office as warden and his purchase of the prison. As he had given securities for the payment of his moiety or half of the purchase price of the prison in 1728, and had entered into debt over building repairs to it, which he was now unable to pay because of the change in his circumstances, he was charged with debts of over three and a half thousand pounds by no less a person than John Huggins, acting as executor to his son. Consequently Bambridge voluntarily surrendered himself to the warden of the Fleet prison in October 1738, and remained a prisoner there until his discharge in July 1740.[78] This in itself is a remarkable testimony to his innocence of those criminal charges laid against him, for several of his alleged victims, including Mendez-Solas and Mackpheadris, were still prisoners in the Fleet when he entered.[79] Surely no man would elect to enter a prison in which there were men wishing to seek revenge against him? Simon Wood, a pamphleteer who wrote a little work on the Fleet for the benefit of would-be prisoners, may well have prepared the way for his reception. He wrote in 1733 that the poorer prisoners were better off under Bambridge than his successor, for "he has been liberal to this sort of people", and had petitioned parliament for their maintenance, though he also added, that he had found this not inconsistent with his interest, "being avavitious...."[80]

Little is known of Bambridge's life after his discharge in 1740; although a note on his life in a book published in 1790 states that he committed suicide twenty or more years after that celebrated but inaccurate inquiry of 1729.[81]

NOTES

1   Report 1729, p 2.

2   Mackay, p 23.

3   See a broadside, BL, pm 515 L2/212. This contains his portrait.

4   *Post Boy*, 30 June 1713: cf Cal TP, 1720-8, p 267. *The Evening Post* of 22 Dec 1713 states that he was also secretary to the Chevalier St George.

5   PRO, SP35/64, fol 333. His petition to sell the prison.

6   Howell, pp 330ff: Mackay, pp 10, 21, 23, "for several years he had been a stranger to his prisoners."

7   It seems his confidence rested more on his financial ability than his possible expertise as a prison keeper [Mackay, p 21].

8   Mackay, p 18.

9   Mackay, pp 31f.

10   Mackay, App XXIII, p viii, dated 20 Nov 1724.

11   Mackay, p 9.

12   Mackay, pp 9f.

13   Mackay, p 25.

14   These rules of 1727 are found in Report 1818, pp 81f. See Appendix 5.

15   Mackay, *et seq*, where not specified.

16   Mackay, pp 2, 14, 25.

17   Mackay, p 10.

18   Howell, pp 619ff.

19   Mackay, p 35.

20   PRO, SP35/64, fols 120, 333.

21   Report 1729, p 3: Cal TP, 1729-30, pp 408, 452; Act 2 Geo II c 32; PRO, SP35/64, fol 333.

22   Act 2 Geo II c 32; Jnl H of C, XXI 352, 513.

23   PRO, SP35/64, fol 333.

24   Mackay, pp 35f.

25   Mackay, p 35; Howell, p 620.

26   Lieutenant Bird, *A Letter from the Shades to Thomas Bambridge in Newgate* (London 1729), pp 25f.

27   Ibid, pp 39f.

28   The publication of his book, *The Villas of the Ancients Illustrated*, dedicated to Richard, earl of Burlington, caused such debts that he was forced into the Fleet as a debt prisoner [F Leslie Church, *Oglethorpe* (1932), p 12].

29   *Daily Journal*, 29 May and 14 June 1729.

30   *St James Evening Chronicle*, 29 March 1729.

31   2 Geo II c 22. Creditors were also required to maintain their prisoners if they refused to permit their release under the insolvent debtors' acts.

32   Howell, p 624: Report 1729, pp 5f.

33   *The Committee's Memorial against Bambridge.*

34   *Craftsman*, 10 May 1729.

35   W J Sheenan, "Finding Solace in Eighteenth Century Newgate", in J S Cockburn (ed), *Crime in England* (London 1977), p 244, quoting BL, MS Stowe 373, fols 42f.

36   Howell, p 308, quoting Jnl H of C.

37   Coll BL, fol 37.

38   Howell: the trials relating to Arne, pp 306 and 370; Castell, pp 383 and 397, and Berkley, pp 563 and 582.

39   William Ashton, deputy keeper of the Marshalsea, was also indicted for four murders. He was found not guilty on every charge. Evidence of his character was given by many prominent men, including a judge of the Marshalsea court and members of parliament [Howell, pp 461, 511, 525, 545].

40   Sean McConville, *A History of English Prison Administration* (London 1981), I 55n.

41   1729 Report (M), p 17; Howell, pp 299, 370ff.

42   1729 Report, p 3; 1729 Report (M), pp 17f.

43   Report 1729 (M), pp 19, 23f; Cal TP, 1720-8, p 279.

44   Report 1729 (M), p 18.

45   *Daily Journal*, 10 Feb 1732; Cal TP, 1729-30, pp 43, 71, 78.

46   Howell, pp 337, 339, 362; Mackay, p 31.

47   Report 1729, p 4; *The Microcosm of London* (London 1904 edn), II 49f.

48   Mackay, p 38.

49   *Weekly Journal*, 1 July 1727; *London Journal*, 1 July 1727; *Daily Journal*, 3 July 1727.

50   Lieutenant Bird's *Letter*, p 39.

51   PRO, SP35/9, fol 207.

52   Mackay, pp 36f.

53   Howell, pp 383ff. *To the Honourable the Commons for Great Britain in Parliament*

now Assembled: the Case of Thomas Bambridge. A bed or mattress had been taken from White's bed and placed on a bedstead in Castell's room. It was too small so it was removed. This occurred a few days before Castell entered that room [Howell, p 442]

54   Report 1729, p 13; *Mr Bambridge's Case against the Bill now Depending.*

55   Howell, pp 581ff. Heard before LCJ Eyre at the Old Bailey.

56   The picture is at the National Portrait Gallery, London. Hogarth's father-in-law, Sir James Thornhill, was a member of the committee. Horace Walpole wrote that the picture showed a session of its committee meeting in the Fleet prison. On the table are shown instruments of torture used in the prison. Oglethorpe addresses Bambridge, whose posture reveals his uncertainty: "villainy, fear and conscience are mixed in yellow and livid on his countenance, his lips are contracted by terror, his face advances as eager to lie, his legs step back as thinking to make an escape; one hand is thrust precipitately into his bosom, the fingers of the other are catching uncertainly at his button-holes ..." [quoted by Church, *Oglethorpe*, p 19].

57   Howell, p 302; Report 1729, pp 9f; *Mr Bambridge's Case.* One Abraham Mendez was one of Jonathan Wild's chief accomplices [F J Lyons, *Jonathan Wild: Prince of Robbers* (London 1936), pp 140, 144, 171f].

58   Howell, pp 606ff.

59   Report 1729, pp 10f; *Mr Bambridge's Case.*

60   Report 1729, pp 11f.

61   *Mr Bambridge's Case.*

62   Coll BL, fol 90.

63   *Mr Bambridge's Case*; Report 1729 (M), pp 19ff.

64   Report 1729, pp 5ff: Report 1729 (M), pp 18f. A manuscript in the CLRO [Misc MS 9.10] shows that these books were badly kept. The names of six prisoners had not been entered; the names of two who had been removed to the King's Bench had not been removed, and five still in the prison were ignorant that they had been discharged by their creditors.

65   *The Case of Mr Bygrave, Late Clerk of Papers at the Fleet* (London 1729).

66   Report 1729, p 9; Mackay, pp 25ff; Howell, pp 302f.

67   Report 1729, pp 5, 18.

68   *The Case of Thomas Bambridge*; *Mr Bambridge's Case*; Report 1729, p 7; Act 2 Geo II c 32.

69   Report 1729, p 13.

70   *Mr Bambridge's Case.*

71   Lord Percival in his diary noted rumours that Eyre had visited Bambridge in his prison

during the course of the trial, and claimed that he had seen a letter that had dropped from Bambridge's pocket, asking how he could buy off the witnesses, and suggesting that Sir George Oxenden might be useful to him in the event of a new trial [quoted in Church, *Oglethorpe*, pp 18f].

72   Quoted in Howell, p 619.

73   Howell, pp 309, 311, 565; Report 1729, p 19.

74   Report 1729, p 14.

75   Jnl H of C, XXI 352, 366. The act was 2 Geo II c 32.

76   *Mr Bambridge's Case.*

77   Cal TP, 1729-30, pp 407f, 451f. Gambier, appointed as the new warden, petitioned the court of Common Pleas to prevent Bambridge molesting his officers and to require him to return various prison documents [BL, pm 515 L15/42; Bambridge's reply in ibid, no 43].

78   PRO, Pris 1/7, fol, 231; and Pris 10/88, for 28 Oct 1738.

79   CLRO, Debtors' list of papers, box 3, petitions for 1737-48. Mackpheadris was still there in 1748.

80   Wood, p 9.

81   *The Memoirs of Remarkable Persons* (London 1790), p 30.

Part One. Chapter Three:

Number Nine, Fleet Market[1]

Bambridge deprived, the court of Common Pleas made new rules for the prison. These forbade turning prisoners out of their chambers or placing them on the common side; prohibited the use of spunging houses and garnish; permitted the prisoners the use of their own bedding, and allowed them to obtain their own food; required the prison books to be properly kept, and ended with the happy, if oft-repeated advice, that the warden was to treat his prisoners "with all tenderness and humanity", and they in turn were to "behave themselves towards [him] with that submission and regard which the law allows".[2] *An Act for the Relief of Debtors with Respect to the Imprisonment of their Persons* was rapidly passed.[3] This, a rehash of an act of 1671,[4] appointed commissioners to enquire into the fees, chamber rent and charities of the prison. It also provided for the relief of deserving debt prisoners, in a similar way to that provided by the insolvent debtors' acts. The courts were required to inspect the prison each Michaelmas term. And furthermore, as some tangible sign of the dawning of a new age, the dungeon in which Arne had died was demolished.[5]

James Gambier, who had been placed in temporary charge of the prison, was appointed warden, to the chagrin of Cuthbert, who claimed the appointment for himself. Cuthbert was deeply distressed to discover that his grant of office, which he believed had extended for his lifetime, had been interpreted by the lawyers as having been cancelled by the same act which had deprived Bambridge. His petitions of protest noted the decline in the profits of the prison through the reduction in fees and chamber rent, and the cost of the necessary repairs to the prison, such as the rebuilding of the women's ward on the common side.[6] By way of consolation he received back from the government his purchase price of the prison of two and a half thousand pounds. But as this sum only amounted to the value of two years' profit from the prison it was small compensation.

In spite of such good intentions, parliamentary and otherwise, the condition of the prison did not improve. This may have been because the question of the fees and chamber rent had been settled in favour of the prisoners, causing financial difficulties to the prison administration, which in any case still preferred to follow the old maxim of increasing profit by decreasing expenditure. Palliative measures rather than reform was the order of the day. In 1731 the warden was acquitted of charges laid against him after a riot in the prison, as a result of which sixteen of the prisoners were ordered to be prosecuted.[7] Simon Wood, writing in 1733,[8] noted some improvements, but made strong complaint about the treatment of the poor prisoners, especially by the bricking up of the begging grate. He noted the continuation of spunging houses under the title of tipstaffs' houses. Two years later the prisoners complained about the tipstaffs' fees. Their plea was accepted by the court, which regulated these fees, and it informed the tipstaffs that they were not to presume to take any more "in any case whatsoever". Fielding's novel, *Amelia*, published in 1751, reveals that vice and profligacy were still to be found in the prison, and such matters as drunkenness, prostitution, bullying, violence and gambling were common occurrences. Smollett's *Peregrine Pickle*, published in that same year, and Paget's *The Humours of the Fleet*, two years earlier, give the same picture.

The reports made by the various prison visitors of the late eighteenth century also lead to the same conclusion. John Howard, although he had found the Fleet better regulated than most prisons (a rather dubious compliment), noted much cause for concern. On 6 April 1776, he found two hundred and thirteen prisoners on the master's side, and thirty on the common side, but wives, "women of an appellation not so honourable", and children added a further four hundred and seventy-five to those living in the prison, which was thus grossly overcrowded.

The prisoners had their own committee which endeavoured to keep the premises clean and decent.[9] Howard suggested that the prison keepers should receive a fixed salary, rather than be reimbursed by fees.[10] William Smith, whose report on the state of the London gaols was published in 1776, around the same time as Howard's, noted the almost complete lack of cleanliness, the lack of an adequate water supply, the failure to provide baths or medical attendance, and suggested that the demolition of the houses in front of the prison would help relieve its atmosphere of sunless gloom. There were three hundred and fifty prisoners in one hundred rooms. Though the prison was better regulated and its prisoners more decent and sober than those of the King's Bench, he found that there were few hours of the night without riot or drunkenness. Finally he added, in faint praise, that while it was said that the warden was a humane man, he was not unwilling to make hay while the sun shone.[11]

By the 1760s those financial difficulties mentioned earlier, linked with the warden's acumen for his own interests, as suggested by Dr Smith, began to tell. The prison building was in a deplorable condition. One of the stacks of the prison house collapsed in 1768, destroying ten chambers inhabited by forty people, some of whom were seriously hurt. Examination of the structure revealed only more conclusively what was already known, that the whole building was in a ruinous state.[12] It was thus proposed to remove the prison to the recently demolished site of Ely Palace in Holborn. The enormous and weighty opposition of the parish of St Andrew Holborn ended this scheme. The vestry argued, for example, that if such a prison was built in that area, then the wealthy parishioners would be driven away, and the parish poor would suffer, for the "many and indigent and necessitous persons ... [in] the *rules* of the Fleet prison ... will be so great as to render the burden of maintaining the poor intolerable". It noted that the inhabitants of the Fleet area regarded the prison as a continual nuisance, and it argued further that if the area became a debtors' sanctuary then rents would rise. However a house rented for seventy pounds to a responsible tenant was of more value that the same house rented for one hundred pounds to a person whose goods were covered by fraudulent judgments and liable to executions. And all this, the vestry concluded, "was in order to better accommodate the Fleet market" which stood in front of the prison house, and which would be rebuilt on its vacant site. Two years later it was proposed to move the prison to St George's Fields in

Southwark, the city exchanging this ground for the site of the Fleet prison. The same kind of opposition ended this scheme as well.[13] The prison, however, had to be rebuilt by the Office of Works between 1770 and 1774 at a cost of twelve thousand pounds. Its original plan was followed, and prison life went on as the prison was rebuilt.[14]

In June 1780 the Gordon riots took place. Prisons have always had a particular fascination for the mob, then and now, but the unusual feature of this mob was that it was polite enough not only to inform the prisoners of their estimated time of arrival, but also to postpone that arrival for a day after receiving word that the prisoners found that time a little inconvenient. The lord mayor having directed Eyles as warden to offer no resistance (although it was said that a few soldiers could have dispersed the eventual mob with little difficulty), and the prisoners having removed their belongings along with their persons, the prison was "captured" without effort, and committed to flames. Although a notice was placed in the London papers ordering prisoners to surrender themselves to the warden at the *Bell Tuns* facing Surgeon's Hall in the Old Bailey at eleven in the morning on the 22 June,[15] and a proclamation issued on 20 June ordering the released prisoners to return, many of them ignored these instructions. Consequently the order was extended to the 5 October, and during the following year those who had failed to surrender were deemed to have escaped.[16] Even then an amnesty was given to allow these people the chance to surrender themselves within twenty-eight days of a similar notice being placed in the *London Gazette* of 16 October 1781, and signed by Lord Stormont, one of the principal secretaries of state.[17] It is not known where those prisoners who had surrendered themselves in obedience to these instructions were initially kept, although a petition of one William Herring provides a clue. Seeking a discharge under the 1781 insolvent debtors' act, which was denied him as he had failed to surrender himself under the above regulations, he argued in his defence that he was one of those who had offered to do so at the *Bull and Garter* public-house in Fleet Market. The keepers, however, "could not give them directions how to act or receive any charge of them". Subsequently he refused to give the clerk, Mr Groves, the half-a-crown required for his name to be entered into a list of the prisoners surrendering, though he had paid a penny as his share of the hire of a room at the *Marquess of Granby's Head* in Fleet Market for a meeting of the prisoners. He continued to reside in the *rules* and always considered himself a prisoner, "having never been one night absent", although he had attended Lord Stormont's office after the destruction of the prison.[18] In all 226 surrendered themselves between 13 July and 1 September, and 190 from that date to the 5 October, but 25 remained as fugitives. In addition, a number endeavoured to pretend they were prisoners, as did George Sussex, in order to avail himself of the insolvent debtors' act.

The prison had once again to be rebuilt by the Office of Works,[19] indicating all too clearly its financial decline. Dr Smith's suggestion about the demolition of the houses in front of the prison was finally effected in 1793, but only after the warden was compensated with an annual grant of two hundred pounds for the loss of their rents, these houses having been annexed to his office.[20] This allowed the prison front to be enclosed by a strong gateway and high walls, as is shown in the early nineteenth-century prints by Shepherd and others of the prison exterior.

Inquiries into the state of the prison still continued, until they became almost an occupational hazard for the warden. And the same recommendations were made, but never implemented. In 1790 the Society for Giving Effect to His Majesty's Proclamations against Vice and Immorality made a report on the prison. It discovered that the prison rules were not obeyed and new ones much wanted. The prison, in spite of its recent rebuilding, was dirty, there were neither bathing facilities nor medical attendance, though at least it had a "convenient" chapel and a chaplain was paid a salary for attending it. Mr Eyles the warden lived at Wimbledon, although his deputy, William Clipson, appeared "attentive to his duty". But the committee was totally unimpressed by this or any other of the London prisons, and earnestly hoped that the taking of fees would be abolished.[21]

A committee of the House of Commons reported on the whole issue of imprisonment for debt in 1792.[22] During the course of its investigations it called evidence from the prison authorities of most of the London debt prisons, particularly those of the Fleet, King's Bench and Newgate prisons. The impression is distinctly given that this committee had a real concern about the condition of the poorer prisoners, for it required details of the medical aid available, the average cost of imprisonment and the working of the *Lord's Act*, which allowed debtors in execution to obtain either their release on stated terms or to claim an allowance from their creditors. The warden gave evidence as to the condition on the common side of the prison, the number of prisoners in the house and *rules,* considered that the average weekly cost for a prisoner was twelve shillings, and gave instances as to how prisoners by the use of the writ *habeas-corpus* were able to winter at the Fleet and enjoy the summer at the King's Bench. But he and others gave harrowing accounts of the plight of the poorer prisoners. The committee, however, achieved little in the way of reform. Public opinion had still to be mobilised, and had no wish to be disturbed by such revelations.[23]

The 1813 Insolvency Act, which allowed a three-month imprisonment before a prisoner was released by an insolvency act, caused considerable difficulty at the Fleet. William Jones, marshall of the King's Bench, argued "it is the facility with which people can get out of gaol, that makes them now anxious to get into it."[24] This appears to have been the case. The number of commitments at the Fleet rose on average to 580 per annum during the 1800s, whereas between 1758 and 1790 it was 200, and in the 1830s, when imprisonment was of even shorter duration, 886 people were committed to the Fleet in 1832, compared to 544 in 1823.[25] The prison became not only overcrowded but also disorderly. It was said that these short-term prisoners contrived to obtain sufficient money to last their time in the prison, and thus they became careless of their behaviour.[26] The position became even more difficult after 1827 when such short-term prisoners were denied the use of the *rules* and the day *rules*.

Further commissions of inquiry into the administration of the Fleet and King's Bench prisons took place in 1814[27] and 1818,[28] each examining in considerable detail the conduct, administration, amenities and problems of the prisons. Henry Grey Bennet, a noted prison reformer, was chairman of both commissions. It is fair to suggest that these inquiries formed part of one extended inquiry whose brief was far wider than that of these two individual prisons. The 1814 committee reported extensively on Newgate and other London prisons. In particular this committee was concerned with the conditions within the prisons, and in particular about the provision of medical and spiritual help, the state of morals, the provision of liquor and causes of disorder, the prison administration and its profits, and it also investigated the prison economy of fees and room renting and letting. It noted of the Fleet, for example, that it had two hundred and nine prisoners, of whom sixty to seventy were in the *rules*, and that the annual income of the warden was over one and a half thousand pounds. It found much to criticise.

The, prison, it reported, was visited by the court of Common Pleas, and if it lacked medical care, nevertheless it possessed whistling or drinking shops, a prisoners' court, and even a school for the children who resided there, but the warden believed that it was also the largest brothel in London. Consequently, there were frequent "scenes of riot, disorder, and the difficulty of altogether preventing them, from the peculiar construction of the prison, and other causes". The warden's power of confining those responsible for such behaviour was of little value, especially as he did not have sufficient power to prevent such outrages. The commissioners praised him for his conduct, although they suggested that the King's Bench prison was better regulated than the Fleet. The report concluded as follows:

> Your committee advise ... that a commission should issue from the crown, to devise new rules and regulations for the Fleet prison. They recommend also the appointment of a surgeon, and an allowance for medicine. And they are of opinion that the manner in which the officers of the prison are reimbursed, is most objectionable.
>
> Your committee however consider the general manner with which Mr Nixon, the deputy warden, conducts the affairs of the prison, as most praiseworthy. It is the system, more than the manner of administering it, of which they complain; and while they consider the deputy warden as a valuable public servant, they trust means will be found to direct his zeal and attention to the management of a prison established on a better plan, and more calculated to increase the comforts and conveniences, and to preserve uncontaminated and undestroyed the morals and habits, of those whom the laws of the country place under his control.[29]

As a direct result of this report an infirmary was established in the prison, though medical assistance was still unavailable, while its officers were obliged to attend the chapel in order to enforce discipline. Nixon stated he could not go there himself, as he held that mixing familiarly with his prisoners would tend to diminish his authority within the prison. Strangers were no longer permitted to use the privies, which had been a source of annoyance to the prisoners, and a large room, furnished with beds, was made available for new prisoners for their first night, at a cost of one shilling each.[30]

The 1818 report spent much time detailing complaints about the strength of the beer supplied to the prison tap room, but it also investigated the separation of male and female debtors, particularly at night, and hoped that further improvements could be made when the kitchens and privies were moved to "more proper situations". The prison was thought to be reasonably clean and well regulated, there being "nothing in our view that we could deem worthy of serious complaint except the want of proper medical assistance", apart, perhaps, from the want of a fire-engine within its walls.[31]

New rules were again suggested by the committee. These permitted the warden to turn prisoners out of their rooms for non-payment, and left the disposal of the rooms to him: he could place the disorderly in a strong room and even use the stocks for punishment. Further rules prevented the sale of spirits in prison and the custom of garnish, abolished spunging houses, and only permitted prisoners' committees to operate if they had the consent of the warden. The warden's use of the writ *habeas corpus* to remove prisoners to the King's Bench was prohibited. The committee required a list of gifts to be put up, an infirmary to be provided, the prison records to be properly kept and accessible to all, rooms to be inspected for health reasons, regulated the tap and the accommodation of wives and children within the prison, and excluded from the *rules* those places where lottery tickets were sold. Most of these rules endorsed or extended existing requirements, and they again ended with the now celebrated exhortation to the warden and his prisoners. It is not known whether these rules were introduced or not.

These two reports not only arose from but also extended the concern of many regarding the whole concept of imprisonment for debt and the conditions of debt imprisonment. In 1815, for example, Henry Grey Bennet obtained an act which abolished fees in prison, requiring the justices to pay the salaries of keepers and prison officers. This act, however, excluded the Fleet and King's Bench from its provisions.[32] Peel's gaol act of 1823[33] established a proper management and inspection of prisons, and required the classification of prisoners. Thereafter there were numerous reports from select committees (one of which in 1836 required the appointment of prison inspectors). By such measures most of the English prisons became the care of, and the expenses formed a charge on, local government.[34]

But not so the Fleet nor the King's Bench. They were exempted from these acts and inspections, as it was assumed they were under the equivalent care of the various courts at Westminster. Furthermore the upkeep of these prisons, should such acts apply, would fall to the Exchequer. As the idea still prevailed that private interests should be respected as much as property rights, it was held that any curtailment of the warden's interest in the Fleet and its profits would need to be adequately compensated. Such finance was not available.

This may well explain the reason for a considerable shift in emphasis between the two reports of 1814 and 1818. The earlier report was scathing about many of the financial practices of a fee-taking prison. Writing about the fees taken at the King's Bench for the use of the *rules* (which netted the marshall two thousand six hundred pounds profit per annum), it commented: "whatever is paid is not paid by them [the prisoners] but by their creditors, to whom the property they are legally worth belongs." Such a sum, it concluded, was "surely much too large to be drawn from the pockets of debtors".[35]

But the 1818 report devised face-saving formulas for such uncomfortable facts. It thus reported on Nixon, who combined in his person three offices of profit at the Fleet, deputy warden, clerk of the papers and chief turnkey (giving him a combined income of two thousand two hundred and more pounds per year), that he was "not overpaid, considering the duties he has to perform, and the responsibility to which he is subject". It held that the system of payment by fees "though it may appear in some respects questionable; yet, we do not find it has been attended by any serious evil or inconvenience, ... we cannot recommend the abolition of fees, and the prohibition of emoluments, which ancient regulations and long usage have established." Bennet must have shuddered while Nixon, to use a modern phrase, laughed all the way to the bank. The reports thus merely regulated rather than reformed that still medieval structure of the Fleet.

The same report gave a list of the prison officers in 1816. It consisted of John Eyles, esq, warden, Mr Nicholas Nixon, deputy warden and clerk of the papers, William Woodroffe, his clerk and clerk of the enquiries, the Revd Richard Edwards, chaplain, a clerk, four court tipstaffs, three turnkeys, and Joseph Foulkes, scavenger, crier and watchman. Eyres had been appointed warden in 1758, during the reign of George II. His patent of office had been renewed by George III, but being "incapable", through age and deafness, of acting in person, he had appointed Nixon as his deputy in 1790, and fourteen years later permitted Nixon to have all the profits of the office, reserving to himself an annuity of five hundred pounds per annum, Nixon, however, being responsible for all escapes. When Eyles died Nixon was appointed his successor, but died in the March of the following year, while sitting in the prison lodge.[36] Various candidates presented themselves for the office, reported *The Real John Bull* in its issue of 7 April 1822. These included Mr Brown, keeper of Newgate, Mr Woodroffe, clerk to the prison, Mr Hall, son-in-law of John Eyles, and Mr Gibbons, a tipstaff at the court of Kings Bench. The paper alleged, rather extravagantly, that the office was worth five thousand pounds per annum, and was in the gift of the chief justice of the court of Common Pleas. It was equally erroneous in its statement that this judge would receive a sum of eight thousand pounds from the successful candidate. Brown was successful, and as a result the Fleet became popularly known as "Brown's Hotel".[37]

The Fleet, of course, was the prison to which Pickwick came, as depicted by Charles Dickens in his first novel, *The Pickwick Papers*. Dickens had had first-hand experience of life in a debt prison, his father having been imprisoned at the Marshalsea, where he was joined by his family. There he was in rather comfortable circumstances, having retained an income of six pounds per week, but Dickens would have seen around him the sufferings of many other prisoners.

Ivor Brown, in his book, *Dickens in his Times*, wrote of Pickwick's experiences in the Fleet:

> Mr Pickwick was first introduced by a turnkey, Mr Roker, to a revolting room. This he was to share with a group, one of whom, in the words of Roker, "takes his twelve pints of ale a day, and never leaves off sucking even at his meals". Obviously here was a debtor with some cash in hand. This caused Mr Pickwick to remark to Sam Weller, "It strikes me, Sam, that imprisonment for debt is scarcely any punishment at all ... you see how these fellows drink, and smoke, and roar. Its quite impossible that they can mind it much." Sam agreed as to some of the fellows. "They don't mind it; its a regular holiday to them - all porter and skittles." But he stressed the sufferings of the others, "them as vould pay if they could and gets low by being boxed up ... them as is always a-idlin' in public-houses it don't damage at all, and them as is alvays a-workin' wen they can it damages too much. 'Its unekal', as my father used to say wen his grog wor'nt made half and half."[38]

Mr Pickwick possessed money, and this magic commodity enabled a room to be found for him, furnished and exclusive to himself, for a weekly rent of seven shillings and sixpence. Nevertheless Dickens spared a thought for the poor prisoner, writing in *The Pickwick Papers:*

The poor side of a debtor's prison is, as its name imports, that in which the most miserable and abject class of debtors are confined. A prisoner having declared upon the poor side, pays neither rent nor chummage. His fees upon entering and leaving the jail, are reduced in amount, and he becomes entitled to a share of some small quantities of food: to provide which, a few charitable persons have, from time to time, left trifling legacies in their wills. Most of our readers will remember, that, until within a very few years past, there was a kind of iron cage in the wall of the Fleet prison, within which was posted some man of hungry looks, who from time to time, rattled a money-box, and exclaimed in a mournful voice, "Pray, remember the poor debtors: pray, remember the poor debtors." The receipts of this box, when there were any, were divided among the poor prisoners; and the men on the poor side relieved each other in this degrading office.

There were also other prisoners, who, neither rich nor poor, nevertheless had an air of listlessness about them, "the careless swagger, a vagabondish who's afraid sort of bearing ....".

The Home Office authorised new works at the Fleet prison during 1814-15 at a cost of nearly two thousand pounds,[39] and this may have included the gas fittings and ranges each chamber possessed by the 1820s.[40] Yet as the facilities of the prison improved, and its amenities and privileges became more substantial, the *rules* being extended in size, the number of prisoners declined, and the length of the average stay in prison became less and less. This was because public opinion was changing and more ready to accept that imprisonment for debt was unjust, with the result that insolvent debtor acts now permitted bail to those seeking their relief. At the same time difficulties were placed in the way of those who wished to enter the Fleet in order to enjoy its privileges. Those who applied for relief to the insolvent debtors' court, established in 1813, were by an act of 1827 not permitted to reside in the *rules* or to obtain day *rules.* The same act imposed restrictions on those who wished to enter the Fleet and King's Bench prisons from the county gaols through the use of the writ *habeas corpus.*[41] In 1833 a parliamentary return into the number of prisoners in custody at the various prisons stated that in the Fleet on 29 September 1831 there were 151 prisoners. Between that date and the same day of the following year 645 persons entered the prison as debt prisoners. But within the same period 622 of these 796 prisoners had been discharged, and five had died.[42] In many cases the duration of imprisonment was a matter of days because of the availability of a permanent insolvent debtors' court. Thus on 1 January 1832[43] there were 220 prisoners in the Fleet, of whom 153 were imprisoned on a mesne process, and 63 in execution.[44] This dramatic fall in the number of prisoners made it uneconomic to continue the prison on its site in the Fleet, though an attempt to transfer it to St George's Fields in Southwark during the 1830s was unsuccessful.[45]

With the abolition of imprisonment under the mesne process in 1838, which the warden considered halved the number of prisoners,[46] it became even more uneconomic to retain three major debt prisons in London. By an act of 1842[47] the prisons of the Fleet, King's Bench and Marshalsea were merged into one, which took possession of the buildings of the King's Bench prison in Southwark. It was not a popular move, especially as the *rules* were only permitted to continue there for a further year, and the use of spirits and private food prohibited in order to enforce a greater degree of order and discipline within the prison. The prison fees were also abolished, and the new governor allowed a salary of eight hundred pounds, according to the Home Office scale, though compensation was paid to those who lost their offices through this new arrangement.[48] The act vested the authority of the prison into the hands of the home secretary, while an official was appointed to replace the warden's duties at Westminster. Though many objections were made to these proposals, little sympathy was afforded to those who wished to continue the old style of luxurious living once permitted in these older prisons.

During those last days of the Fleet prison one Philip Bell, a chancery prisoner, wrote a ballad entitled *The Last Days of the Fleet!* It was set to the tune "The fine old English gentleman", and went as follows:[49]

> I'll sing to you a bran new song,
> Made by my simple pate,
> About the end of the good old Fleet,
> Which on us now shuts its gate.
> It has kept confin'd the choicest lads
> That e'er together met -
> Of merry, jolly, rattling dogs
> A regular slap up set.

Of jovial Fleet prisoners,
All of the present day.

This good old prison in every room
Contains a merry soul,
Who for his doings out of doors
Is now drop't 'in the hole.
But surely this is better far
Than your simple plodding way,
Get deep in debt, go through the Court,
And whitewash it all away.
Like a jovial Fleet prisoner,
All of the present day.

Some right good-hearts are rarely found
As round me now I see;
With such I'm most inclined to say,
Hang liberty for me.
For T...y, S.....y, V....h,
In spirits who excel?
How could we better live than here
Where friendship weaves her spell?
Amongst jovial Fleet prisoners,
All of the present day.

To racquets, skittles, whistling shops,
We must soon say farewell;
The Queen's assent, to her prison bill,
Has rung their funeral knell;
And Bennett, Gray and Andrew too
Must close their welcome doors,
For sing-song and tape spinning now,
This damn'd new act all floors,
For the jovial Fleet prisoner,
All of the present day.

But to her gracious majesty
You'll long be loyal and true,
Altho' the latest act of hers,
Must be felt by some of you.
Speed through the court, or compromise
Like gallant Captain T.....h,

> Or else you'll soon be sent to grieve
> Your guts out in the Bench.
> All melancholy prisoners.
> Unlike those of the present day.

In spite of various attempts to save the prison, including a proposed subscription list to prevent its closure, its prisoners were removed to the new Queen's prison in 1842, two of those transferred having been Fleet prisoners for over thirty years.[50] Another, a more recent prisoner, was Richard Oastler, who provides us with an account of the prison in its last days. Described by his biographer, Cecil Driver, as a Tory radical, he was otherwise known as the "king of Yorkshire". Many suspected that the government had used the device of an "honourable debt" to remove from the public scene one whose strictures on the new poor law had won much popular support.

When Oastler arrived at the Fleet in 1841, he immediately commenced his *The Fleet Papers,* a weekly review addressed to his creditor, Thomas Thornhill, esquire, of Riddlesworth in Norfolk. His first number describes how his solicitor's clerk took him to the Fleet and helped him with the necessary arrangements, so that, having paid his admission fees, he found himself in number 12, coffee gallery. These papers received a wide circulation, which resulted in so many visitors coming to see him that he was forced to establish "At Homes" on three afternoons in the week, and to publish a "rent roll" of his benefactors and their gifts. Such gifts enabled his wife to join him in his imprisonment and allowed them to live in comfortable circumstances.

The bill to unite the three debt prisons came as a great shock to him. Regarding it as an attack on the rights and privileges granted to him by British law, Oastler argued that the matter had been done without the consent of those most involved, namely the prisoners. It was equally wrong, he suggested, for the secretary of state to take over an authority which properly belonged to the judges, who would be shorn thereby of one of their noblest attributes, that of the guardianship of prisoners. "The warden", he wrote, "has received notice" that the marshall "has had direction for the removal of prisoners from this prison, which is stated to commence tomorrow...." He was comfortably settled at the Fleet, had "never received an angry look or word from any officer", and his wife had settled in with him, and thus it was with strong but dignified protest that he allowed himself to be placed in the carriage taking him to his new abode. At the new prison he was received by the head turnkey, Mr Colwell, who entered his name into his books, inspected his face and person, and he was asked to walk forwards

As Oastler's wife had remained at the Fleet to take care of his furniture and papers, he was unable to have a bed for four nights, sleeping in an old armchair in the coffee house. Eventually he was chummed in one of the better rooms, but he found it overcrowded, filthy and swarming with bugs. And this, he added, was the Queen's prison! Eventually he was reimbursed for the cost of cleaning his room, and the Board of Works cleansed the whole prison.[51]

The building which Oastler had left with seventy-two others was purchased by the city of London for a sum of twenty-nine thousand pounds, and was demolished during 1845-6, though, for some reason, part of its Farringdon Road facade remained. The site was again sold in 1864 to the London, Chatham and Dover railway company for sixty thousand pounds, and part of it was used for the building of the viaduct to Holborn station.

The Queen's prison remained a debt prison until imprisonment for debt was abolished as an offence. After this it became a military prison until its demolition in 1879. Montagu Williams in his book, *Round London*, describes the prison when it was the main debt prison of London. His friend Ralph Bythesea was therein, and Williams went to visit him in what was familiarly known as "Hudson's Hotel", this being in honour of the governor's name. The kitchen "resembled that of a West-End club more than anything else", and was presided over by a chef of "considerable distinction". Some time was spent in the tap room, open between one and two and five and six, although the prisoners were not permitted to have more than one quart of ale or one pint of wine per day. Finally they went to Bythesea's room:

> It was a funny little room, with a table in the middle, an iron camp bedstead behind the door, a chest of drawers against the window, and three or four Windsor chairs standing here and there. In a few minutes the laundress, an untidy, middle-aged woman, made her appearance with a snow-white table-cloth, and proceeded to set out a plain but substantial luncheon. While she was thus engaged we were all looking out of the window, watching the racquet players.
> "See that dapper-looking little fellow in flannels?" said Ralph. "That's the tailor of Cork Street. Overdid himself a little with discounting, not to

mention a great partiality for Cremorne and a villa at Barnes. That stout fellow with him is the heir to the earldom of W.... No distinction of rank here, I can tell you!"

He continued, "Now I'll tell you about my arrest. I was coming out of the Travellers and was jumping into my tilbury, when a very common-looking fellow put his hand on my shoulder and exclaimed: 'Very sorry, my lord, but you are my prisoner. *Ca sa* unsatisfied judgement - suit of one Joel'. First of all I felt inclined to knock him down, but, remembering that if it were not the enterprising Joel, it would be somebody else of the same calling, I yielded to fate, hailed a four-wheeler, and was whisked off, in company with the myrmidons of the law, to Slowman's, the sponging house in Cursitor Street, Chancery Lane. Ah, my dear fellow, you've never seen a sponging-house! Ye gods! what a place! I had an apartment they were pleased to call a bedroom to myself certainly, but if I wanted to breathe the air I had to do so in a cage in the back garden - iron bars all round, and about the size of one of the beast receptacles at the Zoo. For this luxury I had to pay two guineas a day. A bottle of sherry cost a guinea, a bottle of Bass half-a-crown, and food was upon the same sort of economical tariff. Well, you know, this sort of thing wouldn't do, so I sent for the governor and talked matters over. He went to his lawyer, who got what they call a habeas for me, whereupon I was brought over here, and here I am. Might have been worse, old fellow, you know."[52]

Indeed it might have been. For the majority of debt prisoners it would have been in any case.

NOTES

1   The street number above the door, which thus became the fictitious address of the prison.

2   See Appendix 3.

3   2 Geo II c 20. This was presumably the final and more general result of the bill for the better regulating of the Fleet prison ordered by the House of Commons in 1729 [Report 1729, p 20].

4   22 & 23 Charles II c 20.

5   Jnl H of C, XXI 513.

6   Cal TP, 1729-30, pp 408, 451; Jnl H of C, XXI 513.

7   *The London Journal*, 3 July 1731.

8   Wood, pp 8, 12.

9   Howard (1777), pp 160, 164.

10   Howard (1780), p 36.

11   Smith, pp 41-3.

12   J P Malcolm, *Londonium Redivivum* (London 1802), I 375f; CLRO, Misc MS 172.12.

13   CLRO, Misc MS, Box 55, item 15.

14   H M Colvin, *The History of the King's Works* (London 1976), p 353.

15   CLRO, enclosed in the 1781 debtors' lists.

16   John Ashton, *The Fleet, its River, Prison and Marriages* (London 1888), p 302, quoting *A Narrative of the Proceedings of Lord George Gordon* (1780); PRO, PRIS 10/137A. At the King's Bench prison 691 prisoners surrendered but 155 did not [Report 1792, p 657].

17   PRO, PRIS 10/155, item 3, front cover.

18   CLRO, Debtors' lists, attached to the 1781 list.

19   Howard (1784), p 221, notes it was rebuilt on the same plan, but the cellar, hall and first floors were arched in brick to make the place fireproof.

20   Report 1814, p 674.

21   *The Report of the Sub-Committee into Prisons of the Society for giving Effect to His Majesty's Proclamation against Vice and Immorality* (London 1790), p 27.

22   Jnl H of C, 1792, pp 640-73, referred to as Report 1792.

23   Report 1792, pp 651, 654.

24   quoted in *Observations on the Laws of Arrest for Debt* (London 1827), p 24.

25   PRO, PRIS 2.

26   David Hughson, *Walks through London* (London 1817), I 126.

27   PP 1814-15 (152) XV 531.

28   PP 1819 (109) XI 325.

29   Report 1814, pp 552, cf 551f, 679, 694, 789.

30   Report 1818, pp 10, 42.

31   Report 1818, pp 7-9, 27. It noted Nixon's kindness and humanity [p 10].

32   55 Geo III c 50.

33   4 Geo IV c 64.

34   S & B Webb, *English Prisons under Local Government* (London 1963), pp 68ff, 73ff, 111f;   Sean McConville, *A History of English Prison Administration* (London 1981), I 247ff.

35   Report 1814, p 538.

36   Report 1818, pp 5f, 75f; GLRO, Misc MS 173.5 (1786), fol 57.

37   *The Times*, 16 Feb 1838.

38   Ivor Brown, *Dickens in his Time* (London 1963), p 65. Pickwick was shown first to a spunging house, until he obtained a writ of *habeas corpus* which permitted him to be transferred to the Fleet.

39   PP 1814-15 (154) IX 190.

40   *Catalogue of the Sale of the Prison* (1845). It included such items as three million bricks, fifty tons of lead and two hundred and fifty tons of glazed windows [GLL, in Pamphlet 3393].

41   7 Geo IV c 57; William Brown, *The Fleet* (London 1843), p 25.

42   PP 1830-1 (142) XII 511.

43   Ibid.

44   *Observations on the Laws of Arrest for Debt* (London 1827), p 21. In that year the King's Bench prison had 855 prisoners.

45   William Leigh, *New Picture of London* (London 1834 edn), p 329.

46   Brown, *The Fleet*, p 25.

47   5 & 6 Victoria c 22. The new prison was to be called the Queen's prison. *The Times* claimed that the closure of the Fleet would save the country £15,000 per annum, "besides getting rid of an ugly object" [issue of 3 March 1841].

48   As the marshall in 1814 had an income of £3,590 of which £2,600 was said to have come from the *rulers*, the sum was reasonably close to the profits of the old prison with the fees from the *rules* deducted [Report 1814, pp 533, 537].

49   Quoted by Aston, *The Fleet*, pp 319ff.

50   Ashton, *The Fleet*, pp 318f, 312n.

51   Richard Oastler, *The Fleet Papers*, see especially nos 374 and 380. In 1842 he was subpoenaed to give evidence at a trial in York, and travelled there by train, escorted by a turnkey. It is an intriguing thought that he should have left an almost medieval institution in order to travel by the then modern technology.

52   Montagu Williams, *Round London* (London 1893), pp 128ff.

The King's Bench prison in the 1820s, showing the main entrance, as drawn by Thomas Shepherd. Collection of the author.

Part Two:

The Administration of the Prison

"An office of inheritance from the crown time out of mind": Warden Ford[1]

The office of warden of the Fleet prison had been established as, and remained as, an office held by grand sergeantry in fee simple, that is, the holding of land or an office on condition of performing certain services. The office was thus a royal appointment, and held on condition of service, but being in fee simple, it could descend in common law to the heirs general, unless this was limited by the terms of the grant.[2] In many respects the wardenship was regarded as a matter of private property, as was maintained by Tilly,[3] and as suggested by an act of 1696-7 which stated that the office "shall be executed by the person to whom the inheritance does belong".[4]

It was further claimed that the prison house was distinct from and not annexed to the office of warden. Harris termed it a freehold,[5] and it is significant that Whitcott rebuilt the prison house at his own expense after its destruction in the Great Fire of London. Tilly was always careful to point out that his purchase of the office of warden and of the prison house were two separate transactions, and added on another occasion that the prison could be kept in any place at the discretion of the warden. Thus *The Lord Keeper's Report* of 1704 stated "the said

Mr Tilly is a purchaser of the said prison, and *also* [my italics] of the said capital messuage or mansion house and garden wherein the said prison is kept." Tilly, when the office had been forfeited because of his deputy's misdemeanours, maintained that the prison house was not affected by this forfeiture, but offered to unite the two together in order to offer a greater security against escapes than that of the "mere office".[6] His claim could not be substantiated, and the patent of office for John Eyles in 1758 clearly linked the two together.[7]

The warden was not only an officer of the three courts of Common Pleas, Chancery, and Exchequer, and, at one time, regarded as the first messenger to the secretary of state and the council,[8] he was also the keeper of the palaces of Westminster. This office and that of the keepership had been linked together from an early period. As Jessop, who edited Harris's *Oeconomy* quaintly put it, "'for the palace, without the warden's licence, none may go in; for the Fleet prison, without his release, none might go out."[9] Although the keepership was a post of responsibility, giving the warden the power of arrest within the area of the palaces, it also provided him with a small revenue from the stalls in Westminster hall and the scaffolding erected there on great occasions, and gave him immunity from arrest. When the then warden was imprisoned in 1592 he was rapidly set at liberty as his services were indispensable in Westminster hall.[10]

The ultimate authority for the prison lay in the king himself, Coke stating that no subject could have a prison himself, but only the king.[11] This authority was shown in part by the appointment of the warden by letters patent from the crown. In medieval times this authority was exercised by the Curia Regis. It still maintained an effective control over the prison during the time of Harris in the 1610s,[12] but by the time of the Restoration the authority for the prison had passed to the courts to which the prison belonged, and in particular to the court of Common Pleas. This court was required to send its officers to enquire into the condition of the prison each Michaelmas term, and to give the prisoners eight days' notice of its intended visitation.[13] The duty of their officers was to see that a list of the rules and regulations was hung up, was accessible to the prisoners and obeyed by both them and the prison keepers, and to report to the judges on the state and condition of the prison. By 1814 this was done each term at the request of the warden.[14] Similar provision was made at the King's Bench, William Smith noting that on one such visit in the 1770s the prisoners had complained about the lease of the tap, the inspection of the prison books, the supply of water, and the lack of a meeting place for their own committee.[15] It is quite clear that the judges wished to establish preventative measures to check any possibility of disorder, and such official visits performed a real service by enabling disputes to be resolved by arbitration rather than by the exercise of power. The 1814 report into the King's Bench prison requested that better records be kept of these visitations,[16] but the 1792 report noted that few of the evils complained of were "within the reach of the courts or the judges".[17] It concluded that these evils were endemic to the system of debt imprisonment rather than due to any maladministration. It was to this court, for example, that the prisoners addressed their petitions during the troubles of the 1720s,[18] and received some satisfaction, for the court insisted that several prisoners should be returned to the master's side from the common side, and that Huggins should return some money extorted from a prisoner.[19] This court also proceeded against Adams, the clerk of the papers, for neglect of duty,[20] revised the prison rules in 1687 and 1729 and the fees in 1727,[21] regulated the prison *rules*[22] and extended them in 1825,[23] and made such orders as that supersedeable prisoners should not be entitled to retain their prison chambers.[24] The warden and his deputy were in constant attendance on this court, which seemed to many to impose some form of regulation upon their conduct within the prison itself. But the 1729 report accused the wardens of purchasing the court's favour by presenting its judges with favours at the end of each year. "Can it be", suggested the *Memorial*, "for any other reason but to purchase unjust favours?" While this was popularly believed, the facts related by Mackay indicate that this court was deeply concerned about the prison and its administration, although there were limits as to how far it could translate that concern into action.

The warden's liabilities were substantial. He was required to keep his prisoners in safe and secure custody, without pain or torment, to produce them to the courts when required, treating them, as the rules indicated, with all tenderness and humanity, and to pay their debts if they escaped from his charge. As Sean McConville writes, "the *sine qua non* of success for a gaoler was the security of bolts and bars."[25] The prison house had to be kept in good repair, while the warden was responsible for paying the taxes and poor rate imposed on this property, ironically required because he let chambers to his prisoners.[26] Although his officers were paid for their services from the prison fees, he was answerable for all their civil offences.[27] His privileges were few [though his recompense great], although one of those privileges was immunity from any debt process. [28]

There was always the risk that his office might be forfeited. Tilly lost his office in 1708 on the grounds that it had fallen "by descent or purchase into the hands of persons incapable of exercising the office of warden",[29] a rather strange turn of phrase to describe one who had acted as warden for nearly twenty years. The act of 2 George II c 32 stated that Bambridge was deposed of his office in 1729 because of the "great danger of escapes ... [and the] continuation of cruelties and barbarities" if he remained as warden. Both these forfeitures took place after parliamentary action, and a vigorous prosecution of the matter by an individual, in the first instance that of Colonel Leighton, whose motives were more those of self-interest than of justice, and in the second case that of General Oglethorpe. The risk was always there.

To assist him in his duty the warden was permitted to arm his watchmen, deprive others of arms, eject prisoners from their chambers for non-payment of rent, and detain their bodies after their creditor's release if such prisoners owed him, the warden, any fees or rent. He seems to have possessed the authority of a magistrate within the prison. Refractory prisoners could be placed in a dungeon or put into the stocks, or, as a last desperate resort, sent to Newgate or Bridewell. These were permitted by each revision of the prison rules.[30] However after 1729 the right to iron prisoners was severely limited, although it was clearly permitted beforehand, and this with other restrictions meant that the warden lacked sufficient power to suppress the riots and disturbances which took place from time to time.[31] The warden always had to remember that any excess of punishment by either himself or his servants could lead to charges of felony or murder being preferred against him.

One result of the prison being an office held by grand sergeantry in fee simple was that the warden was required to make a living out of the prison in order to reimburse himself for his expenses. It was a time-honoured principle, of course, that prisoners were required to pay their own expenses of imprisonment. The logical development of these two facts was that the prison became regarded as a profit-making concern. This was further aggravated by the knowledge that the selling and leasing of the prison caused a situation in which the buyer or lessee would endeavour to make up his outlay in the shortest possible time.

All contemporary writers on the Fleet prison agreed that while the office of warden was one of great responsibility, it was also one of great value.[32] During the closing years of the sixteenth century it was claimed that the "profits" of the prison amounted to six hundred and twenty pounds per annum.[33] Harris in the 1610s claimed that while he could clear two thousand and two hundred pounds on the prison each year, he did so on lower rates than those taken by his predecessors, alleging that one of them, Anslow, made nearly twice that amount when the profits of the Westminster keepership were added to the total. He added, however, that the expenses of office always equalled the income.[34] Tilly, it was claimed, made an annual profit of between eighteen and twenty-two hundred pounds,[35] although another report alleged that with such fees as twenty or thirty guineas for an "enlargement" he was able to obtain eight thousand pounds in gratuities and perquisites within two years.[36] This may have represented the income of the prison rather than its profits, but these were clearly sufficient to encourage an adventurer like Colonel Leighton to spent vast sums of money over many years to gain the office of warden for himself. Though the 1729 committee grossly over-estimated the prison's profits as four thousand six hundred and thirty-two pounds,[37] Simon Wood, a few years later, allowed that the profits could be up to two thousand pounds per annum.[38] This may well have been a gross rather than a net figure.

Although some of this money came from the rents of the Westminster hall stalls and the various houses belonging to the prison, valued at four hundred pounds per annum by the 1729 report, and some smaller amounts were derived from the lease of the prison cellars and coffee room,[39] the bulk of the money came from the debt prisoners themselves. Their payments of chamber rents were said in 1729 to have produced a sum of eight hundred and ninety pounds, and the commitment and discharge fees were estimated in the same year at seven hundred and sixty-six pounds.[40] Besides these there were the various fees for the use of the *rules* and day *rules*. Nevertheless the 1729 figures represent the high water-mark of the prison's finances, for it was then crowded with prisoners, many of whom left in the following year through an act of insolvency. After that date the fees were severely reduced. The commitment fee for the master's side, for example, was reduced to £1.6s.8d. from the earlier £2.4s.4d., and the chamber rent from a weekly 2s.6d. to half that sum.[41] The many acts of insolvency passed throughout the mid and latter years of the eighteenth century reduced not only the number of prisoners, but the length of imprisonment, and thus the profits, considerably. In 1729 when there were 611 prisoners the profits were probably in the region of three thousand pounds. By 1779 there were only 346 prisoners, and allowing for the reduction in fees, the profits could hardly have amounted to one thousand pounds. It was from these "profits", however, that the money required for the repair and maintenance of the prison was found, as well as the monies to meet the various taxes and duties imposed on the prison.

Thus the 1818 committee of investigation into the prison stated that the office was not overpaid considering its duties and responsibilities.[42] This, however, seems to be a case of special pleading, for both the 1814 and 1818 reports gave detailed figures of the prison income, averaged over the previous three years.

Table One: Average Profits of the Warden of the Fleet

	1814 [43]	1818 [44]
	INCOME	
	£	£
entrance fees	792	107
discharge fees	212	213
chamber rent	333	342
for *Rules*	985	961
for Day *Rules*	145	138
Treasury allowance for demolition of houses 1793	200	200
sheriffs fee	18	18
profits on tap	not recorded[45]	326
	OUTGOINGS	
losses by escapes	not recorded	300
taxes	368	368
chaplain & clerk	40	40
servants wages	313	313
scavenger & watchman	43	43
lamps candles coals	60	60
	TOTAL PROFIT	
	1561	1804[46]

If the amount of fees for the *rules* appears excessive from this table, compared to the other prison fees (and those at the King's Bench amounted to a sum four times greater), the warden suggested an answer in a return of 1830:[47] "the fees taken from those having the privilege of the *rules*, form a part of his resources, to compensate him for his labour and services, responsibility and risk, to enable him to defray the necessary expense attendant upon, and keeping up the establishment of the said prison, for salaries to officers, wages to servants, payment of the parliamentary and parochial taxes, contingent law charges, losses by escapes, and all other expenses appertaining thereto." In spite of such pleading he later admitted that he and his predecessors held an office of "considerable emolument and advantage".[48] Nevertheless his point of view was probably more that of a nineteenth-century gentleman rather than an eighteenth-century adventurer, for he added, "though of course they had their corresponding liabilities, and the duties attached to these were frequently anxious and painful".

From the 1820s onwards the income of the warden was considerably reduced because of the reforms in the debt laws. While the number of prisoners remained about the same, the length of imprisonment became less and less, causing a substantial drop in the income from chamber rents, the tap and the fees for the *rules* and day *rules*. In 1818 these items collectively amounted to seventy-six percent of the income of the prison, consequently any diminution in this income became a matter of concern. Thus in 1826 the income from the *rules* was only four hundred pounds, and in 1826 but one hundred and thirty-three.[49] No warden who depended on an income from fees could survive such a loss in income for any length of time.

It has already been noted that these profits came from debt prisoners. It is hardly surprising that these prisoners should, from time to time, point this out in forceful detail. As early as 1690 William Gery stated that such profits came from "'the livelihoods, fortunes and estates of men in a miserable and wanting condition".[50] Others accused the warden, as did Lilburn, of neglecting the unprofitable prisoners for the profitable.[51] It was frequently noted that the only gainer in debt imprisonment was the prison keeper, for he took what rightfully belonged to the creditor. The wardens frequently replied to this assertion that there were cheaper prisons and thus no necessity for any debtor to enter the Fleet prison with its more expensive fees and by the costly writ of *habeas corpus* if he was really honest in his desire to repay his debts.

A further result of the wardenship being an office in fee simple was that it could be sold, leased or mortgaged. The only check on this was that any new purchaser was required to obtain letters patent to enable him to hold the office.[52] From 1559 when it was sold for four thousand pounds,[53] every other warden purchased the office. Some ten or so years later the two Lello brothers jointly purchased it for eleven thousand pounds, and Henry Lello subsequently purchased his brother's share for eight thousand pounds.[54] Huggins obtained the prison for a bribe of five thousand to Lord Clarendon, indicating its declining value, and after endeavouring to find a purchaser for many years considered himself fortunate to sell the prison for the same sum to Bambridge and Cuthbert in 1728.[55]

The office and its profits were frequently used to provide security for a mortgage. This was done on many occasions, especially towards the end of the seventeenth century, although many regarded the practice as being caused more by the warden's desire to avoid his responsibilities towards the relief of the creditors of his escaped prisoners than as a serious financial matter.[56] In 1678 Bromhall, then warden, mortgaged the prison house and the office of warden for a consideration of two thousand and more pounds. Though this mortgage was ordered to be sold by the 1693 act which permitted the sale of the prison, Tilly, the new purchaser, renewed it for the security of his purchase money.[57] Saving clauses regarding these mortgages were obtained by the mortgagees of both the Fleet and King's Bench prisons. They were inserted into the act of 8 & 9 William III c 27 for the relief of creditors in the case of escapes, and which allowed such creditors the right to sequestrate the profits of the prison for the debts of an escaped prisoner. However the saving clause made any sequestration impossible by reserving these profits to the mortgagees until the mortgages had been redeemed. This act was thus rendered ineffectual, and it is probably true that many creditors were ruined because of the escape of their debtors.[58]

Although Tilly did not go as far as did the authorities of the King's Bench prison in their attempt to frustrate those who endeavoured to obtain financial redress for the escape of their prisoners, he certainly imitated their use of trustees. Ford (who had served as a deputy warden), Fanshaw, and Mason are the names of some of the trustees he appointed.[59] He even used a prisoner, Fox, to sign all his legal papers and to act as the so called "warden" of the Fleet.[60] Tilly was thus frequently described by his accusers as the "real warden" rather than Fox, the "pretended" warden. Berisford accused both prison authorities of "private articles" and "secret trusts". He also argued that there were such "frequent shiftings" and "transferrings of the mortgages and other securities" that it was as impossible to "reach" the profits of the prison as it was to know against whom to proceed. He added that the judges were equally at a loss about the profits of the prison, for they were continually informed that they "must be excused for they are pre-engaged".[61] When a verdict was obtained against the warden in the case of an escape in 1694, an inquest had to be held in order to discover who was the warden of the prison.[62] The position was equally complicated by the use of deputy wardens. Berisford thus wrote, "in pursuing of that statute some persons have recovered judgments in actions of escapes, against those officers, yet here also they are come to their journey's end, and after all their tedious and expensive travel, find nought but labour for their pains... ."[63] It is not surprising, therefore, that the House of Commons resolved that whoever had the "fee" of either the King's Bench or the Fleet and executed the same in person or by deputy, was the person "answerable" for his prison to the house. [64]

The mortgages of the prison were ended in 1708 when the office of warden was sequestrated and awarded to Leighton.

The office of warden had been administered by deputy from medieval times, particularly as many of the wardens preferred to reside at their Westminster residence. The first recorded instance of a warden being permitted to employ a deputy occurred when the then warden joined the 1202 crusade.[65] The deputy warden assumed full control over the prison, and was often described as the "warden". The actual warden, however, still held the legal responsibility for the safe imprisonment of his prisoners, a matter clearly emphasised by the legislation of 1696 already mentioned. This, incidentally, gave parliamentary approval to this practice. The warden, to cover himself, frequently required his deputy to give a bond against the escape of prisoners and his failure to pay the rent.[66] Indeed the trust demanded of a deputy was so great that Huggins engaged Guybon for a trial period of six months and required a deposit of one thousand pounds.[67]

Under Tilly the practice developed of the warden declining to hand over all his prisoners to his deputy, and instead reserving their fees to himself. Church, in 1697, discovered that only sixty-eight prisoners on the master's side and twenty-eight on the common side were handed over to his custody. Declining to accept responsibility for those prisoners not named on his schedules, he accordingly neglected them so that some escaped.[68] However a deputy could not plead such innocence in another well-known practice. In order to make up his fees he permitted prisoners to escape for some consideration to him. When a series of judgments against him were pending, and it was impossible to forestall matters by the use of delaying tactics, such as the question as to who held the wardenship, he fled. Fox absconded during the 1690s when there were twelve judgments against him to a value of two to three thousand pounds, as did Church for the same reason soon afterwards.[69] Indeed it seems that the same situation applied at an earlier period in the prison's history, during the third quarter of the sixteenth century, when it was said that Babbington had so many deputy wardens that the prison suffered from the continual changes.[70]

Most deputy wardens leased the prison for a definite sum from the warden, reserving for themselves the fees allocated to the office of warden. Many wardens must have followed Huggins's practice of preferring this arrangement to that of running up an account with a deputy which they were unable to check.[71] Nevertheless the problems of leasing the prison for a fixed annual sum were substantial, as the number of prisoners, and thus the profits, varied from year to year. Furthermore this practice assumed that the prisoners were diligent in the payment of their dues and fees. This assumption was never justified. And yet in view of what has already been related about the history of the prison, it comes as no surprise to discover that the annual rent of the prison was nearly always in excess of what could be legally gained through its legitimate revenues. In 1603-4 the Fleet was leased for a sum of eight hundred pounds per annum, although its profits were returned in the same document as averaging six hundred and twenty pounds between 1596 and 1598.[72] Fifty years earlier the prison had been leased for ten per-cent of that sum.[73] During the 1690s Tilly obtained from Church and Gery a fine of one thousand pounds and an annual rent, paid monthly, of fifteen hundred pounds, though they complained Tilly still sent his agent, Holland, a man of bad character, into the prison to collect rents and fees on his behalf, so defrauding them.[74] Guybon paid Huggins a similar fine but a much reduced rent of nine hundred pounds, but this included the rental of Westminster hall and various house rents which took up four hundred pounds of the above rental.[75] The rental had dropped, therefore, by two thirds over a period of thirty years. The situation was similar to that of the King's Bench prison, whose. rental of seven hundred and fifty pounds was said to be so extortionate that no person of good substance would take the office. The legitimate profits of that prison were estimated by the 1729 committee to be but three hundred and fifty pounds per annum.[76] The lord chief justice of the Common Pleas criticised the letting of this prison at such extraordinary rents, particularly to "obscure" people who did not possess sufficient security to take on the office.[77]

This situation meant that the deputy wardens were none too scrupulous as to how they obtained their profits. As far back as 1597, when the prison was farmed out to John Harvey and Joachim Newport, described as poor men, it was claimed that they lived "by secret bribing and extortion".[78] Harris, who recorded this, extended this stricture to others besides these two men. Deputy Ford also found considerable difficulty in adjusting his books, and like Guybon, who had similar problems in making up his rent, practised various extortions, permitted escapes, and required Christmas presents from his prisoners. It was alleged that Huggins connived at Guybon's practices in this direction, confident in the expectation that his rental would thereby be paid.[79]

It is quite clear that little check was made by the court of Common Pleas, or by any other responsible body, to ensure that the profits of the prison could justify such a high rental. In addition, of course, the deputy wardens expected to make a further profit for themselves out of the prison. The result of this system is summed up best in the words of a writer on the King's Bench prison. He complained that the prison had become "a merchantable commodity, and the buyers often fought to indemnify themselves for their purchase, at the expense of the unhappy prisoner."[80] The position changed, so far as the Fleet was concerned, for the better after 1729. Daniel Hopkins, for sixty years deputy warden until his death in 1781 aged ninety,[81] justified Simon Wood's comment of 1733[82] that he had formerly been an agent of Huggins, "but we hope that [what] he hath seen amiss in them, he will amend in himself". The last deputy warden, Nicholas Nixon, appointed in 1790, eventually leased the whole prison from the then warden, Eyles, allowing Eyles an annuity of five hundred pounds, but taking over himself all the responsibilities of the warden's office.[83]

The warden appointed his own officers. As their remuneration came from

the often substantial fees paid them by the prisoners, they acquired such a value
that prior to 1729 they were openly bought and sold. This was prohibited as a
result of the inquiry of that year. It had found that Adams had paid eight hundred
pounds for the clerkship of the papers, and Bygrave, his successor, paid Adams
seven hundred and fifty pounds for the reversion of his interest. Cotton, who had
succeeded Bygrave under some rather dubious circumstances, paid twice that
amount for the office.[84] Richard Bishop had purchased the office of tipstaff to the
court of Common Pleas from Huggins for two hundred pounds, although
Richardson paid over seven hundred and fifty pounds to the same person for the
corresponding post with the court of Exchequer.[85] A tipstaff's place was sold by
Tilly in 1696 to Francis Duncomb for three hundred and fifty pounds. He was
described by witnesses as the son of a Buckinghamshire parson, a failed apprentice
and a horse thief who had been arrested for buying sheep and cattle in other men's
names.[86] All these appointments were made for the lifetime of the holder, or in
the case of Huggins, for that of his own life and of his son or successor. However
some check against unsuitable persons was made. The court of Common Pleas
certainly vetoed the warden's choice of deputy on one occasion and on another
passed a judgment against an officer for neglect of duty.[87] It also appears that an
incoming warden had some right to eject an officer who met with his disfavour.
Thus Bygrave was dismissed from his clerkship as Bambridge considered him
unsuitable.[88] The circumstances of this dismissal and of Bygrave's consequent loss
have already been mentioned.

The most substantial office in the prison, after that of the deputy warden,
was that of the clerk of the papers. Nixon, as deputy warden, also held this office,
having a private clerk to do this work for him at a salary of one hundred pounds.[89]
The clerk was responsible for keeping the prison books relating to the entries,
commitments and discharges of prisoners, together with the various writs of
habeas corpus and the papers relating to the *rules* and the day *rules* of the prison.
By law he was required to make these books available to members of the public,
though many, including William Smith in 1776, complained that such free
inspections had been refused.[90] Bygrave estimated that the value of the office in
the 1720s was three hundred and fifty pounds per annum.[91] This amount was
made up from such fees as half-a-crown for each discharge writ, five shillings for a
certificate of discharge, one shilling for a copy of every cause charged against a

prisoner, up to three, and thereafter four pence each, and one shilling for every day *rule* granted.[92]

The office of clerk of the inquiries was valued at one hundred and fifty pounds per annum, and was often held with another appointment. Hopkins, the clerk in 1729, was also a clerk in the court of Common Pleas. His function was to enquire into the discharges and the securities of prisoners. The only fee permitted was that of half-a-crown for every discharge fee when that discharge had been made by a creditor rather than by *supersedeas*. One would imagine that those who had their securities checked by this official, in order to take advantage of the prison *rules*, provided some recompense to enable that work to be facilitated. It was claimed that the office was of recent origin in the 1720s. This may well have been so, for the office was later merged into that of the clerkship of the papers, and it may be presumed that its origin was an attempt to relieve that official from some of the more demanding aspects of his work.[93]

The prison had two turnkeys in 1729, whose places were said to be worth fifty pounds per annum.[94] As Duncomb is said to have paid Tilly three hundred and fifty pounds for this office in the 1690s this was probably an underestimate.[95] These men received two shillings from each entry fee and half-a-crown from the dismission fees. It was claimed by the prisoners in 1729 that they demanded five shillings for the latter, whereas the legal fee was but one shilling.[96] By 1817 there were three turnkeys, each of whom received a guinea weekly in lieu of fees, and a room in the prison rent free.[97] They each furnished the rooms with beds in order to accommodate new prisoners who had to await chumming arrangements for a room. Joseph Wilkes, one of these turnkeys, had four beds in one part of his room, separated by a partition from another half where his family lived. He charged fourteen shillings per week for the bed, fire and candle, in term time, but only half a guinea out of term. The junior turnkey, whose room was in the lodge and thus inaccessible to most prisoners, made up beds wherever he could, charging seventeen shillings for a double bed and ten shillings for a single, but argued that the costs of moving them took a great part of his profit away.[98] Such men were forbidden to take garnish, which their predecessors had demanded at a rate of six shillings per prisoner for a bowl of punch.[99] During this period Nixon acted as the chief turnkey as well as deputy warden, and estimated his income thereby as sixty-one pounds.[100] While some of these turnkeys were former prisoners, as was the case in 1729, there is no evidence to suggest that any actual prisoner was ever engaged in this capacity, though it obviously happened elsewhere as it was a practice condemned by Howard.[101] The turnkeys seem to have spent much of their time in the lodge of the prison, between the inner and outer gates, checking visitors in and out, ensuring that prisoners did not escape or that contraband or weapons were let into the prison, while it was also their task to keep the prison quiet.

The five prison tipstaffs were each attached to a particular court, and their task was to conduct prisoners to and from these. A charge of thirty shillings is recorded for taking one prisoner into custody, although the more normal fee was ten shillings for taking a prisoner to a court or a judge's chamber,[102] while a lesser fee, of six shillings and eight pence, was charged by another tipstaff whose particular task was to "take in" the rulers whose security had been withdrawn.[103] Each place had its separate value. The 1729 report alleged that the tipstaff to the court of Chancery had given three hundred and twenty-eight guineas for his office, and another had been sold for seven hundred and fifty-seven pounds, although the three other places were said to have cost their holders between one hundred and two hundred and ten guineas only.[104]

The task of the chamberlain was that of allocating prisoners to the chambers, and arranging the system of "chumming" by which prisoners were required to share rooms. For this the chamberlain received a fee of one shilling per writ on the entry of every prisoner. In 1729 this official was said to have paid an annual fee of forty pounds for his office to the warden.[105] His office does not appear to have survived that report. There were also a considerable number of waiters who were required to accompany prisoners who had obtained the day *rules*, or those, who in earlier days, were permitted to "go abroad" by the warden. As better securities were given the number of these men decreased. The fee for accompanying the day rulers was fixed at five shillings, which the prisoners regarded as excessive when they had already given security for their safe return. The fee for "going abroad" was subject to negotiation, another matter equally unacceptable to the prisoners. These waiters were also available to obtain food and other such commodities for the prisoners from the outside world; the scale of charges laid down for this service has not survived, although the prisoners regarded it as excessive.[106] The post of watchman was one usually given to a prisoner, even though he received the liberty of the gate and was allowed to carry a weapon. Barnes, a prisoner, served in this capacity during the 1720s, to the latter discomfort of the then warden, as Barnes implicated Huggins in the murder of Arne. By 1817 a prisoner combined this office with that of prison scavenger and crier, for which he received the sum of half-a-guinea a week. As crier his task was to summon prisoners to the lodge to meet those who did not wish to be contaminated by entering the prison, for which he received a small tip. As scavenger he was required to keep the staircases and the "offices" of the prison clean, while as watchman he was required to go on duty when the gates shut at night, and do a regular round every half hour, though Nixon, philosophically, accepted he often fell asleep.[107]

Many writers commented on the situation created by the sale of these offices. It was their constant complaint that people were appointed to them not because of their suitability for the office but because of the money they could command. It is hardly surprising that it was alleged that the main object of those men who obtained these appointments was to gain the maximum return on their investments in the shortest possible time. Hence the many complaints, all too justified, of extortion. Guybon is a not too untypical example. Unsuitable for the office of deputy warden, for he had no command over his prisoners and refused to enter the prison for fear of them, he was ignorant of the law and thus within the power of his attorney, Welland. His main qualification, in the opinion of his contemporaries, was that he knew how to obtain or extort money in order to make up his rental of the prison.[108]

James Berisford may have exaggerated when he wrote in 1699 that the "mischiefs and distractions" which took place at the Fleet were "not less dangerous to our constitution, than a standing army".[109] Nevertheless his assertions that the office of warden had become a merchantisable commodity, that the prison had developed into a business enterprise, and that the warden's main concern was speculation on a large and profitable scale, were not too far short of the truth. Concerned only with profits the warden often neglected the poor prisoners in order to pander to the wishes of the rich, and made the common side deliberately uncomfortable in order to persuade as many prisoners as possible to choose the more expensive master's side. As part of the profits of the prison came from the lease of the tap, drinking was encouraged, even though riot and disorder thereby increased.

The parliamentary commissioners of 1729 thus maintained that virtually all the abuses in the administration of the prison could be attributed to the venality of the appointment and method of fee payment to the prison officers. "The warden ... does ... repair his own charge and loss at the wretched expense of the ease and quiet of the miserable objects in his custody", they noted in their report.[110] Simon Wood argued from his own experience that a prisoner was "as much put to his shifts to raise money to clear the demands of the prison, as before to satisfy the plaintiff",[111] while the *Craftsman* observed that debtors could easily mistake "their new keepers for their old creditors".[112] There were many who realised that this position would only be changed when the whole system of fee taking was abolished. Howard recommended that a proper salary should be given to the gaoler and his officers, in lieu of the profits derived from the tap and other such perquisites. Many other writers shared his concern.[113] It is not surprising, therefore, that the 1814 inquiry strongly objected to the whole practice of fee taking, and although the following was written about the King's Bench prison, it applied equally to the Fleet:

It is the decided opinion of your committee, that the mode of remuneration arising out of fees paid by the prisoner, and by emoluments made at the expense of those who are confined to his charge, is the most objectionable means by which a salary is given to the keeper of a prison. His interests are thus set invariably against his duty; and his profits are made at the expense of those whom the law supposes to be penniless, and whose property belongs not to themselves, but to their creditors. The marshall of the King's Bench and his officers are public servants, and as such they ought to be paid at the public expense. The allowing a gaoler to make a profit from coffee-houses and taverns, and on the sale of beer and wine, within the prison, is also most objectionable. He thus becomes interested in the promotion of drinking; and his emoluments increase in the degree that sobriety and good conduct cease to exist among those whom the law places under his care. An act of parliament declares, that no keeper of a prison shall be a publican; why then is there to be an exemption made in favour of the marshall of the King's Bench? ..... Your committee are however aware that the marshall holds his office and these emoluments for life, as long as he shall behave well; they therefore recommend some arrangement should take place, by which a just compensation should be made to him; that the fees exacted from the prisoners should be put under some regulation, or abolished altogether; and that the mode by which the gaol is supplied with malt liquor should no longer continue. The marshall should have a control over everything, a personal profit on nothing.[114]

If this recommendation raised some expectation that fees would be abolished, it was short-lived. Though an act of 1815[115] abolished prison fees it had a saving clause exempting the Fleet and King's Bench prisons from its requirements. This was because they were prisons of the Westminster courts, and there was no public fund to compensate their officers for the loss of their fees. In itself this was a tacit acknowledgement of a long-established custom and the legality of these prisons as offices of profit. Thus the 1818 report, faced with such a financial restraint, commented that while such a system was objectionable, it had not been attended by any serious evil or problems, and consequently it did not recommend the abolition of these fees. Such matters as these were at the centre of conflict between the early nineteenth-century reformers and the upholders of the old order of *laissez-faire*. As Sean McConville comments: "fee giving was at the heart of public administration .... Between the gaoler who bought office in order to squeeze his income from misery and the colonel who paid for the cost of his commission by half-starving or half-dressing his men, there were many more similarities than contemporaries may have wished to realise ... ."[116]

Such a system was not without its compensations, however, as Joanna Innes points out in reference to the King's Bench prison. If the system of fee payment caused a "proprietorial attitude" in the prison officers, allowing them to run the prison as a "private business", and thus resenting outside controls, it also meant they regarded their prisoners more as clients and were unlikely to be harsh or rigorous in their attitude to them.[117] It may be added that the comments of the 1818 report that no serious evil had resulted from the system were probably true in so far as the Fleet was concerned, for all who entered this prison were aware of its position. Most of the prison keepers were themselves humane men. Many of the wardens, Bambridge included, were known to be kind to the poor. Both Nixon and Brown frequently declined to press for the fees of indigent prisoners, and released many who could not pay their prison fees, as well as attending to the sick at their own cost. Philip Staygould was probably more representative of the prison officers than such a person as Barnes (of 1729 fame), for his obituary noted his "friendship, humanity and good nature".[118]

One matter still needs to be resolved. The officers of the prison and their duties have been described, but how was the prison actually run on a day-to-day basis? The warden was often an absentee, and for many years of the early nineteenth century the deputy warden, Daniel Hopkins, who died in that office aged 95, must also have been an absentee. Nicholas Nixon, deputy warden for nearly thirty years, acted for John Eyles, who had been unable to visit the prison through old age for the last sixteen years of his wardenship. It was Nixon who testified to the committee of 1814 that he did not wish to enter the prison and mix with his prisoners, as this could cause an impression of favouritism and also tend to diminish his authority in the prison.[119] He lived however in the lodge of the prison, whose rooms overlooked its courtyard, and by that date the prison turnkeys also resided in the prison in their respective rooms.[120] This in itself was a substantial change from the previous century, for when the gates were then locked at night, none of its officers had access to the prison, which was in control of the nightwatchman.[121]

It will have been realised already that a warden or his deputy, two or three turnkeys, and a nightwatchman, were alone responsible for the care and security of well over three hundred prisoners at any one time, even excluding their families who "lived-in". The tipstaffs and waiters need to be excluded from their number because their function lay outside the prison, and they had little concern with its internal affairs. It will also have been noted that when matters got out of hand, and an external authority was brought in, such as the court of Common Pleas or the military, the warden invariably complained that a "conspiracy" of prisoners was the cause of his problems. Huggins complained, for example, that some prisoners had set up "a court of inspectors". However there is considerable evidence to suggest that there was always a prisoners' committee in existence throughout the latter history of the Fleet. Howard mentions it and was not happy about it, nor was William Smith, while its existence was reported to both the 1814 and 1818 inquiries.

All this suggests that Joanna Innes's thesis regarding the King's Bench prison was also true of the Fleet. She comments that the prisoners themselves "filled the vacuum created by the absence of an effective formal presence in prison life." The prison officers were seen as "a weak body whose effective exercise of authority depended upon the support of the prison population", who acted as a constraint upon their practices. Thus a viable working compromise was needed between the prisoners and the prison officers as to their respective share of responsibility. As will be noted later, the prisoners seemed to have claimed the right to make rules and enforce their discipline for the good order of the prison inhabitants, in the same way as a junior common room would operate today in an Oxbridge college. There was thus a delicate balance between both sides, each of whom had a vested interest in permitting the status quo to continue. That the system worked well enough for it to be little recorded was due to the common sense of both parties to it: the prison officers in that they did not exploit their position, perhaps turning a blind eye to the drunkenness, gaming and immorality in their midst, and endeavouring to use the way of conciliation and mediation rather than that of conflict in order to resolve differences; and the prisoners, who accepted that the privileges they enjoyed were secured to them because of a fee-paying system and one in which they were required to maintain themselves. But this balance could be adversely affected if either side stepped out of line: the prisoners endeavouring to affect the working of the prison in their own interest, as in the allocation of rooms in one instance of the 1720s, or the warden overstepping his traditional role and endeavouring to establish a greater authority over the prison than his prisoners believed necessary. It was when this working relationship broke down that trouble ensued, as it did in particular during the 1720s. But by and large both sides accepted that they needed each other's co-operation in the working of the prison. The warden needed the prisoners' consent to govern his prison with the minimum of resources, while they needed his favour in order that their traditional privileges could be continued.[122]

It is clear that Howard and Smith never understood this delicate balance, nor did the courts, who imposed various orders which tended to give the warden a greater authority than this system allowed. Innes notes one occurrence with respect to the King's Bench prison, which was also true of the Fleet. The court ordered that all women who were not prisoners should leave the prison when its gates were closed for the night. The order was quietly ignored by both sides. The prisoners had no wish for such an order, and the prison officers knew that to impose it would break down the good harmony which prevailed.[123] The same also applied to the sale of spirits in the Fleet. Although forbidden by the regulations, it was allowed to continue as a clandestine operation, and little check was made to prevent spirits entering the prison. Only when information was given to the warden did he feel obliged to act.

In spite of these redeeming features in the prison administration, most gaolers had a bad press, and were subject to popular disapproval. This was probably more the unfortunate legacy of Bambridge and of some of his predecessors than a just appraisal of his successors. Their "greatest mercies are cruelties" wrote one in the 1690s,[124] and another writer of a later period claimed that such men only desisted "from their former violent methods when they find they can no longer pass uncensored".[125] Lilburn, whose full remarks on this score have already been quoted, ended by stating that because of such gaolers, "though the law of England be a law of mercy, yet it is now turned into a shadow".[126] The shadow remained, sometimes disturbed, always dormant, until the prison was closed and the type of office it permitted finally abolished with it.

NOTES

*

1   Cal SPD, 1700-2, p 443.

2   R B Pugh, *Imprisonment in Medieval England* (Cambridge 1970), pp 156f; Harris, p ix; F W Maitland, *Collected Papers* (London 1911), II 365.

3   *The Warden of the Fleet's Case in Relation to Mr Baldwin Leighton's Petition to the Honourable House of Commons.*.

4   8 & 9 William III c 27, clause xi.

5   Harris, p xiii.

6   PRO, SP35/5, fol 124. This was denied by an earlier jury which found that the messuage was pertinent to the office [PRO, SP/Scotland/Series II I, fol 7a]; cf *Some Considerations Humbly Offered in Relation to the Bill now Depending in Parliament for the Further Relief of Creditors in Cases of Escapes.*

7   Report 1818, pp 85f.

8   PRO, SP35/68. fol 80.

9   Harris, p ix.

10   Margery Basset, "The Fleet Prison in the Middle Ages", *The University of Toronto Law Journal*, V (1944) 384; Maitland, *Collected Papers*, II 365.

11   Edward Coke, *The Institutes of the Laws of England* (London 1642), II 589.

12   Harris, p 69.

13   Because of this the prison was not subjected to the numerous acts of the early nineteenth century which endeavoured to reform the prisons.

14   Report 1814, pp 551, 682.

15   Smith, p 42.

16   Report 1814, p 545.

17   Report 1792, p 652.

18   Mackay, pp 5, 14.

19   Mackay, pp 25, 35.

20   *The Case of Mr Bygrave, late Clerk of the Papers of the Fleet.*

21   Mackay, pp 39f; Report 1818, p 81; see Appendix 3.

22   Report 1792, p 643.

23   CLRO, Misc MS 173.5, fol 10.

24   Report 1814, p 785.

25   Sean McConville, *A History of English Prison Administration* (London 1981), I 5.

26   The warden lost his case regarding poor rates for the parish of St Brides for this reason [*Universal Magazine*, 10 Feb 1784]. In 1814 the poor rates amounted to £360 per annum [Report 1814, p 673]. A further appeal took place in 1825 [GLRO, Misc MS173.5 (1825), fol 14].

27   Howell, p 453.

28   Berisford, p 4, quoting *Sid Rep* 68.

29   Report 1729, p 2.

30   *The Debtor and Creditor's Assistant* (London 1793), p 51.

31   Report 1814, pp 551, cf 695 and Report 1729, App 3, nos 5, 7, 10.

32   Brown, *The Fleet*, p 13; *The Microcosm of London* (London 1802), II 46.

33   BL, MS Addit 38170, fol 261.

34   Harris, p 17.

35   Jnl H of C, XI 677.

36   Jnl H of C, XI 643.

37   Report 1729, pp 17f. In this calculation various fees were duplicated, and an assumption made that all the fees were paid. No account was given as to how a figure of £1,500 was arrived at to cover the sums alleged to have been collected in new year gifts and other fees by the warden.

38   Wood, p 10.

39   Report 1729, p 17. The coffee room produced an annual rent of £14, the cellars of the prison £80, while the sheriffs of the county of London paid the warden an annual fee of £8 for his custody of Westminster Hall and £10 for the prison.

40   Report 1729, pp 17f.

41   cf Report 1729, pp 17f; Howard (1780), p 156.

42   Report 1818, p 6.

43   Report 1814, pp 788f.

44   Report 1818, p 77. The income of the marshall of the King's Bench was even more substantial, being returned at £3,590, and being made up of such items as income from the *rules* of £2,600, the day *rules* £223, and the tap £872, less expenditure. This made the marshall one of the wealthiest inhabitants of the county of Surrey.

45   The profit on ale and porter was said to be £200 per annum, but it was not estimated in this report through the failure of the warden's agent [Report 1814, p 548].

46   Nixon also received an additional income as clerk of the papers and as chief turnkey. In 1818 this amounted to £2,238 [Report 1818, p 6].

47   PP 1830 (342) XXIII 385.

48 Brown, *The Fleet*, p 13; even though by this time the Westminster hall rents had been lost, the houses demolished in 1793, and the sale of offices forbidden.

49 PP 1830 (342) XXIII 385.

50 William Gery, *Abuses Discovered*, in BL, MS Addit 38856, fol 127.

51 John Lilburn, *Liberty Vindicated* (London 1646), p 28.

52 2 Geo II c 32. A licence to sell the prison is in BLO, MS Rawlinson B386, fol 47b.

53 Bassett, *The Fleet Prison*, p 386, quoting Harris, p 17.

54 Brown, *The Fleet*, pp 7f.

55 Report 1729, pp 2f.

56 Berisford, p 4; cf 8 & 9 William III c 27.

57 *The Case of John Clements* [1693]; Jnl H of C, X 823, XII 686f; PRO, SP34/6, fols 110, 113.

58 Berisford, pp 2, 20f: *Considerations regarding the Bill for Regulating of the Prisons of the King's Bench and the Fleet: Reasons why the said Bill should Pass without the Clause Proposed by Edmund Boulter.*

59 *The Present Lord Keeper. His Report to Her Majesty upon the Petition of Mr Tilly and Mr Leighton* (1705); Jnl H of C, XI 676; PRO, SP32/6, fol 113).

60 PRO, E/134/11 Anne/Mich 37.

61 Berisford, pp 4, 18ff.

62 *The Lord Keeper's Report*; PRO, E/134/11 Anne/Mich 37.

63 Berisford, p 2.

64 Jnl H of C, XI 646.

65 B Honeybourne, "The Fleet and its Neighbourhood in Early and Medieval Times", *London Topographical Record*, XIX (1947) 24f; Bassett, *The Fleet Prison*, p 385.

66 Howell, p 367; PRO, E/134/11 Anne/Mich 37.

67 Howell, pp 333, 361. William Penrice, deputy marshall of the King's Bench, was required to find a bond of £2000, even though he himself was a debt prisoner therein [*The Extraordinary Case of William Penrice, late Deputy Marshall of the King's Bench Prison* (London 1768), p 13].

68 Jnl H of C, XI 677, cf XII 684 regarding Ford. This happened at the King's Bench as late as 1724, when Richard Mullens only handed over 77 prisoners in the house to his successor [Report 1729 (KB), p 20].

69 Jnl H of C, XI 643, XII 684. Others appear to have formally entered their own prisons as debt prisoners [Report 1729 (KB), p 7].

70   Bassett, *The Fleet Prison*, p 386.

71   Mackay, p 10.

72   BL, MS Addit 38170, fol 261.

73   Bassett, *The Fleet Prison*, p 386.

74   Jnl H of C, XI 644, 677. Leighton offered one Cuthbert, if he gained the office of warden, the position of deputy, for a fine of £1,000 and an annual rent of half of the profits of the prison [ibid, XI 678].

75   Howell, pp 333, 361f.

76   Report 1729 (KB), pp 6, 19.

77   Report 1729 (KB), p 18.

78   Harris, p 160, appendix I, quoting BL, MS Landsdown 85.

79   Mackay, p 10.

80   *The State of the King's Bench Prison* (London 1765).

81   *Gentleman's Magazine*, June 1781.

82   Wood, p 7.

83   Report 1818, p 5.

84   *The Case of Mr Bygrave*; Report 1729, p 18; Jnl H of C, XI 676.

85   *The Committee's Memorial against Mr Bambridge*. Bishop had previously held a fifth share in the office of the marshall of the King's Bench [Report 1729 (KB), p 16].

86   Jnl H of C, XI 676, 679.

87   *The Case of Mr Bygrave.*

88   Ibid. He claimed he had a life interest in the office.

89   Report 1814, p 548.

90   Smith, p 42.

91   *The Case of Mr Bygrave.*

92   Report 1729, p 15; Mackay, pp 16ff, 26f, 39.

93   Report 1729, p 15; Mackay, pp 27, 31.

94   Report 1729, p 18.

95   Jnl H of C, XI 676.

96   Report 1729, p 16; Mackay, pp 26f.

97   David Hughson, *Walks through London* (London 1817), I 124; Report 1814, p 548.

98   Report 1814, pp 672, 697f.

99   Report, p 5.

100   Report 1818, pp 6, 77.

101 Howard (1780), p 33.

102 Mackay, p 19; Report 1729, p 4.

103 Howell, pp 401, 438.

104 Howell, p 356; Report 1729, p 18.

105 Report 1729, pp 9, 15, 18; Report 1729 (M), p 22.

106 Mackay, pp 5, 21; Jnl H of C, XI 676.

107 Howell, pp 320ff.;Hughson's *London*, I 124; Report 1814, pp 548, 672.

108 Howell, p 340; Mackay, p 10.

109 Berisford, p 29.

110 Report 1729, p 14.

111 Wood, p 13.

112 *Craftsman*, 10 May 1729.

113 John Howard, *An Account of the Present State of the Prisons in London and Westminster* (London 1789), p xi.

114 Report 1814, pp 546f.

115 55 Geo III c 50.

116 Sean McConville, *A History of English Prison Administration* (London 1981), I 69f.

117 Joanna Innes, "The King's Bench Prison in the later Eighteenth Century", in J Brewer and J Styles, *An Ungovernable People* (London 1980), pp 268, 270.

118 Coll BL, fol 47.

119 Report 1814, p 685; Report 1818, p 42. This does not mean, however, that he was remote from his prisoners, who had access to him at the lodge. He also visited the prison at night. This was also the position at the King's Bench prison. The 1814 Report accused its marshall of taking £3,590 from a prison he hardly ever visited [Report 1814, p 547].

120 Report 1814, pp 551, 672, 697f; Report 1818, p 6. The lodge appears to have been built for the warden's use in 1793.

121 Report 1792, p 662.

122 Innes, *The King's Bench Prison*, pp 251, 286, 297.

123 Ibid, pp 286f.

124 *Reasons against the said Bill Supposed, for Relief of Creditors, and Preventing Escapes* (1698).

125 *A Speech without Doors, on Behalf of an Insolvent Debtor in the Fleet Prison* (London 1729), p 23.

126 John Lilburn, *Liberty Vindicated against Slavery* (London 1646), pp 8f.

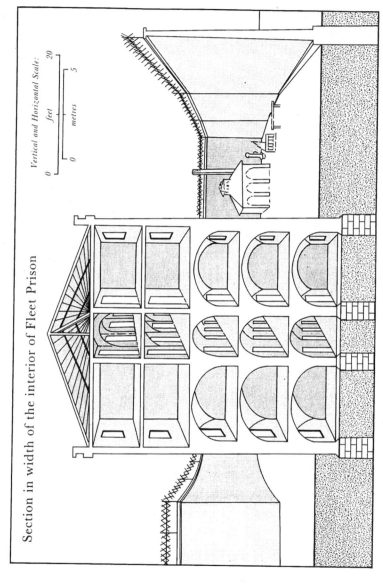

Section in width of the interior of Fleet Prison

Vertical and Horizontal Scale:

A section of the interior of the prison in 1780, redrawn by Gary Llewellyn from the original engraving by Rotalde.

Part Three:

"The Most Lingering Death":[1] The Prisoners

"I will say but little to what the law is in this case", stated Mr Justice Page to the
jury at the trial of Huggins for the murder of Edward Arne in 1729; "a prisoner for
debt is only taken like a distress, and kept there till he or his friends can pay the
debt for him. Imprisonment is no punishment, it is not taken as part of the debt;
for let a man lie ever so long, his heirs at law cannot be exempt from the debt, but
if they have effects, are answerable for it. He is kept only in such manner as he
may be forth-coming and safe."[2] Thomas Macdonald writing much later in his
Treatise on Civil Imprisonment in England, argued that the purpose of debt
imprisonment was to coerce the debtor to discharge his commitments.[3] In essence
both took the same view that a debtor was imprisoned so that, as a condition of
obtaining his liberty, he distributed his property for the benefit of his creditors.

Two forms of process and imprisonment evolved with this purpose in mind.
By mesne process the debtor was imprisoned as a defendant in an action, often
because of his failure to put in an appearance after the original writ had been
served.[4] This process either gave the debtor time to rearrange his affairs by
obtaining a bail-bond, in double the sum of the writ and provided by two sureties
who were housekeepers and worth double the amount for which they stood
surety, or required him to wait in gaol or a sheriff's spunging house until his

plaintiff proceeded against him.[5] It was a grossly unfair situation, for if the debtor
had been arrested in the trinity vacation his plaintiff was allowed seven months in
which to give him the declarations showing the cause of the action, while twelve
months could elapse before the case was brought to trial. The plaintiff was not
required to give security that he would prosecute his action, nor to provide
damages if the cause was shown to be malicious. If the plaintiff did not proceed
with the action during that time the debtor was entitled to be superseded, or
released, but he was still required to pay the costs of his arrest, court appearances
and imprisonment,[6] and even more unfairly, the writ of his release.[7] It was
difficult to obtain redress, as the "debtor" had to prove he had been maliciously
arrested, while the damages he could obtain never equalled the costs of his
imprisonment and defence.[8]

By the final process of execution the guilty defendant was imprisoned as a
debtor, so that his body should satisfy his creditors as a substitute for the
repayment of the debts he owed. There was no restriction on time in taking this
action, nor of the amount of debt, and one Fleet prisoner was mentioned in 1792
as having been imprisoned for nine years for a sum of ninety shillings.[9] This
process could only be taken against the debtor's body, not against his estate or
goods, which were protected against the actions of his creditors. This gave so
little benefit to the creditor that it often appeared that such imprisonment was
more an act of private satisfaction on his part than an attempt to regain the
outstanding debts.[10] Nightengale argued, for instance, that knowing the conditions
of the prisons only "sheer ignorance or unmixed malignity" could be the motive
which influenced creditors to "seek such redress for their losses ... Who, that
knows the real states of these prisons, would confine a man here to correct
him?"[11]

The laws of debt imprisonment were extremely defective. As Joanna Innes
writes, the complicated process often appeared to be more a system of legalised
bullying on the part of the creditor than a court supervised arbitration which
enabled a settlement to be made.[12] Worse, they failed to distinguish between the
fraudulent and the unfortunate debtor, although Dr William Smith, a real
benefactor to the London debtors, considered that five-sixths of the debt prisoners
in England were fraudulent. He wrote, for example, that "when they can carry on
their trade no longer, and some of their frauds are likely to come to light, they run

to gaol not empty handed, where they live in luxury and riot, and declare open war against every law of God and man, and lay aside all rules of decency and good order."[13] In a similar vein Nixon, then deputy warden of the Fleet, wondered if any man had ever taken the benefit of an insolvency act "conscientiously". He maintained that these acts held out "great inducements" for people to take out credit, and then to take advantage of the insolvency acts in order to avoid these debts.[14] On another occasion he suggested that many of those who entered the prison on friendly actions did so in order to take advantage of an insolvency act, adding, "nor is it an uncommon thing for the warden ... to receive both the plaintiff and the defendant in the same prison".[15] Nevertheless there were unfortunate debtors and the law certainly appeared to punish poverty and misfortune as a crime without the benefits received by a criminal or a bankrupt trader.[16] The position was well summed up by a writer in the *Middlesex Journal*. He argued that by the laws of England if a man owed ten pounds he is left to die in gaol, but if he owed over ten thousand pounds he became a bankrupt, "obtains his certificate, and begins again". The writer asked, "what has the small debtor done that his punishment should be greater than that of the large one?"[17] His was a legitimate question.

A Plea for the City Orphans and Prisoners for Debt, of 1690, argued that most prisoners were imprisoned because of misfortunes or through injustices; many had been "maliciously prosecuted and detained in prison by vexatious suits and litigious pretensions". Perhaps more to the point Moses Pitt estimated that imprisonment for debt was futile as only one in ten debts were paid through imprisoning the debtor. It seemed to many that the only people who derived any advantage from debt imprisonment were the "attorneys, solicitors, gaoler, bailiffs and followers" who gained their living thereby.[18] But there were still many, especially tradesmen, who defended the existing laws of debt. Actions were usually brought only after appeals and arbitration had failed to persuade a person to discharge a contractual obligation. The creditor thus using "an enhanced coercive negotiating power" consequently summoned the debtor, and the threat of court proceedings generally gave the debtor a powerful incentive to arrange his affairs and so avoid a perilous situation. In 1790 out of twelve thousand bailable writs issued in London and Middlesex, only ten per cent resulted in imprisonment. While some may have been abandoned because of difficulties, the average tradesman would argue that such a success rate, indicating that these debts had been settled, meant that the debt laws served a useful purpose, and that the whole system of credit would be at risk if they did not exist. Those who were imprisoned as a result were the failures of the system, who refused or were unable to settle with their creditors. Their eventual plight acted as a warning to others not to transgress the laws of credit too hastily. Such arguments gained even more validity when it was noted that most of those who were imprisoned were charged on mesne proceedings only. In 1791 sixty-four per cent of the nineteen hundred and fifty-seven prisoners in the London and Middlesex gaols for debt came into this category. For most of them such imprisonment served as a sharp and severe shock, and many took the opportunity of making an early settlement with their creditors either voluntarily or within the terms of an insolvency act. Others were released as their creditors realised that imprisonment was having little effect in encouraging them to settle their debts. The small number of prisoners in execution may be described as the disaster end of the process, and many of them would have learnt to exploit their position to the full.[19] But it must be admitted than many unfortunate people crept into the system, and found it almost impossible to extradite themselves.

It may have seemed at the time that the whole advantage of the laws of debt lay with the creditor, for often ignorance forced a debtor to come to his creditor's terms.[20] His only defence was to obtain a writ of error which removed the action into one of the higher courts in the hope that the increased cost of this might either drive the creditor beyond the limits of his purse, or cause him to reconsider his position.[21] Others used the system to their own advantage, and moved themselves into the Fleet prison, determined to exist as comfortably as possible on their available resources, instead of reducing themselves to poverty by settling with their creditors. Jones Pierce wrote that a new prisoner would discover as he entered the Fleet that his education had begun: "he will learn more law in a week than a man out of prison all his life."[22] Smith noted that the dishonest debtor might have been planning for his dishonest retreat for years before his eventual imprisonment, deceiving his creditors and conveying his property to his children. Of such men, he wrote, "plenty decks his table [in prison], while riot and drunkenness distinguishes his apartment."[23] Some prisoners certainly took advantage of the law of debt and elected to remain prisoners for life in order to

enable their estates to descend intact to their heirs. This was in spite of the act of
21 James I c 24 which allowed creditors the right to proceed against the estates of
imprisoned debtors who had died in prison. The preamble of this act stated, "and
forasmuch as daily experience doth manifest that divers persons, of sufficiency in
real and personal estate, minding to deceive others of their just debts, for which
they stood charged in execution, hath obstinately and wilfully chosen rather to live
and die in prison than to make any satisfaction according to their abilities..."
Alexander Harris maintained that it was regarded as "a holy maxim" by such men
that the man "is cursed that selleth his patrimony or his possessions (though
bought with other men's money) to pay his debts withall".[24] One illustration of
this was given by the 1792 report. A prisoner who had been in the Fleet for nine
years for a debt of ten thousand pounds, was proved before his commitment to
have been worth four times that amount, and generally worth ten times it. He thus
"saves five hundred pounds per year as the interest of the debt by which he is
imprisoned, and which his creditor has no means of obtaining".[25]

In theory at least the law of debt imprisonment meant that some could face a
lifetime's imprisonment. In order to relieve this situation, and also to meet the
growing concept that personal freedom was a human right that stood on a higher
plane than private property, parliament passed at frequent intervals various acts for
the relief of insolvent debtors, in the realisation that not all were fraudulent or
dishonest. Between the first of these acts in 1670-1[26] and the year 1781 they
were passed on average every four and a half years, but from 1781 until 1793 no
acts were passed due to the hostility caused by the alleged abuses of the system.
The 1792 report was probably instrumental in persuading parliament to the
contrary.[27] The procedure became permanent in 1813, when prisoners of three
months or more standing were able to apply to a special court for their
discharge.[28] Perhaps nothing could show more clearly the absurdity of debt
imprisonment than these acts, and possibly the sympathy given to debtors by the
general public, for as in Innes' phrase, "ubiquitous credit meant that almost every
Englishman was a potential candidate for imprisonment for debt."[29]

The procedure of these acts hardly ever varied, and they were similar in
composition to the bankruptcy laws as defined by Blackstone in his
Commentaries.[30] The debtor was required to give a schedule of his possessions,
which after his wearing apparel, bedding and trade implements to the total value of

ten pounds were deducted, were sold for the benefit of his creditors. He could not be re-arrested on these charges, but he was still required to pay the amount of his outstanding debts after his schedule had been effected. In 1830 it was noted that the average dividend was five farthings in the pound.[31] One wonders how much it might have been had imprisonment not been imposed. Those who made fraudulent declarations, were debtors to the crown, or had debts over a certain sum, one hundred pounds in 1724 and two hundred by the 1790s, were exempted from the provisions of these acts. This was seen as a great hardship. The prison keepers were required to provide schedules of all prisoners in their custody on a certain date, and at whose suits they were charged. Severe penalties were placed on those keepers who entered the names of non-prisoners into these schedules in order to enable them to take advantage of the acts. Thus Church, deputy warden, was bound over in the 1690s for falsely swearing a man to be his prisoner in order to afford his discharge under one of these acts, while a person paid a sum of £7.10s. to the marshall of the King's Bench to be so entered.[32]

After 1711 the names of all the debt prisoners who applied for the benefit of these acts was inserted in the *London Gazette*. If a creditor refused to allow the discharge of his debtor under the terms of one of these acts he was required to provide a maintenance for him, originally of four pence per day, and later of sixpence. But the expense of obtaining these "groats" could cost from between two to three guineas, and the Thatched House Society (a benevolent society) reported that each year on average it helped 150 debtors to obtain this relief, who were entitled to it, but from want of means were unable to sue for it.[33] Even one creditor, out of several, could prevent the discharge of a debt prisoner, though his other creditors were willing to permit his release.[34] The result was that frequently creditors paid more in groats to their debtors than the debt was worth.[35]

It proved impossible to compel those who wished to remain in prison to apply for their discharges, as will be noted later, even though the 1755 act provided that a refusal to do so would be punished by death as a felon without benefit of clergy, and another act offered an alternative of transportation for seven years. There is no evidence that such penalties were ever enforced. Clause II of the 1750 act (*8 Geo II c 24*) put another problem as neatly as any bitter creditor might have done: "to prevent persons from lying in prison until they have spent their substance wherewith they could satisfy their creditors and afterwards taking the benefit of the said act when they have nothing to deliver up to their creditors". To solve this problem it was ordered that the names of all eligible debtors be inserted into the schedule of the next insolvency act after they had been charged in the final debt process of execution. One condition of an insolvency act of 1703 (*2 & 3 Anne c 16*) is worth mentioning. Debtors would be discharged only on condition that they served or procured a person to serve with her majesty's fleet or army and to continue that service for the duration of the war.

As the century progressed, however, the cost of obtaining the benefit of these acts became more and more prohibitive. William Jones, marshall of the King's Bench, protested in 1827 about its cost to the individual prisoner. Thirty years ago, he argued, the cost of a discharge under one of these acts never exceeded one and a half guineas, and court fees and other expenses no more than three guineas; even this was sufficiently large to compel prisoners to raise money for their discharge. Now, with five to six hundred attorneys brought into the insolvency court as agents, charging at least six pounds even to start the necessary proceedings, the total bill would be twenty-five pounds at least. Not only did this offend against the act, which stated that no fees were to be taken save those allowed by the commissioners, it also created new debts. The clerk of the court obtained half a guinea from each discharge, with the result that in five years he had amassed nearly nine and a half thousand pounds for work which a turnkey could do. Brokers appointed by the court to receive the surrendered goods charged one shilling in the pound as commission, and often sold these goods for less than a third of their value. Jones stated that one discharged debtor with debts of ninety pounds had had to pay court expenses of thirty-seven, and another who failed to obtain a discharge was still required to pay expenses of between forty and fifty pounds. The then current insolvency act, Jones maintained, had been productive of more frauds and perjuries than any other act ever passed, and it was hardly possible for any insolvent debtor to take advantage of it without being guilty of perjury.[36]

Until the nineteenth century these insolvency acts were few and far between. As a result many petitions were sent to parliament by the "distressed" debtors in the Fleet and other prisons requesting further legislation for the discharge of prisoners. The reasons they gave hardly ever varied. The release of the debtor, it was argued, gave the creditor a better remedy than imprisonment, while it enabled the debtor to provide for himself and his family, pay taxes to the crown, and do his duty to the nation. In 1690 it was maintained that there were over forty thousand debtors in prisons, and in addition one hundred and twenty thousand dependants, most of whom had to be supported by parochial relief. Each petition, in order to offset criticism, made a careful distinction between the unfortunate debtor and those who made the prison into an asylum for their debts. Each endeavoured to outdo all previous petitions by painting a gruesome picture of the conditions within a debt prison. Many prisoners, they argued, were confined solely for their prison fees. Unlike the criminal the debtor was confined without limitation of time, and was treated "worse than the most odious offender". A number of such men had become incapable of retrieving their misfortunes or of being of "public utility", because of the "idleness and other ill-habits" contracted whilst in prison. And there was always "reason to dread fatal consequences from the fullness of the prisons, which, when the weather becomes warm, will probably increase and cause a general mortality". It was claimed that some prisoners were held on fictitious claims made with the "collusion of wicked attorneys". If some of the general public doubted these statements about conditions inside prisons, the prisoners alleged that creditors were deliberately kept in ignorance of their debtor's miseries, their lawyers having argued that a little restraint would soon enforce payment. Furthermore to avoid such imprisonment many had fled overseas, especially seamen and manufacturers, and were now giving help to the enemy. James Stephen in his book, *Considerations on Imprisonment for Debt*, written while he was a debt prisoner at the King's Bench in 1770, argued even more originally, and endeavoured to prove from Magna Carta and the common and statute law of the realm that debt imprisonment was both invalid and illegal.

The Fleet prisoners found other arguments over and above these "common stock" ones in an attempt to convince parliament about the futility of debt imprisonment, and so provide them with legislative relief. Alleging that a debt might be for no more than twenty pounds, it was argued that the cost of the necessary actions and of removal to the Fleet prison ("for he cannot without danger to his life abide in a common prison"), together with the prison fees and the care of the debtor's wife and family, would amount to over one hundred pounds per annum. This argument could be put another way. The retention of the present system of debt enforcement, at even "a modest computation'" with its bailiffs' and court officials' fees and expenses, together with their "vicious and profuse way of living", cost an annual and rather precise sum of one hundred and fifty-six thousand and three hundred pounds. All this, it was argued, "if rightly applied, would satisfy all the debts of that year". A further argument was presented in the 1720s, probably as a means of drawing attention to the prisoners' dispute with the warden. Those who had protested about the extraordinary fees and the abuses in the prison charities had been "most inhumanely and barbarously locked down in the common side wards, without ... the benefit of air, water or going to divine service, by which means the wards are become so full as to endanger a contagion in the approaching hot weather".

These arguments, together with the supporting evidence of prison conditions, were given in petition after petition. It was suggested that the only people who would oppose such an act were the angry "revengeful" creditors, the gaolers who were "greedy" of their extravagant fees, and the "busy inferior lawyers" who would lose some of their profit. If such arguments could not suffice then an appeal was made to the fact that no other European nation imprisoned debtors without requiring their creditors to support them. And, if all these failed, there was still an appeal on the grounds of religion, justice, and mercy.[37] Yet the fact that so many of these petitions were successful is due not so much to the force of their arguments, but rather to the fact that these sentiments were shared by many within parliament itself, all of whom probably had some friend or relative who had experienced these miseries at first hand. Besides this, there was the continuing fear of pestilence arising from the prisons, a fact actually asserted in the act of 1670. Consequently, whether on the grounds of mercy or fear, these acts were normally granted to the petitioners.

As it was impossible to distinguish between the honest and the fraudulent by these acts, it was said that rumours of one would fill the gaols, many obtaining friendly actions in order to enter the prison.[38] This was noted in the 1814 report, which also alleged that if such persons "happened to be foiled" in their intention, they would discharge themselves as soon as they discovered they were not included within that act's schedule.[39] Their position might be defined by a comment made in the *Gentleman's Magazine* of 1747:[40] "many vile and extravagant persons, ... who have run into debt without any intention of ever paying, ... caus'd themselves to be put in prison, on purpose to defraud their honest creditors, in hopes of being discharged by an insolvent act." It added that a number of creditors not only lost their debts by such dishonesty, but were sometimes "seized" by their lawyers for their outstanding fees. Lord Mansfield thus argued in 1781, for example, that these bills had produced "a considerable deal of fraud and villainy" and had proceeded from a sense of "mistaken compassion".[41] Nixon's similar comment has already been recorded. The anonymous writer of *A Speech without Doors* suggested there were others, apart from debtors, who had an interest in "the rumours of an act", though it needs be remembered he was writing in the wake of the 1729 controversy. These rumours, he claimed:

> awakened the conscious gaolers, those nefarious butchers of their fellow-citizens; they seem now to be ashamed of a tyranny they can no longer maintain; they desist from their former violent methods, when they find they can no longer pass uncensored. Out of a tender compassion now, forsooth, they turn out, in shoals, those miserable objects of slow cruelty, who are their prisoners, when they have no further prospect of gain from them; in order, that when they come to make a due return of the numbers of their shackled subjects, they may appear less upon paper.[42]

It was not, by this date, fair comment.

Those who had fled "abroad" in order to avoid imprisonment for debt were also permitted to take advantage of these acts. "Abroad" meant not necessarily out of the country, for the term also applied to those who sheltered in the Mint and at the other debt sanctuaries of London.[43] Such people had to surrender at various named prisons, of which the Fleet was one. Two hundred and sixty fugitives surrendered for the 1748 act at the Fleet, and fifty-four for that of 1772, this number being just over one third of the total released under that act for this prison.[44] The 1729 act discharged, on a national scale, over six thousand debtors, of whom one tenth were fugitives.[45]

Many noted, however, that the sufferings of the prisoners discharged under these acts did not cease upon their release. The writer of *A Speech without Doors* wrote of debtors being "choked up and killed by an idle life, ill air, and most pinching hunger ...". In prison the debtor saw his family suffer, and he became aware that it was "just, equitable and reasonable in the prisoner not to pay the creditor, but to keep his estate in gaol, to defend his own, his wife's and children's lives from perishing through want". Thus "soon deprived of all spirit, courage, and industry", and surrounded by "desperate people abandoned to all forms of wickedness ... he falls into the way of living by his wits (as they call it)" which sort of wit is "whetted by necessity". He continued, warming to his theme: "his spirits grow debased, his understanding soon fades away, his will becomes depraved, and every other faculty of his mind is weakened. Memory, indeed, is the last power of the mind the poor miserable wretch retains, and that serves only to complete his calamities."[46] These habits of idleness and resentment were carried over into the debt prisoner's ordinary life after he was released, as another writer maintained of a slightly later period. This anonymous writer argued that such men left their imprisonment with "all the desperate principles contracted in them, with minds at enmity against all mankind for the treatment they have met with". Ruined by idleness, no one would give them credit. They thus became "enemies to society" or sank into poverty, becoming "a useless burden to themselves and to the community until they die". "I am tired", he continued, "of describing what the law, as it stands, gives cruel minded creditors of doing to their helpless debtors."[47] Simon Wood echoed these sentiments. Such men, he stated, were "rendered useless when at liberty, which often engages them to take bad courses". Frequently drunk with liquor, they were "prepared for any act of desperation" rather than return to their families "without a penny for their relief".[48] William Smith, from his own experience, argued that a prisoner through long confinement "became liable to the consequences of habitual indolence, filth and vice, and is often unwilling to return to labour when he overcomes his liberty."[49] No contemporary writer preserved statistics to indicate the percentage of prisoners who found themselves back in a debt prison after having been discharged under one of these acts. Undoubtedly there were many, but for the vast majority, the honest debt prisoners, these acts must have been received with profound gratitude as they enabled them to have a fresh start to life and to be free of the corrupting influences of prison existence.

It is not too surprising that many men became so attached to prison life that they managed to obtain so-called "friendly actions" in order to remain within the prison, one commentator stating: "there being nothing they dread more as the fear of being turned out".[50] Some of these men, who were technically supersedable, that is, able to obtain their discharges, followed this procedure in order to hold onto their rooms, finding, it is said, "its inheritance ....more beneficial" than if "they were out of doors", as they were able to make a living within the prison economy by letting out their rooms.[51]   This practice was equally true in the Elizabethan gaols, when it was reported, "we hear of fellows who .... would not be persuaded to leave, who kept themselves loaded with suits for debt to cover their own knaveries",[52] as it also was true of the King's Bench prison in William Smith's day. He wrote, in 1776, words which were equally applicable to the Fleet:

> Many whose actions are supersedable and dischargable, have caused detainers and declarations to be lodged against them for pretended debts, occupying rooms, keep shop, enjoy places of profit, or live on the rent of their rooms a life of idleness, and being indulged with the use of the key, go out when they please and thereby convert a prison, intended for confinement only, into an alms-house for their support, and by making their rooms life-hold estates, are thereby enabled to purchase freehold possessions for their children, to the great distress of real prisoners, who sometimes have no place to lay their heads.[53]

One such prisoner was James Holt. He kept a small shop in the Fleet prison, and though he admitted he could claim the benefit of an insolvency act, he maintained that not being a younger man and not having money to enter into business, he would suffer more inconvenience by going out than by staying in.[54] He may have been more genuine than most, but there were many who shared Holt's sentiments. The 1792 report thus noted that many of these supersedable men lived in the *rules*, having been turned out of the prison house (as required by a ruling of 1787[55]), but had obtained "friendly actions" permitting them to remain on the books of the prison. Fifty-eight of the eighty prisoners in the *rules* were then said to come into this category. The report added: "there are other circumstances which prove, that to debtors of the worst description a prison is no punishment; but, on the contrary, that such persons find an interest, or a gratification, in remaining in a situation full of misery to the honest."[56] Perhaps these commissioners may have misunderstood some of the difficulties that confronted a Fleet prisoner when faced with his discharge, in having to give up his position in the prison economy and learning to fend for himself outside, and thus were unfair in considering all such people dishonest. Few prisoners, however, accepted the argument that these men constituted the majority of their number.

The number of prisoners in the Fleet fluctuated widely. Until the end of the eighteenth century the prison was always overcrowded, in spite of the numbers who took advantage of the *rules* in order to live outside the prison house. The existence of the *rules* in itself was an acknowledgement of the overcrowding of the prison. In 1815 it was estimated that the prison house could only hold two hundred and fifty persons comfortably.[57]

It is best to give the number of prisoners within the prison at any one time in tabular form, and Table Two (see page 154) indicates the great fluctuation in numbers even within one year, often caused by an insolvency act emptying the prison.

Howard calculated in 1776 that there were over two thousand four hundred debt prisoners in England and Wales,[81] and a report of 1792 gave a figure of nineteen hundred and fifty-seven such prisoners.[82] The Fleet and the King's Bench prisons had between one third and a half of all such prisoners. This is verified in part by the prison books of the Fleet, which indicate, for example, that between 1758 and 1790 an average of two hundred people entered the prison each year; between 1797 and 1803 the average rose to three hundred and twenty-five, and between 1804 and 1834 to five hundred and sixty.[83]

Such numbers indicate that the prison was severely overcrowded, but it must be remembered that these figures relate only to the number of prisoners, and not to the number of actual residents, as many prisoners' wives, children and servants also lived in the prison itself. The 1818 report stated there were two hundred and fifty prisoners on average, but three hundred and sixty-five residents, a proportion of nearly one resident "visitor" to every two and a half prisoners.[84]

The system of chumming, which allowed a prisoner to obtain a room to himself, though at high cost, added to the overcrowding, as did the habit mentioned by Mackay in the 1720s of the rulers being permitted to hold chambers in the prison, as well as the warden's practice of permitting non-prisoners "refuge" within the prison.[85] A report of 1698 indicated that there were five or six people in a chamber formerly shared by two, and some of these had to lie on the floor.[86] Though the prisoners were meant to "lie like prisoners, two in a bed together", according to the 1561 rules, Rochford in the 1720s alleged that he had to lie with two others in a bed, without pillows and with only one blanket, for which all three were each required to pay the full chamber rent.[87] The position was even worse

Table Two: The number of prisoners within the prison at given times

Date	total number prisoners	number of prisoners in prison-house	% of total	number of prisoners in the *rules*	% of total
1653[58]	230				
1695[59]	c1000[60]				
1728	611				
1731[61]	200				
1737	478				
1742-3	512				
1747-8	364	219	61%	145	39%
1755	458	233	51%	225	49%
1757[62]	298	110	47%	188	63%
1774[63]	242	171	71%	71	29%
1776[64]	350+	350			
1776[65]	319	241	76%	78	24%
1778[66]	195	143	73%	52	27%
1779[67]	184	147	80%	37	20%
1780[68]	250				
1787	195	121	62%	74	38%
1789[69]	211	131	62%	80	38%
1790[70]	c380	c190	50%	c190	50%
1796	147				
1800	250	190	76%	60	20%
1801	320	250	78%	70	22%
1804	314	256	81%	58	19%
1807	231	178	77%	53	23%
1810	269	221	82%	48	18%
1811[71]	405	305	75%	100	25%
1814[72]	233				
1815[73]	261	209	80%	52	20%
1816[74]	303				
1818[75]	330	250	72%	70	28%
1822	260				
1824	199				
1826 10 Ap	256				
1826 15 Nov	360[76]				
1828[77]	253				
1829[78]	275				
1830[79]	242				
1832[80]	255				

at the King's Bench, where prisoners were again required to lie three to a bed, but many were forced to sleep in the chapel and other such places for lack of accommodation.[88] It has already been noted that one of the principal reasons always given for the need of an act of insolvency was this overcrowding, with its consequent dangers of disease and mortality, not only to the prisoners, but to the population at large.

****

The majority of the Fleet prisoners were debtors, including those who were debtors to the warden or the prison officers for their fees, as was Thomas Roberts in 1742,[89] or Thomas Periom, who was charged in debts of forty thousand pounds to the crown.[90] Others were there for contempt of court or for various financial and other offences against the crown or the exchequer.[91] Thus many smugglers found their way to the Fleet on writs directed against them by the court of Exchequer. These smugglers caused much trouble at the Fleet. James Brown of Galway in Ireland arrived at the Fleet in the 1740s charged with exporting wool from Ireland to France[92] while Robert Blackman and several others also entered the prison charged with the "running of wool".[93] Gabriel Tomkin, a notorious smuggler, under sentence of transportation, was also committed here,[94] as was Charles Pease of Marsh Chapel in Lincolnshire in the 1740s for "running goods", probably tea.[95] Richard Holdsworth entered during the same period, charged with a similar offence,[96] though William Priggs of Kent, who was likewise accused of smuggling, was soon released having provided the authorities with "information".[97] John Mason, having delivered up property to the value of three thousand pounds to meet his liabilities to the receiver of taxes for Cambridge-shire, petitioned for his release in the 1710s after fourteen years imprisonment, being afflicted with "the stone, dropsy, scurvy and rheumatism",[98] and Robert Weemis of Newcastle, charged with evading a sum of fifteen hundred pounds in salt duties, successfully persuaded the Treasury to accept one hundred pounds in composition of his debts, he being in "mean circumstances". But David Boys, fined twenty five thousand pounds for smuggling, and taken to the Fleet as a notorious offender, was equally able to compound his debt, indicating the wealth available to those engaged in this activity.[99] The Treasury was frequently more merciful to its debtors than many creditors, as some other cases illustrate. In the

1710s one Gilliat, a Lincolnshire man, aged and almost blind, incapable of paying his debt, was released.[100] James Brain, a once considerable trader whose business had declined because of "war losses", absconded with debts of £5,785.12s.. But when he was eventually apprehended he had his assets of thirty-eight pounds nineteen shillings seized and his person imprisoned. But as Brain had to be "maintained in prison by his friends and relations" and his debts had been caused through acting as surety for another merchant, now deceased, and he was not thereby indebted to the crown on his own account, he was released.[101] William Tate, searcher of the port of Carlisle, bound in a sum of three thousand and more pounds, who at first had fled to Scotland, then been arrested in Cumberland and brought to the Fleet, was released as he had "no effects ... in the world".[102] And finally there is the case of Sir Alexander Anstruther, baronet, who had been arrested on a charge of high treason for "washing and diminishing the coin of the kingdom" in 1725. The Treasury permitted him to be transferred from Newgate to the Fleet, for at Newgate he had been lodged with the "common malefactors" and his life was considered to be in danger through being imprisoned there at his advanced age.[103]

The Admiralty also sent prisoners to the Fleet. Two naval captains were sent there in 1665 to await charges of neglect and cowardice in not capturing some Dutch vessels.[104] The city of London placed two ships' masters engaged in the Newcastle coal trade, John Grey and Edward Dorsell, in custody at the Fleet on their refusal to sell coal at prices laid down by a statute of 1663.[105] The Fleet even housed state prisoners, particularly during the aftermath of the 1715 rebellion, when both the Tower and Newgate were overfull. Seventy-two prisoners were then lodged at the Fleet and the King's Bench, including Sir William Cockburn and Charles Radcliffe, esq.[106] Quakers were also lodged in the Fleet during their years of persecution,[107] as were the papists, one of whom, Wyat, a poor prisoner, was particularly befriended by a deputy warden, Howard, of the same persuasion, who allowed him his chamber rent and fees free of charge.[108]

The vast majority of these debt prisoners entered the prison by voluntary consent, surrendering to the warden or one of his officers in one of the three courts to which the prison was attached. Many of these, having been successfully sued on a mesne action in an inferior court, were proceeded against on the writ *habeas corpus ad satisfaciendum* by their creditors, who wished to bring them up to some superior court to charge them with the process of execution. Alternatively the prisoner, having been sued in "some inferior jurisdiction", obtained the writ, *habeas corpus ad faciendum et recipiendum,* and so removed the action into a superior court, possibly as a means of harassing his creditor. The safeguards imposed to prevent the superior courts from being overrun with business in this way were never really effective.[109] Both these writs meant that not only was the action transferred to one of these superior courts, but that the prisoner's body was also transferred to the prison of the court concerned, either the Fleet or the King's Bench.[110]

Although a few prisoners undoubtedly obtained these writs in order to harass their creditors, more must have obtained them to avail themselves of the amenities of the prisons involved, and so avoid the horror of the provincial prisons. Edward Hatton wrote about the "pleasantness" of the Fleet prison in 1708, with its gardens and the large extent of its *rules,* and added, "it is preferred before most other prisons, many giving money to turn themselves over to this [prison] from others".[111] Some of the horrors of the others prisons are described by an act of 1670:

> And where it is become the common practice of jailers and keepers to lodge together in one room or chamber or bed, prisoners for debt and felons, whereby many times honest gentlemen, tradesmen and others, are disturbed and hindered in the night time from their natural rest, by reason of their fetters and irons, and otherwise much offended and troubled by their lewd and profane language and discourses, with most horrid cursing and swearing much accustomed to such persons, be it enacted by the authority aforesaid, that it shall not, be lawful hereafter for any sheriff, jailer or keeper of any jail or prison to put, keep or lodge prisoners for debt and felons together in one room and chamber, but that they shall be put, kept and lodged separate and apart from one another in distinct rooms.[112]

The act was a dead letter from its commencement, as no procedures for enforcement of this, or any similar act, were provided until the 1800s.

It is not surprising to find that the charity of some benevolent persons enabled various prisoners to be sent to the Fleet by the use of this writ. The duke of Marlborough so acted with regard to Daniel Beamont, of Eaton in

Buckinghamshire, a starchmaker, who in 1730 was a prisoner in Aylesbury jail. Although charged at quarter sessions with starch duties of sixty-three pounds, nobody appeared to prosecute him, but he had no money nor friends whereby the writ against him could be withdrawn, and remained imprisoned in deplorable conditions. The duke, therefore, presumably unable to do anything about the original charges, procured a writ for him and so "got him to the Fleet", and also assisted the petition which eventually secured his release from imprisonment.[113]

Berisford writing in the 1690s implied that many of the prisoners in the Fleet entered by the use of this writ.[114] Through its use many came to the Fleet from Newgate and the other city prisons.[115] Several transferred themselves from the King's Bench or Marshalsea prisons by using this writ, sometimes because they were required to answer cases in the court of Common Pleas.[116] Others came from provincial prisons, taking advantage of the procedures which enabled them to transfer to a better class of prison. Elizabeth South thus wrote to her father, Daniel Hutson, imprisoned in Bedford gaol, asking whether he was liable to be discharged, or if not, whether he had a mind to be transferred to the King's Bench or the Fleet, and promising that if he had, the business would be facilitated in the next term.[117]

Two main objections were made to these writs. The first was that it was inconvenient for those creditors in the more remote counties such as Yorkshire or Cornwall, whose debtors had obtained the writ of *habeas corpus* and transferred action and person to London, to pursue them there. Ironically, when it was suggested in 1702 that this writ should be discontinued, it was argued that there would need to be a "Westminster hall" in every locality.[118] Many cases must have gone by default by reason of the inability of the creditor to follow his debtor's progress, though his expense in so evading his creditor must have been considerable. The second objection, made by the debtors, concerned the cost of such writs. In 1690 the cost was about three pounds for a prisoner in a London prison, and ten to forty pounds from the country (depending on the length of journey and expense of escort). By the 1720s the cost for a London prisoner had risen to nine pounds.[119] A pamphlet of the 1690s, *Some Brief Reasons Offered to Parliament, for Passing an Act Relating to the Discharge of Prisoners and the Regulation of Gaols and Gaolers*,[120] provides more detailed figures. The actual writ cost four pounds, the removal to the Fleet, including the judge's fees and the prison commitment fees, in excess of eight pounds, and the cost of the proceedings to enable one to be charged in execution was at least twenty-three pounds. The report of 1792 was less specific: it simply reported the "very considerable expense" of these writs.[121] Many attempts were made to end this practice, but it was not until 1827 that they were successful.[122]

****

The prisoners who came to the Fleet were from every social class, from artisans and tradesmen to knights, baronets and even some peers.[123] In 1661 the renowned Praise God Barebones was in the Fleet, and report was made that he frequently visited his co-prisoners and religious compatriots, Vavasor Powell and Major Breman. The same informer added that another celebrated prisoner, Colonel Nathaniel Rich, had been given liberty to go abroad when he wished, "even nine days at a time" as if he was not "a most dangerous prisoner".[124] In 1684 Prince Don Mario Plati wrote from the Fleet soliciting the favour of Archbishop Sancroft of Canterbury,[125] and seven years later Lord Falkland petitioned the king on behalf of his son, then in the Fleet, writing that "your forgiveness of this wild young man, now come to his senses, [would] turn your greatest offender into your greatest lover."[126] During the period 1738-42 the following names are found in the Fleet books: Sir Robert Clifton, Sir Tanfield Leman, Sir Robert Adams, Sir Alexander Anstruther, Sir William Rich, and Sir Francis Bickley, representing the noble order of baronets; Sir Edward Leighton, Sir Alexander Comings, Sir John Boyce, and Sir John Cuthbert the knighthood, together with Lord "Ossoulstone", the earl of Belfast, Baron Hans Minckwitz, the marquise of Spireto, Le Chevalier d'Olivera, and the Hon Willoughby Dormell.[127] Peregrine Pickle, in Smollett's novel, found in the Fleet coffee house an officer, alchemist, attorney, three proprietors, three underwriters, a brace of poets, a baronet, and a knight commander of the bath. A more accurate list of notables is provided by cuttings in the Noble collection of the Guildhall library.[128] The list includes the names of the Chevalier Dessesau, a Prussian dwarf, well known to London society, who died in the rules in 1775; Mrs Cornelly, the "high priestess" of fashion at Carlisle house, Soho square, in 1797; Benjamin Pope, who died there in 1794, called "plump Pope" for the vastness of his wealth, but cast in damages of ten thousand pounds for his usurious practices, refused to pay, entered the Fleet, and continued there his miserly habits; Sir Nicholas Nixon, baronet, once a fashionable figure in eighteenth-century London, who died in the prison in 1811,[129] and the celebrated if fraudulent princess Olive Wilmot Serves of Cumberland, who entered the prison in 1822. A few members of parliament found their way to the Fleet, but were soon released, the wardens noting a precedent of 1603 when one warden was sent to "little ease" in the Tower for failing to release Sir James Shirley, a member of the House of Commons.[130]

Although it was popularly believed that most of the parsons engaged in the clandestine marriage trade around the Fleet prison were Fleet prisoners, this was not the case. Admittedly several of them had had a brief imprisonment in the Fleet for their activities in officiating at the marriages of wards of court, but they were never permanent residents of the prison. Parson Keith of May-Fair, whose establishment rivalled the Fleet marriage centre for many years, was sent to the Fleet prison as an excommunicated person, and although he managed to sign his impressive if invalid licences of marriage in his prison chamber, the actual marrying was left to his May-Fair curates. It was from the Fleet, however, that an official of the future king George IV obtained a clergyman to marry the then prince to Mrs Fitzherbert in 1785, for which he had his debts paid, and the unfulfilled promise of a bishopric in the next reign.[131]

In order to show the variety of prisoners and the distances some travelled to take advantage of the Fleet's amenities, particular note has been made of the many Welshmen who became Fleet prisoners. Amongst the gentlemen of Glamorgan who frequented that place during the reign of the first Elizabeth were Edward Vann and Edward Kemys, who were ordered to the Fleet until they had paid fines of one thousand and five hundred pounds respectively "for causing riots and misdemeanours",[132] and William Mathew of Radyr who was sent there after accusing the president of the Court of the Marches, the earl of Pembroke, with partiality during his trial for concealing a murder.[133] Edward Ellis and Griffith Apparry, yeoman, were undoubtedly Welsh recusants who were recorded as being in the Fleet in 1580,[134] and other recusant prisoners there from Wales included Hugh Griffith of Penmark, Glamorgan, and Sir Charles Morgan of Arkston.[135] Edward Morgan, a Jesuit priest, born at Hanmer, Flintshire, was imprisoned from 1628 to 1642, writing that he suffered much from the "loathsomeness" of the place, and for want of "all necessities".[136] Hugh Nanney of Merioneth, unable to pay a large fine imposed on him for cutting down part of a royal forest, found himself in the Fleet,[137] as did John Wynn of Gwydir in 1603, and Bishop Bayley of Bangor in 1621, for an unknown cause.[138] George Barlow of Pembrokeshire in the early seventeenth century was placed here for not answering a bill exhibited against him by his opponents.[139] Fourteen years later Richard Parry of Llanfallteg in Carmarthenshire was fined one thousand marks by the court of high commission, and on its non-payment was taken to the Tower chamber of the Fleet prison.[140] During the late seventeenth century two Monmouthshire Quakers, Roger and Thomas Jenkin, declined to pay tithe, and spent long periods in Monmouth gaol and the Fleet.[141] Sometime before 1671 Sir Sackville Crow, baronet of Laugharne castle, once Charles I's naval treasurer, died in debt in the Fleet prison.[142] Joshua Edisbury, a former high sheriff of Denbighshire, who died in 1718, was a Fleet prisoner from 1712 onwards,[143] while Sir Rowland Gwynne, a stout Whig eulogised in Macaulay's *History*, who served as member for Radnor and Brecknock in several parliaments, died in grave financial straits in the Fleet in 1725.[144] Richard Morris, one of three brothers who exercised a powerful control over Welsh literature in their day, and a clerk in the navy office, spent a year during the 1730s in the Fleet prison. Here he wrote many *englynion*. In one of them he wrote about his anxiety and sleeplessness, together with his hope of release under an insolvency act.[145] Thomas Johnes of Abermad in Cardiganshire got himself transferred to the Fleet from Cardigan gaol. It was written of him as he lay in the Fleet, "he is in some old dirty stinking loft with little room to turn and without a messenger or the convenience to go out and see anyone, nor to do anything else ... he is in the midst of a crowd of people, the same kind as himself, listening to their wicked talk, but possibly not too wicked for a man of his kind." Released in 1760 he marched out of the Fleet in great triumph.[146] Sir Edward Mansel of Stradey near Llanelli, a person of weak intellect, was charged with a debt of eight hundred pounds and removed to the Fleet in 1763 in order to allow his agent to better control his affairs and prevent a projected marriage.[147] Sir John Powell Pryce died in the Fleet prison in 1776, but his body was buried at Newtown.[148] Morien, a nineteenth-century follower of the druids and a disciple of Dr Price of cremation fame, claimed that his great-grandfather had been deprived of property in the Rhondda valley by the Llewelyn family of Baglan, and that after a short time in Cardiff prison he had been sent to the Fleet in 1812, where he had died and had been buried within the prison walls.[149] Some years later, Sir Watkin Lewes, a prominent London Welshman, sometime member for the city and a lord mayor, fell into adverse circumstances and died in the *rules* of the prison in 1821 aged 85.[150]

The prison also accommodated female debtors. These were single women or widows, that is, independent people, for married women were not responsible for their debts. Their number was never inconsequential. In 1727, for example, 52 (8.5%) of the prisoners were women; in 1737, 32 (6.7%); in 1755, 28 (6.1%), but in 1778 only eight (4.1%).[151] Of the 867 prisoners discharged or admitted in 1813-14, 32 were women (3.5%).[152] On the common side these women had their own ward, but on the masters side there was no such segregation.[153] There were also, of course, many other women living in the Fleet as well as these women debtors. Some, but not all, were the wives of prisoners. Thus, while Nixon in the 1818 report on the prison is quoted as saying that there were many disturbances due to women of bad character being intoxicated and rioting in the galleries (or corridors), and that the Fleet prison was "the largest brothel in the metropolis",[154] there is no reason to believe he was referring to his women prisoners.

If John Lloyd in a petition of 1571 wrote that he must end his days in "this place",[155] and *The Debtor and Creditor's Assistant* of 1793 suggested that the debtor did not "murmur against imprisonment for debt", but rather against "perpetual and everlasting confinement",[156] both were speaking of the exception rather than the rule. Though there were some debtors who remained at the Fleet for a considerable number of years, the number of those prisoners who remained for more than ten years was hardly two per-cent of the total intake. The exceptions were always fondly remembered and quoted by the petition writers. In 1719 one debtor had been in the Fleet for twenty-one years, in 1755 one was there after forty-three years, and in 1743 a prisoner died who had been imprisoned for twenty-six years.[157] Nixon in his evidence of the 1810s referred to one person aged eighty who had been in the prison for over thirty years, but being a prisoner charged with contempt of chancery he could not take advantage of the insolvency acts.[158] The twin assertion made by the same petition writers, of whom Moses Pitt may be quoted as a typical example, that the debtor must remain a prisoner "so long as it shall please God to lengthen out his life",[159] was equally fallacious.

Three per-cent of those who entered the Fleet in 1686 and 1710 died during their imprisonment, six per-cent of those who entered in 1727, eight-per cent in 1747, and three and a half per-cent in 1779.[160] It must be remembered too that there was no age limit for entry to the Fleet.

The average stay of a debtor in the Fleet prison was comparatively short. It was probably of a similar duration to those at the King's Bench prison, where it was said in 1792 that the average period of confinement was between two and three years.[161] This was partly due to the frequency of the insolvency acts, and also because the initial imprisonment on mesne process was often used to give a short and sharp reminder to a debtor in order to encourage him to settle his affairs to the satisfaction of his creditors. In 1778, 161 (92.4%) of the total number of the Fleet prisoners were discharged by an insolvency act, and two years later the names of 89.2% of the prisoners were entered into the schedules of a similar act, although the number of those actually discharged under it is not known. Although it might be thought that those who missed one insolvency act were required to wait several years in prison until the next was enacted, there appears to have been little difference in the length of imprisonment between the two groups. Those debtors who entered the Fleet between January and March 1743 were able to obtain the benefit of the insolvency act of that year. Those who entered in October and December of that same year were required to wait for the 1748 act. However within twelve months of entry to the prison 60% of the first group and 62% of the second group had been discharged; within two years the numbers were 78% and 68% respectively, and within five years 82% and 76% respectively. Even in 1794 when the first insolvency act for twelve years was passed, only 232 prisoners were recorded in its schedule, as compared to 246 in 1780. Of their number, 16.8% had been imprisoned for more than two or three years.[162] There were obviously unseen pressures which permitted the early release of prisoners without an insolvency act.

The following tables shows the number of prisoners entering the prison and their comparative length of imprisonment. Table Three makes use of material from the Fleet prison records;[163] Table Four from the debtors' lists and schedules contained within the papers of the various acts of insolvency,[164] and Table Five is derived from the parliamentary papers and reports which related to the Fleet prison.[165]

Table Three: Comparative Length of Imprisonment 1686-1779

Date	no. entered in year	left within one year	%	after one year	%	after two years	%
1686	139	34	31	29	58	7	65
1710	317	33	10	63	31	8	33
1727	330	13	4	61	26	55	43
1747	232	26	11	116	61	41	78
1779	251	21	8	75	36	38	52

Table Four: Comparative Length of Imprisonment 1728-1813

	1728	1737	1748	1760	1772	1780	1794	1806	1813
Total number of entries	618	453	360	311	134	246	232	198	308
imprisoned over 10 years	38	7	6	8	6	3	2	4	7
as %	6.1	1.5	1.6	2.5	4.4	1.2	0.8	2.0	2.2
8-9 years	18	24	11	6	3	1	8	2	1
as %	2.9	5.2	3.0	1.9	2.2	0.4	3.4	1.0	0.3
6-7 years	61	51	22	9	4	2	8	6	8
as %	9.8	11.2	6.1	2.8	2.9	0.8	3.4	3.0	2.5
5 years	37	39	37	24	7	4	10	6	....
as %	5.9	8.6	10.2	7.7	5.2	1.6	4.3	3.0	....
4 years	52	58	43	33	10	5	11	6	6
as %	8.4	12.8	11.9	10.6	7.4	2.0	4.7	3.0	1.9
3 years	99	89	42	45	25	5	19	12	6
as %	16.0	19.6	11.6	14.4	18.6	2.0	8.1	6.0	1.3
2 years	92	88	65	57	28	36	32	30	14
as %	14.8	19.4	18.0	18.3	20.8	14.6	13.7	15.1	4.5
over 1 year	148	97	134	73	51	120	107	106	62
as %	23.9	21.4	37.2	23.4	38.0	48.7	46.1	53.5	20.1
in same year as recorded	73	NR	NR	56	NR	70	35	26	206
as %	11.8			18.0		28.4	.15.0	13.1	66.8
month when recorded	Sept			Oct		June	Feb	Feb	Nov
longest time imprisoned [years]	20	25	36	13	25	19	12	21	28

A further table can be drawn up using material supplied by the parliamentary papers for the period 1813-22:

Table Five: Comparative Length of Imprisonment, 1813-22

Date	no. entered in year	discharged within same year	%	after 11 weeks	%	by an insolvency act	%
1813	700	297	42				
1819	620	516	83	252	40	257	41
1820	613	527	86	210	34	222	36
1821	657	571	87	311	47	327	49
1822	604	522	86	266	46	279	46

Other figures may be given. In the 1653 schedule of prisoners, 230 in number, 159 (69%) had entered since 1651; 56 (24%) between 1646 and 1650, and two had entered in 1624 and 1627 respectively.[166] During the first half of 1748, 364 prisoners entered the Fleet prison; 9% of these left within six months. Of the 134 prisoners who entered between October 1760 and March 1761, 17% left within that same period; while for the first half of 1778 18.5% of the 195 prisoners who entered the prison during that period obtained their discharges within the same year.[167] A return of 1830 indicated that only fifty-four prisoners had been imprisoned for more than one year, twenty-three between one and two years, but only five for over ten years. In that same year 515 prisoners entered the prison.[168]

Further figures may be quoted for the year ending September 1832. On 28 September 1831 there were 151 prisoners. Within the next year 645 entered, but 622 were discharged. Allowing for the five deaths which occurred during that time, there were 169 in custody on 29 September 1832.[169] In 1836 the warden was required to give a return of the number of debtors in custody for six months and upwards. He had ninety-four, of whom thirty-eight had been there since the previous year, and a further thirty-seven who had been in custody for the previous two years and more.[170]

Surprisingly there is no correlation between the length of imprisonment and the amount of debt. A check made on fifty-eight debtors who entered the Fleet in 1747 shows that one who owed over one thousand pounds was imprisoned for one month before being discharged, while one with a debt of one hundred and fifty pounds remained imprisoned for the next twenty years. All but five were released after two years, nineteen after two months (32%), and thirty-seven (64%) after a year.[171] On the other hand it was more probable than a person with substantial debts would remain longer in the prison, either because of the difficulty of meeting his commitments, or because of some fraudulent intention. Thus in a return of 1830 the five prisoners noted who had been in the prison over ten years had debts totalling £138,900.[172]

These figures about the length of imprisonment are too incomplete for any statistical purposes, yet they show that even during the second half of the seventeenth century, when the insolvency acts were few and far between, and certainly thereafter, the popular idea that imprisonment for debt was inevitably like marriage, a lifelong affair, could not be substantiated. From Table Four it will be noted that for the earlier period, the number in prison at any given time who had been there for three years and more averaged around forty to fifty per-cent, and in one year it was as much as fifty-nine per-cent. From 1780 onwards this average rapidly declined. Table Five indicates the great change caused by the existence of the permanent insolvent debtors' court from 1813 onwards, when it became possible to apply for a discharge after three months' imprisonment. But, equally, a significant number of those imprisoned for debt even prior to that date so managed their affairs that they were discharged within a short period of time. Indeed, for many in the nineteenth century such imprisonment was but a matter of weeks. It was claimed that this alone would justify the existence of debt imprisonment. But others might stress the misery caused to a family and its finances of even a short stay in prison, and would point to those who lingered on in prison for many years. While they were a minority, their story was quite a different one.

NOTES

1   Simon Wood argued that the bankrupt "stands this chance, to be hanged if he conceals, to be starved if he parts from all; the latter is certainly the most lingering death". [Wood, p 14].

2   Howell, p 355.

3   T Macdonald, *Treatise on Civil Imprisonment in England* (London 1791), p 132.

4   The devices adopted by debtors to avoid arrest are depicted by Tobias Smollett in chapter 97 of *Peregrine Pickle*.

5   The cost of this bail was about £8 for one action, but it was said in 1792 that the average cost was over £40. Those who offered such bail could surrender the debtor, as he could do himself, to a prison pending the action. By this time many debtors had become insolvent through what they had expended in trying to avoid imprisonment for as long as possible [Report 1792, pp 643, 645, 649].

6   The cost of even the court charges could be substantial, with tipstaffs and clerks fees. The writer of *Observations on the Law of Arrest for Debt* (London 1827) suggested that the average cost of debtors imprisoned in the London and Middlesex prisons in 1826 was £15 each, and thus with 12,097 entries in that year, £181,455 had been paid in such charges.

7   *The Debtor and Creditor's Assistant* (London 1793), pp 23ff. The society for the relief of debtors imprisoned for small sums (The Thatched House Society), formed in 1772, existed to help such people. Within the first twenty years of its existence the society facilitated the discharges of over 700 prisoners per annum at an average cost of 45s. each, and of these 700 an average of 130 were those who had been discharged from imprisonment but could not find the money to gain their liberty because of outstanding gaol fees [Report 1792, pp 646, 648]. The number of Fleet prisoners in this total is not known.

8   Report 1792, p 642. Families were often ruined as a result [ibid, p 647].

9   Report 1792, p 647.

10   For the law of debt see Macdonald, *Treatise*, pp 46-9, 115-18, 131f: *Observations on the Laws of Arrest for Debt*, pp 7ff; William Holdsworth, *A History of English Law* (London 1966), VI 407f, VIII 229-38, XI 595-602; Report 1792, pp 640ff.

11   J Nightengale, *London and Middlesex* (5 vols, London 1810-16), III 734. Dr Samuel Johnson, quoted in *Observations on the Law of Arrest for Debt* [p 6], stated that creditors often imprisoned their debtors only because of their "wantonness of pride, malignity of revenge, or the acrimony of disappointed expectations". Some creditors, declared the author of *An Oration on the Oppression of Jailors* [p 14] in 1731, "rather see their debtors perish than be paid the debt".

12   Joanna Innes, "The King's Bench Prison in the later Eighteenth Century", in J Brewer and J Styles, *An Ungovernable People* (London 1980), p 253.

13   W Smith, *Mild Punishments Sound Policy* (London 1778), p 64; cf 1792 Report, p 653, which stated about such men that they "conduct themselves as men who think they have no longer any interest in being honest, and know that the law, by imprisoning their persons, has spent its force against them". Thomas Decker was equally concerned in the 1630s at the way debt prisoners lived at the expense of their creditors [quoted by Dobb, Thesis, pp 19f].

14   Quoted in *Observations*, p 28.

15   Report 1814, p 676.

16   Macdonald, *Treatise*, p 57;   M D George, *London Life in the Eighteenth Century*, (London 1951), pp 307-12; Holdsworth, *English Laws*, XI 600. Professional men, farmers, and artisans were unable to take advantage of the bankruptcy laws until 1861. The bankruptcy commissioners could not commit to the Fleet, only to the county gaol, so that bankrupts had to enter the Fleet through the use of the writ *habeas corpus* [Jnl H of C, XII 684].

17   *Middlesex Journal*, 29 June 1769, quoted in Brewer and Styles, *An Ungovernable People*, p 153.

18   Moses Pitt, *The Cry of the Oppressed* (London 1681), preface; *A Speech without Doors*, (London 1729), p 14, cf p 20: "what rest, what quiet, would it give to the land", if these men, the bailiffs, were under "a fresh gale bound for Guinea or some of the plantations".

19   Innes, *The King's Bench Prison*, pp 251ff, and quoting Report 1792, pp 645, 647.

20   Robert Neale, *The Prisoners' Guide* (London 1800), p 15.

21   William Leigh, *New Picture of London* (London 1823 edn), p 66; Neale, *The Prisoners' Guide*, pp 8f. Often neither defendant nor plaintiff could afford the costs. Jones Pearce, in his *A Treatise on the Abuses of the Laws* (London 1814), estimated that for a debt of £15 the cost to the plaintiff was £59, and for the defendant £39 [p 139]. He recommended that the creditor accept the first offer of the debtor, for the longer he remained in prison the more desperate he became, and caring little about the amount of the debt and the costs of the proceedings, he would endeavour to put his creditor to all the expenses he could.

22   Pearce, *A Treatise*, p 93.

23   Smith, p 91.

24   Harris, p25; Macdonald, *Treatise*, p 165; cf Clifford Dobb in *Shakespeare Survey*, XVII (1964) 93, quoting Thomas Savile, *The Prisoners Conference* of 1605, "in those cases, I think a man may embrace the prison in the case of his children." The 1792 Report [p 644] made clear that it was impossible to prevent a man dissipating his estate whilst in prison for debt.

25   Report 1792, p 652.

26   This was a Cromwellian precedent, while Dobb notes that Elizabethan commissioners were appointed to clear the prison by forcing an equitable settlement between creditor and debtor [Thesis, p 18].

27   The clauses of the 1670 act, 22 & 23 Charles II c 20, were repeated with little amendment in all the subsequent acts, save that from 1678 onwards the acts also applied to those on mesne process. Acts for the relief of poor and distressed prisoners for debt and for the relief of debtors with respect to the imprisonment of their persons were similar in form to these insolvency acts.

28   Between 1813 and 1827 50,733 debtors took advantage of these acts [*Observations*, quoting a parliamentary return of 1827 (no 430]. A commission set up in 1832 by Lord Brougham recommended the abolition of imprisonment, while the preamble to the *Debtors' Act* of 1869 stated that while its original objective was the abolition of such imprisonment, this had proved impossible to effect as it had been shown that the recovery of small debts would be rendered impossible without such a threat remaining on the statute book.

29   Innes, *The King's Bench Prison*, p 257.

30   William Blackstone, *The Laws of England* (edition of R M Kerr, London 1857), II 482; Report 1792, pp 644f, 649f.

31   Leigh's *New Picture of London* (1834 edn), p 44.

32   Jnl H of C, XI 677, 679.

33   Report 1792, pp 649f.

34   *Debtor and Creditor's Assistant*, pp 31f. This applied even if the effects of the debtor had been surrendered and the costs of the discharge paid.

35   Report 1792, p 650.

36   William Jones, *Observations on the Insolvent Debtors' Acts* (London 1827). He noted further that witnesses were required to prove that the court papers had been delivered to the creditors, whose expenses could come to a guinea a day.

37   Such petitions are found in the BL, press marks 356 m2/64; 357 b8/55, 109, 111; Cup 645 b11/34; 816 m15/17f, 41; BL, MS Addit 33054, fol 186; *A Plea for the City Orphans and Prisoners for Debt*; GL, broadsides 7.145 and 18.19; *An Oration on the Oppression of Jailors spoken in the Fleet Prison* (London 1731), pp 13f.

38   *Observations*, p 27. Frequently creditor and debtor were often discharged under the same act. See also Macdonald, *Treatise*, pp 115-18.

39   Report 1814, p 646.

40   *Gentleman's Magazine*, XVII (1747) 78.

41   Holdsworth, *English Law*, XI 598n.

42   *A Speech without Doors*, pp 23f.

43   9 Geo I c 28. See also R L Brown, "The Minters of Wapping", *East London Papers*, XIV (1972) 77.

44   CLRO, Debtors List and Papers, Box 3, for 1748, and DS/15/24-7 for 1772; *A Speech without Doors*, pp 20ff, notes the number who fled "abroad", and Wood [p 6] alleged that many tradesmen even turned to highway robbery and housebreaking in their desire to avoid debt imprisonment.

45   Holdsworth, *English Law*, XI 597n.

46   *A Speech without Doors*, pp 14, 17.

47   *Considerations on the Laws between Debtors and Creditors* (1779), pp 33f; *The Case of Debtors now Confined* and *The Humble Petition of Debtors in the Fleet*.

48   Wood, p 6.

49   Smith, p 65.

50   *The Debtor and Creditor's Assistant*, pp 42f; Smith [reporting on the King's Bench], pp 52ff.

51   Report 1814, p 676; cf Report 1818, p 9, and Report 1792, p 663.

52   Aydelotte, quoted by Sean McConville, *A History of English Prison Administration* (London 1981), I 17n.

53   Smith, pp 52f.

54   Report 1814, p 691.

55   Report 1814, pp 785, cf p 676.

56   Report 1792, pp 646f.

57   Joseph Nightengale, *London and Middlesex* (London 1815), III 736. The King's Bench prison house held about 500 prisoners [Report 1792, p 653].

58   *A Schedule or List of Prisoners in the Fleet* (1653).

59   Jnl H of C, XI 642.

60   Jnl H of C, XII 686.

61   BLO, MS Rawlinson C743, fol 99.

62   CLRO, Debtors' Lists. The schedule for 1747-8 is the first to distinguish between prisoners in the *rules* or in the house. Between Nov 1760 and June 1761 there were 134 new prisoners.

63   Howard (1777), p 156.

64   Smith, p 41. On p 52 he states there were only 52 prisoners in the Fleet.

65   Howard (1780), p 177.

66   CLRO, Debtors' Lists.

67   Howard (1780), p 177.

68   CLRO, Debtors' Lists.

69   Howard, *An Account of the Present State of Prisons in London and Westminster* (London 1789), p 4.

70   *Report of the Sub-Committee Respecting Prisons ... of the Society for Giving Effect to His Majesty's Proclamation against Vice and Immorality* (London 1790), p 27.

71   Nield, p 218.

72   PP 1814-15 (106) XI 3. In 1813 over 700 people entered the prison.

73   Report 1814, p 549, cf p 680.

74   PP 1816 (513) XVIII 269. The King's Bench had 753 prisoners.

75   Report 1818, p 9. These are the average figures.

76   PP 1826-7 (424) XIX 352. These indicate that half the annual commitments took place in May and November.

77   PP 1828 (76) XX 181.

78   PP 1829 (69) XVIII 275.

79   PP 1830 (632) XXIII 189. But 515 entered [PP 1830-1 (142) XII 511].

80   PP 1830-1 (142) XII 511; and PP 1833 (494) XXIX 257. In the King's Bench there were 486 prisoners.

81   Howard (1777), p 35.

82   Report 1792, p 647.

83   PRO, PRIS 1/2.

84   Report 1818, p 9.

85   Mackay, p 22.

86   Jnl H of C, XII 202.

87   Mackay, App V.

88   *The State of the King's Bench Prison* (London 1765), and Smith, p 55.

89   GLRO, Debtors Lists and Papers, Box 3, for 1742.

90   Report 1729, pp 2f.

91   In 1728, 5.1%, 1748 10.8%, 1755 8.7%, 1778 9.2% of the prisoners came into this category [GLRO, Debtors Lists], and a return of 1816 mentions 34 such prisoners [PP 1816 (515) XVIII 271].

92   Cal TB & P, 1739-41, p 16.

93   PRO, SP35/9, fol 207.

94   Cal TP, 1720-8, p 98; PRO, T11/22. fol 310.

95   Cal TP & B, 1742-5, p 355. He was later released on account of the distressed condition of his wife and five children.

96   Cal TB & P, 1739-41, pp 343, 522.

97   Cal TP & P, 1739-41, p 546.

98   Cal TP, 1714-19, pp 61, 252.

99   Cal TB, 1714-15, II 518, 564; Carl Winslow in D Hay (ed), *Albion's Fatal Tree* (London 1975), p 148.

100 Cal TB, 1714-15, II 146.

101 Cal TB, 1716, II 121, 217.

102 Cal TB, 1717, III 624f; 1718, II 272.

103 Cal TP, 1720-8, p 296: PRO, SP35/60, fol 52; SP35/76, fol 136.

104 Cal SPD, 1664-5, p 370.

105 *Remembrancia of the City of London*, index volume, p 88.

106 PRO, SP35/7, fol 181; SP35/9, fol 140. Earlier precedents are found in PRO, SP35/68, fol 80, and Cal SP, 1661-2, p 103.

107 Cal SPD, 1664-5, pp 35, 120: W Braithwaite, *The Second Period of Quakerism* (York, 1979), pp 201, 208.

108 Cal SPD, 1680-1, p 661.

109 cf 28 Geo II c 13, clause XXXIV, of 1755.

110 Blackstone, *Laws of England*, III 130: *The Debtor and Creditor's Assistant*, pp 68f; Holdsworth, *English Laws*, IX 108ff; *An Enquiry into the Nature and Effects of the Writ of Habeas Corpus* (1758). It was alleged that the *Habeas Corpus Act* of 1679 caused many to remove themselves "from most of the gaols of England" into the Fleet and King's Bench prisons [PRO, SP35/68, fol 80]. This act possibly regulated an existing use of the writ. A further writ of *habeas corpus* was required to take a debt prisoner to the courts of Westminster or Guildhall to answer further charges. The books known as PRIS/10/88-110 among the Fleet prison records at the PRO are the registers concerned with the issuing of these writs. They note writs issued to enable prisoners to be escorted not only to the Westminster courts, but also to the Surrey, Kent, and Lincoln assizes, etc, to appear as witnesses in cases.

111 E Hatton, *A New View of London* (London 1708), II 745.

112 This is section XIII of the act and is quoted by Eric Stockdale, *A Study of Bedford*

Prison (London 1977), p 46. A pamphlet of the 1690s, *Some Brief Reasons offered to Parliament for Passing the Act relating to the Discharge of Prisoners*, states that the prisoner cannot "without danger to his life ... abide in a common, close, noisome county or corporation gaol".

113   PRO, T1/310, fol 54.

114   Berisford, p 24.

115   CLRO, DS/15/8-12.

116   *The Debtor and Creditor's Assistant*, pp 68f. Of fourteen who are noted as entering the Fleet prison by the use of this writ from others prisons in 1729, eight came from the King's Bench and two from the Marshalsea [CLRO, Misc MS 9.10].

117   Cal SPD, 1677-8, p 336.

118   *Some Considerations relating to the Bill for Regulating the King's Bench and Fleet Prisons*; cf Holdsworth, *English Law*, XI 601.

119   Hodgkins' Papers, BL, MS Addit 38856, fol 127; BLO, MS Rawlinson D1051, fol 22.

120   BL, pm 816 m15/41.

121   Report 1792, p 643.

122   For example, Jnl H of C, XII 687, XIII 542; cf 19 Geo III c 70, of 1779.

123   Innes, *The King's Bench Prison*, p 263, notes an assessment of that prison's population made by the prisoners themselves. Of 800 prisoners 60 (8%) were military and naval personnel, 40 (5%) mercantile, 50 (7%) manufacturers, 110 (14%) mechanics, 160 (20%) agriculturalists, 150 (19%) tradesmen, and 200 (25%) labourers. She is equally surprised by the non-appearance of professional people!

124   Cal SPD, 1661-2, p 82.

125   BLO, MS Tanner 33, fol 65.

126   BLO, MS Ashmolean 830, fol 128.

127   CLRO, Debtors Lists; PRO, PRIS/1/7, 8, 10, and 10/49.

128   GLL, Noble Collection, C43 Fleet.

129   He is probably the one mentioned beforehand in the 1792 report. Henry Brooke, in his *The Fool of Quality* [London 1872 edn, pp 22f], noted an earlier precedent, of one who had amassed enormous wealth, by which he could have easily paid his debts, but preferred to remain in the Fleet in a state of luxurious defiance, waited on by his man in livery while his creditors starved.

130   GLL, broadside 7.90.

131   John Brooke, *King George III* (London 1974), p 504.

132 *South Wales and Monmouthshire Record Society*, I (1949), 96f, 112.

133 *Morgannwg*, II (1958) 45; cf Ralph Flenley, *The Register of the Council in the Marches of Wales*, (London 1916), p 31, for another example.

134 *Catholic Record Society*, XXII (1921) 131.

135 R Mathias, *Whitsun Riot* (London 1963), pp 15, 33.

136 Henry Foley, *Memorials of the English Province of the Society of Jesus* (London 1878), IV 517. He was arrested in 1642.

137 T P Ellis, *Dolgelley and Llanelltud* (Newtown, 1928), p 85.

138 *Calendar of the Wynn (of Gwydir) Papers* (Aberystwyth, 1926), nos 244, 972. Clifford Dobb quotes SPD, James I, vol 122, no 23, which alleges that he had disputed with the king about the sabbath [Thesis, p 99].

139 Brian Howells in *Pembrokeshire County History* (Haverfordwest, 1987), III 82.

140 J E Lloyd, *A History of Carmarthenshire* (Cardiff 1939), II 133f.

141 G H Jenkins, *Literature, Religion and Society in Wales, 1660-1730* (Cardiff, 1978), p 212.

142 *The Carmarthenshire Historian*, IX (1972) 33.

143 M Waterson, *The Servants' Hall* (1980), pp 22ff.

144 *The National Library of Wales Journal*, XXI (1979), 169f.

145 W J Gruffydd, *Y Morysiaid* (Cardiff, 1939), p 41; J H Davies, *The Morris Letters* (Aberystwyth, 1907), pp xviiif.

146 quoted in B Phillips, *Peterwell* (Llandyssul, 1983), pp 127, 129.

147 M V Symons, *Coal Mining in the Llanelli Area* (Llanelli, 1979), 152f.

148 *Montgomeryshire Collections*, 16 (1883) 290.

149 Morien (Owen Morgan), *History of Pontypridd and the Rhondda Valleys* (Pontypridd, 1903), pp 320ff. There is no foundation in his later claim that prisoners were buried within the precincts of the prison.

150 R T Jenkins and H M Ramage, *A History of the Honourable Society of Cymmrodorion* (1951), pp 52f.

151 CLRO, Debtors Lists, and DS/15/35-6.

152 PP 1813-14 (320) XIII 1-7-30.

153 Report 1729, p 3; Report 1814, p 551. The 1818 report [pp 8, 42] said that however desirable it was to separate these rooms, it was not practicable because of their limited number.

154 Report 1814, p 21. There were then 50 women and 77 children living within the prison walls in addition to prisoners.

155 Cal SPD, 1671, p 573.

156 *The Debtor and Creditor's Assistant*, p 55.

157 PRO, PRIS/1/10; CLRO, Debtors Lists.

158 Report 1814, pp 675f. This was Thomas Williams of Radnor, who served as chapel clerk. He had entered the prison in 1785 and died there in 1817.

159 Moses Pitt, *The Cry of the Oppressed*, preface.

160 PRO, PRIS/1/2, 3, 10, 11.

161 Report 1792, p 658.

162 CLRO, Debtors Lists.

163 PRO, PRIS/1/1a. 2. 3. 10, 11.

164 CLRO, Debtors Lists.

165 PP 1814-15 (106) XI 3; PP 1823 (28) XV 185, and (67) XV 187; PP 1826-7 (424) XIX 351 and PP 1830-1 (142) XII 511. The figures provided are not always consistent. This is because so many more prisoners entered the Fleet in latter years compared to previous years [Table 3], but after 1813, when a permanent insolvency court was established, the period of imprisonment was much shorter and charitable societies would defray some of the expenses of obtaining the benefit of the act. 95% of those discharged by this court left within eleven weeks of imprisonment.

167 These figures are derived from the debtors papers at CLRO, and DS/15/8-12 and 35-6.

168 PP 1830 (342) XXIII 385. On average 1684 prisoners entered the King's Bench prison each year between 1820 and 1826.

169 PP 1833 (13) XXIX 221.

170 PP 1836 XLIII 147.

171 CLRO, Debtors Lists. 42% of these persons were detained on a single suit.

172 PP 1830 (342) XXIII 385.

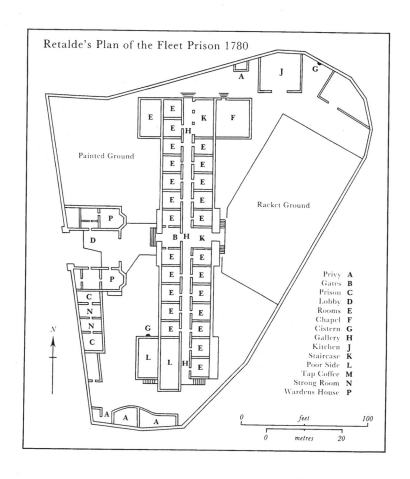

Retalde's Plan of the Fleet Prison 1780

Painted Ground

Racket Ground

Privy **A**
Gates **B**
Prison **C**
Lobby **D**
Rooms **E**
Chapel **F**
Cistern **G**
Gallery **H**
Kitchen **J**
Staircase **K**
Poor Side **L**
Tap Coffee **M**
Strong Room **N**
Wardens House **P**

N

0   feet   100

0   metres   20

Rotalde's plan of the Fleet prison in 1780, redrawn by Gary Llewellyn.

Part Four:

"The Prince of Prisons"[1]

"Then take no care but only to be jolly.
To be more wretched than you need is folly."[2]

"In short, this community is like a city detached from all communication with the
neighbouring parts, regulated by its own laws, and furnished with peculiar
conveniences for the use of the inhabitants."[3]

"There are infinite abuses, extreme licentiousness, and extreme misery,
within the walls of a prison."[4]

The Fleet prison was a building set behind a row of houses on the east side of the
Fleet ditch, which when culverted over, became more dignified under the title of
the Fleet market. It is now called Farringdon Street. The houses in front of the
prison were demolished in 1793, to be replaced by a twenty-five-foot-high wall
and the lodge entrance made familiar by the Shepherd prints of the 1820s. This
allowed an additional courtyard in front of the prison, gave much extra and badly
needed light and ventilation to its main building, and provided a house for the
warden's residence.

The building was always notorious for its ill state of repair. This was
undoubtedly due to its hasty and cheap reconstruction after the Great Fire of

London. Complaints were made continually about its condition, exacerbated by the refusal of the wardens to spend the money required for its repair. Mackay's report suggested that the simpler repairs were carried out by the prisoners themselves,[5] although it was reported that Bambridge owed eighteen hundred pounds to a building contractor for repairs done to the prison house.[6] The King's Bench prison was in an even worse condition. Not having been destroyed in the great fire it was probably still utilising its medieval buildings. After a petition by the prisoners to the House of Commons, in which they described its ruinous condition, receiving the support of its marshall (who expressed his concern for the safe keeping of his prisoners), the Office of Works reconstructed the prison house on a new site in St George's fields in Southwark, half a mile from the former prison, during 1753-4.

This activity on the part of the Office of Works, and its readiness to finance the rebuilding of the King's Bench prison, undoubtedly encouraged the warden of the Fleet to petition the Treasury about the dilapidated state of his own prison. In 1768 part of the building collapsed, destroying ten chambers. An examination of the structure showed it was in a ruinous state, and it was considered inadvisable to lay out any more money on its repair.[7] Accordingly the warden wrote to the Office of Works stating that his "inmates had [so] worn out the prison that nothing short of a total rebuilding was likely to be of any avail". A first thought was to remove the prison to St George's fields, Southwark (and thus to be almost alongside its sister prison), and move the Fleet market to the site of the prison house, but the prisoners objected, and the city demurred at its suggested contribution of five thousand pounds for the prison site. Similar proposals to remove the prison to Ely gardens in Holborn floundered on the counter-petitions produced by the local inhabitants.[8] It was finally decided to rebuild the prison on its existing site. The work was carried out between 1770 and 1774, and cost nearly twelve thousand pounds. Throughout the whole time of rebuilding the prisoners remained within the prison, and this is probably why the new building so closely followed the design of the old.[9]

During the Gordon riots both prisons were reduced to shells. On the urgent prompting of the judges the rebuilding began immediately, and was completed by June of the following year. For greater security against fire, and presumably against the efforts of further rioters, the lower storeys were arched in brick, and the floors and staircases constructed in stone. The estimated cost of thirteen thousand pounds was probably exceeded.[10]

The building itself was long and narrow. It contained four floors, together with a cellar or semi-basement. Dark and narrow passages, termed galleries, seven feet wide, in the middle of each floor, went the length of the prison. On the ground floor were a hall and a tap room. The cellar contained a kitchen and a public dining-room popularly known as Bartholomew's Fair. The kitchen was later placed in the courtyard. A coffee room and the chapel were on the first floor, and an infirmary was later made out of several chambers on the third. On the four main floors of this the master's side, there were one hundred and ten chambers or rooms. Each was 14½ by 12½ feet, and 9½ feet high; a few, over the chapel, were larger. Each had its own fireplace. These were regarded as being larger rooms than at any other prison in the kingdom, the King's Bench rooms being much smaller, hardly having enough room for two beds.[11] With some restrictions, the prisoners were free to move around the prison at will. They even had their own locks on their chamber doors, one warden [Nixon] actually stating that he had no master key to the rooms for fear that the prisoners might accuse him or his officers of theft. However, he claimed the right of entry to any room, "but we do not [enter] without their opening ... to us".[12] The prison was thus more like a lodging house or some "squalid rents" than a penal institutions of the present century, as H M Colvin has suggested.[13]

The southern wing of the prison contained the common side. Its commitment fee was less than that of the master's side, and its inhabitants paid no chamber rent, had to provide their own furniture and bedding, and were required to separate themselves from the master's side from 9.00 pm when a bell was rung for that purpose, though its summons was rarely obeyed. The prisoners on this side were not permitted either to join the "college" or the prisoners' society, which was exclusive to the master's side.[14] This common side was kept purposely in a deplorable state as an inducement to new prisoners to enter the master's side with its greater commitment fees and chamber rent, and, of course, to remain on that side. A petition of the 1690s stated that it was used as a "curb upon the rest to pay those great rates the gaoler exacts, he unmercifully threatening all for non-payment with dungeons and irons".[15] For want of five guineas, claimed another during the 1720s, his friend was turned over to the common side, placed in irons and chained down onto the floor.[16] Dr Smith, writing in general about prisons in 1776, claimed that most common sides were "places much more unhealthy and not much cleaner than a pig's stye".[17] Those few prisoners who had sworn themselves to be worth less than five pounds in order to take advantage of the prison charities had no option but to reside here, but the common side was never confined to their number, so that in 1814 it possessed twenty-three prisoners, of whom only seven or eight were in receipt of the prison charities.[18]

The four floors of the common side contained three wards 24 to 25 feet square, each having seven sleeping cabins on one side of the room. An extra ward was added in the 1770 rebuilding.[19] The wards of the earlier building were called, at various times, the upper and lower chapel, Julius Caesar's, the lion's den and the women's ward. A cellar intended as a kitchen had become a lumber room, while rooms on the chapel stairs had been taken from the common side and given to the master's side by the 1720s. It is not surprising that at times the common side was overcrowded and uncomfortable. In the 1690s its inmates petitioned that they "all promiscuously are clapt up close, without liberty of discharging the offices of nature with convenience".[20] The 1729 report proclaimed that the whole side was "very noisome and in very ill-repair",[21] and a prisoner's song of 1738 went as follows:

> A starving life all day we lead,
> No comfort here is found,
> At night we make one common bed
> Upon the boarded ground;
> Where fleas in troops and bugs in shoals
> Into our bosoms creep,
> And death watch spiders round the walls
> Disturb us in our sleep.[22]

Though this song was not composed with the Fleet in mind, its vivid description came a little too near the truth for comfort for those on the common side of this prison.

ENTERING THE PRISON

As soon as a new prisoner entered the Fleet, he was placed on view for half an hour before the prison officers, in order that they might become acquainted with his person, and so prevent his departure or escape through the lodge gates along with the many visitors to the prison. Peregrine Pickle, in Smollett's novel, "was obliged to expose himself a full half hour to the eyes of all the turnkeys and doorkeepers, who took an accurate survey of his person, that they might know him again at first sight". A century later Mr Pickwick was told by the turnkey, "'We're capital hands at likenesses here. Take 'em in no time, and always exact'", as several turnkeys inspected him "narrowly", and "studied his features with most intent and thoughtful faces".[23]

The new prisoner was then offered the choice between the two sides of the prison, and informed about his commitment fees, the cost of a chamber, and the chumming arrangements if he entered the master's side. He could defer his decision, however, or play for time, by entering a spunging house.

Spunging houses were a widespread institution of the prison world. They were houses, frequently taverns, kept by prison officers or by sheriffs' or bailiffs' underlings. It was claimed that these houses gave facilities of comfort and convenience that the prisons could not allow, particularly for those who wanted time to settle their affairs without having to enter a prison and thus having to pay its commitment fees. Although strictly controlled by legislation, which required that no person be sent there without consent, or charged for wine, liquor, tobacco or anything whatsoever, unless requested, nor charged greater prices for lodging and food than those laid down by the local quarter sessions,[24] many believed with Simon Wood that their real purpose was to obtain as much of the debtor's money as possible.[25] One such unfortunate said this about them: they "draw out your blood to the last drop, and plead their mercy that they do not send you to a common prison".[26]

There were three or four spunging houses attached to the Fleet prison during the time of Bambridge's wardenship, though there is no reason to believe that either he or Huggins had introduced their practice to the Fleet. Bambridge insisted that he never permitted prisoners to enter one of these houses unless they had made a specific request. While their purpose was similar to that of the other spunging houses, they were also used by prisoners who awaited security for the use of the *rules,* or by those who were expecting a more desirable room in the prison house than would be theirs at their first entry. There were, of course, counter-claims that prisoners were brought into them contrary to their wishes.[27] Simon Wood noted one of the inducements given to persuade new prisoners to enter these houses: "it is buzz'd in your ears, the nauseous smell of the prison, the uncertainty of a room."[28] Their costs were heavy, the wardens claiming that not being a legal part of the prison, the regulations laid down for the prison fees did not apply to them. The 1729 committee endorsed such complaints, and incorrectly argued that their existence was contrary to an act of 1671. The warden, it asserted, refused to admit prisoners into the prison, and took them to the spunging houses without their consent, allowing these places to become a "terror" to the prisoners. Here they were forced to call for more liquor than they were inclined to drink, and to spend more than they were able to afford, "to the defrauding of their creditors, and the distressing of their families, whose substance they are compelled there to consume". It added that the prisoners were "better or worse treated" according to what they could pay, some being allowed "a handsome room and a bed to themselves", while others were "stowed in garrets, three in one bed, and some put in irons". The report even alleged that many prisoners were prepared to pay large sums of money in order to be removed into the prison, for the warden kept them in these houses "until he squeezes from them all the money than can possibly be got" from them or by the charity of their friends.[29] But this was only one side of the story, for the wardens never put their case to the committee.

Four of these spunging houses are named in the various trials of this period. The Vine tavern adjoining the prison, and whose windows backed onto the prison yard, was one. Mary Whitwood rented another of the warden for thirty-two pounds per annum, which Bambridge increased to sixty on the promise that her house would be full. She claimed, however, that she had to bribe him for this promise to be even partly fulfilled, with a present of forty guineas and a model of a Chinese ship "made with amber and set with silver". Brown had seven beds in his house, but only four to five prisoners, while Corbett, a turnkey, kept his twenty-six inmates in two linked houses, which he rented from the warden. Presumably these were the houses in front of the prison. A chamberlain, Mr Holdsworth, looked after the prisoners in these houses, together with Mrs Corbett. Only two of these prisoners had beds to themselves, but at additional charges. In the case of Mr Sinclair, Corbett charged one shilling for a night's lodging, but it is not certain whether this fee was for a private room or for a garret shared with the servants of the house. It was probably for the latter, for the 1729 report alleged that he charged two shillings for the hire of a room and one shilling for "firing". The price of dinner was one shilling, and as Corbett refused his inmates permission to obtain their own food, the minimum charge at his house was fourteen shillings per week. His house was probably a victualling house, for a club was held in it which officers of the prison, including Bambridge, as well as his prisoners, attended. The Vine was much cheaper at five shillings per week, while at another house a bed cost sixpence per night. Joseph Jennings paid Mrs Whitwood in 1724 seven shillings a week for his lodging, as well as three shillings and sixpence to the deputy warden, Guybon, for the privilege of so residing there. Corbett is said to have earned over five hundred pounds per annum from his enterprise, but this was probably at a time when the prison was overcrowded and many prisoners were glad to avail themselves of his services.[30]

The legality of these "prison" spunging houses was long disputed. Lord Chief Justice Raymond at Bambridge's trial for the murder of Castell, an inhabitant of such a house, ruled that as the houses were within the confines of the prison *rules* they were places of proper confinement. He qualified this by saying that unless such imprisonment was with the consent of a prisoner, it would be illegal, and that the houses must be kept by a proper tipstaff.[31] Although the revised rules of the prison, established after the 1729 inquiry, and the legislation which followed, permitted the use of these spunging houses provided that the criterion of voluntary consent had been obtained,[32] the houses do not appear to have survived for long thereafter. Wood, admittedly, described them as tipstaffs' houses,[33] and a prisoner died at Corbett's in 1738,[34] but by this time these houses were probably used as accommodation for rulers rather than as spunging houses. However such houses long continued outside the actual prison set-up, being used by sheriffs' officers for similar purposes and at equally outrageous prices.[35]

A new prisoner was expected to pay garnish to his fellow prisoners. This was a financial contribution, contrary to all prison regulations, and had been officially abolished in 1752 as a "great oppression".[36] Howard, twenty years after its supposed abolition, discovered it was two shillings towards wine and one shilling and sixpence for "the use of the house" at the Fleet.[37] It was an immemorial custom, which fully justified the remark of Gayton in his *Wil Bagnalls*

Ghost of 1655 that "our fellow prisoners lie heaviest upon us .... If your pockets
have not [the garnish] the outward furniture of your body, hat or cloak, must
supply."[38] The well known song about a debtors' prison contains this stanza:

> Welcome, welcome, brother debtor,
> To this poor but merry place,
> Where no bailiff, dun or setter,
> Dare to show their frightful face.
> But, kind sir, as you're a stranger,
> Down your garnish you must lay,
> Or your coat will be in danger,
> You must either strip or pay.

A modified form of garnish was exacted from Mr Pickwick. He was
relieved of half a guinea in order to provide cigars for his room mates. But not
only was garnish to be paid to one's fellow prisoners; until 1729 the tipstaffs
required a payment from each prisoner of six shillings, which they spent on a bowl
of punch.[39]

FINDING ACCOMMODATION

There were 102 chambers on the master's side of the prison, excluding the so-
called chapel rooms. Several others were reserved for the prison turnkeys who
generally partitioned their rooms into sections and let them to prisoners, thus
supplementing their own income.[40] An additional number, fifteen, in the basement,
were let to the tapster as part of his lease. These, in turn, were sublet to prisoners
at exorbitant rents, Howard noting from between four to eight shillings per
week.[41] In 1815, still described as the rooms in "Bartholomew's fair", though
damp and dark, they were "given away" by the deputy warden to those prisoners
who were poor and had large families.[42] By this time, however, the tapster had
become the warden's servant and not his lessee.

It is not surprising that the prison was often overcrowded, with many
chambers accommodating up to six persons, a position made much worse by the
number of wives and children of prisoners who took up residence with them.[43]
Those who could not obtain the use of a chamber because of this overcrowding,
or because, like Elizabeth Lepointz, were turned out of one as a consequence of a

dispute about fees,[44] were often forced to move into a room on the topmost floor of the prison called Mount Scoundrel. Smollett called this "an apartment most miserably furnished, in which they lay promiscuously admidst filth and vermin until they can be better accommodated by rotation". William Paget in his poem *The Humours of the Fleet*, written in 1749, wrote about this place as follows:

> To them succeeds the chamberlain, to see
> If you and he are likely to agree,
> Whether you'll tip and pay your master's fee.
> Ask him how much? Tis one pound six and eight;
> And if you want, he'll not the two-pence bate.
> When paid, he puts on an important face,
> And shews Mount Scoundrel for a charming place;
> You stand astonished at the darkened hole,
> Sighing, the Lord have mercy on my soul!
> And ask, "have you no other rooms, Sir, pray?"
> Perhaps enquire what rent too you're to pay:
> Entreating that he would a better seek,
> The rent (cries gruffly) half a crown a week.
> The rooms have all a price, some good, some bad;
> but pleasant ones at present can't be had;
> This room, in my opinion's not amiss.
> Then cross his venal palm with half a piece,
> He straight accosts you with another face.
> 'Sir, you're a gentleman; - I like you well,
> But who are such at first, we cannot tell;
> Though your behaviour speaks you what I thought,
> And therefore I'll oblige you as I ought.[45]

He shows the new prisoner to a room and introduces him to a "chum" with whom he must share it.

With such a scarcity of rooms, a delicate and complicated system of room sharing developed known as "chumming". Each person who paid the full commitment fee for the master's side would receive a chum ticket entitling them to a share of a room. This system endeavoured to allocate rooms on as fair a basis as possible without distinction of rank, although it was alleged that at the King's Bench prison a poor applicant was generally chummed with one who could buy him out, and so enable him to have a small income from the prison economy. There is no evidence that this practice was followed at the Fleet. The system worked in this way. When all the chambers or rooms were occupied by a single prisoner each, or by two or three each (in this calculation families were not counted), the occupants of each chamber were required to take a new member of the master's side on a rota system, starting from the first room on the ground floor. Women, however, were only chummed with women. The tapster's and the turnkeys' rooms were exempted from this arrangement, as at a later date were those rooms occupied by sick or insane prisoners.

The senior person in each room was regarded as the room master or owner. His colleagues were called his chums. When a room became vacant any master was entitled to apply for it, and the most senior person applying for it received it. His room was then offered to the most senior "double chum". If he declined it he would lose his seniority as a chum. Each person in a room had an equal share in its management, as to whether a lodger should be taken, a family admitted, or the room let to others. But none had the right to prevent a "chum" being admitted through the rota system described above. The profits from lodging or letting were shared by the inhabitants, but if the room was let furnished, and the master had provided the furniture and bedding disputes must have arisen. Neither was there any way in which a prisoner, having fitted up his room in an expensive manner, could choose a person to succeed him in it and so obtain from him some recompense for the money he had expended.

In the 1720s it appears that the prisoners administered this system themselves.[46] A chamberlain appears to have done so thereafter, until the warden gave up furnishing the rooms and providing beds and bedding. Thereafter it is probable that the prisoners themselves did so, following the customary pattern, subject to the oversight of the prison officials.

A new inmate, entering with his chumming ticket, had three options available to him. He could accept the arrangement offered to him and move into the chamber, buy out the room master and the chums, or allow himself to be bought out. This meant that the inhabitant/s of the room paid him a weekly sum of 3s. 6d. (it was later increased by sixpence) to make other arrangements and, in Howard's phrase, "shift as best as he could for himself".[47] It was alleged, however, that the going rate was considerably more than the official rate laid down by the prison authorities. There were many alternatives available to the prisoner who had to shift for himself. There was Mount Scoundrel, when that was available. In the

King's Bench prisoners were permitted to sleep in the tap room after it had closed, and this was probably true of the Fleet as well. But most of these prisoners either found lodgings with others, or resorted to those rooms which had become semi-official lodging "houses" for their sort, being kept by their room masters for this purpose, and providing them with a small income thereby. The same applied to those prisoners who entered the master's side without paying their full commitment fees, which appears to have been allowed by the end of the eighteenth century. James Newham protested about this arrangement, and his comments were incorporated into the 1818 report. Unable to pay his full fees, he had entered the master's side, but was not permitted a chumming ticket. He was thus forced to find alternative lodgings within the prison, at great expense, and if he were to be turned out of them, he "must either walk the galleries, sleep upon the stones, or go to the poor side". He paid a guinea for his lodging during the first week of his imprisonment, fourteen shillings for the next, and thereafter half a guinea, but was only permitted to sleep in the room.

This system of chumming suited those who wanted privacy and who could afford it to obtain it, either by buying out their chums or by renting a room from another prisoner. The price was regulated in the 1790s at 8s.4d. for an unfurnished apartment, and one guinea furnished, but by 1815 it was 8s.3d. and 15s.3d. respectively. The furniture, one supposes, was provided by the room master. These were the "official rents", and the fact that some regulation was needed indicates that not only was the practice widespread, but that it had become a seller's market. But both the reports of the 1810s noted that these official charges were hardly ever observed, and while the prison authorities endeavoured to ensure that these charges were the only ones made, and that no prisoner had more than one room, in his name or in that of others (taking away such rooms if these matters were violated or if a prisoner became supersedable), Nixon commented, "I believe I am often defeated." The 1814 report suggested with more truth that if a new prisoner entered the prison and wanted his own room, he would probably discover that "a room scantily furnished" might cost more than a first floor in the "best street in London". It was later added that at a time when numbers were few in the prison, so that many prisoners had rooms to themselves, many found the weekly rent of 1s.3d. an extra burden on their limited resources. Beforehand, under these arrangements, that sum would be shared by several.[48]

Dickens gives a vivid description of this system at work in *The Pickwick Papers.* Mr Pickwick was first chummed with three others, including a butcher and a parson, in a room which had on the outside door the likeness of a man being hung while smoking a pipe. Inside there was no cupboard, carpet, curtain nor blind, the room was dirty and smelt intolerably close. Such filthy, noisy and drunken types did not suit Mr Pickwick, and as soon as it was realised he could pay for solitude he was offered "a capital room" in the coffee room flight for a pound a week. For an additional seven and sixpence a week, a carpet, six chairs, a table, a sofa bedstead, a tea-kettle, and other small articles of use and comfort were provided. The room rent was paid to a chancery prisoner of twenty years' imprisonment, who, needing bread, willingly accepted this arrangement, and agreed to pay out of the same sum the costs of paying out any prisoner chummed on Pickwick. He soon calculated that the prison apartments were the equal in annual value to a small street in the suburbs of London.[49]

Continuous complaints were made during the 1720s about the amount of rent charged for these rooms. The weekly rent then appears to have been 2s. 6d. as fixed by an act of 1696, which also provided that the warden should forfeit a sum of twenty pounds if he offended against its terms.[50] Although this act had been passed after a long period of unsettlement about these fees, a considerable number of disputes now arose about its application. Mackay, stating that the warden demanded this sum of 2s.6d. from every prisoner, whether they possessed a chamber or not, claimed that this sum was the fee for the chamber alone irrespective of the number of prisoners within it, and should be divided between their number.[51] Ancient practice suggests that Mackay was wrong in this instance: Moses Pitt complained, for example, of being charged 8s. for a chamber whose fee he said was 2s.4d.[52] Mackay argued further that the chaplain's weekly due of four pence was included in this sum and was not to be added to it.[53] Furthermore he and his colleagues insisted that the rent of the chamber also included the use of furniture, and that the additional charge for this item of 2s.6d. per week was illegal. The act of 1696, it was suggested, did not specify a bare room for a rental of 2s.6d.[54] The claim was also made that a room could not be obtained without a bribe to the warden, while it was noted in the 1729 report that many paid more than the weekly sum of 2s.6d. for their rooms.[55] This was probably more the result of chumming arrangements than a deliberate attempt at

A Fleet prison chamber in the 1820s. Collection of the author.

extortion.

The state of the furniture provided by the warden caused further disputes. It was so poor, claimed many prisoners, they were forced to obtain their own.[56] The inventories of several rooms furnished by Huggins are recorded by Mackay. One chamber possessed a bedstead, feather bed, two blankets, a quilt, grate, two tables and a shovel and tongs. Another had a bedstead, a feather bed, blanket and rug, cupboard, two chairs, table and grate. Robert Rochford said he and two others paid 2s.6d. each to lie three together in one bed without pillows and with only one blanket, in a room where there was no table, chairs, curtain nor grate. These lists may be compared with the inventory of Elizabeth Berkley who furnished her own chamber herself. It included such items as two cane and two stuffed chairs, an easy chair, looking glass, three pairs of dimity window curtains, a chocolate mill and various items of silverware.[57] The warden was also required to provide bedding for his prisoners. The chamberlain was responsible for these arrangements, and received an entry fee from each prisoner. He charged 5s. for the first pair of sheets, and 2s. thereafter, even if the prisoner used his own.[58] Many claimed that the blankets the warden provided were never "sufficient for keeping warm",[59] while James Wilkinson said he was required to lie on the bare boards.[60] But even this may have been better than the fate of some of Paget's friends who lay on "beds of musty straw, where vermin crawl".[61] The general prison legislation of 1729 permitted prisoners to obtain their own bedding at no extra charge to themselves.

Huggins claimed that he had spend nearly one thousand pounds in refurbishing the prison when he became warden, but that the prisoners "so break, tear to pieces and burn his goods that he is obliged to be continually furnishing some or other of his rooms".[62] The new regulations and fees after 1729 reduced the rent to 2s.6d. for each furnished room, and half that if unfurnished, irrespective of the number of inmates who therefore shared its rental between themselves.[63] This represented an outstanding "victory" for the prisoners and a considerable loss of income to the warden, though the change was entirely at variance with previous precedents. By 1805 the cost per room was said to be 1s.3d. for the room and an additional seven pence for the furniture, but it was added, probably with reference to the chumming arrangements, that matters were so arranged as to make it cost ten to thirteen shillings instead.[64] In 1828 the following fees were recorded: if the warden found the bed 2*s*.6*d*., with the bed to oneself, or half that sum if two to a bed; but if the prisoner provided his own bed and bedding 1*s*.3*d*. on his own, and half that in turn if shared with anyone else.[65]

By 1814 the warden had given up providing bedding, as the report then mentioned:

> Is there any provision, to oblige the keepers of the King's Bench and Fleet to provide bedding for the prisoners? - Yes, there is such a provision, but it never has been complied with; the warden never found any bedding, and the judges excused him, because they said it would be attended with such an expense that the warden could not bear it; the prisoners, in that case, would be wasting the warden's substance, and selling the beds and blankets continually.

Two further reasons were provided by the 1818 report. Firstly, it was argued, perhaps a little incorrectly, that such bedding had not been provided for the previous sixty years, and secondly, that to re-introduce the custom now would be disadvantageous to the "poorer sort" of prisoner who had started up a business of letting out beds and bedding to prisoners, at the rate of 1*s*.6*d*. per night. The warden exercised a right, though not provided for in the rules, of inspecting bedding and ordering the destruction of any that were infested with vermin. It was also noted that those prisoners who brought in their own furniture normally sold it when they left, often to those who made a business out of letting furniture to other prisoners.

THE FEES OF THE PRISON

At the same time of entry into the prison, as the accommodation was being sorted out, the new prisoner would be told about the fees of the prison. For not only was the prisoner expected to support himself, he was also required to contribute to the costs of the prison establishment, and hence the profits of the warden's office. This, of course, was a time-honoured device of the medieval world which applied to every aspect of local and national government. These fees were a frequent source of contention and dispute between the warden and his prisoners, and none more so than during the 1720s. Much of the controversy of that period which led up to the inquiry of 1729 may be traced to these disputes. Simon Wood's argument that the prisoner was as much "put to his shifts to raise money to clear the demands of the prison, as before to satisfy his plaintiff", [66] was echoed by many others, including, as one would have supposed, Mackay.

These disputes of the 1720s were occasioned by the differing interpretations placed on the various fee tables of the prison, in particular as to which fee table was the applicable one. The lists are laid out in Table 6. The 1561 and the 1636 tables graded the fees according to the social rank of the prisoner, but these distinctions appear to have been abolished in 1641 with the fall of the Star Chamber court,[67] although one Captain James Martin claimed that the 1636 table of fees still hung in the hall of the prison in 1726.[68] A revision was made in 1686 as a result of the act *22 & 23 Charles II c 20* which permitted prisoners to obtain their own food. It also ordered that a table of fees should be hung up in every prison of the realm, so that no greater fees than these should be demanded or received.[69] Until that date the warden provided "commons" for his prisoners, at a set fee which all were required to pay, whether they chose to eat his food or provide their own.[70] As a result of this legislation the court of Common Pleas reduced the 1636 commitment fee from £3.6s.8d. to £2.4s.4d. on the master's side, and from £1.14s.4d. to £1.7s.4d. on the common side, thus excluding the first week's commons provided in the original fee.[71] It appears that those committed by the Council, and possibly by the courts of Exchequer and Chancery, still had to pay the original commitment fees.[72] These were termed the customary fees.

To complicate matters still further, Lord Chief Justice Herbert had issued a table of fees in 1651.[73] This stipulated that the fee for the liberty of the house and irons was £1.6s.8d. and 7s.4d. for the dismission fee.[74] These meant a commitment fee of £1.16s.4d. for the master's side. This table, the prisoners claimed, was the legal one, as it had been ratified by parliament in 1693, and could not be superseded by any rule made by the court of Common Pleas.[75]

There was much confusion and ambiguity, therefore, about the whole question of the fees, and as to which table was the correct one. If on the one hand the prisoners campaigned for the 1651 table, probably devised by some humanitarian Commonwealth official, they were wrong in their claim that this had received parliamentary sanction in 1693. On the other hand they claimed, a little

Table Six: The fees of the prison

	liberty of house and irons	first weeks commons	commitment fee	chaplain	clerk's fee	entering name & cause	porter	chamberlain	jailor	dismission fee	turnkey	totals where given
1561												
master's	£3.6.8	16s.8d.	£3.6.8		2s.4d.	4d.		1s.	1s.	7s.4d.		
yeoman	£1.14.4	16s.8d.			2s.4d.	4d.	-	1s.	1s.	7s.4d.		
common	17s.4d.	6s.10d.			2s.4d.	4d.		1s.	1s.	7s.4d.		
1636												
master's		[£3.6.8]										
yeomans		[£1.14.4]										
poor box		[7s.4d.]										
1651												
master's	£1.6.8					4d.	1s.	1s.	1s.	7s.4d.		£1.16s.
yeomans			13s.							7s.4d.		
1686												
master's	£2.4.4											
common	£1.7.4											
1724												
master's	£2.4.4			2s.			1s.	3s.		12s.6d.	2s.6d.	£3.5.4
1727												
master's	£2.4.4			2s.		4d.	2s.	1s.		7s.6d.	2s.6d.	£2.19s.
common	£1.6.8			1s.		4d.				7s.6d.	2s.6d.	£1.18s.
poor box		7s.4d.										
1729												
master's	£1.6.8								2s.	7s.4d.		
common	13s.								2s.	7s.4d.		
1813												
master's	£1.8.6									7s.4d.		

[plus clerk of the papers, at so much a writ]

DISCHARGE FEES

Clerk for every action of discharge	2s.6d.	clerk of papers for discharge	2s.6d.
copy of cause, first three, each	1s.	clerk of enquiry for discharge	2s.6d.
others, thereafter, each	4d.	turnkey for discharge	2s.6d.
Certificate for discharge	2s.6d.	clerk of papers for *hab.corpus*	5s.4d.

Return of first cause 4s., and others 2s.

SOURCES: Mackay, pp 39f: Report 1729, pp 15f. These fees were still being charged in 1814 save for the fee for the clerk of enquiries [PP 1813-4 (320) XIII 30].

SOURCES:

1561: Malcolm's *Londinium Redivivum*, I 286. This table was revised in 1686 to exclude the commons fee from it.

1636: BLO, MS Rawlinson D1123, fol 28b.

1651: Report 1729, p 9: Mackay said this was given parliamentary approval in 1693 [pp 34, 39].

1686: Report 1729, p 9.

1724: Mackay, p 39 [of LCJ King].

1727: Mackay, pp 39f: Report 1729, pp 15f.

1729: PP 1813-14 (320) XIII 30.

confusingly, that the 1686 commitment fee of £2.4s.4d., as it was substantially more than the total fees settled by the 1651 table, represented the whole commitment fee, and thus insisted that the additional items separately provided for in the 1561 and 1651 tables over and above the commitment fee for the liberty of the house and irons, was included within it. These were the fees for the clerk, jailer, dismission fee and so forth. The prison authorities insisted that the commitment fee of £2.4s.4d. represented only the fee for the liberty of the house and irons, and the additional items were extra to it and not included within it. The warden claimed that he had prisoners who could swear that these fees had been charged for the previous twenty to twenty-seven years.[76] The prison authorities were quite correct in this, as the 1686 revision merely took away from the warden's commitment fee the cost of commons, but obviously continued the other fees included within the tables. In 1724 Lord Chief Justice King accepted the warden's case, but the prisoners were clearly not prepared to accept his judgment and continued to press their demands.

After a further period of conflict, the dispute was referred once more to the court of Common Pleas in the Trinity term of 1727. Bambridge was then deputy warden, and as his figures were accepted by the court (with a reduction of 5s. in the dismission fee), the prisoners claimed they were required to pay double fees for such items as the fees to the chamberlain, gaoler and the dismission fee, believing that all fees were contained in the initial fee for the liberty of the house and irons.[77] But Bambridge had only entered into office as deputy warden a few weeks before this hearing, and undoubtedly presented to it the fees he found in use in the prison, which had been accepted by the prothonotaries' report of 1724, and also by Lord Chief Justice King.[78] Bambridge's assertion that he had "taken no fees but the old established fees such as were not, fraudulently but fairly and upon great and mature deliberation confirmed and settled" was more correct than some of his contemporaries may have wished.[79]

These disputes about the prison fees continued. The prisoners organised themselves against the prison administration, basing their claims on the 1651 fee list, and declined to pay their fees and chamber rents until the dispute was settled in their favour. They spent much time endeavouring to show that the fees charged were extortionate and wrongfully extracted from the prisoners. It was even suggested that the ancient constitutions of the prison still applied and that there should be a yeomans side between that of the master's and the common side, with a correspondingly reduced commitment fee, though the 1636 table was the last to use that category, and the 1651 one merely used the term as a polite euphemism for the common side. Others again argued that the commitment fee still included the first weeks' commons, or that no fees at all were due from those on the common side.[80]

Equally strong complaint was made that a fresh set of commitment fees had to be paid for each surrender or charge entered against a prisoner.[81] Thus the commitment fees of John Dudley amounted to over forty-five pounds, and those of Samuel Siddale with three surrenders to over ten pounds, though these sums included the fees paid at the judge's chambers. Elizabeth Lepointz paid nearly fourteen pounds for five surrenders.[82] A similar protest was made that new commitment fees were required from any prisoner who had left the Fleet for another prison by the use of the *habeas corpus* writ and then returned, even on the same day. Archibald Paterson had to pay these fees though he returned from the King's Bench three days after being sent there from the Fleet. This procedure was a favourite trick of creditors to encourage their debtors to settle their affairs with them.[83] A further dispute was occasioned by the warden's appointment of a clerk of the enquiries to assist the clerk of the papers. The prisoners protested about the new set of fees caused by this appointment, which they felt was totally unjustified. Another constant complaint was that the warden retained the corpse of a prisoner, as well as his possessions, until his relatives had paid any outstanding fees due to him.[84] Although this was not mentioned in the 1729 report, it was forbidden by the new rules occasioned by it, as much on medical as on humanitarian grounds, for often the smell became so offensive that "none could go near the corpse". A more persistent complaint was that the table of fees, ordered to be displayed in a prominent position by the 1670 act, was never set up. Huggins answered this with the assertion that his prisoners "were pleased to burn, tear to pieces, and obliterate" these lists.[85]

Some of these complaints may have been justified. The 1729 report contains a list of extortions,[86] while as a result of the 1724 prothonotaries' report Huggins was required to return various monies to his prisoners. One Jennings, for example, received seven or eight guineas.[87]

It is not surprising that after such a long conflict, and the general feeling engineered against the prison authorities in 1729, that the court of Common Pleas should have reduced the fees and charges of the prison. The chamber rent was reduced to ls.3d. per week, unfurnished. The fees for the master's side were fixed at £1.6s.8d., together with 2s. for the turnkey, 7s.4d. dismission fee and 2s.6d. for the clerk's fee, and for the common side 13s.4d. plus the additional fees named above. However, those who were eligible to take advantgae of the prison charities paid no fees whatsoever. It was also agreed that there was only one commitment fee, and not one multiplied by the number of actions against a prisoner. This scale of fees remained in force, with little modification, until the end of the prison in 1842: the act of 1815 which abolished fees in prisons not applying to the Fleet or the King's Bench.[88]

With such disputes about the prison fees and the chamber rent, it is hardly remarkable that many prisoners declined to pay, and accumulated substantial arrears. This had always been the case. In 1698 the warden argued that while at one time the profits of the prison were considerable, it was no longer so, and with the chamber rents fixed at 2s.6d. per person, he was only able to obtain fifty-five pounds or so for a half year from this source, for few of the prisoners thought themselves obliged to pay anything.[89] The same situation occurred in the 1720s, and was made more acute by the fact that there was no one certain method by which prisoners could be forced to pay. The warden reacted to these disputes in various ways. The chamber of Captain Allen Ascough was padlocked against him for his refusal to pay his outstanding rent. Archibald Paterson was forbidden the use of the day *rules* until he had paid his outstanding chamber rent. Others, like Wood, were ejected from their rooms, and forced to "walk the prison to keep warm", or turned over to the common side, ironed and placed in dungeons, as Jacob Mendez-Solas claimed, or found the outstanding fees "extracted from their pockets or distrained from their effects". Barbara Bush, although released by her creditor as she was in a starving condition, was sent to a spunging house by Guybon as she was in dispute with him about her chamber rent to the tune of thirty pounds or so. She claimed that as she was forced for a time to share a room with a "common woman of the town ... a raving mad woman", the warden was entitled to claim only half of his weekly demand of 2s.10d. Eventually for want of bail at the warden's suit she was transferred to the Wood street compter, where it was later alleged she was "in a starving condition".

Other prisoners, though discharged by their creditors, were detained in the prison for their fees at the suit of the warden. Henry Topping, a linen draper of Westminster, claimed this had happened to him in respect of chamber fees, although he had rented a room from John Ferryman, who kept the tap house, for 1s.6d. per week, and had paid the clerk of the enquiries 10s. for checking his discharges. The same also applied to those who, while discharged by their creditors, were unable to meet the cost of the fees of their release from prison, though in later years the Thatched House Society (founded in 1772) met these costs for deserving cases. In 1814, for example, Nixon alleged that where one poor prisoner paid his own discharge fees, twenty were paid by the public charities. But this did not apply in the 1720s. Thomas Goldby, a coachman of St Giles in the Fields, claimed that he was required to pay fees of £1.12s.6d. to the various prison officials to enable them to enquire into the legality of his discharge, even though Mr Head, a turnkey, was prepared to vouch that he had seen the attorney sign the discharge papers. He was only released when he threatened to complain to Lord Chief Justice Eyre.[90]

The more drastic, if ultimate remedy of retaining the corpse of a prisoner until his family had paid the outstanding fees has already been noted. By the 1800s a more civilised method was adopted to deal with those who were in arrears with their chamber rents. They would not be turned out of their rooms until a quarter's rent had accumulated. This threat was said to be generally sufficient. But it was also noted that the warden, being a "humane" man, would often compound with such people for their debts in rent and fees, often taking five pounds instead of the fifteen owed, particularly so when their creditors had discharged them.[91]

The problem which lay behind all these disputes was not only that the prison fee tables could be easily misconstrued, or did not adequately convey the charges they were required to make clear, but that the warden needed as much financial income as he could obtain in order to run the prison (and live luxuriously himself), while the prisoners, being debtors, wished to remain in the Fleet for as little expenditure as possible. Yet the warden was probably right to feel extremely annoyed that his prisoners were prepared to dispute these fees which enabled them to enjoy the privileges which his prison allowed, for they had willingly entered the Fleet knowing it was the most expensive prison in the kingdom.

THE PRISONERS' FINANCES

It must not be assumed that all the prisoners who entered the Fleet had sufficient resources to provide their own food, bedding, blankets, fuel, and all the other incidental expenses of life. For such items no allowances or concessions were given by the prison, not even to those who entered the common side of the prison with its reduced commitment fee and lack of chamber rent.[92] Those who were unable to meet the prison's commitment fees were probably refused entry, and therefore had to make their abode in one of the other London debt prisons, such as Newgate or one of the compters. At a later stage it appears that such people were admitted, though if they chose to live on the master's side they were refused a chum ticket, and were required to pay their commitment fees before they were discharged.[93] Many prisoners who entered the master's side must have run out of funds and been forced into the common side. Simon Wood was one of these.

It was estimated in 1793 that it cost on average twelve shillings a week to live on the master's side. This was a basic amount and it meant that such a prisoner had to "live hard [and] seldom know a good dinner".[94] But others spent up to five guineas a week, "for everything can be purchased in a gaol except quiet and retirement", it was reported, "[for] those who have money without honesty ... have there no inducements to refrain from extravagance, but every temptation to the contrary".[95]

If some entered the Fleet with considerable amounts of money at their disposal, a much larger number entered with extremely little. Their situation was rendered all the more difficult by the horrific fact that the Fleet was, until 1813, the only prison in England and Wales whose prisoners received no relief from national or county funds. A county allowance for debtors had been established since the days of Elizabeth I, and an act of 1738 extended its provisions to the King's Bench and Marshalsea prisons, but not for some reason to the other non-county prison, the Fleet. "Mr Thornton's Act" of 1813, admitting that there was no adequate relief for prisoners in the Fleet, extended this allowance to its prisoners. It permitted those not charged in execution (for whom "groats" were available from their creditors) and not entitled to be discharged by an insolvent debtors' act, on swearing they were not worth ten pounds, and after due examination by the city magistrates, to receive a sum of 3s.6d. per week. It was not available to those who benefited from the prison charities.[96] The overseers of St Brides parish, in which the prison was situated, and to whom the warden paid poor rates, refused to accept any liability for such poor prisoners, though it was said they gave some assistance from time to time.[97]

Relief from the county fund only applied to those imprisoned on mesne process, and it came rather late in the day so far as the Fleet was concerned. For those debtors imprisoned on execution writs some provision had been made since the insolvency act of 1670.[98] This required the creditor, if he refused to release his prisoner under the terms of an insolvency act, to provide four pence a day (the "groat") for his maintenance, later increased to sixpence in 1792-3. If more than one creditor was involved each was required to pay 2s. per week. It was not easy to obtain these groats, and the Thatched House Society assisted many such people, who had found themselves unable to meet the cost of two or three guineas required to sue for this maintenance, to obtain them. In 1792 only eighteen of the Fleet prisoners were in receipt of such relief.[99] If the money was not paid before ten each Monday morning the prisoner could be released by the court. Thomas Macdonald considered that this payment was simply "to keep the body of [the] debtor alive", and he continued, "the sullen price of a low tyrant is gratified by the price; it makes the prisoner still more his own; he throws down his groat, and while he has a daily groat to give, his wretched debtor's imprisonment is prolonged, and may continue, during the tedious course of a vile existence."[100] Such statements were quite understandable in view of the fact that many creditors paid out in "groats" far more than the debt was worth.[101]

Few of the Fleet prisoners had property or an income to support them in prison, in spite of many allegations to the contrary.[102] The income from the county funds or the "groats" was never sufficient for their needs in such an expensive establishment. And, it must be remembered, such sources of income only applied to a few before 1813. Many relied on allowances given them by their families and friends; indeed the 1815 report infers that some wives living in the prison adopted prostitution in order to support their husbands and families. A few prisoners, who had the room and ability to do so, were able to use their professional or craft skills within the prison, as did many more who lived in the *rules*, as will be noted later. Nixon stated that he permitted "all to work that can work" though he noted that the prisoners were in general "an idle disorderly set of men".[103] Robert Tailor was one of the first to be noted as making use of his imprisonment in order "to profit himself by trade", to the annoyance of his fellow prisoners.[104] This was in 1586-7, but his example could not have been followed by many, for the restrictions of space and access were not easy to overcome.

Many others found a living within the prison economy. Though the details of this are mainly found in the reports of 1792, 1814, and 1818, it must have been operating at a much earlier period. This generally centred on the provision of rooms, always at a premium in an overcrowded prison. There were those who had allowed themselves to be chummed out for a payment of 3*s*.6*d*. or more per week, some to avail themselves of lodgings provided by other prisoners in their rooms. Those who made a living out of providing such accommodation in these rooms were able to take up to six people at charges which varied from 10*s*.6*d*. to 14*s*. or even a guinea a week, deducting, one assumes, some amount for their furniture, and sharing the remainder with their chums, and possibly being required to buy off any new prisoners chummed onto that room. The 1792 report noted a prisoner who had let out his room at a charge of one guinea per week, and found accommodation for himself at the cost of one shilling per week. At such rates bedding was probably provided, but those who found individual lodgings and needed furnitire, bed, and bedding could hire them from other prisoners who had set themselves up as dealers in these matters. "A numerous class of persons", said Nixon, "gain their livelihoods" in these ways. He also stated that many of these people deliberately detained themselves in prison, even if supersedable, by friendly actions, in order to retain their room and profit thereby. "I suppose", he added, "his inheritance [by it] is more beneficial then if he was out of doors." One assistant turnkey in the King's Bench prison, a former prisoner, maintained his prison chamber for this express purpose.[105] Others within the prison economy acted as scavengers, cooks and servants to the more wealthy prisoners, and possibly to the prison staff, while others served as prison watchmen. Many of these were prisoners on the common side.[106] Howard noted a prisoner who had converted his room into a billiard room.[107] Others, as noted later, acted as shopkeepers, tap keeper, cooks, or opened profitable if illegal gin shops. By such means, Feltham argued, confirming Nixon's statement, "some gain more than they would out of doors, after they become acquainted with the ways of the place."[108]

Two possibilities still remained open for the desperate, though not before they had been in the prison for three months, and who could swear that they were not worth more than five pounds per annum and had no other means of subsidence. Had they declared themselves to be such as they entered the prison, no commitment fee would have been payable after 1729.[109] These people were required to live on the common side and to beg at the grate in order to participate in the prison charities. Their number was never large, for it was argued that many declined to accept such entitlement for fear of the disgrace it would bring upon themselves and their families. Howard in 1777 found sixteen prisoners of this description, in 1793 there were twelve, and in 1814 seven or eight, while in one month of 1815 there were but four.[110]

Those who begged at the grate (the first of the two possibilities mentioned) were required to sit in rotation for twenty-four hours at a time in a small chamber which had a window overlooking the Fleet market. Here they would peer through its bars and beg for alms, crying, "pray remember the poor prisoners". John Feltham in his guide to London of 1803 requested the charitably disposed to "liberally contribute to this box",[111] while Simon Wood noted another source of income to its inhabitants, for many non-prisoners used the begging grate as a means of communicating with their friends inside the prison, and would give a small tip for that privilege.[112] Those who took part in this and the other charities (the second of the possibilities) elected their own steward to see to the fair distribution of their proceeds amongst themselves. The steward, on behalf of the prisoners, retained one key to the box, and the warden the other, with the result that the prisoners claimed that under Huggins the head turnkey demanded half a crown from every pound donated to the box. The receipts were reported in 1814 to be of the annual order of one hundred and thirty pounds, though three hundred pounds had been recorded in one particularly good year. By 1814 the individual on duty was permitted to take all he collected for himself, and no further account was taken. The old system was restored, however, by 1829, when the amount was shared out monthly between all the "charity" prisoners. In July of that year, for example, four prisoners shared the receipts of £8.8s.5d. collected at this box. If these figures are correct the "charity" prisoners, considering their low number, were wealthier than many on the master's side.[113]

The charity prisoners also employed several men to collect alms for them outside the prison. These men wore distinguishing badges. Tempest's *Cries of*

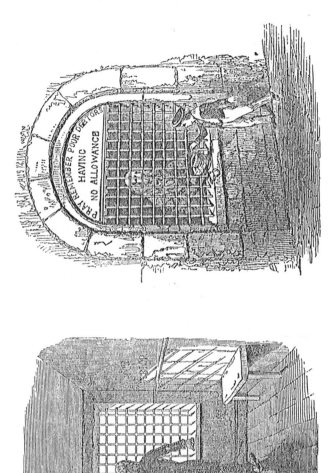

The interior and exterior of the Fleet prison grate, where the poor debtors cried for assistance from the public. From the *Illustrated London News* of 14 March 1846.

London depicts such a person carrying a basket for bread and food and a box for alms, shouting, "Remember the poor prisoners", while another description continued his cry, "bread and meat for the poor prisoners, bread and meat".[114] The custom was of medieval origin. In 1375 the prisoners of the King's Bench prison were permitted to have a "proctor" to collect alms for them, provided he was not a prisoner.[115] Such "running boxmen", as they were termed, employed by the Fleet prisoners at Christmas, Easter, and Whitsunday brought in a sum of £3.12s.6d. in 1727.[116] On one occasion the box travelled far afield, for John Taylor, a woolcomber of Milverton, Somerset, implicated in Monmouth's rebellion and suspected of being involved in some plot, testified he was not a Fleet prisoner, but had come some one hundred miles in order to serve his friends by carrying the charity box of to the Fleet with him.[117] It may have been special pleading, but for others the task was not without its hazards, as one lord mayor committed several such men to Bridewell as public nuisances.[118]

There were a number of prison charities. Some provided an annual sum for the relief of the poor prisoners, and others provided a capital sum in order to discharge the honest and poor amongst them. Judge Price left provision for a three half pence loaf of bread a week for sick prisoners.[119] Edward Thatcher gave the income of forty shillings per annum from a house rental to relieve the poor debtors;[120] and Lord Chief Baron Pengally left a sum of five hundred pounds to the King's Bench and Fleet prisons in order to release needy prisoners on condition that their debts did not amount to more than fifty pounds.[121] Warden Nixon said that he received up to £100 per year from various individuals for the relief of the poor prisoners.[122]

A list of the charities awarded to the prison is given in the 1729 report. The court of Common Pleas gave three pounds a term, and the Exchequer court 6s.8d. per term. Edward Thatcher's gift is recorded, but with the deduction of house tax its value was £1.16s.; Mr Parker gave thirty shillings, paid through the Merchant Tailors' company, but also subject to a similar deduction of tax; John Grubben was recorded as giving three pounds (less ten shillings towards the repair of a sea wall in Somerset); Mr John Kenrich thirty shillings, and the master of the Rolls two pounds. Mr Dawson's gift of nine shillings had not been paid for some years, nor had Mr Carter's of seventeen shillings, which allegedly was paid by the churchwardens of the parish of Underhurst. The Leather Sellers' company gave eighteen shillings, while thirty-three penny loaves were given each Christmas by an unspecified party. The total amount, including the income from the running box-men, came to £29.5s.6d.[123] In 1828 the list of charities was returned as follows:

	£	s.	d.
Court of Chancery	15	15	0
Court of Common Pleas	12	0	0
Court of Exchequer	1	6	8
Draper's Company*	1	10	0
Company of Leather Sellers	1	8	0
Saddlers' Company	1	10	0
Archbishop of Canterbury*	1	0	0
St Bartholomew's Hospital*	1	13	0
St Ethelburga's Parish		9	0
An unknown person	2	0	0
Mr Thomas Stuckley (every three years)	2	0	0
Executors of Mrs Misson in lieu of 48 stone of meat at 2s.8d. per stone*	4	6	0
Warden of the Fleet*	1	1	0
(* at Christmas time)[124]			

W K Jordan, in his study of the London charities, has suggested that the citizens of London devoted 1.84% of their charitable wealth to the relief of prisoners, and mentions one benefaction of interest, that of a London grocer, Robert Chichele, who left enough money to provide each prisoner in the London prisons with a half penny loaf each week for two years.[125]

Complaints were continually made that the list of charity monies was not displayed in the prison as required by the 1670 act, and that this money was often given to the people who were "little in need of them".[126] Smith complained in 1776 that only about ninety pounds of the four hundred pounds due to the charity prisoners was distributed, but he may well have been misled as to their extent, or possibly added into the total figure the amount from the begging grate box.[127] Similar complaints had been made in the 1720s. The warden was accused of taking money from benefactors in order to release prisoners, but then of retaining these prisoners at his own suit for the outstanding fees they owed him. Barbara Rush's case has been noted. She had been recommended to a Miss Crisp as an object of charity, but Guybon retained her for the chamber rent she owed.[128]

The conditions under which these charity prisoners were required to live were dreadful even by eighteenth-century standards. In petition after petition they described their plight and begged for an alleviation of their situation. In one such petition, jointly made by the poor debtors in the Fleet and King's Bench prisons to the House of Commons, they wrote:

> Many of the poor said prisoners have neither friends or money to help them, but live by begging at the grate, and are in much worse condition that the common beggars are abroad, being scarcely able to subsist thereon, and when that charity fails, they starve, as is well known, there being no care taken of them, that scarcely a week passes by but some sad examples of that kind [occur] ... [129]

William Young with six others petitioned the lords of the Treasury in 1715. They had been removed to the Fleet as "owlers" for exporting wool. A further six of their number had died in the Fleet between June and July of that year for want of necessities. Their petition went on to relate that their wives and families were forced to live "on the parish". As their solicitor had been directed to allow them sixpence a day to keep them from starving this meant they were debarred from the common charity of the prison. They consequently begged for greater assistance.[130]

The friends of some of these prisoners even advertised on their behalf in the London press. Two may be quoted, although their dates are not known:

> A gentleman, with his wife and child, who are next to starving in the prison of the Fleet; the poor gentlewoman in order to prevent their perishing, has been to the houses of several persons craving some relief, and as she was passing in the Strand, in Charing Cross, on the 19th of February last, had the misfortune to be squeezed between two coaches, and has kept her bed ever since in most tormenting pains, not having a penny to pay for physic, or any manner of support; any persons willing to relieve them, may be convinced of the truth hereof, by calling or sending to see them in the said prison.

> The poor prisoner in the Fleet, whose wife and child have been so long sick in one bed, is now himself so ill as to be unable to help himself, and is, together with them, in the greatest distress imaginable: He only lies for his fees, and is destitute of money either to discharge him, or to aid him in his present miseries. The truth of this advertisement will appear in the infirmary

room, or by enquiry of the turnkey of the Fleet prison.   The smallest,
pittance will claim the deepest thanks and gratitude.[131]

Other examples may be quoted. Simon Wood wrote in his book *Remarks
on the Fleet Prison* that he had been forced to give up his room for lack of
chamber rent, and was now "forced to walk the prison to keep warm within him,
during the winter season".   He had been clothed from the gifts of his fellow
prisoners, and he received a loaf of bread and a plate of meat from a Ludgate hill
chemist every Sunday. Any profits from his book, published in 1733, would be
spent on obtaining his discharge or the support of his family of three children.[132]
Pierce Egan, in his description of the Fleet during the 1810s, given in his *Life in
London*, noted an honest tradesman whose wife had come to prison with their
three children, to tell him that she has pledged the last article she had left, a
waistcoat, to purchase bread. Dr Smith noted how many such families went on
pawning one thing after the another, until they "melt down and convert every part
of their substance into money to support them while in confinement".[133]   Richard
Oastler, one of the last prisoners to enter the Fleet, noted as he arrived a prisoner
whom he had known as a prosperous merchant, but who was now a beggar in
prison through no fault of his own. He had not tasted food all day.

Those who were unable to benefit from the charity money of the prison,
whether they were on the common side or not, were probably as hard pushed to
survive as those who received such charity monies.   Many clearly lived at
starvation level,[134] although the situation was never so grim at the Fleet as it was
at other prisons.   The 1729 committee discovered three hundred and fifty
prisoners at the Marshalsea prison, who were, it claimed, literally dying of
starvation, many of whom subsequently died. Ten years earlier another
parliamentary inquiry claimed that three hundred prisoners had died at that prison
in less than three months,[135] and in 1740 *Hookes' Weekly Journal* estimated that
five hundred prisoners died of starvation in English gaols each year.[136] Yet
although there were probably real cases of suffering by Fleet prisoners, and many
had to accept a standard of life lower than they had enjoyed beforehand, the
impression one receives is that for many the real problem was more of boredom
than of deprivation.

DRAINS, CHAPEL, AND BEER

Though the Fleet offered many amenities for the relief of boredom, it is surprising that the more necessary provision of an infirmary and medical care was almost totally ignored. It is equally surprising that with this neglect, accompanied by the lack of proper sanitation within the prison and its overcrowding, no major outbreak of gaol fever ever took place, though the writer of *A Speech without Doors* of 1729 considered that the prison distemper was more frequent and more certain than "the smallpox".[137]

The report of 1729 stated that for want of an infirmary many prisoners, even those with smallpox, were required to share the beds of others or to lie upon the floor.[138] The new rules thereafter ordered that no prisoner should be obliged to lie in the same bed as a diseased person.[139] But no infirmary was provided until the late eighteenth century, when it was placed in the larger rooms over the chapel. It was described by Pickwick as a large, bare and desolate room, with a number of stump bedsteads made of iron in it. The prisoners, in a petition of 1791, pointed out the anomaly of having an infirmary without any medical supervision,[140] perhaps hinting that this conflicted with a statute of 1774 which required the appointment of a surgeon.[141] The 1814 report provides the same story. There was still no medical assistance, unless provided by one of the prisoners who had a medical training, while no provision was made for the supply of medicines, unless provided by the prisoners or by Mr Nixon.[142]

The sanitary condition of the prison was appalling by any standard. Time after time and year by year the writers on the prison mention its dampness, lack of wholesome water (which came from the river or through pumps), the vermin that abounded throughout the prison, and the stench from the open dunghill, which Mackay suggested was not removed until forty tons of "the stinking soil" had accumulated. Part of the 1774 act was complied with, namely the whitewashing of the walls, but this was done by the prisoners (though Nixon claimed he had it done once every three years), while the prisoners also claimed that they paid for some of their number to clean the drains and necessary houses, sinks and yards, sweep the yard and galleries, and to set up the lights, although all this was the responsibility of the warden as outlined in the 1729 rules. As a result, they claimed, they were driven to an expense of several pounds a week for the sake of their health.   The warden at least tried to enforce some cleanliness on the prisoners, for he posted the following notice in the prison during July 1807:

> In consequence of various complaints having been made to the warden, of dirt and filth being thrown about the prison-house and yard, he has thought it necessary to give this public notice, that any person who shall hereafter sweep or throw any dirt, ashes, filth, or rubbish in any of the galleries, or on the stairs of this prison, or who shall cast any filth in any part of the yard, or at any of the drains therein, except at the place appointed for the reception of such filth at the south end of the building, or who shall carry any water, either dirty or clean, up or down the front stairs, shall, if a prisoner, be deprived of his or her room or chummage, and, if a stranger, shall be locked out.[143]

The general rule of cleanliness is expressed by a comment made by the commissioners in 1814: that "each person keeps his room in the state of dirt or cleanliness agreeable to his own habits".   They recommended that the health of the prisoners would be "improved if more care was taken upon the subject".   The warden believed, however, that he had the right to inspect bedding and burn all that was infected with vermin.[144]

It may have been thought more fitting that a chaplain should have been provided instead of medical care, and a chapel rather than an infirmary. As there was no parish church within the limits of the *rules* the chapel was available to the rulers as well.   The chaplain was supported in the traditional manner, through payments made by the prisoners. He received in the 1720s two shillings from each prisoner's commitment fee, and thereafter four pence a week.   As this weekly sum was added to the chamber rent paid by each prisoner on the master's side during the 1720s, it must be presumed that it was not required of those on the common side. During that period it was claimed that these fees should have amounted to upwards of nearly nine hundred pounds per annum, but Huggins had only paid the chaplain, Dr Francis, who was also dean of Bedford, forty guineas, with an additional forty guineas if he supplied a chaplain to care for the prisoners. Huggins explained this by stating that a previous chaplain had compounded his fees for this sum because of the difficulties he found in collecting them. He added that he never received any greater sum from the prisoners than what he paid the chaplain, simply as many of the prisoners refused to pay their fourpences.[145]

After 1729 the two shilling entry fee for the chaplain was reduced to one shilling, and only required of those on the master's side, while the four pence weekly charge was forgotten.

The chapel duty was normally taken, it appears, by clergymen who were debt prisoners in the prison. During the 1690s one of these, Elborrow, who served as assistant chaplain, in association with the chapel clerk, Bartholomew Bassett (who renting the prison kitchen gave his name to the public dining room), exploited the "pretended" lack of episcopal jurisdiction over the chapel, and entered the clandestine marriage trade. Legislation of 1711 forbade the use of the prison or its chapel for these marriages, but they continued within the *rules* until the passing of Lord Hardwicke's marriage act of 1753.[146] During the time of Moses Pitt one Thomas Beverley, a prisoner, preached in the chapel every Sunday, and. received the sum of five shillings from the warden for so doing. He may have been a nonconformist minister.

A service was performed twice on Sunday in 1731 by a Mr Patterson, who was described as "the minister" of the chapel, but not a prisoner.[147] In the time of Howard the chaplain was Mr Horner, and he added to his duties by taking a weekday service on Wednesdays; but by the 1810s, under the care of the Revd Manley Wood, the services were reduced to one on Sunday at one o'clock in the afternoon, apart from services on the greater festivals of the church.[148] His salary, provided by the warden, was thirty pounds, and a clerk was paid ten pounds. The services were very poorly attended, by half a dozen or so, which the chaplain put down to the fact that that time was too early for most of the prisoners, few of whom would have got up by that time and had their breakfasts. The 1814 committee felt that this was not a sufficient explanation, and expressed considerable annoyance that neither the warden nor his officers attended the services, and that while the prison gates were shut during the time of divine service the coffee houses remained open. This, they wrote, "they cannot too strongly condemn". The turnkeys, replied Nixon, were employed in driving away idle boys and people from the chapel door so that there might be peace within, though a prisoner, John Welsh, added that those inside were so disgracefully behaved, with "scoffing, coughing, laughing, and acting like a parcel of boys", that the clergyman was often unable to continue with the service.[149]

If most prisons possessed chapels, few had the other amenities found in the

Fleet. A coffee house had been formed from the great hall in 1732, and to suit the convenience of the times, its bar was built in the place of various pews from the chapel which then adjoined it. New premises had to be obtained after the rebuilding of the 1770s, for Howard states that it was neatly made out of two rooms. An Old Bailey trial report of 1740 shows that the coffee room provided newspapers and journals, thus confirming Simon Wood's comment that it was as complete as any in town. Possibly it was outshone by the coffee house of the King's Bench prison. Here an ordinary was held in the 1800s each day at the price of two shillings per head, together with a pint of porter. Masonic meetings were also held in this coffee house. It was rented from the marshall at a sum of £105 per annum, and one would assume that this also applied to the Fleet coffee house, although the amount of its rental is not known.[150] The tap room was another long established prison institution, although Howard hints that it had been newly furnished in the 1770s. Although the tap ended at 11.00 pm (an hour later by 1809) wine and beer clubs were held on a weekly basis, and these not only continued until the early hours of the morning, to the annoyance of the more sober prisoners, wrote Howard, but also attracted to them many strangers from outside the prison. An act of 1784 which forbade the gaolers of the county prisons to offer alcohol for sale never applied to these great London prisons, and the last warden of the Fleet, Brown, having the licence to sell beer and ale to his prisoners, discovered to his annoyance that they called his prison "Brown's hotel".[151] Robert Cruickshank based his painting, "The Evening after a Mock Election in the Fleet Prison, 1 June 1835", in this tap room. It depicted, amongst others, Captain Wilder, RN, Harry Holt, a prize-fighter, Mr Palmer, cutler to George III, Captain Oliver, a smuggler and the tapster, and Mr Hutchinson, a Liverpool draper. Cruickshank was also a prisoner.

The committee of 1814 had the pleasure of listening to Mr Nixon give details about these arrangements. He himself purchased the ale and beer coming into the prison, as the brewer would not trust the prisoners with any credit. He received a profit of five shillings per barrel. On average this would amount to two hundred pounds per annum. The cellar head, with its four cellars, was not kept by a prisoner, though it once had been, but its keeper sold the beer and porter to both the tapster and the coffee house keeper, who were prisoners. Though Nixon endeavoured to prevent these men taking more for these items than they cost outside the prison, namely ale at eight pence a pot and porter five pence, he knew that while they did not ask for more, yet they would take more if it was given, usually an extra penny, which he hinted was expected of the purchaser. However these beverages were sold at the "street price" at the cellar head, provided one took one's own pot to be filled. John MacGee, master of the coffee room, explained that the additional penny was a voluntary contribution, "not one gentleman in twenty ever refuses to give it", which covered his cost of providing coals and candles for the place, even though he was allowed ten shillings by the prison per week for this, and for supplying knives, forks, and salt. Incidentally this and the taproom were the only two public places in the Fleet where fires were kept, apart from Bartholomew's Fair. He paid no rent for the room, and had applied to the warden for the office, being the warden's servant more than his lessee. He also sold a limited amount of wine, two or three bottles a week, for few could afford it, and those prisoners who could normally sent out for it. In addition he sold tea and coffee and would dress a beefsteak if required. Newspapers were also available here, and the place appears to have been the centre of the upper society within the prison. Prisoners were at liberty to send for beer "outdoors" though Nixon would not allow them more than a pot at a time. Nevertheless he felt that this was rarely done, for the beer he supplied was of the best quality. Yet in 1818 the quality of this beer was subject to enquiry, the prisoners having complained about it. The complaint was regarded with sufficient seriousness for the brewer and some of his employees to be called to give evidence, possibly because at about the same time there had been near-riots at the Kings Bench over this very matter. It was still drunk, however, to the tune of 870 barrels of porter in that year, and 63 of ale, providing the warden with a profit of £326. The committee was rather critical of such profits arising from the sale of alcohol, as this could only encourage the warden to be interested in increasing his profits at the expense of good order.[152]

The sale and use of spirits in prisons had been barred by an act of George II's reign, and this applied to the Fleet and King's Bench as well as to the county gaols. In 1730 a newspaper reported, "On Tuesday a woman was detected by the turnkey of the Fleet prison carrying some spirituous liquors into that gaol, contrary to the act of parliament, and being brought before Slingsby Bethel, esq., at Guildhall, was committed to Bridewell. She's the first convicted in this city since the act commenced."[153] Further legislation imposed penalties on the warden if such liquor entered his prison, but his prisoners felt no such restraint, with the result that by the 1800s they had formed "whistling shops" where rum, gin, and other such spirits could be purchased. This term is explained in Pierce Egan's *Life in London*. His friend, the haberdasher, kept such a shop in his room, which "always abounds with some prime articles", but for which the customer was required to "whistle".[154] Here would resort the racket players for their "whet". Mr Pickwick discovered from Sam Weller that the turnkeys took good care to "seize the hoard of everybody but them as pays 'em", and took his master to a room where a flat stone bottle, "which might hold a couple of quarts", was produced from beneath a bedstead. A pamphlet, *Poor Logic in the Fleet Prison*, in the Guildhall Noble collection, has a woodcut cover depicting such a shop. In it are shown the master and mistress of the whistling shop, the racket players, a poor tradesman, smugglers, and debtors, all with their glasses of "tape", white for "max" and red for cognac, all "contraband articles". Nixon was examined carefully on this score too by the 1814 committee. He admitted that it was easy to smuggle gin into the prison: "we never search any persons coming into the prison, and the women will very easily bring it under their petticoats." If he heard of any gin shops he would take the room from its occupier, and stave in the barrel in front of the prisoners. But he was well aware that they existed, normally opening after the tap and coffee house had closed. One has the impression that the prison officers would only act on information supplied to them.[155]

The public kitchen, once in the basement, later in the courtyard, was where meat and provisions were sold; and a cook, elected and employed by the prisoners on a half-yearly basis (in case they became too impudent in office) was required to boil or roast meat free of charge until two in the afternoon, after which time it would cost two pence to heat a meat or pie dish, and one penny to dress vegetables. The cook also agreed to provide boiling water free to prisoners for breakfasts and teas, of up to two quarts per person per meal. The old kitchen was leased to the tapster, along with fifteen prisoners' rooms. These were all in the cellar, as was the public dining room known as Bartholomew's Fair, which adjoined the kitchen. In 1775 John Cartwright had leased these at public auction. In this kitchen, wrote Tobias Smollett in his *Peregrine Pickle*, "there are some hewers of wood and drawers of water ... who have had forests or fishponds of their own". A bakehouse had been provided by 1815. Nixon let it be known that he had no profit from any of these amenities.[156] There were other places where people could eat, such as the coffee house or the tap room, but the Fleet never seems to have imitiated the practice of the King's Bench prison, where several enterprising prisoners opened restaurants in their rooms. It was noted that prisoners would move from one place of eating to the other, "when they are in debt in one place they go to another, and when they are able to pay off the debt, they come back again", so repeating in prison, as Joanna Innes observes, the very practices that had characterised their life beforehand.[157]

Although the Fleet did not possess the privilege of having its own market and stalls within the prison yard as did the King's Bench, provisions could still be bought in the courtyard where they were cried as "in the public streets". The warden provided servants whose task was to obtain the prisoners' requirements in the market outside the prison without fee or reward. The prisoners regarded this as an unsatisfactory arrangement, and felt that these servants went to the first rather than to the cheapest stalls. Two chandlers' shops for dry goods were operating in the prison by 1814. These had the warden's permission, and it appears they were of recent date. James Holt, who kept one of these shops, had applied for it when it was available for letting, paying his predecessor twenty-three pounds for the fixtures, scales, and shelves, but this price did not include the "good will" of the business nor any stock. He kept his shop in number two, the hall gallery, paying the master of the room 8*s*.3*d*. per week and allowing him his own room besides. Though he kept his prices down as far as possible to those applying "outside", many prisoners still went "out of doors" for all they needed, and the 1818 report suggested that either the average charge of these shops was two or three pence in the shilling dearer than those outside, or the weight or the purity of the articles was likely to be adulterated. The other shop keeper wanted to be able to sell small table beer in his shop, "something cheaper than porter", but the 1818 report made it clear that such beer had always been sold there and there was no inhibition on its sale.[158]

Various entertainments took place within the prison. One was in celebration of the 1729 report, sponsored by the ringleaders of the anti-warden party. A newspaper cutting states:

Last night a may-pole in 90 foot of length, adorned with garlands, their majesty's arms, and a fine vane, was erected at the Fleet prison, at the joint charge of Captain Macpheadris, Captain Sinclair, and other gentlemen there residing, as a monument of their gratitude and commemoration of their deliverance from insufferable hardships. A large quantity of punch and of other liquors was likewise given to the prisoners in general, and all imaginable demonstrations of joy was expressed on the occasion.

On another occasion in the 1740s an entertainment was given by the warden:

On Thursday the warden of the Fleet gave a very sumptuous entertainment to the gentlemen of the master's side, and a sirloin of beef and strong beer to the prisoners of the common side, and the women had plenty of wine among themselves; their majesty's and all the royal family's healths went merrily round, and almost every room in the house was illuminated.[159]

Such activities continued until the closing of the prison, taking place on such occasions as the granting of insolvency acts, when the prisoners generally subscribed towards the cost of such an entertainment.

When Mr Pickwick first entered the prison yard, on his first coming into the Fleet, he found that "dirty, slipshod women passed and repassed, on their way to the cooking house, in one corner of the yard; children screamed and fought, ... the tumbling of the skittles, the shouts of the players, mingled perpetually with these and a hundred other sounds; and all was noise and tumult." This yard, at the back of the prison, was known as the *bare*, while the courtyard in front of the prison, in Pickwick's time, was called the *painted yard* as an artist had painted on its high walls various scenes of men of war in full sail. On the *bare* tennis, rackets, "Mississippi", fives, skittles, and other games were played,[160] possibly taking the place of the bowling green of which John Taylor, the water poet, wrote: "'or bowling, there's large space."[161] This yard was probably a survival of the medieval garden of the Fleet, where Moses Pitt would "walk and read in the little garden of the Fleet", which was praised by Hatton for its pleasantness,[162] and about which Huggins complained that his prisoners tore up the bowling green and uprooted the trees.[163] The prisoners elected on a half-yearly basis a racket and a skittles master. They received a small fee from each player, as well as the fines of two or three pence for those who put their balls "over the wall". In all they probably obtained a guinea a week.[164] The election address of John Aldridge, of two

The rackets court or the prison yard. As depicted by the *Illustrated London News* of 14 March 1846.

coffee gallery, for this post, was printed in 1841. He told his fellow prisoners he realised his responsibilities if elected, for the health as well as the amusement of many of his fellow prisoners would be entrusted to him.[165] Many strangers also joined the prisoners on these courts, for the Fleet prisoners were regarded as eminent players.[166] Several of the prisoners opened up their rooms for indoor billiards or card games. Howard noted that the large room over the chapel was kept as a billiard room by a prisoner, who also resided and slept in it. Paget in his poem thus describes the "amusements" of the prison:

> Therefore cabels engage of various sorts,
> To walk, to drink, to play at different sports;
> Here on the oblong table's verdant plain,
> The ivory ball bounds and rebounds again;
> There at backgammon two sit *tete-a-tete,*
> And curse alternatively their adverse fate;
> These are at cribbage, those at whist engaged,
> And, as they lose, by turns become enraged:
> Some of a more sedentary temper, read
> Chance-medley books, which duller dullness breeds;
> Or politics in coffee-room, some pore
> The papers and advertisements thrice over:
> Warmed with the alderman, some sit up late,
> To fix the insolvent bill and nation's fate.[167]

VISITORS AND FAMILIES

Visitors were admitted freely into the prison, provided they were sober, and they were permitted to join in all the prison activities. Howard found butchers from the Fleet market allowed into the Fleet "as at another public house", and, not unnaturally, considered that this lessened the dread of confinement.[168] Warden Eyles, petitioning in 1742 against his prosecution for the escape of a smuggler from the prison, wrote:

> all persons are at liberty to resort to the prisoners till ten at night and as there
> are two hundred prisoners within the walls the number of people who come
> are sometimes three thousand a day, and very often above one thousand
> people come in the winter time from the close of the evening till ten o'clock,
> which makes it extremely difficult to guard against the escapes of smugglers

who are desperate fellows and by a small disguise may easily escape through the gates of the prison.[169]

Hughson in 1817 considered that the prison gates were opened "once a minute".[170] Those who entered the prison were the rulers, prisoners' wives, relations, friends and attorneys, tourists, those who came to play rackets or to participate in the various clubs run in the coffee house or tap, and even those who wished to make use of the prison for its other conveniences, of whom it was said, "When the filthy butchers' boys come in, there are no gentlemen who would like to sit down after them."[171] The gates were opened at five a.m. in summer and two hours later in winter, while they closed at ten, when strangers were required to quit the prison as the cry went forth, "Strangers all out". But the gates never closed until half-past ten, and the requirement that the "oil, candles and fires" be put out at eleven in the tap and coffee house was rarely observed.[172] Many visitors, including women, stayed overnight, for with such numbers resorting to the prison it proved impossible to ensure any adequate check, with the result that, as Nixon remarked, the Fleet had become the largest brothel in the metropolis. It appears that until the late eighteenth century there was no supervision at all during these night hours.[173]

Many prisoners brought their families into the prison to reside with them, for it was cheaper than running two households, while accommodation outside the prison walls was expensive and limited.[174] This trend appears to have been a recent one by the 1760s, and a short-lived attempt was made to regulate it in the 1790s. In 1793 it was reported that the crier gave warning half an hour before the gates closed that all the women and children should leave the prison, for they were not permitted to remain within its walls by night.[175] But this rule of court was ignored by all parties within the prison, as it was impossible to enforce and would, in any case, antagonise the prisoners and cause many considerable hardships. The number of such people living in was always considerable. Howard found that on 6 April 1776 there were 213 prisoners on the master's side, 30 on the common, together with 475 wives (including those "of an appellation not so honourable"), and children. In 1792 200 children, without schooling, resided in the prison with their parents. In 1803 Neild discovered 229 prisoners, 148 wives and 391 children, 768 in all, while in 1815 there were 50 women and 77 children actually living within its walls.[176] Jones Pearce complained that these wives insulted the turnkeys and caroused with other prisoners, sitting half the day in the lobby.[177]

A chamber observed by Pickwick was probably typical of many. In it a man and his wife and a whole crowd of children were making up a scanty bed on the ground, while the younger children passed the night on a few chairs. In many instances the rooms were shared in addition by the prisoners' chums, and in 1815 it was said that the practice of two married couples and a single man sharing a room was common. It was argued, however, that any chum had the right to refuse this arrangement and so prevent a family moving in or even entering the room during the daytime.[178]

Many children were brought up in the prison. One was Charles Lewis whose obituary notice mentioned a friend of his, an orphan, Tom Clarke, whose parents had died in the prison and who was accordingly brought up by the prisoners' bounty. He "made himself useful in the fives court and tennis courts, making the balls and rackets required".[179] Such children, argued Oliver Nugent, a King's Bench prisoner, in the 1792 report, though they could be very useful to their parents as messengers, were being brought up in a prison. This, he concluded, was "very prejudicial to their morals". He felt that if they were sent to their parishes, to be cared for by the parish overseers, "it would be better in every respect".[180] Schools had been established for the children of debtors in the neighbourhood, reported Nixon in 1814, and if he was informed by a parent, he would send the children there at his own expense. He added that he had the power to compel their attendance at chapel, and if they misbehaved, to lock them out of the prison.[181]

Sam Weller had a friendly action brought against him so as to be with his master, Mr Pickwick, and though the circumstances of his entry were a little different from most, many debt prisoners brought in their own servants to attend to their needs.[182] In addition Howard discovered that the tapster and several of the prisoners kept dogs.[183]

This vast number of family members, domestic retainers, and canines accompanying the debt prisoners, could only make a difficult and overcrowded situation even more intolerable, and must have been a powerful source of friction. The 1814 report relating to the King's Bench suggested that these factors "must augment every inconvenience to a most alarming degree",[184] and in 1818 this was reported of the Fleet:

> The only certain remedy for this inconvenience would be found in the entire exclusion of all women (not prisoners themselves) from sleeping in the prison; but though this has been adopted in the King's Bench prison, where it has been recommended by the additional motive of procuring better accommodation for the prisoners, we have not thought ourselves called upon to extend this prohibition to the Fleet, where the number of rooms is much more adequate to the demand; and considering the hardship of the prisoners being deprived of the society of their wives and families, the difficulty, and in many cases the impossibility of procuring lodging and subsistence for them near enough even for occasional visits at the prison, especially in cases where the usual residence and settlement of the prisoners are in distant counties, together with other inconveniences attending the separation, and the impossibility of preventing the access of women in the day-time; we incline to think that the admission of women and children may be controlled, as far as it is expedient to do so, by the regulation which we have suggested for this purpose.[185]

This regulation was a projected rule that prohibited all but married couples from living in the same room without the warden's permission. The King's Bench rule was never enforced. Nixon, in fact, discovering that the wives could be as riotous and troublesome as their husbands, had on occasions told prisoners that they must provide for their families outside the prison house, and threatened to lock them out.[186] But it was never an easy situation.

A DISORDERLY HOUSE

An overcrowded prison, filled with restless, idle, and under-occupied men, many of whom were regarded as dishonest, could only lead to a state of disorder. The anonymous writer of *A Speech without Doors* described many prisoners as "choked up, killed, I may say murdered, by an idle life, ill-air, and a most pinching hunger", living in despair; with "business lost and reputation gone for ever, ... contaminated and corrupted". Such men could easily lose all restraint about following dishonest practices.[187] The position was exacerbated by the availability of alcohol.

Though much of this disorder, the prisoners claimed, was caused by the high spirits of their fellow prisoners, being more in the nature of misdemeanours than violent outbursts, the actual position appears to belie this statement.[188] Warden Harris in the late 1610s complained that whatever his prisoners did "they can but be in prison",[189] and his catalogue of their abuses appears very similar to those described by Huggins a century later. Huggins complained that his prisoners broke his furniture; threw filth out of the windows; destroyed the prison stocks, notices, and the new houses of easement; tore up the trees in the courtyard and around the bowling green; kept their rooms in defiance of his officers, and amongst other outrages, libelled his good name.[190] Dennis Planchy, writing from the Fleet in 1664, argued that he had been in most of the prisons in Europe, but "had learnt more roguery in that ... than in all". He continued, "the citizens of London cannot too soon know the intrigues they are gulled with", adding that compared to the seven "arrant rogues" who were his fellow prisoners "in a dank hole", he was almost honest.[191] While one may suspect ulterior reasons for his statement, since he asked for a private chamber, the liberty of the prison and an allowance in exchange for some information, his sentiments about his fellow prisoners are confirmed by many others. Moses Pitt wrote of his fellow prisoners that "they turn night into day and day into night, by drinking, whoring, dicing, roaring, swearing, cursing, blasphemy, and all other ways of debauchery."[192] Howard noted how much riot was occasioned by the beer and wine clubs. Their reputation was well known. At the trial of Margery Akers at the Old Bailey in 1740 for the theft of a gold watch from a fellow prisoner of her husband, Mr Murden, it was said that Murden requested the turnkey to send for a constable. The reply was made, none would come, for the constables were apprehensive "of being ill-used at the Fleet".[193] William Smith wrote "there are few hours of the night without riot and drunkenness", and Paget described in his poem, "some sots, the ill-mannered drunk, a shameless fight! Rant noisy through the galleys all night."[194] Scenes of rioting, drunkenness and disorder, pickpocketing, robbery, fighting, and prostitution, were complaints made by both Harris in the 1610s and Nixon two centuries later. The prostitutes who made the Fleet "the largest brothel in the metropolis" often caused riots within the prison, and it was noted that one crier stole in order to obtain the reward for finding the stolen article. Many of the prisoners complained of these scenes of riot and noise, particularly at night, but Nixon made clear that he and his turnkeys would never interfere in such matters, nor had they ever been called in to "quell any disturbance".[195] David Hughson in his *Walks through London* of 1816 argued that these disturbances had become worse since the passing of the insolvency act of 1813, which permitted a three month-imprisonment before a person was released by a permanent insolvency court. "The prisoners are less moral than they were before", he wrote, "for prisoners in general contrive to procure money to maintain them during the three months, and they are less careful of their behaviour."[196] Nixon clearly agreed with this statement, adding that there was more intoxication since the "late act",[197] while the 1818 report recommended:

> Instances, however, of riot and disorder have occasionally occurred from the unrestrained admission of women, from the effects of liquor, and other causes; these disorders are stated to have been much more prevalent of late, in consequence of the number who have procured themselves to be thrown into prison to take the benefit of the insolvent act passed in the fifty-third reign of your majesty, ... and who, during the three months of their imprisonment mentioned in the said act, have been induced to squander the money they possess in dissipation, instead of reserving it for their creditors. These disorders it may be difficult and indeed impossible entirely to prevent; and though we hope they may in some degree be lessened by the further regulations that have occurred to us, we are well aware that the most effectual remedy must be expected from the constant and active vigilance of the warden and other officers of the prison, and from the due exercise of the powers vested in the warden and deputy warden, of punishing all offenders by such means as the regulations of the prison gave them the opportunity of resorting to.[198]

Perhaps the real offence was that these men were using the money which rightly belonged to their creditors for their own comfort and advantage whilst in prison. The Fleet was an admirable prison from their point of view, and this may be why it received a greater intake of prisoners during its Indian summer of the 1810s and 1820s than ever before.

Although the Fleet never reached the level of the King's Bench prison when Sir John Holt, lord chief justice at the King's Bench, in order to suppress the "mutinous factions, clamours and otherwise of the ill behaviour, by means whereof diverse insolences and bloodsheds do often happen to be committed within the said prison", permitted the marshall to summon to his assistance "all mayors, sheriffs, bailiffs, constables and headboroughs, and to all other his majesty's officers and ministers whom these may concern",[199] it did not fall too far short. In

1705 an attempt was made to evict a turnkey;[200] twelve years later military assistance had to be summoned in order to deal with various smugglers who had "grown very outrageous" and had threatened to break the gaol,[201] and in 1727 Bambridge also had to call in military aid to suppress a great riot and mutiny in the prison.[202] Military assistance was again requested by the warden in 1822 to quell a riot caused, it was said, at umbrage at his conduct, but this information came from the scurrilous *Real John Bull*.[203] But the wardens generally preferred to use the methods of arbitration and compromise rather than resort to force.

Individual prisoners also caused considerable problems to the warden. These included the counterfeiters,[204] and those concerned in seditious organisations.[205] One incident may be noted. It concerned two Fleet prisoners, P W Duffin and Thomas Lloyd, a citizen of the newly established United States of America. They had published what was made out to be a libellous publication by a government frightened of any revolutionary movements in that dramatic year of 1793. This "libel" related to the republic of France's glorious example and wished success against all tyrants. It had been placed on the chapel door of the Fleet. For this they were pilloried, amidst a great demonstration, and transferred to Newgate. Though it was alleged that they had conspired to break out of the prison and escape with others, the riot in fact was no more than a demonstration against the laws of debt imprisonment.[206]

Smugglers always caused anxiety to the wardens, partly because their debts, mainly to the Exchequer, were substantial, and also because they were strong and desperate people. There were two serious incidents which concerned smugglers, one of which was thought worthy of note by a government department. In 1742 the excise officers became aware that a group of Fleet prisoners, accused of smuggling, had managed to continue their profitable operations inside the prison. They therefore searched the premises, and discovered about one hundredweight of tea. The official report continued:

> But before the seizure was made, the turnkey who attended them and pretended to assist them, gave signals to the other prisoners in the yard, who attacked the said officers in great numbers, by whom the said officers were so mobbed and beat that they were forced to relinquish their seizure.

This was in the April of that year. In the following September information was received that:

> Run tea was again lodged there. Some excise officers, with a party of forty soldiers from the Tower for their assistance, went to search, but when they came to the prison gate they were denied entrance for a considerable time, and till a great quantity of tea might have been carried off, which probably was the case, the room, where our officer had information the tea was lodged, smelling as strong as any tea warehouse.
>
> That on the 14th past [of November] on another information of a large quantity of rum being lodged in the said prison, several excise officers with a party of fifty soldiers, endeavoured to make a search, but the officers and soldiers were obstructed in their duty and so abused by the prisoners by throwing brickbats, dirt and tearing their clothes that they were obliged to retire.

The attorney general, to whom this paper was addressed by the excise solicitors, was reminded that the warden had failed to give any effectual assistance to the searchers, "under pretence", as they put it, "that it is not in his power to keep his prisoners in order, or to prevent such tea coming in". But the hint was made, that if not he, certainly his officers, were in league with the smugglers.[207]

Another similar incident took place in 1778. A newspaper report read:

> Yesterday morning at about five o 'clock, by virtue of an information, custom house officers, assisted by a file of musketeers, entered the Fleet prison, in search of run goods, on which the prisoners were much alarmed, and some little resistance was made; but after the soldiers had knocked two or three of them down, they retired, and left them to search for the goods. They found in two rooms a quantity of tea, laces, piece goods, etc, to a considerable amount, which they took to the custom house. The officers had obtained leave from the chief justice of the Common Pleas to enter with their arms to prevent any mischief being done to them by the prisoners.[208]

THE PRISONERS' COMMITTEE

The existence of a prisoners' committee had already been noted, and the suggestion made that its co-operation was needed for the good ordering of the prison. Such a society was by no means unique.[209] One existed at the King's Bench prison in the 1600s. Here the prisoners had formed a court, with the oldest debt prisoner as the presiding judge. In one instance a prisoner who had served a writ against a fellow prisoner was brought before this court, and sentenced to forfeit his cloak (which was pawned for drink) and to eat the writ. If he declined he was to be pumped and shaved.[210]

The relationship between the gaoler and his prisoners was always a delicate one under these arrangements, and when either side went beyond the limits of that carefully monitored balance, trouble would ensue. This was seen in the activity of 1724-8 when a weak deputy on the one hand, and a strong warden on the other (who tried to redress the position and turn it to his own advantage), were resisted by a strong "committee" of prisoners. Huggins complained of their absolute government, in which they acted in open defiance of his authority as warden; kept chambers by force and disposed of others; appointed a steward and a court of inspectors and held a mock court, all in order, as he put it, to better support their "turbulent behaviour and effect their conspiracy and design".[211] This court, Huggins declared, demanded 5s. a term from each prisoner in order to pay the expenses of their case in the court of Common Pleas for a reduction in the fees of the prison; inflicted punishments on prisoners who declined to obey their orders or conform to their sentiments, and terrified the others into a "seeming compliance" with their views. The deputy warden, Guybon, was so terrified of their influence that he declined to enter the prison without their leave, and removed his office completely outside the prison house. Not surprisingly, Huggins traced all the disorders in the prison to the existence of this society. His assessment does not appear to be unfounded, though the prisoners concerned regarded it as no more than an agreement amongst themselves to support good behaviour.[212]

This society of prisoners appears to have continued its activities after its triumph with the 1729 committee, undoubtedly with enhanced prestige, though it never received any official recognition and little is recorded of its history. Wood, writing in 1733, does not mention it, although Smollett in his *Peregrine Pickle* describes a "court of enquiry" which comprised the more respected inhabitants of the place. This sentenced two offenders. One, a solicitor, was "pumped" for pickpocketing, and the other, a naval lieutenant, accused of riot, was handed over to the warden for his own sentencing. Howard, when he visited the prison in 1776, discovered such a society which had its own committee room, and regarded its task as that of obtaining peaceable government within the prison; the hearing of disputes and complaints; the production of petitions for acts of insolvency; the levying of fines for blasphemy, swearing, riot, drunkenness, and damaging the light; acting as a channel between the prisoners and the warden, and providing scavengers to keep the prison clean and to light the lamps provided by this committee. In one sense the committee fulfilled the same function as a court leet or trade guild, and probably received the assent of most of the prisoners. Howard and the other prison visitors, while they considered that some of the committee's activities were good, especially those which eased the day-to-day condition of prison life, criticised its demand of garnish from each new prisoner on the master's side, of two shillings for wine and eighteen pence for the use of the house (its major source of revenue), its use of fines and the pump for punishments, and its refusal to allow the common side prisoners to associate with members of the master's side or to share their facilities.[213]

A similar but far better organised society at the King's Bench prison printed a list of thirty-seven rules "to be obeyed and observed by every member of the college", many of which, thought Howard, were "arbitrary and improper".[214] Its regulations concerned the allocation of rooms and the custom of chumming, the provision of criers and the arrangements about the cleaning of the prison. In addition "members" were not permitted to write in the name of the prisoners to any body without the consent of a general meeting. The Fleet probably had similar rules. It is not known, however, if that society's stipulation that the protection of its "court" would not be given until each new prisoner had paid a shilling to each of its various officials, was also observed at the Fleet.[215]

The Fleet society, when co-operation was achieved between it and the prison warden, clearly worked for the general good of the prison. This emerges in the report given of a general meeting of the master's side debtors held in the coffee room of the Fleet, in 1808. This meeting appointed a committee consisting of three representatives from each gallery, and their task was defined as keeping the house quiet, peaceable, clean, and wholesome. The warden accepted various resolutions from this meeting, designed to improve the conditions of the prison. These referred to the cooking of meat and vegetables, the use of the coffee room, the price of ale and porter, and the provision of cooking facilities. Mr Nixon was thus thanked for his "assistance and the prompt manner adopted by him for redressing the wrongs and injustices experienced by the prisoners". However he refused to grant two of their requests. Stating that he was forced to bury the bodies of prisoners who had died in the prison, whose relatives did not claim them, at an average cost to himself of between ten and twenty pounds, he felt unable to relinquish his right to receive a fee from relatives who claimed the corpse of a prisoner from him.   He also felt unable to furnish the chambers with beds, bedsteads, and bedding, without fee, as no authority could be adduced for such a claim.[216] The college probably continued until the end of the prison's existence. As Innes writes of the King's Bench "college": it "did much to fill the vacuum left by the indolence of the prison officers", though she notes that the court of King's Bench endeavoured on several occasions to limit the rights of these prisoners' societies.[217]

A vivid description of the way the prisoners' court operated is provided in evidence given to the 1814 committee. John Welsh, who called its members "a set of men, who had left honour and integrity at the gates", complained about their activities. "In what way?" asked the chairman, to receive the reply:

> By threats; and by those threats, arising from different causes; if any exaction shall be made in the prices of the rooms, and a man shall dare to make a complaint to the warden, whose ears are ever open to the complaints of the prisoners, that man is immediately treated most insultingly, and is in danger when he walks the place; I have (and that is known to Mr Nixon) been ill treated twice, because I have stood forward to oppose the irregularities. Mr Nixon has been kind enough to open the gate and give me the *rules*, this he did on one occasion some time back, as well as on a late occasion; I have had two hundred people hooting me through the place.

Another incident concerned one Perry Price, which related to the private arrangements made regarding room rents by the various chumming procedures. He too felt he had been charged more than was warranted, and accordingly complained to Nixon. Walsh, who was informed of this, testified:

> A man of the name of Price ... had been obliged to make a complaint to Mr Nixon of the exorbitant charges that were made for his room; Mr Nixon, obeying the orders of the court, took the room from the parties who had oppressed this man; this was immediately communicated to the other prisoners within the walls, and there was a hue and cry immediately; the man could neither go in nor out of his room without being in danger; at last they prepared a mock trial; they had all the symbols of a court of justice, constables and tipstaffs, etc, etc; they condemned him; directed him to pay a

fine of 20s. to the man he complained against, and ten gallons of beer; he refused to pay it, and they put a sack on him, and then the ordeal was to put him under the pump; they actually put the sack over him and drew him away; I had a friend of mine who dined with me, and we heard the noise, and got up to the window, when we saw the man acting as tipstaff, with a staff in his hand, holding Price by the collar, with threats, and the others were standing round him, and another man came up, whose name is White, he got 20s. of Mr Price, and he was to return him 10s. for as they approached the pump, they mitigated the penalty from 20s. to 10s. ... [on gaining the money] they led the man away with a great deal of hooting, and then they turned the corner, and I saw no more of him; but I afterwards heard he was had into the tap room, and the ten gallons of beer was had in, and they got terribly drunk.

Perry Price, with grave reluctance and obviously anxious to play down the whole incident, stated that his offence was that, in wishing to dress for dinner, he put on his shirt in front of a woman in his room. No mention was made of any complaint he had made about the room charges. Nixon replied that this was an exceptional case.[218] Under these circumstances it is hardly surprising that the suggested new rules of 1818, said to have been at the warden's insistence, ordered that no assembly of prisoners for the examination of the conduct of any prisoner or for any reason whatsoever, or for any other purpose, should be had without the permission of the warden or his deputy.[219] It probably had little effect, for the prisoners continued to meet, probably to mete out "justice" to those who complained about the prison economy, and to elect their officers, such as the cook and the racket masters, in the usual manner.

PUNISHING THE DISORDERLY

The right to punish their fellow prisoners for minor offences was obviously one claimed by these societies. All major offences were dealt with by the warden, although most of the holders of that office complained that their punishments had little effect in quieting the prison.[220] For lesser offences the warden was permitted to turn prisoners over to the common side, dispossess them of their rooms, restrain them from the liberty of the "yards and walks" or place them in the stocks, which though allowed by the new rules of 1729 was regarded even then as an obsolete custom.[221] More serious offenders were placed in the dungeon. This

had been rebuilt in the time of Bambridge, contrary to the instructions of Lord
Chief Justice King who had turned down an application for its building by Huggins
and Guybon on the grounds that there should be no prison within a prison,
although the rules permitted the warden to have a strong room or dungeon in the
prison house in order to ensure the quietness of the prison.[222] Its building had
been requested for keeping those prisoners safe who were in danger of escaping,
and hence King prefaced his remarks by the words, forgotten later, "they might
raise their walls higher". The judges later commanded Gambier to rebuild the
dungeon after he had on his own authority pulled it down, although Oglethorpe
was disgusted by their attitude. Smollett in *Peregrine Pickle* described the
dungeon as situated on the south side of the ditch, infested with toads and vermin,
and "surcharged with noisome damps and impervious to the least ray of light".
Others complained of its lack of a fireplace, and its odious smell (caused by being
next to the prison dunghill), and also by being the place where the dead were kept
before the coroner's inquest. Most prisoners placed in this dungeon were also
ironed, for both Huggins and Bambridge claimed that this was the only effective
means of restraining disorderly prisoners and of keeping the prison in quiet and
safety. The use of irons was prohibited after 1729, though they had been upheld
as necessary by the court of Common Pleas but five years earlier (or so Bambridge
alleged).[223] The strong room built by Gambier on the coffee room landing was
described as "sufficiently secure, well lighted ..., provided with a fireplace", by the
1818 report, though the plans of the building in 1820 also indicate another strong
room alongside the beggars' grate.[224] In one of these rooms Thomas Lloyd was
placed in 1793 after his alleged attempt to open the prison. He claimed he was
given no chance to obtain his bed, and was not permitted a jug of water or even an
urinal.[225]

        Although Ford, deputy warden in the 1690s, alleged that discharges were
given to prisoners in order to quieten the house, he probably meant no more than
that they were transferred to other prisons. Guybon thus wrote that when
prisoners "were turbulent and unruly or quarrelsome ... it hath been usual for the
safety and quiet of the house to procure *habeas corpus* to remove them from one
place to another".[226] This place was normally the King's Bench prison.[227]
Nevertheless it was still possible for the removed prisoners to obtain their own
writ of *habeas corpus* and remove themselves back to the Fleet, so defeating the

warden's object. However the cost of their removal was often prohibitive. It included the charge for the writ, the tipstaff's fees, a set of discharge fees at the King's Bench and a new set of commitment fees at the Fleet. Those in the *rules* also had to find a new set of securities for their safe imprisonment.[228] Archibald Paterson, removed by the warden to the King's Bench in 1726, returned three days later, expressing his surprise at the warden's demand of £2.6s.8d. as a new commitment fee. Major Wilson, some years earlier, on his return, discovered he was not particularly welcome, for he was assaulted and placed in a dungeon. His injuries were so serious he claimed that he had to be bled for the preservation of his health "in his chains".[229] The 1729 rules forbade the warden to use this practice of obtaining *habeas corpus* transfer writs for his prisoners, but it is obvious that the practice still continued.

The number of prisoners who were transferred to the King's Bench from the Fleet by the use of this writ was substantial.[230] Of the 138 prisoners who entered the prison in 1686, 26 (18%) were so removed; in 1743 six out of 146 (4%); in 1779 25 out of 251 (10%).[231] In 1772, for example, a considerable number of prisoners who were transferred to the King's Bench by the use of this writ returned the same day or soon afterwards by bringing their own writ and paying a new set of commitment fees. Fisher Littleton was sent there twice, in February and June, but returned on the same day on both occasions. Charles Douglas Bowden did the same in February, as did Corfield Clare the following November.[232] The rules of the prisoners' society at the King's Bench provided for this eventuality. If a prisoner was removed to the Fleet he would forfeit his room unless he returned within seven days.[233] However, it must not be assumed that all these people were sent to the King's Bench by the warden as a form of punishment, particularly so as that practice was outlawed by the 1729 rules! Many prisoners transferred themselves, spending winter at the Fleet and summer in the more salubrious area of the King's Bench.[234] Judges disliked this practice, and were known to have remanded those prisoners whom they suspected had brought "their *habeas*" on a friendly action or merely for their own pleasure.[235] Others were sent there by their creditors as a means of harassment, perhaps with the aim of forcing their debtors to reconsider the advantages of putting their affairs in order when placed in a more unfamiliar setting. Mackay noted this practice which he thought occasioned a great hardship to poor prisoners and was most unreasonable.[236]

ESCAPES, SUCCESSFUL AND UNSUCCESSFUL

The warden's main task was to keep his prisoners secure, and thus escapes were regarded as an abuse of his office and offences against the law of credit. Consequently the most persistent complaints against the wardens of the prison and their officials, at the end of the seventeenth and the beginning of the eighteenth centuries, concerned the number of escapes by prisoners in their charge, escapes in which it was widely held they were implicated. This accusation was known in the earliest days of the prison, for an act of Richard II made prison gaolers who permitted escapes liable to the forfeiture of their office.[237] The preamble to the act of 1702 which endeavoured to further regulate this matter stated that many prisoners "by bribes and illegal practices" frequently obtained "liberty to escape" to the great damage of honest creditors, the decrease of personal credit and discouragement of trade, as well as offending against "all the good and wholesome laws heretofore made to restrain such practices".[238] Parliamentary concern was not only expressed by the numerous acts which endeavoured to prevent escapes, but also in the inquiries into the Fleet prison which took place during the 1690s and 1729. It was equally and as vividly expressed by the dismissals of Tilly as warden in 1708 for permitting escapes, and of Bambridge in 1729, who merited the following sentence in the statute which relieved him of his wardenship: "through the great danger of escapes and of the continuance of the cruelties and barbarities before mentioned" should he continue in office.

An escape was defined as a prisoner leaving the prison house save by a writ of *habeas corpus* or by a rule of court, and by implication, for those who had security to enter the *rules*, in passing beyond its defined bounds. An escape by a prisoner on mesne process was not regarded as seriously as the escape of a debtor who had passed to the final process of execution. In the latter case the warden was responsible for the debts of such an escaped prisoner.[239] The failure of the warden to produce such a prisoner within one day also constituted an escape, for which, as he was reminded in the writ of *supersedeas* which admitted each prisoner to his care, "you will answer .. at your peril". Even the temporary absence of such a prisoner, irrespective of whether he returned or not, was regarded as an escape.

The 1696 act, noted earlier, was passed by an anxious legislature in an attempt to deal with this problem of escapes from prisons, and in particular from the Fleet and the King's Bench. By it gaolers were prohibited from delaying processes laid against them for escapes by the use of writs of error. Creditors were permitted to sequestrate the prison profits in order to obtain the amount of the debt and the costs awarded to them in the escape actions. No retaking of a prisoner could be pleaded; no writ of error was to be brought without special bail, and the gaoler was held liable for any of his deputy's or officers' actions regarding escapes, unless oath was made that such action had been taken without his knowledge. Finally the act ordered that any gaoler or his officers who permitted and assisted escapes would forfeit a sum of five hundred pounds each, and be rendered incapable of holding any such office in the future.[240]

Both the warden of the Fleet and the marshall of the King's Bench evaded these requirements by the use of trustees, deputies, and mortgages. It became impossible, as a result, for the agitated creditors to discover who was responsible for the payment of the debts of their escaped prisoners. John Berisford well expressed their frustration: "All the mighty advantages which that act was thought to produce prove imperfect and abortive, and our great expectations are dwindled into air."[241] One creditor, however, took matters into his own hands. When judgment was made against the marshall of the King's Bench, Lentall, for the escape of his prisoner, Paine, with debts of over two thousand pounds, George Moore seized part of the marshall's estate in Oxfordshire, and sold goods worth one hundred pounds before he was turned out.[242] However, the seventy pounds cost of an action awarded against Church, deputy warden of the Fleet, for the escape of one Warr, was paid in part to his creditor John Praed, but the creditors lost in all a sum of nearly six and a half thousand pounds, as the warden successfully claimed that Warr had been theoretically transferred to the King's Bench prison before he had escaped from the Fleet. Church eventually fled after a number of adverse judgments had been made against him.[243]

This situation was not ended until the Fleet mortgages were abolished and Tilly deprived of his office of warden in 1708, while the King's Bench mortgages were not ended until a further commission of inquiry into that prison, pursued by the still redoubtable General Oglethorpe, in 1754. Until that earlier date, so far as the Fleet was concerned, numerous complaints were made about the warden's compliance in the escapes of his prisoners. Tilly, it was alleged in a case already mentioned, had allowed a Mr Barkstead to escape to Pennsylvania for a sum of fifty pounds. Barkstead had had to transfer to the Fleet to obtain such a bargain, as the marshall of the King's Bench required "ten times that amount" for the same privilege. There was even an added bonus with the Fleet, for Tilly offered to go to the buoy in the Nore to see him on board.[244] Though these circumstances were denied by Tilly, the fact that it gained currency is probably a reflection on the warden's conduct in other cases. Yet it must be admitted that if a prisoner escaped from the *rules* his debts were paid by those who had entered into securities for his safe imprisonment, provided they held good and had been taken, while escapes from the prison house were extremely rare. This is not to deny, however, the warden's willingness to permit escapes, a matter which is well documented in the pamphlets of the period as well as in the parliamentary reports.

There can be no doubt that the penalties of the 1696 act were rigorously applied after the mortgages had been resolved. Huggins paid the debts of escaped prisoners on numerous occasions, although he was sometimes able to purchase what was termed the "crown title" if the prisoner was held as a debtor to the king or by exchequer proceedings.[245] One escape cost him five hundred pounds, and he narrowly escaped paying the debts of Sir Alexander Anstruther, of nineteen thousand pounds, only because his was a "technical" escape, and the debtor-knight had received the benefit of "his majesty's grace and favour".[246] Bambridge complained that such escapes were "highly penal to him", and even after his day his successor was charged with the debts of an escaped smuggler, David Boys of Portsmouth, which amounted to over twenty-five thousand pounds, and also those of his two companions. Again Boys's escape seems to have been a "technical" one in that he had been seen several times outside the prison, although he was still within the custody of the warden. In this case the warden wrote an urgent petition to the Treasury requesting that the debts might be compounded into a smaller sum or he be released from his responsibility of finding them. It is not known whether he was successful, though the Treasury possibly regarded this compounding business as a means of reminding the warden of his responsibilities and fining him for his neglect.[247] Even in the late 1810s the warden was still paying out on these escape writs; in 1818 it was estimated that on average these writs cost three hundred pounds per annum.[248] On one occasion the warden's liability was almost turned against him by one Robert Jacques. Jacques had arrested a friend in a fictitious sum of eight hundred pounds and then helped him to escape. For this he was placed in the pillory for one hour, and imprisoned in Newgate for three years.[249]

It was almost impossible to prevent escapes, particularly those from the *rules*. There were only two effective penalties to make prisoners think twice before embarking on such an adventure. Those in the *rules* knew that those who had trusted them by standing as their securities would be required to reimburse the warden to the full amount (and even more) of their guarantee. They were also aware that if they were caught their securitors had the right to imprison them as their debtors on the amount of money they had lost through them. If the securitors failed to meet the debts of the escaped prisoner then the warden had the right to imprison them as his debtors, as also the original debtor for the costs he had incurred.[250] Secondly, the gaoler had the right to send a recaptured prisoner to the county gaol of the county where he was taken. There he was to remain until he had rendered satisfaction. Richard Girling was one of many who discovered this to his cost. He was sent to Newgate on a warrant of escape from the warden of the Fleet.[251] In such a case there was no possibility of returning to the Fleet, even though conditions in Newgate were harsh and gruesome. An act of 1743 provided penalties for those who assisted persons to escape from prisons, whether that escape was successful or not. If the prisoner was held for treason or felony those assisting his escape would be adjudged guilty of felony, and be transported for seven years. Otherwise it would be a misdemeanour, to be punished by a fine or by imprisonment.[252]

There appears to have been little check made on the whereabouts of the prisoners. No roll-call ever seems to have taken place. Indeed the parliamentary commission of 1814 had the pleasure of informing the marshall of the King's Bench that one of his most important prisoners, Lord Cochrane, had escaped.[253] Immediately a prisoner was known to have escaped, a search would be ordered by the warden. This would permit the warden to make a special plea in the subsequent proceedings taken by the creditor for the recovery of his debt. The diligence of the search may be noted from a newspaper cutting of 1741:

> The warden of the Fleet, having had intelligence that James Maule, esq., who lately escaped from that prison, and fled to France, was re-embarked for

England, caused his officers and many other persons to be posted in several
parts of Kent, and other places, to intercept him; some had the good luck to
take him between Greenwich and Shooter's hill, and brought him back to the
Fleet, where he is again closely confined. [254]

Advertisements were placed in the public papers to assist the warden in his
search. One went as follows, and this extract enables us to see why such a strict
examination of a new prisoner's features took place on entry into the prison:

> Escaped out of the Fleet prison, on the 9th day of January instant, Richard
> Taylor, and had not yet been retaken. He was captain of the Loyal Pitt,
> privateer, fitted out at London, and afterwards repaired at Dartmouth. He
> formerly dealt as a lumper at Radcliffe, and had a place in the custom house;
> had been a prisoner in the Marshalsea, whence he was committed to the
> Fleet; appears to be about five foot, five inches high, of a pale complexion,
> white eyebrows, hair light coloured, and has a blue mark on his nose, betwixt
> his eyebrows, and on his cheeks, more on one cheek than the other, seeming
> as if burnt by gunpowder; his nose large, and chin pecked, is long and is
> aged, and stoops in the shoulder, round bodied, but no way bulky, swears
> almost at every word he speaks, and that very hastily.
>
> Whoever will give intelligence of him, so that I may thereby cause him to
> be secured, and brought back to the Fleet prison, shall receive a reward of
> twenty guineas for their trouble, which I hereby promise to pay. Dated the
> 26th of January, 1762. John Eyles. Warden of the Fleet prison. [255]

When a prisoner was recaptured he might, if a judge's warrant had been
obtained, be sent to the county gaol of the county in which he was captured. If he
was brought back to the Fleet he might be confined in his room, placed in the
strong room, sometimes even ironed, but more frequently the unfortunate person
was placed in a tub at the prison gate for public exhibition. [256]

Huggins found it "impossible to enumerate" the number of escapes from the
prison during the long period of his wardenship. [257] Some idea may be formed,
however, from the lists of prisoners presented by the warden to the London
sessions as required by the insolvency acts. These give a schedule of the
movements of the prisoners between two separate dates, thus noting those who
were still prisoners, and those who had been discharged or had escaped. Thus
only the successful escapes are noted. Out of the 64 prisoners who entered the
prison between October and December 1743, one had escaped in the same period

(1.35%). In 1753 three who had escaped had been recommitted, but on different actions, possibly by those whose securities for their safe imprisonment had been called in. Of the 298 prisoners in October 1760 three had escaped by the end of May (1%),[258] and of 135 prisoners recorded in January 1772 nine had escaped by the June (6.6%); one from the house, one via the day *rules*, and seven from the *rules*.[259] The warden, in every such schedule, was always careful to note that they had escaped without his knowledge, privity, or consent.

It is not to be wondered at that most of the escapes took place from the *rules*. As far back as the time of Harris complaints were apparently made about the number who escaped when allowed out of the prison through the use of the writ *habeas corpus*, which probably antedated the use of the *rules*.[260] When a check was made in 1753 of the 88 persons then residing in the *rules*, 28 were not to be found: "Skipman Trafford had the *rule* many years ago, and has never been seen since"; John Jordan was one of several who had run away; George Menrell kept a shop on Ludgate hill but went away soon after a commission of bankruptcy had been issued against him; Daniel Bristow ran away upon an accusation of murder and Thomas Costell "it is to be imagined ... was either hanged or transported".[261] The comments "gone away" or "not to be found" occur time after time in the margins of the Fleet entry books. The court of Common Pleas was so concerned at the number of escapes from the *rules* that in 1719 it ordered that any prisoner who left the *rule* without a writ of day *rule* should be taken up and "carried into the prison there to remain in safe custody until by due course of law he shall be discharged".[262]

No precautions could be taken against the escape of the rulers except by the taking of securities which would be forfeited if they escaped. Tilly argued that such an escape from the *rules* was "no more a voluntary escape by the warden's consent than for a prisoner to escape over the walls of the prison house", but he added significantly, with reference to the securities taken, that in one instance "it hath been owed by the plaintiff to be a benefit more than if he [the prisoner] had not escaped".[263] This was confirmed by a writer of the same period: "debts have often been paid by these means, and by the benefit of securities they have taken, when the prisoners were wholly insolvent."[264] The only persons to lose with such escapes were the unfortunate securitors who had trusted the ruler, for the prisoner, if successful, gained his freedom, the creditor his debt, and the warden a substantial profit, for the securities were always fixed to an amount higher than the actual debts of the prisoner.

Few successful escapes ever took place from the prison house, though those that did received substantial publicity. Though some concern was expressed at the proximity of the walls to the houses around the prison, its walls were 25 feet, later 40 feet high, with a *cheveaux-de-frize* on top of them, so that the committee of 1729 felt there was "no seeming possibility of any prisoner" escaping that way.[265] But some did. Several smugglers on the common side were discovered making a hole in the prison wall in 1733,[266] and seven years later Thomas Batterson managed to make an escape over the wall by using a rope.[267] A Frenchman, M. Verteillac, escaped in 1791 by using a rope ladder with steel steps provided by two accomplices, and then passed through a dwelling house into the Belle Sauvage yard. The warden had to pay out two thousand, five hundred pounds in penalty clauses as a result.[268] Edward Johnson, arrested as a debtor and then identified as a smuggler, was placed in the strong room preparatory to being moved to Newgate. He managed to escape by cutting the panels of its door, throwing a line over the wall, and then cutting the iron railings on top of its forty-foot height. It was assumed he had accomplices.[269] Most, however, of the escapes from the prison house took place through the prison gates by the use of some form of disguise as the turnkeys on duty there had carefully studied the profiles of the prisoners as they entered the prison. Alfred Morris left this way with the aid of a wig and a Spanish cloak in 1838, but Sir William Boyd failed some years later to disguise himself realistically as an old woman and then as a Jew.[270] But such escapes were not many, Nixon believing that as most came to the prison for their own benefit, there was little point in escaping, unless it was "by a foreigner who has no residence in this kingdom" or a smuggler "who can live anywhere".[271] He may well have been right.

****

For many people entering the Fleet was a disaster both to themselves and to their families, but others were able to accommodate themselves to its society and values.[272] Describing themselves as the "collegians of the Fleet" they established their own way of life in that little and self-centred community; a "body politic" as one called it.[273] Some stood out against the prison ethos, which contrasted so much with the expectations of society, or at least of the commercial world. That ethos was summed up by a statement made in the 1792 report: "many insolvent debtors in prison either profusely dissipate, or avariciously hoard up, the money which they ought to apply in payment of their debts."[274] By the time many had entered the prison it was too late to do anything else, and the debtors' ethos accepted the dictum, "better live reasonably well inside than starve outside". The prison conditions of overcrowding, drunkenness, and immorality were the standards accepted by contemporary society. As the Webbs suggested, "most contemporaries took such conditions, abuses and privileges, as a matter of course. They were time honoured, sanctioned by years of custom."[275] The report of 1792 was correct in its statement: "there are other circumstances which prove, that to debtors of the worst description a prison is no punishment; but, on the contrary, that such persons find an interest, or a gratification, in remaining in a situation full of misery to the honest."[276] But this was a late eighteenth-century view. An earlier generation might have suggested that debt imprisonment was more an accommodation than a punishment and the prison more a community than a gaol.

NOTES

1   W Paget, *The Humours of the Fleet* (1749); cf Stow's description,"the best prison of any in this city" [Strype's edition of Stow's *London* (1720), III 280].

2   Samuel Speed, "A Fellow of the King's College in Southwark", *The Prisoners' Complaint, or the Cries of the King's Bench* (London 1673), p 7.

3   Tobias Smollett, *Peregrine Pickle*, chapter 97.

4   Report 1729, p 650.

5   Mackay, pp 16, 29; cf Howell, p 362: "'Who did the repairs?' 'I know not'."

6   Jnl H of C, XXI 328.

7   J P Malcolm, *Londinium Redivivum* (London 1803), I 375f; *London Magazine*, November 1768, p 573.

8   CLRO, Misc MS 172.12.

9   The descriptions of Simon Wood in 1733, Tobias Smollett [in his novel *Peregrine Pickle*] and of others of the same period, closely resemble later descriptions such as *The Description of the King's Bench, Fleet and Marshalsea Prisons* (London 1828), and the plans of the later reconstruction, such as Rotalde in 1845, and the Surveyor Justice plans [no I 61-2] at CLRO. A plan of the earlier building is at the BLO [MS maps Eng A2 map 2]. This indicates that the major alteration in the rebuilding was the placing of the chapel on the NW corner of the prison house.

10   This section owes much to H M Colvin, *This History of the King's Works* (London 1976), V 351-4.

11   Report 1814, p 681; Report 1818, p 28.

12   Report 1814, p 679.

13   H M Colvin's phrase in *The King's Works*, V 350.

14   Report 1814, p 682; Howard (1977), p 164.

15   *Some Brief Reasons offered to Parliament for passing an Act relating to the Discharge of Prisoners and the Regulation of Gaols and Gaolers*; cf Wood, p 9.

16   *A Speech without Doors on behalf of an Insolvent Debtor in the Fleet Prison* (London 1729), p 3.

17   Smith, p 4.

18   Report 1814, p 790.

19   Report 1792, p 654; Report 1814, p 677.

20   Jnl H of C, XII 202; cf Report 1729, p 3; Smith, p 42, still noted the lack of the kitchen.

21   Report 1729, p 3.

22   Quoted by John Ashton, *The Fleet, its River, Prison, and Marriages* (London 1888), p 297. The common side at the King's Bench was in an even worse state. It was below ground, subject to flooding, and so "smoking" that prisoners were either liable to choke to death or to perish with cold [*The State of the King's Bench Prison*: 1765].

23   Charles Dickens, *The Pickwick Papers*, chapter 40; cf Paget, *Humours*, p 17. This practice also enabled the warden to print detailed descriptions of escaped prisoners.

24   Many different acts regulated their use, such as 2 Geo II c 22, and 32 Geo II c 28.

25   One Marshalsea spunging house was alleged in 1774 to have charged a woman £2.6s.8d. for three days' lodging. This represented 55% of her debt [Coll BL, p 27]. Although prisoners were not permitted to stay for more than forty-eight hours in such places, many endeavoured to remain until they had exhausted their financial resources, believing that their creditors would never release them if they thought they possessed any money.

27   Howell, p 385.

28   Wood, p 12.

29   Report 1729, pp 6-8; Howell, pp 385, 397.

30   For details regarding these spunging houses see Report 1729, pp 4, 6-8; Report 1729 (M), p 19; Howell, pp 301, 363, 401f, 404f, 407, 421, 429, 432, 441f, 454; Mackay, pp 12, 15, 18, and App VIII, IX. Louden's house may have been a spunging house too; he kept a boarding house and boarded many prisoners there at five shillings per week [Howell, p 363].

31   Howell, pp 451, 454.

32   Rule no 14.

33   Wood, p 12.

34   PRO, PRIS/1/7, fol 195.

35   Report 1792, pp 641f.

36   S & B Webb, *English Prisons under Local Government* (London 1963), p 25n. Dobb suggests it had been introduced in the Compter during the early 17th century, and spread to the other prisons thereafter [Thesis, p 70].

37   Howard (1777), p 164.

38   pp 37f: cf Richard Steele's *The Lying Lover*, set in Newgate. Storm says to Simon, "'We'll drink his coat off. Come, my little chemist, thou shalt transmute this jacket into liquor.'"

39   Report 1729, p 5.

40   Report 1814, p 672.

41   Howard (1777), pp 157f.

42   Report 1814, p 548. They had no fireplaces.

43   Jnl H of C, XII 201f; Mackay, pp 16, 18, 22, 34; Howard (1777), pp 157f; Smith, p 42. John Berisford wrote that until the 1697 act the warden required prisoners in the *rules* to take chambers in the prison, which made the position even more acute [p 8].

44   Mackay, App IV.

45   Paget, *Humours of the Fleet*, pp 17f. Mount Scoundrel did not survive the rebuilding of the prison in the 1770s. It seems it was much missed, for it was recommended in 1818 that the warden should provide an equivalent for those who entered the prison too late for chumming arrangements to be made. He accordingly provided them with beds and bedding [Report 1818, p 9].

46   Mackay, p 31, App II; Howell, p 342.

47   Howard (1780), p 178.

48   For details of the system of chumming see Mackay, pp 14, 18; Paget, *Humours of the Fleet*, pp 18ff; Howard (1777), p 158; Wood, p 13; John Feltham, *The Picture of London* (London 1803), p 175; *Debtor and Creditor's Assistant*, pp 17, 22; Report 1814, pp 548f, 675-8, 686-8, 784f; Report 1818, pp 4f, 45f.

49   Dickens, *Pickwick Papers*, chapter 42.

50   8 & 9 William III c 27 s 14, and 22 & 23 Charles II c 20 s 10, provided that fees and chamber rent should not be greater than required and be determined by two out of three of the lord justices. The fees at Ludgate were 2*s*.6*d*. if in a bed by oneself, and half that price if not. At the King's Bench it was 2*s*. per week, bed and sheets provided, half price if two in a bed, but it was claimed that the full fee was charged even to those who "lie on the boards in the lumber room" [BLO, MS Rawlinson D809, fol 116; *The Case of William Penrice*, (1768), p 40].

51   Mackay, p 22, App I; Report 1729, p 4.

52   Moses Pitt, *The Cry of the Oppressed* (London 1691), p 86. In 1621, 2*s*.4*d*. was charged per person each, even if sharing a room [Wallace Notestein, *Commons Debates 1621* (New Haven, 1935), V 510]. John Lilburn mentions that at the King's Bench 5*s*. to 10*s*. per week was charged, and if six in a chamber in three beds 2*s*.6*d*. each per week [*Liberty Vindicated against Slavery* (1646), p 26].

53   Mackay, p 28; Report 1729, p 18.

54   Mackay, pp 7, 22.

55   Report 1729, p 17; Howell, p 359, notes 5*s*.

56   Mackay, pp 6f, 22, 28, 33.

57   Mackay, pp 7, 22, App V.

58   Mackay, p 26.

59   Howell, p 602; Mackay, p 6.

60   PRO, PRIS/10/49, fol 194. This was a frequent occurrence on the common side [Report 1729, p 3].

61   Paget, *Humours of the Fleet*, p 12.

62   Mackay, p 22; cf Report 1729, pp 4, 16.

63   Jnl H of C, XXI 513.

64   The fee in 1814 at the King's Bench prison was 1s. per room, and this sum was shared amongst its inmates [Report 1814, p 534].

65   *Description of the Fleet, King's Bench and Marshalsea Prisons* (London 1828), p 19.

66   Wood, p 132.

67   Report 1729, p 2. The tables are to be found in BLO, MS Rawlinson D1123, fol 289, and *The Microcosm of London* (London 1904), II 55f.

68   Mackay, App XI.

69   The same requirement about the list of fees being put up was made in the general prison act of 1729, 2 Geo II, c 22. Howard (1777), p 160, said the only table in the Fleet was one dated 1727 which concerned the the clerk's fees.

70   BLO, MS Rawlinson D1123, fol 289.

71   *Microcosm of London*, p 58.

72   Report 1729, p 9.

73   Report 1729, p 9.

74   The dismission fee was not a discharge fee. Rather, as Huggins claimed, it was *dimmittere in custodiem*, freedom of the house, and thus rightly included within the commitment fees [Mackay, p 30)]

75   Mackay, pp 34f, cf pp 6, 35, 39; Report 1729, p 9. They possibly took as a precedent an order of 1693 which required the fees of the Westminster courts and offices belonging to them to be as those established in the reign of Elizabeth I, and thus reformulated by Herbert in 1651 [Jnl H of C, XI 3].

76   Mackay, p 34.

77   Mackay, pp 3, 35ff, App II.

78   Mackay, pp 14ff.

79   *Mr Bambridge's Case against the Bill now Depending* (London 1729).

80   Mackay, pp 15, 19, 25f.

81   Mackay, pp 16, 26, 30, App II; Report 1729, p 9. The judges in 1729 accepted that this

practice of taking separate fees for each commitment was justified by ancient practice.

82   Report 1729 (M), pp 21f; Mackay, App II. Siddale paid three surrenders at £3.8s, 10s.6d. to the tipstaff, commitment fees of £6.10s., 3s. to the chamberlain and 2s. to the turnkey.

83   Mackay, p 6.

84   Mackay, p 29, App VI; Pitt, *The Cry of the Oppressed*, p 85; Wood, p 14. The practice clearly continued after 1814. Nixon in 1808 stated he did not do this, and added that he even paid between £10-20 for the funerals of prisoners whose relatives did not claim their bodies [Joseph Nightengale, *London and Middlesex* (1815), II 733].

85   Mackay, p 8, App XI.

86   Report 1729, p 18; Report 1729 (M), pp 21f, where it was alleged that extortions were practised at the Fleet regarding commitment fees, but this may have been no more than the charging of a new commitment fee for each action in which the debtor was charged.

87   Mackay, pp 24f.

88   Wood, p 9; Howard (1780), p 177.

89   *Considerations Humbly Offered in relation to the Bill now Depending in Parliament for the Further Relief of Creditors in Cases of Escapes.*

90   Mackay, pp 9f, 19f, App III, V IX; Howell, pp 581, 612ff, 623; Report 1729, pp 9f, 13f; Pitt, *The Cry of the Oppressed*, p 85; Wood, pp 9, 11, 16. In 1824 one of the 126 prisoners was detained at the suit of the warden, in 1747 it was thirty out of 364 [CLRO, Debtors Lists].

91   David Hughson, *Walks through London* (London 1817), I 125; Report 1814, pp 549, 677; CLRO, Misc MS 173.5 (1786), fols 31, 65.

92   By 22 & 23 Charles II c 20 s VIII, the gaoler was required to allow prisoners to provide their own food and bedding, etc. After this date the warden probably ceased to feed his prisoners.

93   Report 1814, p 549.

94   *Debtor and Creditor's Assistant* (1793), p 45. It added that some of the prisoners could not support themselves on a weekly 30-40 guineas.

95   Report 1792, pp 653f.

96   *The Debtor and Creditor's Guide* (London 1813), pp 21-4; Wood, pp 5, 12. These funds were provided by the county treasurers. Glamorgan, for example, paid three pounds each to the Fleet and King's Bench prisons, but not to the Marshalsea. But out of this sum, if the Fleet debtor had a room of his own, he had to pay 1s.3d. in chamber rent.

97   Ashton, *The Fleet*, pp 310f, quoting *The Morning Herald*, 12 August 1833.

98   An act of 1670, 22 & 23 Charles II c 20, required a maintenance of 18d. per week, and

later legislation increased this to 2*s*.4*d*., but it was difficult to enforce this requirement, as was acknowledged by the so called Lord's Act [32 Geo 2 c 28], which set the same scale.

99   Robert Neale, *The Prisoner's Guide, or every Debtor his own Lawyer* (London 1800), pp 12ff; Report 1792, pp 649f, 657.

100   Thomas MacDonald, *A Treatise on Civil Imprisonment in England* (London 1791), p 110.

101   *The Debtor and Creditor's Assistant*, p 78.

102   Those who had often hoped to obtain a composition from their creditors [BLO, MS Rawlinson D1051, pt 1, fol 4].

103   Report 1814, p 681; cf King's Bench, where it was reported that 470 of 570 prisoners were idle [Report 1792, p 652].

104   *Acts of the Privy Council*, 1586-7, pp 306f.

105   Report 1792, pp 651f; Report 1814, pp 535f, 549, 676-8, 688; Report 1818, p 48; *Debtor and Creditor's Assistant*, p 17; *Smith*, p 53 [regarding King's Bench].

106   Report 1814, pp 677, 682; Hughson, *Walks in London*, I 124.

107   Howard (1777), p 158.

108   Feltham, *Picture of London*, p 175.

109   Report 1792, p 654; Report 1814, p 550.

110   Howard (1777), p 159; *The Debtor and Creditor's Assistant*, pp 21f; Report 1814, pp 550, 677; Report 1818, pp 7, 42.

111   Feltham, *Picture of London*, p 176.

112   Wood, p 8.

113   Wood, p 8 [he complained of it being blocked up]; Mackay, p 32 [he notes p 17 a further dispute when the warden claimed that the steward of the box was "highly prejudicial" to its success)]; Howard (1777), p 159; *Debtor and Creditor's Assistant*, pp 21f; Hughson, *Walks*, I 125; Report 1814, pp 550, 677. The begging grate book survives for the 1820s, see PRO, PRIS/10/9. An account book of 1627-31 is also at the PRO, E215/1593. It reveals that in March 1628 twelve prisoners shared £18 and in December £3.3*s*.8*d*..

114   Cf Clifford Dobb in *Shakespeare Survey*, XVII (London 1964) 98; Jnl H of C, XII 202; Cal SPD, 1635, pp 75f.

115   Cal Pat, 1374-7, p 95.

116   Report 1729, p 17. Ludgate prison had a similar "running post". He received a penny per month from each prisoner [*The World Display'd and Mankind Painted in their Proper Colours, to which is Added, a Description of a Prison* (London 1742), p 19].

117   Cal SPD, 1700-2, p 442.

118   Jnl H of C, XII 202.

119   Wood, p 11.

120   Cal TB, 1685-9, VIII-III, p 1179.   The prisoners complained that the Exchequer had taken this money and they requested its return.

121   *Daily Journal*, 2 February 1731.

122   Report 1818, p 42.

123   Report 1729, p 17.

124   *A Description of the Fleet, King's Bench and Marhsalsea Prisons*, p 20.

125   W K Jordan, *The Charities of London, 1480-1600* (London 1960).

126   *An Oration on the Oppression of Jailors* (London 1731), p 10.

127   Smith, p 46.

128   Mackay, p 18, App IX; Report 1729 (M), pp 18f.   Bambridge received 36 guineas from the Exchequer at three guineas each for twelve prisoners as a special favour to the poor, but is said to have demanded from them all fees over and above that sum.

129   BL, pm 816 m15/17. Another petition [BL, pm 357 b8/109] stated that the prisoners resembled "starved carcasses ... mere walking shadows".

130   Cal TP, 1714-19, p 98.

131   Coll BL, fol 29.

132   Wood, p 16.

133   Smith, p 3.

134   Jnl H of C, XII 202; Lilburn, *Liberty Vindicated against Slavery*, p 13.

135   Quoted by M D George, *London Life in the Eighteenth Century* (London 1951), p 307.

136   Issue of 10 January 1740.

137   *A Speech without Doors*, p 19.

138   Report 1729, p 4.

139   Wood, p 10.

140   Malcolm, *Londinium Redivivum*, I 376. A room on the common side had been provided as an infirmary for many years previously.

141   14 Geo III c 59. It also required that prisons be whitewashed and hot and cold baths provided. But the act was neglected as no system of inspection was provided nor effectual penalties for its neglect.

142   Report 1814, pp 550f, 673, 693; Report 1818, pp 42, 44. There was neither infirmary nor medical care at the King's Bench [Report 1815, pp 539f].

143 Mackay, p 29; Smollett's *Peregrine Pickle*; Howard (1777), p 182; Smith, p 41; *Description of the Fleet*, pp 18ff; Report 1814, pp 683, 689, 693, 787. Neild in his *State of the Prisons* [p 220] noted in particular the state of the staircases and lobbies. But there was plenty of water.

144 Report 1814, p 552.

145 Mackay, pp 11, 28, 31, 33; Report 1729, pp 16, 18. The stipend of the minister was provided by the grant of the prison in 1667 [Cal SPD, 1667, p 496]. The 1818 report [p 6] noted that these arrangements had been discontinued for many years.

146 See R L Brown, "The Rise and Fall of the Fleet Marriages", in R B Outhwaite (ed), *Marriage and Society* (London 1981), p 117.

147 BLO, MS Rawlinson C743, fol 99.

148 Nightengale, *London and Middlesex*, III 734: Report 1814, p 680.

149 Report 1814, pp 552, 680, 685, 695. Neild in 1815 found only eleven prisoners at the chapel service, accepting the general excuse that it was too cold. He believed the provision of a fireplace and fire would fill the chapel in order to hear "the excellent preacher" [p 219].

150 Bryant Lillywhite, *London Coffee Houses* (London 1963), pp 208f, 313f; Wood, pp 7f; *London Sessions Papers*, 1740, p 98; Howard (1780), p 157; Report 1814, pp 680, 685; Report 1818, pp 8f, 19, 42.

151 *The Times*, 21 February 1838.

152 Report 1792, pp 652, 657; Report 1814, pp 546, 674, 690, 694, 697; Report 1818, pp 8, 48-50, 77. Nixon had given up the wine licence, although in 1792 over 130 dozen bottles were sold in that year. Even in 1620 the warden had obtained 200 marks profit from the sale of beer in the prison [Notestein, *Commons Debates*, I 374].

153 Coll BL, fol 7.

154 Pierce Egan, *Life in London* (London 1812), chapter 8. In the King's Bench Smith [p 49] found thirty such gin shops and estimated that 240 gallons were sold weekly.

155 Report 1814, pp 679f, 690.

156 Howard (1777), pp 157f; Paget, *Humours of the Fleet*, pp 25f; Hughson, *Walks*, I 125; Report 1814, pp 675, 786.

157 Report 1815, p 590; Joanna Innes, "The King's Bench Prison in the later Eighteenth Century", in J Brewer and J Styles, *An Ungovernable People* (London 1980), p 276.

158 Report 1814, pp 675, 690f, 697; Report 1818, p 27; Hughson, *Walks*, I 125.

159 Coll BL, fols 88, 90.

160 Paget, *Humours of the Fleet*, pp 13-16; Howard (1777), p 159; *Debtor and Creditor's*

Assistant, p 46; Hughson, *Walks*, I 125; Report 1818, p 43; BL, MS Harleian 4031, fol 31; The
Noble collection at GLL and Coll BL provide further references.

161   Dobb, *Shakespeare Survey*, p 87.

162   Hatton, *A New View of London*, II 745.

163   Mackay, p 8.

164   Hughson, *Walks*, I 125; Report 1818, p 43.

165   GLL, Noble collection, C43/T1841: Ashton, *The Fleet*, pp 305f.

166   Report 1814, pp 678f.

167   Paget, *Humours of the Fleet*, pp 13f.

168   Howard (1777), p 159.

169   PRO, IND/4625, fol 207.

170   Hughson, *Walks*, I 126.

171   Report 1814, pp 680, 689f.

172   Paget, *Humours of the Fleet*, pp 35f; *Debtor and Creditor's Assistant*, p 19; Hughson,
Walks, I 125f; Report 1814, p 679.

173   Report 1792, p 662 [clearly stated here regarding the King's Bench].

174   Report 1792, p 654.

175   *Debtor and Creditor's Assistant*, p 19.

176   Howard (1780), p 179 [he found at the King's Bench 395 prisoners, 279 wives and 725
children]; Report 1792, p 652, cf p 654; Report 1814, p 551; Report 1818, p 9. In 1776 Smith [p
62] found only 52 prisoners in the Fleet, but 25 wives and 46 children.

177   *A Treatise on the Abuse of the Laws* (London 1814), pp 108f.

178   Report 1814, p 551f; Report 1818, p 43; cf King's Bench prison where on one staircase
with 16 rooms there were 140 people residing [Report 1792, p 661; cf Report 1814, p 544].

179   *Gentleman's Magazine*, May 1794.

180   Report 1792, pp 659, 661f. It was later feared that female children in the King's Bench
prison could be introduced to prostitution [Report 1814, p 543].

181   Report 1815, pp 681, 685.

182   As noted in Smollett's novel, *Peregrine Pickle*, chapters 41-3.

183   Howard (1784), p 221.

184   Report 1814, p 543.

185   Report 1818, p 8.

186   Report 1814, p 679; Report 1818, p 43.

187   *A Speech without Doors*, pp 12f.

188 The prisoners said of themselves, that they were "to a wonder, quiet and peaceable under their afflictions and unhappy circumstances ... considering the several mixtures of mankind among us, we live in as much sobriety, order and good behaviour among such a number of persons as can anywhere be found" [Mackay, pp 23, 34].

189 Harris, p 9.

190 Mackay, pp 8, 20, 22, 31f.

191 Cal SPD, 1663-4, p 604.

192 Pitt, *The Cry of the Oppressed*, preface.

193 *London Sessions Papers*, 1740, p 98.

194 Howard (1777), p 159; Smith, p 43; cf Paget, *Humours of the Fleet*, p 15.

195 Report 1814, pp 551, 679, 681, 685, 694; Report 1818, p 41. Though he added, unless there was a riot in the prison or a prisoner was taken sick [Report 1814, pp 679, 685].

196 Hughson, *Walks*, I 126.

197 Report 1818, p 42.

198 Report 1818, p 7; Report 1814, p 679.

199 BLO, MS Rawlinson A290, fol 46. This was in 1696.

200 CLRO, Misc MS 8.16; PRO, SP34/5, fol 225.

201 PRO, SP35/9, fol 207.

202 *Mr Bambridge's Case*; Report 1729 (M), p 20.

203 *The Real John Bull*, 27 October 1822.

204 Jnl H of C, XI 645f, 678. Another later 19th-century gang of counterfeiters used the Fleet to forge notes [Ashton, *The Fleet*, pp 316f].

205 Cal SPD, 1661-2, p 236; PRO, SP44/274. fol 46.

206 *The Trial of P W Duffin and Thomas Lloyd for a Libel in the Fleet Prison* (London 1793), *in passim*. Innes notes that these two had caused a substantial riot in that prison, and had been affected by the writings of James Stephens [*The King's Bench Prison*, p 294].

207 PRO, T1/309, no 12; cf T11/22, fol 310. Three of these prisoners subsequently escaped [Cal TP, 1742-5, p 151].

208 Contained in the Noble collection, C43F, at GLL.

209 Such a society had worked so well in the government of Ludgate gaol in 1633 that the court of aldermen ordered one to be established at Newgate, with monthly meetings [W J Sheehan in J S Cockburn's *Crime in England* (London 1977), p 233]. Thomas Buxton discovered such a society in the debtors' side of Newgate in 1818 [*An Enquiry ... into Prison Discipline* (London 1818), p 48f], though it hardly conformed to the expectations of 1633. A

prisoners' court had been established for offences against the community. It was presided over by the oldest prisoner who wore a hat draped with knots on either side of his head in imitation of a wig, and who punished offences by fining the offenders.

210   J S Burn, *The Star Chamber* (London 1870), p 98. For a later case of 1739 see PRO, PRIS/1/7, fol 466. The eight culprits were sent to the Fleet.

211   Mackay, p 31.

212   Mackay, pp 31f; Howell, pp 340, 342, 362.

213   Howard (1777), p 164; Smith, p 42; Innes, *The King's Bench Prison*, pp 281ff.

214   Howard (1780), p 211.

215   GLL, pm pamphlet 5339. It was abolished in 1779.

216   Nightengale, *London and Middlesex*, III 733.

217   Innes, *King's Bench Prison*, p 286.

218   Report 1814, pp 694-6.

219   Report 1818, pp 21, 41.

220   Harris, pp 8f; cf William Brown, *The Fleet* (London 1843), p 15; Report 1814, p 551.

221   Harris, p 43; Report 1729, p 13.

222   Mackay, App VIII; Report 1729, pp 10, 13; Report 1729 (M), p 17; *Mr Bambridge's Case*.

223   Percival's Diary, quoted by Leslie F Church, *Oglethorpe* (London 1732), p 21.

224   Report 1818, p 4; *The Portfolio*, 1824, p 357; *Description of the Fleet, King's Bench and Marshalsea*, p 19. The King's Bench strongroom had no fireplace, but straw was provided if the prisoner had no bed [Report 1814, p 544].

225   *Trial of P W Duffin and Thomas Lloyd*, p 9.

226   Mackay, pp 28, 32.

227   Mackay, pp 28, 32; Report 1729 (M), pp 19. At one time such prisoners were sent to Newgate, especially escapees [Report 1729, p 6], but the 1814 report alleged that the warden had no power to do so [Report 1814, p 695].

228   Mackay, pp 17, 29, 32.

229   Mackay, p 28, App VI, XXIII; Report 1729, p 16.

230   Those who needed to be transferred in order to appear before the court of the King's Bench were able to use a "speedy *habeas*", devised for them, and which cost 12 guineas. This enabled them to be technically transferred and acknowledged to be in the custody of the other prison, without any practical transfer having taken place [Jones Pearce, *A Treatise on the Abuse of the Laws, particularly in Actions by Arrest* [London 1814], pp 90f].

231 PRO, PRIS/1/1a, fols 3, 11.

232 PRO, PRIS/10/158.

233 GLL, pm pamphlet 5339 (of 1779).

234 Report 1792, p 651.

235 *Debtor and Creditor's Assistant*, pp 69f. A case in point may have been that of Sir John Pretyman, a debtor to the king. His application for a writ to transfer him from the King's Bench to the Fleet was opposed by the attorney general, who also requested the lord keeper to see what could be done to prevent such writs from being granted. The Treasury finally ordered the lord keeper not to grant such writs to any one imprisoned as a crown debtor [Cal TB, 1667-8, II 62, 123, 136, 154].

236 Mackay, pp 6, 23; Report 1792, p 657; *Debtors and Creditor's Assistant*, pp 69ff; Pearce, *A Treatise*, p 90.

237 1 Richard II c 12.

238 1 Anne stat 2 c 6.

239 Howell, p 357; BL, MS Harleian 6840, fol 249; 8 & 9 William III c 27 s 1; Coke's *Institutes*, (1671 edn), II 382. If a prisoner on a mesne process escaped the warden was only responsible for any damages sustained, if such could be proved, but not for the debts themselves.

240 8 & 9 William III c 27.

241 Berisford, p 2, cf pp 18ff; Jnl H of C, XII 684f.

242 Jnl H of C, XII 686.

243 Jnl H of C, XIII 685; cf Cal TB, 1681-5, p 641. Warr's escape may have been more a "technical" one in that he had provided securities for his safe imprisonment "outside" the prison house.

244 Jnl H of C, XI 677.

245 Cal TP, 1720-8, p 279 [as in the case of Perrin]; Howell, pp 353, 366.

246 PRO, SP35/76, fol 136.

247 Cal TB & P, 1720-30, p 43. Other "memorials" of the wardens to the Treasury praying they may not be prosecuted for such escapes are in Cal TB, 1716, II 504; PRO, T/11/22, fol 310; T29/29, fol 146; IND/4625, fols 173, 207, 225.

248 Report 1818, p 77.

249 *Gentleman's Magazine*, July 1790.

250 An Exchequer case of 1475 stated that if a debtor in execution escaped, and the creditor successfully brought an action against the gaoler, the debtor would be cleared of his debt to the creditor, but not, in practice, to his gaoler [*Select Cases in Exchequer Chamber*, II 34, quoted by

R B Pugh, *Imprisonment in Medieval England* (Cambridge 1970), p 245n].

251 Middlesex county records, sessions papers 622, fol 277. Other cases will be found at the PRO, PRIS/1/3 for Samuel Jackson 1743, and PRIS/1/6 for Francis Dutton, fol 26b. See also Report 1729, p6.

252 16 Geo II c 31.

253 Report 1814, pp 541f.

254 Coll BL, fol 111.

255 Coll BL, fol 54.

256 Howell, pp 306, 354; Report 1729, pp 3, 13.

257 Report 1729, p 3.

258 Derived from PRO, PRIS/1/9.

259 The schedules are at the CLRO, Debtors Lists, and DS/15/22-3. The Fleet prison fugitive book 1748-50 [PRO, PRIS/10/158] is probably more a list of rulers, whose descriptions are given in some detail in case of escapes.

260 By inference from Harris, pp 78, 101ff, cf p 52.

261 PRO, detached note attached to cover to PRIS/10/134.

262 PRO, SP35/16, fol 245.

263 *The Warden of the Fleet's Case in Relation to Mr Baldwin Leighton's Petition to the Honourable House of Commons.*

264 *General Considerations relating to a Bill for Regulating the Abuses of Prisons and Pretended Privileged Places* (London 1697).

265 Report 1729, p 4; Report 1814, p 680; Report 1818, p 4.

266 Coll BL, fol 2.

267 PRO, IND/4625, fol 173.

268 Lillywhite, *London Coffee Houses,* p 188; *Gentleman's Magazine,* November 1791; Report 1814, p 680.

269 *Portfolio,* 1824, p 357.

270 *The Times,* 16 February 1838; cf PRO, IND/4625, fol 207. His debts were said to be £2,600.

271 GLL, Noble collection, C43F. This formed the basis for one of the plots in Rowcroft's novel, *Chronicles of the Fleet Prison* (London 1847).

272 Report 1814, p 680.

273 *An Oration on the Oppression of Jailers,* p 7.

274 Report 1792, p 652.

275   S & B Webb, *English Prisons under Local Government*, pp 31f.

276   Report 1792, p 647.

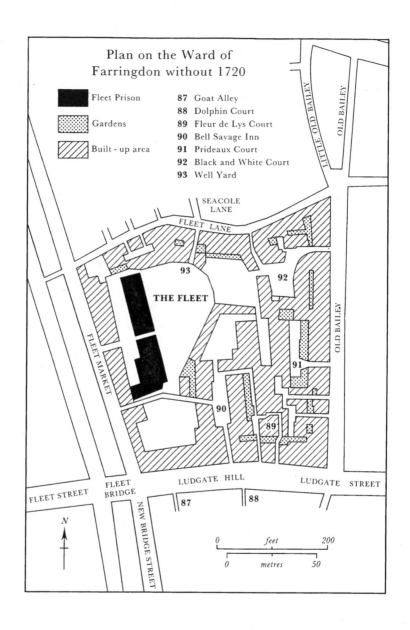

A plan of the ward of Farrington Without in 1720, showing the area surrounding
the Fleet Prison. Drawn by Gary Llewellyn from the map in Stype's edition
of John Stow's *Survey of London*

Part Five:

The Privileges of the "great and terrible Leviathan"

"This great and terrible Leviathan, who thus disturbs our peace and cracks the sinews of the body politic."[1]

The Fleet was a debt prison. The task of its warden was to produce the prisoners committed to his care if and when required without fail. He made a distinction between the prison house and the custody of his prisoners by claiming that he could keep them wherever he found more convenient. He also asserted that he could allow his prisoners considerable leniency from the terms of strict confinement. Although this picture had been modified by the beginning of the eighteenth century, mainly through the pressures of commercial and legal interests, two aspects of it continued to the end of the prison; namely, the use of the day *rules* and of the *rules* itself. The origin of both probably lay in an extension of the writ *habeas corpus*, although even this may have been an attempt to regulate a custom which dated from the earliest days of the prison.

There were three particular usages of this writ of *habeas corpus* applied and utilised for debt imprisonment during the seventeenth century. One was used to enable a debt prisoner to enter the Fleet from another prison, or more technically, from the jurisdiction of one court to another. Another was the writ known as *ad testificandum* which was used to take a Fleet prisoner to a court of law. Major Wilson complained in the 1720s that Guybon refused to permit this writ to two of his fellow prisoners without a fee of two guineas being first paid. As they were required to give evidence on his behalf at the Guildhall it meant he lost the case by default.[2] The third use of the writ was to enable a prisoner to leave the prison for a length of time.[3] This writ was granted on the assumption that a prison could be at any place where a prisoner was restricted from a full exercise of liberty.[4] Not unnaturally, the use of this writ was highly sought after, while its application in favour of any prisoner depended on the goodwill not only of the authority which had committed him, but also of his gaoler who was still responsible in law for his prisoner's custody.[5] Thus James Harris, who had been removed to the Fleet by a *habeas corpus* from the lord keeper, requested that official to permit him to go with a waiter to "peruse his writings in Devon".[6] It also appears that this writ was available from the warden during legal vacations, and he presumably had power to grant it in urgent cases, though in most cases it would be granted by the court.[7] This writ was not confined to prisoners of the Fleet and King's Bench prisons, as were the *rules*.[8]

Its usage was of great antiquity, for what had probably started as an abuse of prison life had been converted into a custom regulated by various rules. Harris, the sixteenth-century deputy warden, suggested that such writs had been granted as far back as 1377, and claimed that his prisoners were entitled to go abroad with a keeper at the warden's discretion.[9] In this he was short by nearly a century, for it was an apparently established custom to permit prisoners to go abroad from the Fleet by 1291, as noted in the case of Matthew of the Exchequer, whose superiors had endeavoured to prevent this privilege.[10] A statute of 1377[11] endeavoured to regulate this custom of allowing prisoners to leave with security or/and with a tipstaff, in order to go into the country about their business, "being out of their prison nights and days ... to the great mischief and undoing of many people". In future those who wished to obtain such writs were required to obtain either the assent of their creditors or a warrant from the king. If the warden permitted prisoners out at large without such a warrant, even though they left "by bail" and accompanied by a tipstaff, the creditor would be allowed to have an action for debt against him, and the warden would lose his office and the "keeping of the said prison". This custom had proved so attractive to many prisoners in other gaols that in order to take advantage of it they had sworn themselves as crown debtors, and accordingly entered the Fleet. From henceforth, ran the statute, such prisoners were to be returned to their original gaols, there to remain until they had settled with their original creditors, and only then to be brought to the Fleet in order to serve their debt imprisonment at the suit of the crown.

The practice of letting prisoners "go at large at their will", still much abused, was again regulated by acts of 1405-6 and 1444. The first noted that the wardens purchased the king's protection and so prevented the creditors gaining their rightful recovery, and thus disallowed this practice.[12] The second permitted the warden or any prison gaoler to take security for a prisoner's safe imprisonment, and this was obviously linked to the provision for permitting prisoners to leave gaol or to "go abroad". A saving clause was inserted for the warden of the Fleet that he should not be prejudiced by this ordinance in the "duty of his office."[13] The 1561 constitutions of the prison permitted the warden to allow a prisoner "to go into the country ... on needful business" between law terms, that is, on his own authority instead of that of one of the courts. The prisoner had to be accompanied by a keeper, and this right was subject to the qualification that the committing court had given no contrary instructions.[14] Harris interpreted the phrase "needful business" as meaning the management of estates, consulting with creditors, bailiffs and other officials, burying members of one's family, making an inventory of goods, or arranging to sell or survey one's possessions. It was added that the courts were aware of the frauds of feoffees and the weakness of wives and children in managing estates.[15] There were thus two forms of this writ, one given by the warden outside term time, and the other by the courts within term. It is impossible to distinguish between them.

Harris gives numerous instances of the use of this writ during the 1610s. He estimated that his annual revenue arising from it was eighty pounds, which at a cost to the individual of 20*d.* per day, suggests Jessop, allows an estimate of at least one hundred prisoners making use of this writ for ten days each during the course of the year. They were still held responsible for their prison fees during the period of their absence. Harris met some opposition to this requirement of an accompanying keeper, for he complained that not only had he to provide two or three keepers for those charged with great debts (some in excess of ten or twenty thousand pounds), but that he was only able to charge for the cost of one.

Furthermore he claimed that he could not in conscience pay a mere three or four pence a day to one of his servants who had to accompany the prisoner "who goeth out early", and unlike his keeper, "who goeth daily before, he is not weried, and would not return late at night".[16] Irregularities in the use of these writs, especially their forging by prisoners and the counterfeiting of the judges' signatures, were noted in the 1635 commission into the prison, which spent much of its time examining such matters. It also expressed its concern at the liberty allowed to the prisoners.[17] During the 1636 plague in London the Fleet prisoners petitioned that they might be allowed the use of this writ in order to enter the country and be out of danger. This was permitted.[18] However it appears that while the prison was housed at Caroon house, Lambeth, after the Great Fire of London, such writs were not allowed, even though the prisoners complained that for "lack whereof many of them are unable to satisfy their creditors and perish for want". The reason for this refusal is not known.[19]

The practice of permitting prisoners to go abroad from the prison by the use of this form of the writ *habeas corpus* was apparently abolished by an act of 1696, which endeavoured to bring some sort of order and clarity to the confused world of privilege and repression that the Fleet and the King's Bench prisons typified.[20] However by that date this writ had been virtually supplanted by the use of the day *rules* and the *rules*. Its suppression soon after was undoubtedly due to the numerous instances of its abuse found by the two parliamentary inquiries into the Fleet prison. A prisoner ordered to be kept in close confinement, Pitcher, was permitted by Tilly to go abroad into the country where he took possession of that land whose rent he had failed to pay and for which default he had been committed to the Fleet.[21] John Evans, a prisoner in execution at the suit of John Jennings, was allowed at large, and found opportunity to abuse his creditor.[22] A further prisoner, Conyers, was alleged to have made terms with Tilly, and freely stated that it had cost him forty guineas for the privilege of being "seen every day in the streets ... without ever going into the Fleet".[23] William Warr, a prisoner, was told by Church, then deputy warden, that so long as he "could feed Mr Tilly with money, he would have liberty to go where he pleased".[24] Miles Larkin, though committed as a debt prisoner in execution to the Fleet, "still lives in his house at Chelsea", and Colonel Dean, with a court order that he be kept in strict confinement, left the Fleet two hours after his admission, went to his creditor's chambers, and thoroughly "abused" him. Even worse, a horrified house heard how a prisoner at the King's Bench, Kellow, had found his liberty and had been taken up in Kent charged with highway robbery, while a Fleet prisoner by the name of Hudson, a "player", had paid one hundred pounds to the warden as security for his safe imprisonment, which was accepted as sufficient liberty for him to act in a local playhouse. A further prisoner, Peter Wade, having been permitted such liberty by the warden, fell sick at Newington Butts. To cover himself in the eventuality of his death, Tilly and his assistant Fox rushed there and forced him to promise and sign a will which gave three hundred pounds and an indemnity to Tilly and his heirs from all escape writs in his particular case.[25] It was also alleged that Fox gave "protection warrants", possibly writs of *habeas corpus*, to those who feared arrest on actions for debt, as in the case of Scoltock.[26] Further complaints were made by Berisford. He complained that a tenant might be taken to the county gaol for refusal to pay his rent, but he "takes his *habeas corpus* to the Fleet", so that he can get the liberty he needs in order to return and take another farm "next hedge to their former landlords".[27] Another complained that debtors, after an expensive law suit, "remove themselves to the said prison, and by agreement with the warden, are immediately set at liberty, and return into the country; there they live in defiance of their creditors, making a jest of the law." By their example they drew others "to extravagant courses and lavishly to spend their creditors' money".[28] To a society concerned about trade and credit it could hardly have been better put. Though many of these stories were undoubtedly embellished, there was probably some grain of truth in all of them.

There are several hints that this custom survived in part after this date at the Fleet and the King's Bench. A broadside of the late 1690s states in connection with the origin of the *rules*, then regarded as of recent date, that prisoners who could not give bail could yet give security to continue in another place of confinement if accompanied by a keeper.[29] This may be illustrated by a later case. A Mr Conway had been admitted to the Fleet, but the prison and the spunging houses were full. He was allowed to stay, therefore, at a friend's house on Ludgate hill, accompanied by a keeper. Two days later, when room was available, he moved into the prison.[30] Huggins clearly believed this right remained, for he was reported as allowing one Perrin, a London merchant in the Virginian tobacco trade, to go to Holland and elsewhere in 1714, on giving security for his safe return.[31] It was said too of Huggins, as Tilly before him, that he permitted prisoners to journey "to any part of the kingdom, on pretence of giving evidence at some trial or assizes". This the 1729 committee considered as "a wicked practice" which was "for lucre only".[32]

These writs, during the time they were lawful, were sued for in the court of Common Pleas, although a more specialised one was obtainable from the court of Chancery for those whose estates were endangered by their restraint. It was said that these writs were of such benefit to the creditors, in enabling their debtors the better to settle their affairs, that they often assisted their prisoners to obtain them.[33]

The length of time a prisoner was permitted to remain outside the prison was obviously well defined in these writs, although due to the substantial distances prisoners had to travel to reach their chosen destinations it must have been a generous allocation in many instances. A warrant issued by the warden in response to such a writ has survived in the Barrington family correspondence. It was issued in November 1653 by the then warden of the Fleet, Harry Hopkins, and reads:

> Whereas John Barrington, knight and baronet, now a prisoner in the Fleet, has obtained a writ of *habeas corpus* issuing out of the high court of chancery directed to the warden of the Fleet, for his going abroad until the 23rd of January ... know ye therefore that I Henry Hopkins, the warden of the prison of the Fleet, do nominate and appoint my servants Humphrey Morris, John Hawkins and Anthony Porrens to do and apply all my office in guarding and attending the body of the above named John Barrington ... and to be his keeper and him safely to bring again to the said prison of the Fleet [on the] 20th day of January next coming or sooner if he be required there; and so that no further order shall be taken for his enlargement willing and requiring all persons, officers and others whom it may concern to be aiding and assisting to my said servants, or any of them in the due execution hereof, given at the Fleet the 28th of November 1653.[34]

It is not known where John Barrington went in furtherance of this writ, but the destinations of some others who went "into the country"[35] with the use of this writ are known. They included Shropshire, recorded because a prisoner, Arthur Powell absconded on his way to a trial there;[36] and Monmouthshire, where Daniel O'Sullivan, having giving security in sums four times greater than his debt of fifty pounds, lost both this and his liberty by being imprisoned by Lord Herbert in Chepstow castle. His complaint, however, was more prosaic, namely that he had been charged for his chamber rent at the Fleet during his year's enforced absence.[37] George Lawson, committed at the queen's suit, was permitted to be "carried" to Northumberland in 1712 by the court of Common Pleas as a witness in a trial. When his keeper was himself arrested for debt at Newcastle Lawson escaped, but was later captured and held close prisoner, with the result that there was an information filed against the warden for an escape, "as though the said Lawson was not so secured".[38] A list of precedents in a manuscript at Queens college, Oxford, includes a statement that Sir William Constable was brought out of the Fleet prison by order of James I in order to be employed as ambassador in the low countries.[39] All these removals, to be legal, would have required the same writ or warrant as Cotes and Hill received in 1671. This permitted them to be at large until the end of term, having given good security to the warden of the Fleet prison for their safe return.[40] Without such a warrant not even the king's demand that a prisoner be freed would be regarded as legal, but with it Tilly's claim that his writ or *rules* ran into Yorkshire or extended to the East or the West Indies could not be disputed.[41]

The warden was still responsible for his prisoners throughout the period of their "being abroad". If they escaped he was responsible to their creditors for their debts.[42] This is the reason why he required not only security or a bond of money for the safe return of his prisoners on the expiration of their writ, probably to a sum far in excess of their debts,[43] but also that they should be accompanied by a keeper. In 1694 a bond was entered into for a penalty of ten thousand pounds, to cover debts worth a tenth of that sum, but this was apparently sufficient for the prisoner Francis Hind to be relieved of a keeper's presence, together with the accompanying charges of his wages, victuals and transport, which was then set at twenty pence per day. But, said Harris, of another and earlier case, "this was no small favour at the warden's peril".[44]

Harris employed special keepers for this purpose. He had twenty,[45] but it was not unknown for a prisoner's own servant to act in this capacity.[46] The writ cost a substantial sum of money. It even seems that a "bribe" had to be given to receive it, and one of one hundred pounds was not unknown.[47] Lilburn, writing of the King's Bench, gives the following costs which had to be met before the writ would be granted. Firstly there was a gift to the marshall's wife. The clerk who checked the securities received ten to twenty shillings. Mr Holland received half a crown for making the bond or warrant. Then there was a weekly sum which would cost between five and twenty shillings. If a prisoner was in execution of his sentence there was a daily sum of half a guinea if out of term time, four shillings for the first day during term time, and three shillings for each subsequent day. To all this had to be added the keeper's charge of two shillings per day, and other costs which might amount up to another ten.[48] The Fleet appears, outwardly at least, to have been much cheaper, with fees of twenty pence per day and half that for a half day. These were the fees according to the 1567 constitutions,[49] though Harris added that the charges could amount to thirty to forty shillings per week. Probably this sum takes into account the prisoner's fees and chamber rent in the prison, which had to be paid unless a composition had been agreed with the warden. The profits from these writs could be staggering. Tilly, for example, claimed that he had received ten, twenty or thirty guineas as the initial "feel", and could make two hundred pounds annually from this source alone. The investigating committee, considering his estimates too conservative, multiplied it by four for the year 1694, and suggested a figure of nine hundred and twenty-two pounds for the following year.[50] One of the reasons why they might have recommended the ending of this practice of giving such liberty to debt prisoners was that they could not accept that any subject of the crown, certainly not a gaoler, should have a virtual licence to obtain such vast amounts of money.

****

Little is known of the origin of the day *rules*. Unlike the writs of *habeas corpus* the day *rules* were confined to the legal terms, and Harris noted that while originally they were only available for those wishing to attend the Westminster courts or to see their counsel, now "late custom hath enlarged their walks all over London".[51] Berisford also linked these day *rules* with the writ of *habeas corpus* when he wrote in 1699 that the writs were now "commonly understood" as the day *rules*. He was not at all happy with this position, and found several legal precedents which appeared, to him at least, to contradict the giving of such liberties to debt prisoners. One was Mostin's case. He had been let out by rule of court, but the warden was not allowed to plead such justification in a subsequent action of escape.[52] Lilburn would have concurred with Berisford's statements, for he too denounced the use of these day *rules*, on the grounds that they permitted a prisoner to live at home, though he was still required to maintain some presence in the prison by paying his fees. Thus his creditors were "cozened and deceived" and prisons turned into sanctuaries and places of security.[53] But both Berisford and Lilburn could only argue such precedents and express their concern, for the 1561 constitutions of the prison plainly allowed the warden to licence prisoners to go abroad, accompanied by a keeper, for either the half day or a full day. The cost of a half day was then four pence, together with sixpence for the keeper, and double both charges for the full day.[54] These writs for the day *rules* are described as day writs of *habeas corpus* in 1635,[55] giving a further clue to their origin. Following these precedents the act of *8 & 9 William III c 27* plainly endorsed and permitted this practice of the day *rules*.[56]

The original purpose of the day *rules* was similar to that of the writs of *habeas corpus* as described above, namely to permit debtors to arrange and transact their affairs with their attorneys or creditors. "The courts have thought it an equal advantage", wrote a pamphleteer of 1697, "both to debtor and creditor, that the prisoners, by day *rules* ... should have qualified LIBERTY (in term time at least) to solicit their law affairs, and dispose of their estates and effects to the best advantage."[57] Berisford, as may be expected from such a soured and embittered creditor, was a little more sparing in his approval. "The prisoners claim", he wrote, as though he disputed it, "that they have extraordinary occasions to go abroad, to direct their attorneys, and advise with counsel about their business and the like."[58]

Application for the use of the day *rules* was made by a prison tipstaff on behalf of the debtor concerned in the court of Common Pleas, on each day that court met. In every successful application the court directed that the warden be made secure against escape. This was done by requiring the attendance of a keeper as well as a note in hand from a friend of the prisoner promising his safe return by nightfall,[59] and to secure and indemnify the warden in a fixed sum if he escaped. Many suspected that the wardens, particularly in the times of Tilly and Huggins, were none too particular about obtaining the court's permission before allowing their prisoners the use of these day *rules*. "Where one goes abroad by virtue of a day writ, forty go abroad without it," was one considered judgement.[60]

The warden's insistence that each prisoner who left the gates of the Fleet by virtue of this writ be accompanied by a keeper was not only a question of greater security, but of more profit to the warden. This was in addition to the bonds for safe return, and similar protests were made about this double imposition as were made at an earlier date with regard to leaving the prison by the writ of *habeas corpus*.[61] Throughout the period of Guybon's deputy wardenship in the 1720s the prisoners mounted a campaign to show the unreasonableness of requiring these two forms of security, the bond and the attendance of a keeper, claiming that the giving of security should be in lieu of a keeper. They also claimed that far more than the legal fee of five shillings for his attendance was often demanded. Furthermore they expressed their annoyance that the securities were required in sums greater than their debts, while the warden would not always accept the securities they offered. James Collett, for example, had urgent need of the day *rules*, but the warden refused to accept the securities he offered (though he had paid twenty five shillings for the bond), nor would he allow him two "waiters" to accompany him, even though Collett promised to pay him for the trouble. The warden's refusal, he claimed, caused him "great loss and damage" for which there was no redress.[62] Had they known Harris's work, then in manuscript, *The Oeconomy of the Fleet*, they might have used for their argument his comment that he only required prisoners to be accompanied by keepers when a "sufficient bond" was not available. His added comment that this was "no small favour at the warden's peril" was more a rhetorical flourish than a practical gesture of goodwill.[63] By 1778 those who had the liberty of the *rules* were able to take advantage of the day *rules* without having to provide further security, as had been the case earlier, and of the sixty-four prisoners who had the use of the day *rules* in that year, fifty-two were already in the *rules*.[64] By the early nineteenth century the point had been conceded, and those who had given security were exempted from the attendance of a keeper.[65]

John Mackay, writing on behalf of the prisoners, declared in 1723 that the cost and difficulty of obtaining the day *rules* made them "ineffectual".[66] They were certainly not inexpensive. In the 1720s the clerk of the enquiries demanded five shillings even to enquire into the securities offered, while the escorting keepers required the same sum per day. This made it unlikely, said the prisoners, that a poor man could ever take advantage of this provision, for in addition to these sums there was a daily charge of six shillings and sixpence.[67] To be true the 1729 report gave a figure which reduced this sum by sixpence for the first and the last days of term, specifying that the ordinary charge was five shillings and sixpence. This was made up of the following fees: the four judges received three pence each; the secondary or deputy warden twenty pence; the warden twelve pence, and the clerk of the papers twenty-two pence.[68] It was his duty to plead for the *rules* in court and check the securities. These charges were later reduced to five shillings and four shillings and sixpence respectively,[69] but by 1828 they had been increased to half a guinea.[70] In addition, by this time, the cost for a bond of security, or a warrant of attorney which had been substituted for it, was now calculated according to a percentage of the debts in which the prisoner was charged, so that if these were under five hundred pounds this expense would be two pounds seven shillings. The total cost was said to be seldom more than five guineas.[71] This had to be paid each term during which the privilege of the day *rules* was required. But it was said that when Nixon was deputy warden and found a person who needed the use of the day *rules*, who was respectable and honest and was in prison for a small sum, he would allow him the benefit of the day *rules* without any other expense than the daily fee.[72] It seems that from the 1750s prisoners who habitually made use of these day *rules* were permitted to run up accounts for administrative convenience. Richard Ryder in Trinity term 1753 owed £3.17s.6d., as did Sir Robert Clifton for the Hilary term of the following year.[73]

The day *rules* permitted a prisoner to travel anywhere so long as he returned by nightfall to the prison gates. This, therefore, was an extension of a grant given for purely legal purposes, which Harris explained had become enlarged by custom to include the whole of the London of his day.[74] Nightfall, too, was gradually extended until it was interpreted as midnight, but by 1818 custom was giving way to order and it was said to be 11 p.m. and by 1828 9.00 p.m.. If a prisoner failed to return by that time he would lose the benefit of the day *rules* in future. The prisoners were permitted to leave by nine in the morning, so with a reasonable horse one could travel a considerable distance. However as these writs had to be granted by the court of Common Pleas, they could only be obtained during those days when the court sat. This excluded the greater festivals of the church and Sundays.

Many took advantage of these day *rules*, in spite of their limited application and prohibitive cost. During Michaelmas term 1748, 329 separate motions were granted: 172 in Hilary term of 1749, and in Easter and Trinity terms of the same year 285 and 201 respectively. Michaelmas term 1754 saw 340 applications, Easter term 1755 465, but Trinity term two years later only 118. The numbers obviously fluctuated according to the number in prison. As many made use of these day *rules* on more than one occasion each term it is impossible to suggest how many individuals benefited from them. But several clearly went out on every possible occasion, as did Gilbert Cuthbert, Thomas Oddy and Sir Robert Clifford, from 1749 to 1757.[75] What had originated as a legal privilege designed to assist debtors in arranging their affairs, had become an opportunity for pleasure for those who could afford to alleviate the miseries of their imprisonment in the Fleet. "Show you my horse", is described by Egan Pierce in his *Life in London* as a cant phrase for these day *rules*, but perhaps it conveys something of the pleasure and freedom this privilege allowed.

****

The *rules* of the prison was a well-defined area outside the prison house in which prisoners were allowed to reside. The 1792 report suggested that their origin lay in a temporary arrangement while the building was being rebuild, but this is an inspired guess,[76] as was Nixon's suggestion that it lay in a rule of court during the time of James I.[77] Strype, in his edition of Stow, published in 1720, states that these *rules* had been granted "for some years since",[78] while writers of the 1690s stress that their origin is to be found in a rule of court made by the court of Common Pleas in 1685 or 1686.[79] But this rule obviously regulated their position rather than initiated it. Lilburn writing in the 1640s suggests there was some confusion in the King's Bench prison between the right to leave the prison by a writ of *habeas corpus*, and the right to "lie within the *rules*" of the prison.[80] Complaints made against the marshall, Glover, in 1680, suggested that one of his alleged offences was that of charging excessive fees for the *rules*, as well as charging some rulers with treasonable activity, placing them in close confinement and ironing them, when he had been given "great sums and goods in lieu" for their use of this privilege.[81] So far as the Fleet was concerned a petition of the 1750s, in which the prisoners requested an extension of the area or limits of their *rules*, states that it had been allowed by a statute of 1686, but that "in great measure ... [it] existed time out of mind and in some sort was endorsed by the patent of 19 Charles II in which the office [of warden] was granted to Whitcott."[82]

In fact we may go back further to the reign of Mary I and the grant of 1558 which permitted the Babington family to sell the Fleet prison and the office of warden to John Heath. This tantalisingly suggests that the *rules* consisted of the houses within and without the close of the Fleet.[83] Nothing written by Harris would suggest that the *rules* operated in his day, unless the matter was so well understood that he saw no need to mention it. Fifteen years after he wrote his *Oeconomy of the Fleet*, Thomas Cranley wrote his *Amanda, or the Reformed Whore*, in 1635. He mentions that various houses in Fleet lane were filled with prisoners, particularly with women debtors. These were "without the prison gate" but he was able to communicate with one female debt prisoner, who lived in the lane, from his prison chamber's window. She asked him "if he sometimes went abroad in the city", and would he visit her?[84] Another petition of the same period protests that the use of the Fleet yard had been taken from the prisoners, and though it was outside the prison gates, it was "a part and member of the prison." This had occurred as the warden, facing enquiries about various escapes, had been forced for his own security to restrain all prisoners in execution "within the gate of the main prison, whereby we are all deprived of the liberty of the *rule* and dwelling without the gate (which is also the prison it serves) and thereby debarred from meeting our friends (who will not come to the house,) or providing for ourselves those things which are needful for us". They prayed for the "ancient, lawful liberties and privileges of the house" to be restored "for the comfort and convenience of the prisoners" who gave the warden security for their true imprisonment.[85]

An attempt to remedy this ambiguity about the legality and the extent of the *rules* was made by a committee of the House of Commons (in the course of an inquiry into the abuses practised in the prison) during 1696. Having heard of the many abuses practised in the use of the writ of *habeas corpus*, the committee demanded that the *rules* of the Fleet be ascertained by act of parliament, and that it should be deemed an escape if any prisoner was seen outside these limits. This was enacted in 1697 by the *8 & 9 William III c 27* which stated that all prisoners were to be detained in either the prison house or in the respective *rules* of the prison, while section five, for example, stated that nothing in the act was to be construed as to make void the securities for living in the *rules*. Thereafter this act was quoted as the legal authority for the existence of the *rules*.[86] Undoubtedly the acceptance of the *rules* by this legislation was the outcome of the realisation that more accommodation was needed than the prison house could provide, and that the various privileges and customs of the past needed regulation. Lord Chief Justice Raymond clarified this position and understanding by stating at one of Bambridge's trials, "every part of the *rules* is a part of the prison, though not within the walls."[87]

However much the *rules* were disliked by the judiciary and creditors, they were tolerated because of the overcrowding of the prison and the consequent fear of pestilence. Even Berisford accepted this, stating that the only authority he could find for the use of the *rules* at the King's Bench was a statement by Lord Chief Justice Keeling. In this Keeling declared that because of the number of "the removals from other prisons" there were more prisoners in the King's Bench than it could contain. Consequently the boundaries of the prison were enlarged by the direction of the court, "which enlargement is called the *rules*, which are houses adjacent, hired by the marshall".[88] Other writers explained the consequences of such over-crowding. It was impossible to dispose of such numbers "in so small a compass" as the prison; "what large buildings and vast [number of] guards must be requisite to keep these numerous shoals of men who in all likelihood will become prisoners, when the Mint, Savoy and Friars are divested of their pretended rights," wrote one, capitalising, as all good pamphleteers must, on contemporary concern, in this case of ending the numerous debt sanctuaries which infested London and sheltered its criminal classes.[89] Another writer played on the real fear of Londoners that their prisons could become a source of pestilence to the city, writing that to place all prisoners within the walls of a prison would be like "putting a quart of wine into a pint pot". Warming to his theme, he pointed out the dangers of "the contagious distempers which may justly be dreaded from a multitude of necessitous persons so strictly to be confined".[90] A further writer played for pity. If the *rules* were taken away then the debtors would be "starved and smothered to death" as the prisons were "not sufficient to contain the prisoners by many thousands".[91] Such arguments had a substantial measure of truth about them. In 1814, for instance, the marshall of the King's Bench allowed a considerable reduction in the cost of the *rules* as a means of "clearing the prison".[92] However, these arguments were set against a background of continuing hostility to the existence of the *rules*; Sir John Pratt typifying the reaction of many in his comment that if the "*rules* be law, all England may be made one extended prison".[93] But as the granting of the *rules* was an outcome of the non-penal nature of debt imprisonment, in which the main emphasis lay on the security each prisoner could offer for his safe imprisonment, it is not surprising that John Howard found other prisons possessed similar privileges for their debt prisoners. Their number included the King's Bench prison.[94]

The territorial extent of the *rules* as defined in the eighteenth century was as follows: from the prison house along the Fleet ditch southwards to Ludgate hill, eastwards to Cock alley on that hill, on the north along both sides of the Old Bailey to Fleet lane, and down both sides of that lane until the prison house was reached.[95] These limits were considerably extended in 1824 so as to include Chatham place, St Paul's, Salisbury court in Fleet street, and Shoe lane. Though the circumference of the new limits extended to one and a half miles, double the previous limit, it was still smaller than the *rules* of the King's Bench.[96] Unlike those *rules*, however, the Fleet rulers were permitted to enter the public houses within their area, and in both they were permitted to reside along the outer streets or within the narrow and squalid courts and alleyways which lay in between.

With the single exception of Ludgate hill, the area of the Fleet rules was always a mean one. The Fleet ditch, which ran in front of the prison, described by Pope in his *Dunciad* as "the king of dykes", a "place of dead dogs", and by another writer as "a nauseous and abominable sink of nastiness",[97] was covered over in 1737 and the Stocks market in the city transferred to this site. It then became a little more respectable. But this never applied to Fleet lane, which Strype described in a memorable phrase as "a place of no great account for buildings or inhabitants".[98] A map of this lane in 1728 shows it containing mean houses, many taverns, and slaughter houses.[99] The rulers later claimed it to be such a "red light" district that no respectable gentleman from the prison could live there.[100] Within the whole area there were also numerous gaming houses, and between thirty to forty public houses, with approximately two hundred and nineteen habitable houses in 1786.[101]

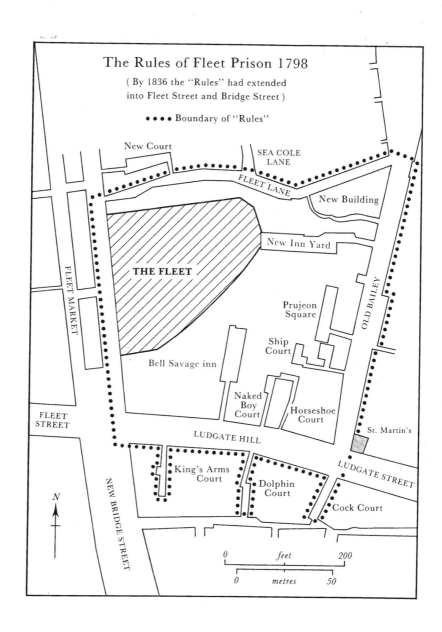

A plan of the extent of the *rules* in 1798.

It was impossible to provide guards at every street corner within the *rules* in an attempt to prevent escapes by the rulers. Indeed such escapes were hard to prevent, especially as the western boundary was an imaginary line drawn through part of the Fleet market, so that an unintentional "shove" could cause a prisoner to be jostled into close confinement. Even to cross from one side to the other of a certain coffee house on Ludgate hill could also constitute an escape, while another house on the same hill could be entered by the back door but not by its front.[102] Nevertheless, Pearce alleged that a prisoner, if seen outside the *rules*, could play a "trump card", that is, a bank-note, and he would hear no more about his misdemeanour.[103]

As the warden was liable for the debts of any escaped prisoner, he indemnified himself by requiring securities from each ruler for his safe imprisonment and for his "forthcoming" in prison when required. By the 1800s this security took the form of a "warrant of attorney to confess a judgement to the amount of the debt with which the prisoner stands charged, with a defeazance on the back, declaring it is to be void in case no escape should take place".[104] The day rulers probably had to give the same form of security. Those who were imprisoned on a mesne process, whose creditors could only recover damages in the case of an escape rather than the debts owed to them, were required to obtain what was termed a single security. But those who were in execution of their sentences needed to obtain double security. This meant that the warden required at least two people to enter into securities for that person's safe imprisonment, the penalty of both being in the same amount of the debts charged against the person concerned. Such securities were always carefully scrutinised, and sometimes rejected, not only on the grounds that they were insufficient, but also for what was later politely termed "the impropriety of conduct" of the debtor who requested the use of the *rules*.[105] As the securities were always made out in the name of the existing warden, rather than to his office, they had to be renewed at considerable trouble and expense whenever a new appointment was made.[106]

Prisoners were called in if any doubt arose about their securities. Equally, when prisoners in the *rules* had further actions for debt laid against them they would be called in and required to pay additional fees for the use of the *rules* as well as to obtain more substantial securities.[107] Mackay alleged that Huggins took two securities but allowed an additional "blank" space on the form, and frequently demanded that rulers find that additional and third security with all the new fees it entailed. But this may have been no more than the need to obtain new securities because of new actions brought against that ruler.[108] Thus Edward Goldney who was charged with an additional action of forty pounds was required to give better security, and John Howells, charged with a new debt of thirty pounds, was required to find an additional five pounds for his use of the *rules*.[109] Robert Castell is another case in point. He entered the prison charged with debts of under one hundred pounds, but later, as a prisoner, he was charged with further debts of over one thousand pounds. But his friends who had offered security for him surrendered that security on learning that he was planning to go abroad with Lord Londonderry. As was usual in such circumstances he was brought in from the *rules* and taken into a spunging house in order that he might have time to re-arrange his securities without having to pay again for the use of the *rules*.[110] Others were also taken up and brought into the prison house at the request of their securitors; some as they no longer trusted their friend, others as they had failed to realise that if the prisoner "went out of the rules [their] security was liable".[111] In such cases the person who had offered the security was responsible for having the prisoner arrested by the tipstaff and for paying the fees concerned.[112]

These securities were nearly always entered into by two persons or more, even if, on one occasion, the additional security was provided in the name of the prisoner himself,[113] or, as on another occasion, by his creditor. This occurred in the case of Castell, whose creditor thought it better "to run the hazard" as there was no possibility that his prisoner could sort out his affairs in the prison house.[114] The cheapest bond available was for a penalty of one hundred pounds, and this was required even if the debts recorded against the prisoner were only ten to twelve pounds. Normally the sum was double the amount of the debt.[115] Edward Kelly was a rare exception, for when he died in the *rules* with debts of twenty-five pounds he possessed no security. Those who had more substantial debts appear to have had more favourable treatment. One with a debt of two hundred and fifty pounds was required to find bonds in double that sum, another in a debt of fifteen hundred pounds in only two thousand. Sir Robert Clifton, with debts of over twelve thousand, gave security of only five thousand. Those who were charged with contempt of court were required to find security in the sum of one thousand pounds. Three further examples may be given. John Clarke, with debts of fifty-five pounds, was required to find security of two hundred. He obtained this from his brother William Clarke. James Ashley, in the following year, 1753, needed security of one thousand pounds to cover his debts of only one hundred and seventy. His son, Lorraine James Ashley, and Benjamin Less, a surgeon of Saffron hill, provided them. Some months later Ashley returned from the King's Bench prison and was required to provide new securities. William Flanders, an innkeeper with debts of thirty-three pounds, had securities in the sum of one hundred entered into by Samuel Clayton, a butcher of Hanover yard, St Giles in the Fields, John Mason of the same, victualler, and John Brindle, another victualler of Hungerford market.[116]

No fixed fees were charged for the *rules*. Instead like the day *rules* an annual charge was imposed based on a percentage of the debts charged against a prisoner. Guybon took two guineas for each one hundred pounds of debt: in 1793 it was five per-cent for the first hundred pounds, and two and a half per-cent for the remainder, but by 1803 it had been reduced to a consistent three per-cent.[117] In addition the stamp duty on the warrant cost twenty shillings, and there was an enquiry fee to the clerk of half a guinea. It was then said that if the debt was large, or if the prospective ruler was an "industrious handicraft man with a wife and large family", a lesser sum would be taken. From such fees the warden of the Fleet gained nearly a thousand pounds in 1814.[118]

In former days it had been customary to make an initial bargain with the warden. This led to many charges of extortion, especially during the 1720s in particular. These "bargains" were said to be anything from five guineas to one hundred pounds, so that the *rules* provided a substantial source of profit to the warden, even forgetting the new year presents the warden was said to expect from his rulers. Huggins admitted he received many such presents, some of fifty guineas or more, but claimed he had never demanded them and had not allowed Guybon to take them. The 1729 report states that such gifts from the 382 rulers amounted to over two thousand eight hundred pounds, and would be three times that sum if all had paid; but in their list of the prison profits this figure was reduced, and even when added to the initial fees for the *rules*, only amounted to fifteen hundred pounds. This was an average of four pounds per ruler.[119]

The rulers in the 1720s made many complaints about further fees, even though Huggins did not require them to maintain a chamber in the prison house, as insisted on by Tilly.[120] Thomas Winston was sorely grieved that for non-payment of the weekly four pence due to the chaplain his securities "were threatened" and the warden had written to one of his securitors suggesting he should surrender him.[121] Huggins, or rather his assistants, were also accused of taking money from prisoners for the liberty of the *rules*, and then denying its application to them. It was further alleged that they carried back rulers into the prison house. It was claimed that in both instances their only motive was to obtain further money by forcing such disappointed persons to make a further application for the use of these *rules*.[122]

Exceptional privileges regarding these *rules* were available to those who could pay for them, as was discovered in the case of Thomas Perrin. An affidavit given to him by John Huggins, warden of the Fleet, in October 1710, reads as follows:

> John Huggins, warden of the Fleet, maketh oath, that Thomas Perrin of London, merchant, shall peaceably and quietly, without interruption or molestation, hold and enjoy to himself the liberty of the *rules* of the prison of the Fleet, without any further charge whatsoever, and this deponent will not permit or suffer the said Thomas Perrin, under any pretence whatsoever (against his will) to be confined within the walls of the said prison, nor shall the said Thomas Perrin be removed to any other prison, by or through the means or procurement of this deponent, by *habeas corpus* or otherwise, to any of his majesty's prison or prisons, place or places of confinement, so far as to the utmost of his this deponent's power can be prevented; and in case a *habeas corpus* be brought to effect, so as that the said Thomas Perrin should be removed, he, this deponent, will use his utmost endeavour to bring him back to the *rules* of the Fleet, that he may enjoy the liberty aforesaid, or to procure for him the liberty of the *rules* at this deponent's own proper charge and expense, and so to be continued to him under Moses Cooke, esq, the present marshall, or any other marshall, so long as the said Thomas Perrin shall continue to be a prisoner, so as that he may either at the King's Bench or Fleet prisons enjoy the liberty proposed, notwithstanding any action or actions, judgement or judgements, declaration or declarations, extent or extents, by means of his late or present misfortunes, or any thing that may or shall happen to or arise therefrom: And that in case this deponent should sell, assign or set over the wardenship or property in the Fleet, That then and in such case, he this deponent will, at his own cost, use his endeavours, so that he shall enjoy the liberty aforesaid, and upon his single security, and that he shall have day *rules* to transact his affairs in term time, as often as his occasions require, without any expense to him the said Thomas Perrin; and

in case of his consenting to be within the walls of the prison, shall be let into the *rules* again whenever he shall require the same, by writing to Mr Samuel Blunt, or any other person immediately.[123]

This affidavit aroused the wrath of the 1729 committee, but in view of the presuppositions already made about the *rules* and the prison, there was nothing essentially illegal about it.

Many attempts were made by the rulers to have the limits of the *rules* enlarged. They were even prepared to engage counsel to plead their case to the court of Common Pleas. In 1735 a petition was sent to that court, requesting that the area be enlarged to include both Holborn and Blackfriars, and the whole of the Fleet market. Commercial opposition caused its failure.[124] The court received a further petition in 1745-6. Learning from the first rejection, the rulers requested only a limited extension to Holborn, and persuaded several householders and tradesmen from the neighbourhood to support them. These argued that the *rules* were a benefit to them by the trade it provided and the possibilities it allowed of using their houses as lodgings. Several of them were stallholders in the Fleet market. In their petitions the rulers complained that many of the tradespeople had removed their shops into the Fleet market. This meant they had only limited access to some nine shops' "back fronts" and to ten warehouses, but they were only able to go three foot deep into the butchers' shops. They claimed that they often had to pay a halfpenny to two pence for a messenger to obtain the foodstuffs and goods they could not purchase themselves, in which, they added, they were frequently deceived, so that a twelve pence shoulder of lamb cost them eighteen pence and three farthings worth of carrots cost another halfpenny to obtain. This complaint was brusquely set aside on the grounds that they still had access to a part of the market. Other traders in the market feared they would lose credit if the rulers were admitted, and claimed they would obstruct their business. Others argued that any extension would increase prostitution in the area, and enlarge the clandestine marrying trade associated with the prison *rules*, although the rulers correctly pointed out that this trade had no connection with the prison whatsoever.[125] The petition failed because of the opposition of the city authorities and the parochial bodies. Indeed, this may have been the occasion about which a later writer wrote, "some years ago an attempt was made to take St Bride's church into the *rules*, whereupon the parishioners' rose to a man" to prevent its application.[126]

~~A~~ later attempt to enlarge the *rules* took place in 1786, when there were only sixty prisoners within it. It was then proposed to extend the limits from Chatham place to Holborn hill, and from the Old Bailey to Snow hill, thus taking in the whole of the Fleet market. Had it been successful it would have tripled the extent of the *rules*, though note was made that the King's Bench *rules* were ten times the size of the Fleet's. A considerable number of reasons, economic, pragmatic, even theological, were offered by the rulers to show the desirability of such an extension. There were not enough shops in the *rules* to justify most of the market's exemption from it; the number of reasonably priced lodgings available was insufficient and there was a lack of room in the prison house, while the accommodation in the prison chapel was insufficient for all the Fleet prisoners. The demolition of seventeen houses in Half Moon court in the Old Bailey to make way for an extension of the Sessions House had meant a grave diminution in the number of lodgings and workshops available. Twelve of these workshops had been used by rulers, who had thereby tried to ease the burden of their imprisonment. Thus is was only right that some compensation be given by extending the *rules* elsewhere.

The same interests as before opposed this application. The traders argued that many rulers infringed the privileges and liberties of the city by working within the *rules*, and thus forced honest and presumably rate-paying craftsmen and traders out of work. It would destroy the credit of many of the market people. The parishes involved feared that if the extension was granted "the manners of the prison [would] daily grow ground", and expressed concern at the great number of prisoners and their dependants who sought relief from the parochial rates. "Every parish", it was claimed, "in which the *rules* are prayed to be extended apprehend great mischiefs from the obvious consequences of inviting a number of necessitous people to come and reside in that part of the town." These were the days of parochial poor relief! In fact this was clearly the major argument, and the rulers were not helped in their case by the warden's successful application for a reduction in the poor rates paid by the prison because of the diminution in the number of prisoners. It was claimed too that there were twenty vacant rooms to let within the *rules*, though the rulers maintained in reply that these were either on Ludgate hill, which they could not afford, or the area of Fleet lane, which was not a respectable area. It seems that a very limited extension was granted, however, bringing the London Coffee House on Ludgate hill into the *rules*, instead of forming only a part of its boundary as before. It may be that the prisoners requested much in order to achieve a limited objective, but even that was denied them with this one slight exception.[127]

And yet surprisingly the prisoners in 1824, when the number of prisoners and rulers was far less than in 1786, and using the same kind of arguments about the lack of shops and the limited accommodation available (due to the vast number of houses unfit for habitation), were successful in their petition to the court of Common Pleas and obtained a substantial enlargement of the *rules*. Although the prisoners had the support of the warden in their application, the real reason for their success was because the city authorities and the local inhabitants, who would have opposed it, were not informed about their application to the court. The city authorities, eventually hearing of the successful application, made strong objections to it in November 1825. The new *rules*, they argued to the court, had been placed in one of the most preferable quarters of the city both for trade and the residence of "opulent and respectable citizens", and in an area which had been greatly improved by the removal of the Fleet market to form a new street. And to add insult to injury, all this had been done when there were only thirty prisoners in the *rules*. The warden, William Brown, replied in a letter still contained in the city archives, refusing to give the information the city solicitor had requested about the number in the *rules*, on the grounds that he could not do so without the sanction of the court. He added that the judges would not have allowed such an extension unless it was for "substantial reasons", and that the opposition had come mainly from two or three people in Bridge street who would not be affected by it.[128] And there the matter rested, the rules enlarged.

Not only did a concerted and organised opposition appear every time an extension of the *rules* was planned, there was always a bitter and continuing protest against its very existence. When an attempt was made to end its use in the 1690s, Tilly insisted that his rulers should make their own contribution to a fund established to obstruct the bill. One Mr Rossiter was said to have given two pounds to this noble cause, though Mr Lentall was fetched into the prison and so "persuaded" of the value of these *rules* to himself and others that he contributed one hundred pounds.[129] He must have been gratified that his money was not in vain. Further bills of 1698 and 1702 were also claimed indirectly to affect this privilege, and these too were successfully resisted.[130] The epithets continued. The *rules* were termed an "asylum for debtors" and "places of refuge", which reduced imprisonment "to a mockery", allowing the rulers "to come and go as they please". Its existence encouraged the debtor to resist his creditors and "live as extravagantly as possible", permitted the manners of a prison to gain ground daily, while it was "not wise to abate the terrors of confinement by making it pleasant".[131] Such sentiments were re-echoed in the 1814 report on the King's Bench prison. Its *rules*, the committee argued, could hardly be called imprisonment, for by it the debtor "eludes the sentence of the law, and may dissipate that fortune which, in justice, is no longer his own".[132]

Prison manners were repeatedly condemned by all these pamphlets and petitions against the *rules*. Those non-prisoners who were so unfortunate as to live in the area of the *rules* lived under an "odious and unmerited stigma", which hurt both their reputation and their credit and depreciated the value of their homes.[133] When a plan was unveiled to transfer the prison to Ely house, in the 1770s, the inhabitants of the parish of St Andrew Holborn claimed that they would become "disreputable like the Savoy" and that "the rich who pay the poor rates" would be driven away. Instead "multitudes of poor" together with their families would enter the parish and require support.[134] What they meant by the term "disreputable" may be illustrated by a householder's petition against an extension of the limits of the *rules* to include the Fleet market. He wrote that the rulers loitered around shops, and:

> utterly hinder our customers, and give a disgust to such of our customers at whose suit any of such prisoners may be confined ... that hinder or prevent their coming to our shops for fear of being abused and insulted by them from whose licentious behaviour as already practised by them in the present indulgences they now enjoy.[135]

Others accused the rulers of planning villainies in the public houses of the *rules*.[136] Berisford painted much the same picture, writing:

> It can't but tease an honest tradesman to his soul to see his debtor, under condemnation, strut it out with his sword and nose him at his very door ... for 'tis the daily practice of all those pretended prisoners in the *rules* to walk

where they please in the several parts of the town, and to be sure they'll cross the street to put their creditors on the fret, and brave it to their faces; besides some creditors on Ludgate hill are so unfortunate, as to have their debtors come and live next door to them: perhaps the creditor and debtor may lodge in the same house, and this is worse than only losing the debt, for he's laughed at to boot ... Can the creditor think anything but that the law is a jest ... He can't think it in earnest sue when it calls his debtor's lodging there an imprisonment, and his debtor a prisoner ...[137]

Berisford may well have known of an actual incident which was reported by one of the committees into the Fleet prison. One Winn, a prisoner "at liberty" at the suit of a Mr Norcortt "had taken a lodging under the plaintiff's nose".[138] Can this, responded Berisford, be "imprisonment in the strict sense of the term?"

Probably the most persistent attacks made on the existence of the *rules* came from the city guilds. The various guilds argued that those who worked at their trades and crafts in the *rules* infringed the common rights of the city by trading without the expenses and apprenticeship required of the city traders. Indeed their "only qualification" to do so was "the non-payment of their debts".[139] A guild member complained about some of the prisoners who kept shops within the *rules*. Using accomplices, he continued, "they procure goods and merchandise thither", and then not only refuse to pay the invoices but keep the goods by force "to the great damage of the creditor so decoyed and to the scandal of the city of London".[140] These guilds had good reason to be alarmed. The number of prisoners who worked in the *rules* was not unsubstantial. The 1792 report quoted Nixon as saying that such men appeared to live with "some degree of decency, and in general by their own industry, as they are chiefly mechanics of some sort or other".[141] It has been noted that the wardens often allowed such men into the *rules* on reduced fees if it would help their circumstances. A list of such prisoners, at a much earlier period, is provided in one of the prison rule books for the 1740s and 50s. The following names and occupations are given in it: George Gillet kept a chandlers shop in the Old Bailey; William Shallcross was a watchmaker in the *rules*; Henry Fowler a tinplate worker at Mr Carlton's in the Old Bailey; John Savery a tailor at the King's Arms; James Crokett a bookseller at Poudgeons court, Old Bailey; Richard Huntmill a law-seller in the same place; Charles Hodges a carpenter in the Old Bailey; Joseph Hilton a staymaker at Dolphin court; Joseph Howell a watch engraver at Mr Lumley's Ship Court, Old Bailey; William Harris a cabinet maker in the Old Bailey over against the Golden Lion tavern; Thomas Holt, attorney, on Ludgate hill (he died there in 1757), while William Flanders and Edward Walker were both inn keepers.[142] Others were known to have worked as printers, for in 1722 Viscount Townshend ordered the warden to restrain certain printers, who lived in the *rules*, from publishing seditious ballads and other papers.[143] One wonders how these men managed to obtain credit. They argued, however, for themselves, that such work prevented many of them and their families from seeking parochial relief, and so increasing the poor rates.

Those prisoners who had taken houses in the *rules* were accused of not paying their parochial dues, even "of bidding defiance to all such demands", and then often requiring support from the parish poor rate for themselves and their families.[144] Joseph Nightengale considered that it ought to be made a law that any person "enjoying this privilege of the *rules* wilfully running into debt, for rent, lodging, or property, with any of the tradespeople having houses or shops within these limits or elsewhere, should be deprived of such liberty, upon complaint made to the warden".[145] St George's parish in Southwark, in whose parish the *rules* of the King's Bench were situated, had obtained a private act of parliament which exempted it from the care of that prison's rulers, but this precedent was never taken in regard to the Fleet, possibly because the prison and its *rules* extended into three separate parishes. St Bride's parish once endeavoured with little result to obtain some financial assistance from St Martin's Ludgate, as the main burden of relieving the destitute rulers fell onto its own poor rate.[146] Malcolm noted that in 1703 the three parishes petitioned parliament for relief against the burdens imposed upon them by insolvent debtors, and thereafter they endeavoured to limit their liability by declining to assist such people.[147] The *Mirror* in July 1833 reported as follows:

> Guildhall. A gentleman complained that the overseers of St Brides had refused to relieve a distressed prisoner in the Fleet. The prisoner was Mr Timothy Sheldrake who had been well known for his skill in treating deformities of the body. He once kept his carriage and obtained four thousand per annum from his practice, but was now quite destitute. He was eighty years of age and of that temper that he would rather starve than make a complaint. When applicant saw him he had actually fasted forty-eight hours. St Bride's parish had assisted him, but denied that he was legally entitled to such relief, applicant contended that as the prison was in St

Bride's parish and rated seventy pounds per annum, it was bound to afford casual relief to those within the walls of the prison, and to recover it from the respective parishes to which those who had been relieved belonged. The vestry clerk said that relief must be given out of the county rate. Sir C Marshall said he would take time to consider the point, but he thought a sufficient relief should be allowed out of the county rate.[148]

Although this extract relates to a prisoner inside the prison house, and not in the *rules*, it illustrates the dilemma faced by the parochial authorities, and their endeavours to limit their responsibilities in this direction.

Another frequent cause of complaint was that the *rules* were used by many people who, for their own purposes, masqueraded as prisoners in the Fleet, often with the purpose of deceiving creditors about their financial position. "It was the constant practice of the warden", complained one of the committees of investigation into the Fleet, "to take yearly two or three hundred persons into the protection of the Fleet though they were never arrested or committed".[149] Berisford added his own typical comment: "Whitefriars and the Mint are not crushed, so long as the prisons of the King's Bench and the Fleet are in being, for 'tis now become a common practice for bankrupts and cheating knaves themselves to run into one, as they did into the other for shelter and protection."[150] Joseph Johnson provides us with an example of this practice. As a householder in the *rules* of the Fleet, fearing arrest for debt, he made an agreement with the warden to be his prisoner in the *rules* for a fee of ten guineas.[151] Another by the name of Scoltock obtained a warrant of protection from the deputy warden Fox, though he was never a prisoner. His two sons with others were appointed his keepers, and his goods were sheltered in the prison house.[152] Many of the Fleet parsons who solemnised marriages in the *rules* claimed to be prisoners for debt in the prison, and thus immune from ecclesiastical sanction, as the prison was said to be a "peculiar" and thus not subject to the bishop of London. The prisoners, who found these marriages a source of offence when they applied for an extension of the *rules*, made it clear that such clergy were "no prisoners [but they] come occasionally and voluntarily within the verges of the prison".[153] Many others were advised by their friends to shelter in the *rules*. J A Randall wrote to his father Robert in 1678 that if he was unable to "be cleared ... I would advise you to remove to the King's Bench *rules* where you will live as well as any citizen".[154]

Richard Savage, the poet, was persuaded to take lodgings in the *rules* of the Fleet in a desperate attempt to deceive his creditors. He received a guinea weekly from his friends.[155] The basic idea of these manoeuvres was to persuade one's creditors that as one was already in a debt prison, there was little point in adding further writs to an already hopeless case. The position was never remedied.

The number of rulers in the Fleet was always substantial. It may be expressed in the form of a table:

Table Seven: The number of prisoners in the Rules *of the Fleet*

Date	Total number	in *rules*	percentage
1729[156]	c 1000	382	38.2
1747-8[157]	364	145	39.8
1755[158]	458	225	49.1
1760[159]	298	188	63.0
1774[160]	242	71	29.3
1776 [161]	195	52	26.6
1779[162]	184	37	20.1
1785[163]	225	93	41.3
1785[164]	400	150	37.5
1790[165]	c 380	c 190	50.0
1792[166]	260	80	30.0
1815[167]	279	60-70	25.0
1825[168]		15-20	
1834[169]	310	60	19.3

Other figures may be quoted. Out of the 134 prisoners who became prisoners between October 1760 and May 1761 26.11% entered the *rules* during that period; in a similar period between January and July 1778 10.28% of the prisoners admitted also entered the *rules*.[170] A return of 1827 gives the number of those admitted into the prison and the *rules* in each year between 1813 and 1826. In 1813 695 entered and 153 were admitted into the *rules* (22%); in 1817 the numbers were 733 and 86 (11.7%); in 1821 660 and 113 (17.1%) and in 1825 566 and 20 (3.5%) respectively.[171] The last year illustrates the effect of the reform of the debt legislation on the Fleet, bringing in few long-term prisoners, while in 1827 it became illegal for those who were imprisoned for the statutory three-month period before taking their cases to the insolvency court to be granted the *rules*. It must be remembered too that these figures relate to those who entered the prison or the *rules* in each year; they do not represent a total figure of the number in either for any given period. It seems reasonably clear, however, that while there were wide fluctuations in the numbers of rulers, there was until the 1820s an average of one third of the prisoners in the *rules* at any one time. This seems to be a much higher average than the King's Bench, where Howard found in 1776 that only 24% of the prisoners had the *rules* (80 of 444) and in 1779 it was but 20%.[172]

Though some in the King's Bench lived in their own homes in its *rules*,[173] most of the Fleet rulers lived in lodgings, which they complained were expensive, poorly furnished, and dirty, and often shared with people of bad character. Two guineas a week was not an uncommon rent, so that the rulers felt able to assert that there were only about twenty houses within reach of their pockets. Some of these were certainly the lodging houses built specifically or altered to accommodate the trade from these rulers. Some of these houses can be readily distinguished in the prison books; amongst them were the Bell and the Green Cannister in the Old Bailey, and Lumley's of Ship court.[174] The householders of the area were generally suspected of obtaining substantial profits at the expense of the poor debt prisoners,[175] perhaps following the spirit of a statement of 1701 which argued that if the *rules* were permitted in any area the inhabitants would probably connive at it, by reason of the profits they would obtain by entertaining such rulers in their homes.[176] Some confirmation and explanation of this statement is found in a printed petition protesting about the proposed removal of the prison to Ely house in the 1770s. This petition replied to several others which had argued that such a move would be beneficial to the householders as it would "raise the rent of the neighbourhood". On the contrary, the petition protested, while a seventy pound house might be rented for one hundred pounds if the move was successful, yet the first sum was far more valuable to the landlord if it brought a responsible tenant instead of one whose goods, "the landlord's best security", might be "covered by fraudulent judgments or liable to executions".[177]

A further explanation of the high cost of living in the *rules* lay in the scarcity of houses available for renting. In the 1780s the total number of houses in the *rules* was 219, but those on Ludgate hill were extremely expensive, and those in Fleet lane so disreputable and dilapidated that it was said no gentleman could live there.[178]   One who did was Francis Place's father.   Impoverished, he had had a friendly action brought against him which enabled him to live in the Fleet rules and lodge at the Elephant and Castle in Fleet lane.   This was a public house which attracted low company.   Here he gambled away all the money he had received from the sale of the lease of his public house, with the result that his wife became a washerwoman in order to provide them with some income.[179]   Huggins's claim that a chamber in the Fleet prison was cheaper and far more commodious than a room in the *rules* was probably true.[180]

The rulers thus lived under considerable disadvantages.   When the Fleet market was opened most of the local shopkeepers moved their businesses therein, but as there was only limited access to this market, for reasons already stated, the rulers were required to employ messengers to purchase their requirements at extortionate prices and often to their great disadvantage.[181]   On the other hand they were allowed to frequent the numerous public houses and vaults in the area, and even to reside at them.   It was alleged by the 1814 report that some of the prisoners entertained at great expense and resorted to the Belle Sauvage public house and the London coffee house, so that their "substance" was "much wasted by expensive living in these places".   Its recommendation that they should be excluded from the *rules*, as at the King's Bench prison,[182] was not implemented because of the strange counter-assertion of the 1818 report:

> ... as to the later, viz. the access to the coffee houses and the public houses within the *rules*, we are much disposed to subscribe to the opinion of the deputy warden, that no very material inconveniences result from it; that irregularities likely to arise there are sufficiently checked by the superintendence of the magistrates over public houses, and the interest of the keepers of such public houses to prevent them; that the prisoners who are disposed to waste their property for their own gratification would have the same opportunity of doing it within the prison as within the *rules*, though at more expense; and that to exclude these places from the *rules*, would deprive the prisoners of a convenience for the meeting of their creditors and the more ready access to their friends, which does not seem to have been abused, without any adequate advantage to the discipline of the prison, or any probable benefit to the creditor.[183]

Nixon had obviously put up a good case to the committee on behalf of his prisoners.   However it was eventually agreed that the houses where lottery tickets were "exposed to be sold" should be excluded from the *rules*, for it was realised that certain prisoners were linked with this trade and being prisoners were able "to escape the provisions made for ... preventing such mischiefs" in that enterprise. The Newgate sessions house was also excluded, as it was reported the rulers went there for "amusement". To visit such places would be regarded as an escape.[184]

Though the protests against the existence of the *rules* were many and influential, and sufficient to prevent any extension to its limits for many years, it proved impossible to end them because the prison house could not hold the number of prisoners committed to it. When in 1698 the warden brought in many rulers into that house it became intolerably overcrowded and all were "close confined".[185] This precedent was continually brought to the attention of all would-be reformers. But by the beginning of the nineteenth century there had been a serious decline in the number of long term prisoners, and hence in those eligible to enter the *rules*. After the strange extension of the *rules* in 1824, the attack against their existence began in earnest. Following the advice of William Jones, the marshall of the King's Bench, an act of 1827 prohibited prisoners from removing to the Fleet or King's Bench by the writ of *habeas corpus*, and, more significantly, prohibited insolvent debtors the use of the *rules* or day *rules* throughout the process of their cases through the insolvent debtors' court, save by its special leave.[186] Strangely no one appeared to notice that one of the reasons for the existence of these day *rules* had been to facilitate that business which the insolvent debtors' court now undertook instead. After the abolition of arrest on mesne process in 1838, and the ruling that those seeking relief through the insolvent debtors' act were to be permitted bail (a procedure which reduced debt imprisonment to a matter of a few days), the number of prisoners drastically declined, and it proved absurd to maintain three large debt prisons in London. By the act of *5 & 6 Victoria c 22*, these three, the Fleet, King's Bench and Marshalsea prisons, were consolidated into one, which took over the buildings of the King's Bench prison. The same act abolished the *rules* though allowing those who were then in possession of them a twelve-month grace. In spite of all the opposition to the existence of the *rules* this time-honoured institution had survived to the closure of the prison, and although convenience was often the slogan for its retention, it might well have been the sheer force of custom which had kept it alive. What had started as a privilege became a long-cherished right which was jealously guarded. And never more so than when its *raison d'être*, namely the overcrowding of the prison, had long since ended.

NOTES

1   Berisford, p 28.

2   Mackay, App IV.

3   Harris called it a charge to render the prisoner at the return of the writ rather than a discharge in the interim, Harris, p 103; cf Cal SPD, 1635, pp 75f. Blackstone in his *Commentaries on the Laws of England*, III 129, has no reference to the use of this writ.

4   Harris, p vii: Berisford, p 10; Clifford Dobb, "London's Prisons", in *Shakespeare Survey*, XVII (London 1964) 99.

5   Dobb, *London Prisons*, p 100.

6   Cal SPD, 1683-4, p 362.

7   Harris, p 52.

8   Debt prisoners at Ludgate also had the use of this writ, and by it, probably, Bunyan was allowed an "unofficial parole" in London whilst a prisoner at Bedford gaol.

9   Harris, pp 106, 110. He was accused of an excessive use of these writs [Wallace Notestein, *Commons Debates, 1621* (New Haven, 1935), IV 277].

10   Those who permitted this were heavily punished; the warden was removed from office and his deputy taken to Newgate, while Matthew was sent to the Tower [R B Pugh, *Imprisonment in Medieval England* (Cambridge, 1970), p 241].

11   1 Richard II c 12.

12   7 Henry IV c 4.

13   23 Henry VI c 9; and see BL, MS Addit 25250, fols 2ff.

14   Harris, p 112. These were the rules numbered 6, 8, and 12f.

15   Harris, pp 106f.

16   Harris, pp viii, 52, 77ff, 101ff, 106ff. In fact their use was more restricted still as he states that only 120 persons had received these writs in a three-year period, and 36 in one particular year [p 105].

17   Cal SPD, 1634-5, p 588. One prisoner had used his writ to visit a playhouse, and another, a close prisoner of the Privy Council, had been permitted to appear in the street in a coach drawn by four horses [Dobb, Thesis, pp 34f].

18   Cal SPD, 1635-6, pp 460, 528.

19   Cal SPD, 1667-8, p 510.

20   8 & 9 William III c 27 s v.

21   Jnl H of C, XI 643.

22   Jnl H of C, XI 642.

23   Jnl H of C, XI 643. An escape judgment was made against Fox for this, though it was probably permitted by the use of a writ of *habeas corpus*.

24   Jnl H of C, XII 685.

25   Jnl H of C, XI 644f.

26   Jnl H of C, XII 643. Tilly, it was alleged, was able to "swear" that prisoners were in prison though they were forty miles away [Jnl H of C, XI 641]. If "prison" meant in the custody of his officers, or subject to security, then Tilly was legally correct in these actions.

27   Berisford, p iv.

28   *A Short View of some Complaints against the Warden of the Fleet Prison* (1705).

29   *Some Considerations relating to the Bill for Regulating the King's Bench and Fleet Prisons*.

30   Howell, p 391.

31   Report 1729 (M), pp 19, 23f; Cal TP, 1720-8, p 279; cf Cal TP, 1714-9, p 107 and Cal TB, 1716, II 504. These allege that Perrin made his escape against Huggins's will, the Treasury having refused his request for his liberty upon giving security to surrender himself when required.

32   Report 1729 (M), p 18.

33   Harris, pp 101, 106f.

34   BL, MS Egerton 2648, fol 225. Another writ is in MS Addit 25250, fols 6ff.

35   In all probability the day *rules* sufficed for visits into the city.

36   Cal SPD, 1635, p 75. It was added that the prisoner had settled with his creditors "no party complains"; cf Cal TB, 1669-72, III-I 195, when a prisoner was allowed bail for a month to attend the Aylesbury assizes in order to "get in money due to him".

37   Cal SPD, 1667, p 411. He was later imprisoned at the warden's suit for these charges.

38   Cal TB, 1712, II 134.

39   The Queen's College, Oxford, MS CLV, fol 368, no 103.

40   Cal TB, 1669-72, III-II 962.

41   Jnl H of C, XI 644; cf Harris, pp 5, 106. John Lilburn, *Liberty Vindicated against Slavery* (London 1746), p 26, suggests that the *rules* of the marshall of the King's Bench "reach sometimes as far as York".

42   Harris, p 148. He notes how Sharpe, an attorney, obtained a false writ, deceived his keeper with it, then brought an action of escape against the warden, endeavouring to lay his debt upon the warden.

43   Cal SPD, 1667, p 441.

44   Harris, pp 77f, 103; BL, MS Egerton 2648, fol 225; PRO, E/134/11/Anne, Mich 37.

45   Harris, p 77.

46   William Holdsworth, *A History of English Law*, VIII 233n, quoting Historical Manuscript Commission, 4th Report, appendix 5.

47   Jnl H of C, XI 644; cf Harris, p 104.

48   Lilburn, *Liberty Vindicated*, p 26.

49   BLO, MS Rawlinson D1123, fol 28b; Harris, p 77; cf Cal SPD, 1664-5, pp 566f, which quotes the warden stating that in answer to a claim that 8*d.* of each 20*d.* fee was due to the poor box, that the full amount had been allowed to the warden by the 1561 grant of the prison.

50   Jnl H of C, XI 643, 677.

51   Harris, p 78.

52   Berisford, pp 13ff, 16f. His reference to Ostin's case is given as *Lord Dyer*, 297.

53   Lilburn, *Liberty Vindicated*, p 28. He notes that several continued with their business or trade.

54   Harris, p 112. This was omitted in the 1729 revision of the rules. Harris estimated he made an annual income of £400 from these writs alone.

55   Cal SPD, 1635, pp 75f, 80f; cf Thomas Cranley's *Amanda, or the Reformed Whore*, edited by Frederic Ouvry (London 1869), pp 29f.

56   Such day *rules* were also allowed at Ludgate and Pountry Compter. The charges at the latter were 1*s.*4*d.* for the keeper and in addition his dinner or 4*d.* in lieu [*Fees of the London Prisons* (London 1709)].

57   *Several Considerations on a Bill for Regulating the Abuses of Prisons* (1697).

58   Berisford, p 16.

59   Mackay, p 31. The cost of the enquiry was five shillings.

60   Mackay, p 31; Jnl H of C, XI 642.

61   Berisford, p 16, notes that a keeper was required.

62   Mackay, pp 5, 7f, 21, 33, App I, XI.

63   Harris, p 103. He added, "though no bond, be so sure as to have the prisoner in the house."

64   CLRO, DS/15/35-6; Report 1814, pp 550, 684; Report 1818, p 4.

65   *A Description of the King's Bench, Fleet and Marshalsea Prisons* (London 1828), pp 16, 20.

66   Mackay, p 5.

67   Mackay, pp 21, 27, 33.

68   Report 1729, p 5. By 1814 the fee was divided as follows: warden 1*s.*, clerk of the papers 1*s.*10*d.*, secondaries of court 1*s.*8*d.*

69   By the 1729 legislation. The Fleet day *rule* books of 1748-57 [PRO, PRIS/10/179-80] show that in the Easter term 1749 the total sum received in such fees was £64. In the same term in 1752, the sum was £134, but the Easter term after that, when an insolvency act had emptied the prison, only £28, of which the warden received just over £6. Yet Tilly considered it a bad day if he did not clear £20 from these writs [Jnl H of C, XI 643]. In 1814 the warden received an annual £145 from this source [Report 1814, p 550].

70   *Description*, pp 16, 20.

71   Report 1814, pp 550, 684; Report 1818, p 4. The 1814 committee regarded the practice of a "renewable bond" as "most objectionable" [p 538].

72   Report 1815, p 550.

72   PRO, PRIS/10/180.

73   Harris, p 78.

74   *Description*, pp 16f; *The Debtor and Creditor's Assistant* (1793), p 11; PRO, PRIS/10/179-80; Report 1818, pp 4, 44. The 1792 Report [p 651] states that the King's Bench court had limited the hours at that prison from 8 a.m. to 9 p.m., and also the number of applications per term to three a prisoner. This was never so at the Fleet.

75   PRO, PRIS/10/179-86.

76   Report 1792, p 643.

77   Report 1814, p 683.

78   Strype's edition of Stow's *Survey of London* (London 1720), II 280.

79   *The Warden of the Fleet's Case in Relation to Mr Baldwin Leighton's Petition to the Honourable House of Commons; Some Brief Considerations relating to the Bill for Regulating the King's Bench and Fleet Prisons.* In 1745 search was made to clarify this understanding of a rule of court having established the *rules* in 1686, but nothing was found, though it appears that only the papers of the courts of Chancery and Exchequer were checked [CLRO, Misc MS 172.15]. However, it is noted that the prisoners had applied for an increase in the size of the *rules* in 1686 [CLRO, Misc MS 173.5, fol 23]. No evidence has been found for this assertion. There might have been confusion with a case of 1666-9 involving the King's Bench *rules*, Lentall v Cooke, which was first recorded in a book published in 1685, Jos Keble's *Reports in the Court of King's Bench* (II 422f). The case was over the question as to whether a prisoner in the *rules* was a true prisoner or not. For Lentall it was argued that his house could not contain all his

prisoners unless they were permitted to enter into the *rules*, which privilege had been known since the days of Elizabeth I.

80   Lilburn, *Liberty Vindicated*, p 26.

81   BLO, MS Rawlinson D1051, pt 1, fols 9ff, 21ff; Dobb, Thesis, p 23n.

82   CLRO, Misc MS 84.21.

83   Cal Patent Rolls, 1557-8, p 229. The area of the *rules* appears to have formed the medieval and historic limits of the Fleet prison, it being stated in the mid-16th century that "all within the inclosure ... is the gaol of the Fleet" [BL, MS Harleian 4031, fol 31; cf M B Honeybourne, "The Fleet and its Neighbourhood in Early and Medieval Times", *London Topographical Record*, XIX (1947) 37].

84   Cranley, *Amanda*, pp 9ff, 28ff.

85   BL, MS Harleian 2017, fols 149f.

86   Jnl H of C, XI 646.

87   Howell, p 451.

88   Berisford, p 11. Yet even then it was an area in which prisoners were allowed to reside, rather than being a kind of annexe to the prison house; see also Jos Keble's *Reports*, II 423.

89   *General Considerations relating to a Bill for Regulating the Abuses of Prisons and Pretended Privileged Places* (1697).

90   *Some Considerations Humbly Offered in Relation to a Bill now Depending in Parliament for the Further Relief of Creditors in Cases of Escapes* (London 1698).

91   *Reasons against the Said Bill Supposed for Relief of Creditors and Preventing Escapes; Remarks upon the Bill for Preventing Escapes out of the Queen's Bench and Fleet Prisons,* (London 1702).

92   Report 1814, p 537; Jones Pearce, *A Treatise on the Abuses of the Laws* (London 1814), p 101.

93   Quoted in Report 1729 (KB), p 8.

94   These were Lostwithiel in Cornwall where the *rules* took in the whole borough; Carmarthen in west Wales, a mile around the whole town, and Newcastle upon Tyne, part of two streets [Howard (1777), pp 386, 422, 468f]. St Thomas's gaol in Exeter also had such *rules* in 1786 [CLRO, Misc MS 173.5 (1780), fol 64].

95   Edward Hatton, *A New View of London* (1708), II 745. Maps of the *rules* are contained in CLRO, Misc MS 173.5.

96   William Brown, *The Fleet, a Brief Account*, (1843), p 18; Leigh's *Picture of London*, (1834 edn), pp 73; CLRO, Misc MS 173.5.

97   Quoted in M D George, *London Life in the Eighteenth Century* (London 1951), p 84.

98   Strype's Stow, III 280.

99   *London Topographical Society*, publication LXXIII.

100   CLRO, Misc MS 173.5 (1786), fol 59.

101   Ibid, fols 17, 25f.

102   Ibid, fol 24.

103   Pearce, *A Treatise*, p 102.

104   Report 1818, p 4.

105   Mackay, pp 10ff; Howell, pp 357, 413, 420, 433, 449f, 455f, 460; *Debtor and Creditor's Assistant*, pp 13f; Jnl H of C, XIV 45.

106   Mackay, pp 10ff; *Debtor and Creditor's Assistant*, pp 13f.

107   PRO, PRIS/10/134, *in passim*.

108   Mackay, p 11.

109   PRO, PRIS/10/134, for 1751.

110   Howell, pp 387, 394, 430ff.

111   Howell, p 413.

112   Howell, pp 401ff, 438.

113   PRO, PRIS/10/157, 18 May 1697, Jacob Barnes.

114   Howell, pp 412f.

115   Report 1729, p 5.

116   PRO, PRIS/10/134; Howell, pp 449f.

117   Howell, p 336; John Feltham, *The Picture of London* (London 1803), p 176; *Debtor and Creditor's Assistant*, pp 13f. By 1814 the sum was once more 5% [Report 1814, p 683]. The King's Bench *rules* were more expensive again, 8 guineas to £100 and 4 guineas for each £100 thereafter, plus stamp bond and fees [ibid, pp 536f]. The fees are laid out in PP 1830 (342) XXIII 385.

118   Report 1814, pp 549, 683.

119   Mackay, pp 10, 12f; Howell, p 325; Report 1729, pp 5, 18; BL, MS Hargrave 125, fols 7ff.

120   Berisford, p 8.

121   Mackay, p 13.

122   Mackay, p 13; cf pp 10ff, App VIII.

123   Report 1729 (M), pp 25f.

124   CLRO, Misc MS 84.21 and 173.5 (1824).

125 CLRO, Misc MSS 84.21, 172.12, 173-5 (1786), fol 35.

126 Case of the rector, churchwardens, and overseers of the parish of Holborn, contained in CLRO, Misc MS 172.12 (1770).

127 CLRO, Misc MS 173.5 (1786); *Debtor and Creditor's Assistant,* p 11.

128 CLRO, Misc MS 173.5 (1824). The market's removal was an added factor which caused substantial problems to the rulers and prisoners.

129 Jnl H of C, XI 643.

130 *Some Considerations Humbly Offered to the Bill now Depending in Parliament in Relation to the Further Relief of Creditors in Case of Escapes* (1698); *Some Considerations Relating to the Bill for Regulating the King's Bench and the Fleet Prisons: Remarks upon the Bill for Preventing Escapes out of the Queen's Bench and Fleet Prisons* (1702).

131 Berisford, p 10; cf Cal SPD, 1665-6, p 367, which notes an incident as a result of which Mr Morice, secretary to the Council, wrote to Sir John Lettall of the King's Bench prison about one of his prisoners, John Sandelands, who was allowed to walk freely abroad. The king considered "such a privilege a scandal to government", and ordered the offending prisoner to be strictly kept, that "he may learn to fear the laws and satisfy his master, or at least that imprisonment may not become a mockery".

132 Report 1814, p 538.

133 CLRO, Misc MS 173.5 (1786), fol 42.

134 CLRO, Misc MS 172.12 and 173.5 (1786), fol 42.

135 CLRO, Misc MS 84.21.

136 *A Short View of Some Complaints against the Warden of the Fleet* (1705).

137 Berisford, pp 9f.

138 Jnl H of C, XI 644.

139 CLRO, Misc MS 173.5 (1786), *in passim,* but especially fols 28, 36, 52.

140 *A Short View of Some Complaints against the Warden of the Fleet.* Jnl H of C, XII 202, noted that the warden forced artificers who had lived in the *rules* and supported themselves by their labours.

141 Report 1792, p 654.

142 PRO, PRIS/10/134. The wide social variety of the rulers may be seen from this selection. The same book suggests that only about 25% of the rulers could be described as belonging to the professional, upper, or commercial classes.

143 PRO, SPD, Entry Book 81, fol 41, quoted by Leslie Church, *Oglethorpe* (London 1932), p 11.

144 CLRO, Misc MSS 173.5 (1786), fol 42, and 172.12.

145 J Nightengale, *London and Middlesex* (London 1810-16), III 735ff.

146 St Bride's Vestry Minutes, GLL, MS 6554-IV, 18 Feb 1718/19.

147 J P Malcolm, *Londinium Redivivum* (London 1803), I 375.

148 *Mirror*, 20 July 1833.

149 Jnl H of C, XI 643.

150 Berisford, p iv. Blackfriars and the Mint were debt sanctuaries. Their "pretended privileges" were abolished by the act of 1696, 8 & 9 William III c 27, which also attempted to regulate the prisons. See R L Brown, "The Minters of Wapping", *East London Papers*, XIV (1972) 77.

151 Mackay, p 12.

152 Jnl H of C, XI 643.

153 CLRO, Misc MS 84.

154 S V Makower, *Richard Savage* (1909), p 257.

155 Cal SPD, 1677-8, p 331.

156 Report 1729, pp 5, 18. As only 102 prisoners are recorded on the masters's side, the initial number may be greatly exaggerated.

157 CLRO, Debtors' Lists.

158 CLRO, DS/15/1-2.

159 CLRO, DS/15/8-12.

160 Howard (1777), p 156.

161 CLRO, DS/15/30-3.

162 CLRO, DS/15/35-6.

163 CLRO, Misc MS 173.5 (1786), fol 12.

164 Ibid, fol 26 (for beginning and end of the year).

165 *Report of the Sub-Committee into Prisons of the Society for Giving Effect to His Majesty's Proclamation against Vice and Immorality* (London 1790), p 27.

166 Report 1792, p 651. In the King's Bench 70 of 570 prisoners had the *rules* (12%).

167 William Brown, *The Fleet*, p 14.

168 CLRO, Misc MS 173.5 (1825), fol 14.

169 Leigh's *Picture of London* (1834 edn), p 74.

170 CLRO, DS/15/8-12 and 35-6.

171 PP 1826-7 (424) XIX 351-3.

172 Howard (1780), p 177; Joanna Innes, "The King's Bench Prison in the later Eighteenth

Century", in J Brewer and J Styles, *An Ungovernable People* (London 1980), p 263, argues the case for one third.

173 Report 1792, p 653.

174 PRO, PRIS/1/3, 10 and PRIS/10/134; CLRO, Misc MS 173.5 (1786), fol 59.

175 CLRO, Misc MS 173.5 (1785), *in passim*; Jnl H of C, XIII 542.

176 Jnl H of C, XIII 542.

177 CLRO, Misc MS 172.12.

178 CLRO, Misc MS 173.5 (1786), fol 59. Feltham in his *Picture of London* (London 1803), p 176, notes that "lodgings are bad and very dear."

179 The autobiography of Francis Place, BL, MS Addit 35142, fol 158f, 238b. This was in the 1780s.

180 Mackay, p 31.

181 CLRO, Misc MS 173.5 (1786), fols 28, 173-5.

182 Report 1814, pp 536, 550, 683f; Report 1792, p 655; William Brown, *The Fleet*, p 18. For a time the King's Bench rulers were permitted to visit the Surrey theatre and other such places within their *rules*.

183 Report 1818, p 8.

184 Report 1814, pp 21, 41, 44.

185 Jnl H of C, XII 201.

186 William Jones, *Obervations on the Insolvent Debtors' Act* (1827).

Endword

The world of the eighteenth-century debt prison is a world apart from our twentieth-century conception of imprisonment. Its closure in 1842 virtually brought to an end one of the last great medieval institutions of our country; one which over six hundred years had retained its basic medieval outlook and structure. Over the centuries, it is true, parliament and the courts had endeavoured to modify and correct this system of imprisonment, but because of the continuous saga of vested interests they were only able to adjust some of the outward circumstances and regulate matters, rather than effectively challenge the assumptions upon which these practices were based.

The claim that the office of warden was quite separate from the prison house, advanced so contentiously by Tilly, and with good precedent on his side, led to the system by which debt prisoners were permitted to leave the prison under licence from the warden or the various courts associated with the prison. Though Tilly's claim was disputed and eventually disallowed, unfair though that may have been, the existence of the day *rules* and the *rules* was a practical outworking of this claim, and without it, could not have been allowed.

Reformers such as Howard, Smith, and Neild, and parliamentary commissioners, all suggested, some implicitly and others more circumspectly, that the problems which occurred at the Fleet prison all had one cause, namely the venality of the office of warden. The prisoners, true to time honoured medieval custom, were required not only to support themselves but also to pay the costs of the prison administration. The system whereby the prison was sold or leased to the highest bidder meant that every warden or his deputy endeavoured to obtain the maximum profit from his undertaking within the shortest possible time scale, at the expense of his prisoners (as they continually asserted). Though the courts endeavoured to establish a scale of fees their interpretation was always a matter of dispute. A further outcome of this practice was that the warden endeavoured to run his prison as cheaply as possible, with the minimum outlay on staff and repairs to the building as well as the provision of care for his prisoners. But as the office of warden had been awarded by patent or by royal grant no government felt able to interfere unless the situation got completely out of hand, as was alleged during the wardenships of Tilly and Bambridge.

The debt prisoners at the Fleet were not prisoners undergoing punishment for their offence, though this often seemed to be the case, but rather they were being held in confinement until they had paid their debts or settled with their creditors. By implication this meant that they were entitled to live as well as they could whilst in their place of confinement. The prison administration was more than willing to acquiesce in this attitude, since the profits of the prison were thereby enhanced. For those with finances the Fleet could be a reasonably comfortable place, with most of the facilities of London society available, the open access of one's friends and the possibility of being joined by one's family.

The unwillingness of the prison authorities to employ too many officers, and the considerable privileges and freedom allowed prisoners, led in all probability to the existence of that tacit understanding between warden and prisoners so necessary for the good management of the prison. It has been suggested that this worked well, even though criticised by Howard, and the lack of much comment about it save when this understanding broke down is probably an indication of its good working. Clearly without the co-operation of the prisoners the prison was utterly unmanageable without undue repression and severity, the cost of which was too enormous, in financial and moral terms, for the warden to effectively contemplate. The system appears to have given considerable support to the prisoners in their effort to manage the prison in their own interests, as far as possible, with the maximum comfort available and the continuation of the long established privileges. And in turn the warden was prepared to turn a blind eye to much of what was going on in his prison.

This co-operation between warden and prisoners was a fragile affair, and when it got out of hand through the mismanagement of the warden or the over-assertiveness of the prisoners, public and even parliamentary concern was soon expressed. Tilly's abuse of the system and Bambridge's enforcement of his authority both led to public reaction, although the reforms established as a result were piecemeal and inadequate. At the most their dismissals warned their successors to act more circumspectly.

The prison was an institution in decline from the early seventeenth century onwards. Its heyday had been the late sixteenth and early seventeenth centuries, when it had been filled with imprisoned recusant gentry. The difficulties of selling the prison in the 1720s, the need for the Office of Works to rebuilt the prison house in 1770, all point to this conclusion. Nevertheless its brief Indian summer just before its closure which brought in a vast number of short-stay prisoners, each of whom was required to pay committal and dimission fees, must have provided the warden with some recompense for its eventual closure.

Although the Fleet was a popular prison for those in debt, its popularity was not shared by the commercial and trading interests of the city of London or by the growing lobby of prison reformers. The numerous inquiries into the administration of the prison bear witness to this assertion, as does the powerful lobby created every time an extension of the *rules* was advocated. Though reforms were instituted and an attempt made to regulate practices, the nature of the *rules* being a classic illustration, little of a tangible nature was effected. It has been suggested this was partly due to the prison being run as a private concern in an age when individual property rights were respected, but it may also be due in part to two other factors. If there was a real difficulty as to how the Fleet could be replaced, there was also a feeling, however subdued, amongst creditors that prisons at least served a fairly useful purpose, as the threat of debt imprisonment or its actual enjoyment generally persuaded the average debtor to settle his affairs in an amiable manner. But equally there was another feeling, not often expressed but clearly present, that when the possibility of debt imprisonment was a real threat to a commercial society which lived on credit in an uncomfortable world, then its existence ought to be made as comfortable and convenient as possible. Circular arguments with such contradictory interests are always hard to challenge, especially when they are buried deeply within the subconscious. Thus it was only when the prison ceased to be profitable, due to the lack of prisoners, that it closed.

The Fleet prison reflected to an extraordinary extent the society around it. Rich and poor co-existed within its walls. Acute poverty rubbed shoulders with accumulated wealth. Though often regarded as a prison for the upper and professional classes, its average inhabitant came from the artisan and craftsman classes. Contrary to even the frequent pleas of its prisoners, few were imprisoned there for more than a few years, and those who remained there for a considerable period of time were either fraudulent or simply unfortunate. Neither were the debtors necessarily poor. True, there was poverty, and acute poverty at that, but many debtors moved to their confinement with substantial resources, and others were assisted financially by friends and family, even if their assistance was slightly selfish as they too might need some reciprocal help on a future occasion. Nor could there be much stigma in being a debt prisoner, particularly when it was possible to live outside the prison house and to receive one's friends and family within it with little restriction whatsoever. It may be safely asserted that the Fleet prison was one of the great institutions of the London scene until its closure, even if it lay a little on the debit side of life.

Appendix 1:
The Wardens of the Fleet

1561	Richard Tyrill
	Sir Jeremy Whitcott
	John Tilly
1713	Baldwin Leighton
1713-1728	John Huggins
1728-1729	John Bambridge
1729-1736	James Gambier
1736-1740	John Garth
1740-1758	John Eyles, senior
1758-1821	John Eyles, junior
1821-1822	Nicholas Nixon
1822-1842	William Robert Henry Brown

Appendix 2:
Copy of the Warden of the Fleet's Patent, 1758
[from the 1818 Report into the Prison, pp 85f]

GEORGE the Second, by the grace of God King of Great Britain, France, and Ireland, Defender of the Faith, &c, to all to whom these presents shall come, Know ye, That We very much confiding in the fidelity, experience and prudent circumspection of our trusty and well-beloved John Eyles, of Hatton-Gardens, in the parish of St Andrew, Holborn, in our county of Middlesex, esquire, of our special grace, certain knowledge and mere motion, have given and granted, and by these presents do give and grant, unto him the said John Eyles the office of Warden or Keeper of the Fleet, and the custody of the prison and gaol of the Fleet, situate and being in the parish of Bridget, otherwise St Brides without Ludgate, London, and of the prisoners committed or to be committed to the prison or gaol of the Fleet aforesaid, and the capital messuage for the custody of the prisoners, and thirteen messuages in the parish aforesaid, and all other messuages, lands, tenements and hereditaments to the said office belonging and appertaining; and all the rent, fee or salary of seven pounds twelve shillings and one penny yearly, payable and to be paid by the hands of the sheriff of our city of London and our county of Middlesex for the time being, for the keeper or the custody of that prison and gaol; and all those other rents or annual payments issuing from and out of the messuages, lands and tenements within our said city of

London and suburbs of the same to the said office and custody of the prison and gaol of the Fleet aforesaid belonging and appertaining, being of the clear yearly value of four pounds, more or less; and all other fees, salaries, rents, profits, emoluments, liberties, jurisdictions, privileges, advantages and hereditaments whatsoever to the said office and prison, and to the keeper or custody of the same, or either of them, in anywise belonging or appertaining; and also all that office of keeper and the custody of our palaces of Westminister, called the Old Palace, and the New Palace in our county of Middlesex aforesaid, and the letting or setting of all shops, galleries and stands, as well within as without the palace or palaces of Westminster aforesaid, to the said office belonging or appertaining, and all that annual rent or fee of ten pounds twelve shillings payable and to be paid by the sheriff of our city of London and our county of Middlesex for the time being, for the execution of that office, in as ample manner and form as any other warden or wardens of the Fleet aforesaid, heretofore having or exercising the said office, hath or have had or received, or ought to have had or received by reason thereof; and all that messuage or tenement, with the appurtenances, situate within the staple known by the name of the wool Staple, at Westminster, called the Tipstaffs House, heretofore in the tenure or occupation of John Jennings or his assigns; and all those other messuages, buildings, tenements, rents, fees, salaries, profits, commodities, emoluments, advantages, jurisdictions, liberties, privileges and hereditaments whatsoever, to the office aforesaid of keeper, or to the custody of our palaces of Westminster aforesaid, in any manner belonging or appertaining, or accepted, reputed or taken as part, parcel or member thereof; and him, the said John Eyles, Warden or Keeper of the Fleet, and of the prison and gaol of the Fleet aforesaid, and Keeper of our palaces at Westminster aforesaid, we do make, ordain and constitute by these presents to have, hold, enjoy and exercise the said offices, messuages, lands, tenements, rents, annuities, fees, salaries, liberties, profits, advantages and hereditaments aforesaid, and all and singular other the premises aforesaid, with their and every of their appurtenances, unto the said John Eyles, by himself or his sufficient deputy or deputies, for whom he shall be answerable, for and during the will and pleasure of us, our heirs and successors, in as ample manner and form as his father John Eyles, esquire, deceased, or any other warden of our prison of the Fleet aforesaid, and keeper of our palaces of Westminster aforesaid, or either of them, heretofore hath had, held, used or enjoyed, or ought to have had, held, used or enjoyed the said offices and other the premises aforesaid, or any or either of them: Provided always, and by these presents we do strictly charge and command that the said John Eyles shall in no case be admitted into nor shall execute the said office or offices without our special licence under our sign manual first obtained in that behalf, nor shall enter into the said prison until he the said John Eyles shall have given good and sufficient security to us for his the said John Eyles' good behaviour in the said offices, or either of them, such security to be first approved by our Chancellor of Great Britain, or the Keeper of our Great Seal of Great Britain, or our Commissioners for the custody of our great seal of Great Britain; our Chief Justice of the Common Pleas, and our Chief Baron of our Exchequer for the time being: Provided also, and we will that the said John Eyles shall enrol or cause to be enrolled these our letters patent in our court before our Justices of the Common Pleas at Westminster, within the space of six lunar months after the date of these presents: Provided likewise nevertheless, that if the said John Eyles shall sell or permit any person or persons to rent or farm any inferior office or offices under him, or take any money, fine, income or reward for or in respect thereof, contrary to the tenor of a certain act of parliament made in the second year of our reign, intitled, "An Act to empower His Majesty, his Heirs and Successors, during the life of Thomas Bainbridge [*sic*], esquire, to grant to office of Warden of the Prison of the Fleet to such person or persons as His Majesty shall think fit, and to incapacitate the said Thomas Bainbridge to enjoy the said office or any other whatsoever;" then these our letters patent shall forthwith cease, determine and become utterly void to all intents and purposes. Lastly, we will, and by these presents do grant to the said John Eyles, that these our letters patent, or the enrolment thereof, shall and may be in all things good, firm, valid and sufficient and effectual in the law towards and against Us, as well in all our courts as elsewhere within our united kingdom of Great Britain, without any confirmations licenses or tolerations hereafter to be procured or obtained from Us, notwithstanding the not reciting any former letters patent granted of the offices or premises, or the not naming or ill-naming the offices, prison, custody, rents, annuities, fees, salaries, and other the premises aforesaid, before by these presents granted or mentioned to be granted of any part or parcel thereof, or any other omission, imperfection, defect, matter, cause or thing whatsoever to the contrary hereof in anywise notwithstanding. Witness Ourself, at Westminster, the twenty-fourth day of November in the thirty-second year of our reign.

By writ of Privy Seal.

Appendix 3:
The Rules of the Fleet Prison
[from the 1818 report, pp 78-80]

RULES AND ORDERS
Hilary Term, 3 Geo. II. 1729.

IT is Ordered, That all and singular the orders and rules hereunder wrote and established, pursuant to an act of parliament made and published in the second year of the reign of our said Lord the King, intitled, "An Act for the relief of Debtors, with respect to the imprisonment of their persons," be well strictly and truly observed and kept, as well by the Warden of the Prison of our Lord the King of the Fleet, and all his Officers and Servants, as by all Prisoners who now are or at any time hereafter shall be committed to the custody of the said Warden. And it is further Ordered, That this rule, with all and every the rules or orders aforesaid, shall be fixed up in the hall of the said prison, for the use, benefit and inspection of the prisoners detained in the aforesaid prison.

By the Court.

CONSTITUTIONS and ORDERS, renewed and established, touching the government of the Fleet Prison, by Sir Robert Catlyn, knight, Chief Justice of the King's Bench; Sir William Cordell, knight, Master of the

Rolls; Sir James Dyer, knight, Chief Justice of the Common Pleas; Sir Edward Saunders, knight, Chief Baron of the Exchequer, and others, by virtue of a Commission under the Great Seal of England, bearing date the third day of June, in the third year of the reign of Queen Elizabeth, and afterwards reviewed and exemplified under the Great Seal the first day of February, in the thirty-seventh year of the said reign, and again declared and established as Rules and Orders by which the said Prison of the Fleet should be governed, by Letters Patent granted to Sir Jeremy Whichcot, of the office of Warden of the Fleet, in the nineteenth year of the reign of King Charles the Second.

1 That it may be lawful to the said warden or his deputy to appoint so many of the household servants as to either of them shall seem good, to open and shut the two outer gates of the Fleet at such hours as the gates of Ludgate and Newgate are accustomed to be opened and shut; and the said persons to carry in their hands halberts, bills, or any other weapon, as shall seem good unto the said warden or deputy within his precinct of liberty.

2 That it is and shall be lawful to the said warden and his deputy to take order from time to time that no person coming there do carry any weapon further than the porter's lodge there, be he a stranger or other, unless they be licensed so to do by the discretion of such as the same warden shall appoint to keep the gate there.

3 That it may be lawful for the said warden or his deputy, and so many of his household as shall be thought needful, to keep watch, in harness, or otherwise, within his precinct, at all times as he shall see cause for his better safeguard, if he shall suspect any prisoner within his custody to intend to make an escape.

4 That it may be lawful for the said warden to take order at all times for such money as shall be gathered at the box, or otherwise generously given to poor men there, for the distribution thereof amongst them, if any contention shall arise; and that the said poor men shall always keep one key of the said box, and another key to be at the warden's appointment.

ORDERS made by the Right honourable Sir Edward Herbert, knight, Lord Chief Justice of His Majesty's Court of Common Pleas at Westminster, and the rest of the Justices of the said Court, Friday, the seventeenth day of February, Anno Domini one thousand six hundred and eighty-seven, concerning His Majesty's Prison of the Fleet.

5 If the prisoners on the master's side refuse or be not able to pay their chamber rent, then and in such case, the warden has liberty to turn them out of his or her chamber into the wards; but no prisoner whatsoever to be confined under the pretence of nonpayment of chamber rent, but all of them to have liberty of walking in the fore-yard, hall and cellar of the house, in the day time without interruption; the ward gates in the day time to stand constantly open, and to be opened, viz. at five o'clock in the morning in the summer, and seven in the winter.

And the said justices do further order, that the warden shall be at liberty to shut the ward gates at nine of the clock at night in the winter time, and at ten in the summer, if he so think fit; provided he keep a watchman constantly to attend there, to let out and in such persons as shall have occasion to go to the necessary house, they returning as soon as he or she has done there.

6 That the warden shall not for the future detain or embezzle any prisoner's goods, but that the said warden has liberty to detain the person of such prisoner or prisoners after they are discharged by their creditors, until all lawful fees and dues shall be fully paid and satisfied.

7 That the warden shall, with all convenient speed, make and provide a confined room or dungeon in the wards, as it was before the great fire of London, for the confinement of persons endeavouring to make their escapes, or guilty of any other great misdemeanour, that the general quietness and liberty of the rest of their fellow prisoners may not be restrained or suffer thereby.

And the persons whose names are hereunto subscribed, having reviewed and considered the said rules and orders, and being informed that a confined room was provided according to the said last-mentioned order, and that the same is boarded, wholesome and dry, do order and declare that the rules and orders before mentioned shall continue to be rules and orders for the better government of the Fleet prison, and be observed accordingly.

AND whereas some further Resolutions, are proper and necessary to be made for the better government of the said Prison, the persons whose names are hereunder subscribed do further order, -

8 That the warden of the Fleet do keep the chapel of the Fleet in good repair, and take care that divine service be performed, and the sacrament of the Lord's Supper administered therein, at the usual and proper times, according to the rites and ceremonies of the Church of England, and all prisoners are required to attend at the times aforesaid, and not to absent themselves from the said chapel without reasonable cause.

9 And it is hereby further ordered, That no chaplain of the Fleet, or any clergyman, being a prisoner within the walls or *rules* of the Fleet, do presume to marry any person, without a licence within the prison or *rules* of the Fleet; and that the warden and his officers do use their utmost diligence to prevent all such marriages.

10 That the warden do cause the stocks to be kept up in the said prison, (as has been anciently practised,) for the punishment of such prisoners as shall blaspheme the name of God, be guilty of profane cursing and swearing, or shall behave themselves in a disorderly manner.

11 That no prisoner do take possession of any chamber within the prison, but with the consent of the warden or his deputy, to pull down any partition, or make any other material alteration there, without the consent of the warden or his deputy; but that the disposal and appointment of the chambers or rooms within the said prison be in the warden or his deputy only, yet so as neither of them do turn any prisoner out of possession who shall be rightfully possessed of a chamber, without reasonable cause; and that every prisoner, on his or her discharge, do deliver over to the warden, his deputy or chamberlain, the key of his chamber, and

all the warden's furniture therein.

12 That the warden, or his deputy, may turn any prisoner out of his chamber to the common side, that shall refuse or neglect to pay his or her chamber rent for the space of three months; and that the warden or his deputy shall in such case cause an inventory to be made of the prisoner's goods and effects (if any) signed by two witnesses, and shall immediately deliver such goods and effects to such prisoner, but the warden may still detain the person of such prisoner, though discharged by the plaintiff, or in any other manner, until his arrears of his chamber rent shall be fully satisfied and paid.

13 That no prisoner or other person shall keep any public room within the said prison for selling any victuals, wine, brandy, punch, beer, ale, or any other liquor, without leave from the warden or his deputy, and if any prisoner or prisoners shall offend in the premises, it shall be lawful for the warden or his deputy to turn him her or them out of their room or rooms, to the common side; and the warden and his deputy are hereby required to take care that good order be kept in such public room or rooms as shall be allowed by either of them to be used as aforesaid.

14 That the warden do take effectual care that every prisoner committed to his custody, be conveyed to the prison of the Fleet, without being carried to any public, victualling or drinking house, or the private house of any tipstaff, officer or minister of the Fleet, or of any tenant or relation of his, without the free and voluntary consent of the person or persons so in custody, and that no garnish or money shall be extorted by any prisoner or prisoners from any person committed, for his coming into the said prison.

15 That the warden do cause a table of the gifts and bequests made for the benefit of the prisoners of the Fleet, expressing the particular purposes for which the same are given, to be fairly writ in a plain and legible hand, to be hung up in the hall of the said prison; and that the warden take care that no prisoner or prisoners be deprived or defrauded of his her or their shares, dues or dividends of the charities so given; and that no cellarman, turnkey or other officer or servant of

the warden shall have any share or part in any charity given to the prisoners, or bear any office in the said prison which may entitle him to any power in, receipt or disposition of such charity.

16 That every prisoner who shall make oath before one of the judges of the court from whence the process issued upon which he or she shall be taken or charged, or before a commissioner empowered by such court, that he or she is not worth five pounds, and cannot subsist without the charities belonging to the prisoners of the Fleet, shall immediately be admitted to all shares, dividends and profits arising from such charities.

17 That two rooms, marked 9 and 10, up the chapel stairs, shall be kept as an infirmary for the use of the prisoners on the common side, who shall fall sick of such diseases as shall require their being removed, to prevent infection, or for necessary care and relief; and that no prisoner shall be obliged to lie in the same bed with a diseased person.

18 That the warden shall keep the prison-house and windows in good and necessary repair, and keep the drains, bog-houses and dunghill as clean and free from stench and noisomeness as possible.

19 That when any prisoner dies within the said prison, the said warden shall forthwith give notice of such death to the coroner, that the said coroner may enquire, according to law, how such prisoner came by his death, and that the said warden shall detain the body no longer than till the coroner's inquest have made their inquisition, which shall be done with all convenient speed; and that immediately afterwards the dead body shall be delivered to the prisoner's friends or relations, if they desire it, without fee or reward.

20 That the warden do not sue, or procure to be sued out, any writ of habeas corpus to remove any prisoner from the prison of the Fleet to the prison of the King's Bench.

21 That the warden shall keep a book, in which all commitments shall be

fairly entered in the words of such commitment, within fourteen days after any prisoner shall be committed.

22 That the warden shall keep another book, containing the names of every prisoner actually brought into the Fleet, and taken into the house, with the name of the party at whose suit he shall be committed, and the time when the prisoner was brought to the Fleet, and received into the prison, specifying withal the court or judge by whose authority he shall be committed.

23 That every tipstaff to whom any prisoner shall be delivered in custody at a judge's chamber, shall keep a book, containing the name of such prisoner, the time when he was taken into custody, to be signed by such judge's clerk; and such judge's clerk shall keep another book, in which the like entry shall be made, signed by the tipstaff.

24 That the warden shall keep a book, in which memorandums shall be entered of all declarations, delivered to the turnkey or porter against any prisoner in the Fleet Prison, containing the names of the parties, the cause of action, and the time when such declaration shall be delivered.

25 That the warden shall keep a book, in which all discharges of prisoners shall be fairly entered: which entry shall specify how such discharge was made, whether by the plaintiff, by supersedeas or otherwise, and such entry shall be made within five days after every discharge.

26 That the warden shall keep a book, in which every writ of habeas corpus upon which the prisoner shall be committed or the custody alterned, with the return of every such writ of habeas corpus, shall be fairly entered.

27 That all the books before mentioned, except the tipstaff's book, shall be kept in the public office of the clerk of the papers of the Fleet; and that all persons shall have liberty to resort to them, and to take copies as there shall be occasion.

28 That no clerk, officer or servant whatsoever belonging to any judge of

this court shall directly or indirectly demand, receive or take any gratuity, fee or reward, for or by reason of any petition, complaint or application that shall be made by any prisoner or prisoners of the said prison, pursuant to or founded upon any of the rules and orders herein-before mentioned, or concerning any misgovernment in the Fleet.

29 Lastly, That the said warden and his officers do treat the several prisoners in his custody with all tenderness and humanity, and that such prisoners do behave themselves towards the warden with that submission and regard which the law requires.

R EYRE,
ROBT. PRICE,
ALEX. DENTON,
J. FORTESCUE.

Appendix 4:
The Prison Fees, 1625
[from Ackeman's *Microcosm of London*. pp 55-6]

AN EXTRACT FROM THE BOOK OF FEES KEPT IN THE FIRST
PROTHONOTARIES' OFFICE IN THE COURT OF COMMON PLEAS.

*Termino Hillar. 21 Jacobi regis, 1625, a comico^{on} having issued from his
maj^{ty} to enquire into fees &c. taken from the 30th of Q. Eliz^{a}.*

Inter alia,

*Fees due and belonging to the warden of the Fleet, and his under officers, as
appeareth by a commission under the great seal of England, from the late Queen
Eliz^{a} in the 3rd year of her reign, and confirmed in the 37th year of Eliz^{a} what
every one in their several degree ought to pay.*

	£	s.	d.
An archbishop, A duke, A duchess are to pay for their commitment fee to the warden of the Fleet, and his officers, having the first week's dyett	21	10	0

also they are to pay for their ordinary			
comons weekly, with wine	3	6	8
A marquess, A marquessess, An earl, A countess,			
A vice Countess,			
are to pay for their commitment fee to the			
warden of the Fleet, and his officers, having			
the first week's dyett	11	11	0
also they are to pay for their ordinary			
comons weekly, with wine	2	0	0
A lord spiritual or temporal, a lady the wife of a			
baron or a lord,			
are to pay for their commitment fee to the			
warden of the Fleet, and his officers, having			
the first week's dyett	10	5	10
also they are to pay for their ordinary			
comons weekly, with wine	1	10	0
A knight, a lady the wife of a knight, a doctor of			
divinity, a doctor of law, and others of like			
callings, are to pay for their commitment fee			
to the warden of the Fleet, and his officers,			
having the first week's dyett and lodging	5	0	0
also they are to pay for their ordinary			
comons weekly	0	18	6
An esquire, a gentleman, a gentlewoman, that			
shall sit at the parlour comons, or any person or			
persons, under that degree, that shall be at the			
same ordinary comons of the parlour,			
are to pay for their commitment fee to the			
warden of the Fleet, and his officers, having			
the first week's dyett and lodging	3	6	8
also they are to pay for their ordinary			
weekly comons, with wine	0	10	0
A yeoman, or any other that shall be at the hall			
comons, man or woman			

are to pay for their commitment fee to the
warden of the Fleet, or his officers, having
the first week's dyett   1   14   0
also they are to pay for their ordinary
weekly comons, with wine   0   5   0

Appendix 5:
The Fees of the Prison, 1727
[from the Report of 1729, pp 15-16]

Serjeants-Inn Hall, Trinity Term, 1727

The TABLE of *FEES Ordered by the Judges to be paid by the Prisoners of the Fleet, to the Warden and his Agents, and to be hung up in the Hall of the said Prison.*

Whereas several Matters in Controversy between the Prisoners and the Warden of the Fleet were heard by the Right Honourable Sir *Robert Eyre* Knight, Lord Chief Justice of His Majesty's Court of *Common Pleas at Westminster,* the Honourable *Robert Price* Esq; Sir *Francis Page* Knight, and *Alexander Denton* Esq; Judges of the said Court, at *Serjeants-Inn* Hall in *Chancery-Lane, on Monday* the 24th Day of *April, on Wednesday* the 26th May of the same Month of *April, on Monday the* 1st Day of May following, and on *Friday* the 5th Day of the same Month *of* May, *in Easter* Term, in the 13th Year of the Reign of our Sovereign Lord King *George,* Anno Domini 1727: Upon which Hearing the Lord Chief Justice of the said Court came to the following Resolutions, viz.

That there is due and ought to be paid to the

	£	s.	d.

Warden of the *Fleet,* for every Commitment-Fee
(exclusive of Commons) from all Persons of the
Degree of an Esquire, Gentleman, or Gentlewoman,
or any other Person under those Degrees who
shall enter on the Master's side of the said
Prison   2   4   4

And that there ought to be paid to the Warden for
every such person, for the Use of the Minister
of the said Prison   0   2   0

That there is due, and ought to be paid to the
Warden of the *Fleet,* for a Commitment
Fee for every Prisoner in Wards, or Common
Side, not taking Part of the Poors Box   1   6   4

And every such Person ought to pay the Warden
for the Use of the Minister of the said Prison   0   1   0

And every Prisoner taking Part of the Poors Box,
ought to pay to the Warden 7*s* 4*d.* and no
more, for his Commitment Fee, and nothing
for the Minister   0   7   4

That there is due, and ought to be paid to the
Warden of the *Fleet,* for every Render in each
Cause £2.4*s*.4*d.* and nothing to the Minister   2   4   4

That there is due, and ought to be paid to the
Chamberlain as his Fee for every Prisoner's
Entrance into the House 1*s.* and no more   0   1   0

That there is due, and ought to be paid to the
Warden for every Prisoner's Discharge,
either by Creditor or Supersedeas, as a Fee
for his Dismission out of Prison, without any
Regard to the number of Causes wherewith
he stands charged, 7*s.*6*d.* and no more   0   7   6

That there is due, and ought to be paid to the
Clerk of the Papers, for every Discharge

of every Action	0	2	6
And for the Copy of every Cause, not exceeding Three	0	1	0
And for every Cause, exceeding three Causes, 4*d*. (besides the 1*s*. a piece, for each of the said first three Causes)	0	0	4
That there is due, and ought to be paid to the Clerk of the Papers, for his Certificate of the Prisoner's Discharge delivered to the Prisoner himself, without any Regard to the Number of Causes he stood charged with, 2*s*.6*d*. and for his Certificate to the Warden for such Discharge 2*s*.6*d*.	0	5	0
That there is due, and ought to be paid to the Clerk of the Enquiries on the Discharge of a Prisoner by the Creditors, and not by Supersedeas	0	2	0
That there is due, and ought to be paid to the Turnkey (who is now both Porter and Gaoler) for the Prisoner's Entrance into the House 2*s*. and for such Prisoner's Discharge to the Turnkey (being Porter and Gaoler) 2*s*.6*d*.	0	4	6
That there is due, and ought to be paid to the Turnkey, for every Declaration delivered to him for a prisoner	0	1	0

That there is no Fee due to the Warden upon his accepting Security, on the Prisoner's having the benefit of Day *Rules*

That there is no Fee due to the Warden for Lodging and Chamber Rent, where the Prisoner has not actual Possession of the Chamber; but there is due to the Warden for every Prisoner or Prisoners, his or their Lodging or Chamber Rent 2*s*.6*d*. per Week, such Lodging

or Chamber being Furnished   0   2   6
That there is due to the Minister that Officiates
and performs Divine Service within the said Prison,
for the Time being, from every Prisoner within the
Walls of the said Prison, or without the Walls, or
within the *Rules*, Four Pence per Week to be
paid to the Warden for the Use of such
Minister; and that no such Minister or any other
Clergyman, being a Prisoner within the Walls or
Rules of the *Fleet*, do presume to Marry any
Person without Licence, within the Prison or *Rules*
of the *Fleet*; and that the Warden and his Officers
do use their utmost Vigilance to prevent all such
Marriages.
That there is no fresh Commitment-Fee due to the
Warden upon the Prisoner's bringing himself
back to the *Fleet* by *Habeas-Corpus*, and
that there is no Fee, Gratuity or Reward due to
the Warden for his returning a *Habeas Corpus;*
but there is a Fee of 5*s*.4*d*. due to the Clerk of the
Papers for the Allowance of every Writ of *Habeas
Corpus*, and 4*s*. for the Return of the first Cause,
and 2*s*. for every other Cause, and no more   0   11   4
That when a Prisoner dies in the *Fleet*, the Warden
shall detain the Body no longer than till the
Coroner's Inquest be finished, which shall be
done with all reasonable Speed; and immediately
afterwards the Body shall be delivered to the
Prisoner's Friends or Relations, if they desire
it, without Fee or Reward.

   That it is the Duty of the Warden, and belongs to him, to keep the Prison-
House and Windows in necessary and good Repair, and to keep the Bog-House
and Dunghill as clean and free from Stench and Noisomness as possible.

That a Table of Gifts and Bequests made for the Benefit of the Prisoners in the Fleet, expressing the particular Purposes for which the same were given, be prepared by the Warden, and hung up in the Hall of the said Prison.

That the Ward-Gates be opened at five of the Clock in the Summer, and seven of the Clock in the Winter, and do stand constantly open in the Day-time, according to the Order made the 17th Feb. 1717.

And whereas this Court, upon farther Consideration of the Premises, this present *Trinity* Term in the 13th Year of the Reign of our Sovereign Lord King *George,* is of Opinion that the said Resolutions are just, It is hereby Ordered that the same be observed by the Warden and Prisoners, and all other Persons therein concerned.

Robt. Eyre.
Robt. Price,
F. Page,
Alexr. Denton.

A TABLE OF FEES, to be taken by the Warden of the Prison of the *Fleet,* for any Prisoner, or Prisoners Commitment, or coming into Gaol, or Chamber-Rent there, or Discharges from thence, in any Civil Action; settled and established 19th day of January, in the 3d year of the reign of His Majesty King George the Second, 1729, pursuant to an Act of Parliament lately made, intitled, "An Act for the Relief of Debtors with respect to the Imprisonment of their Persons."

	£	s	d
Every Prisoner charged with one or more Actions (who, at his own desire, shall go on the Master's Side) do pay to the Warden for Commitment Fee	1	6	8
Every Prisoner charged with one or more Actions (who shall go on the Common Side) not being entitled to partake of the Poor's Box, to pay	0	13	4
Every prisoner entitled to partake of the Poor's Box, nothing			

Every Prisoner to pay for his Discharge	0	7	4
Every such Prisoner on the Master's Side who, at his own desire shall have a Bed to himself, to pay for Chamber Room, use of Bed, Bedding, and Sheets, to the Warden, per Week	0	2	6
If two in a Bed, and no more, for Chamber Room, use of Bed, Bedding, and Sheets, each to pay to the Warden, per Week	0	1	3
If the Prisoner finds his own Bed, Bedding, and Sheets (which the Warden is in no sort to hinder him of) then he shall pay for Chamber Room to the Warden, per Week	0	1	3
If there be two Prisoners in one Bed, finding their own Bed, Bedding, and Sheets, then each of them to pay to the Warden, per week	0	0	7½
Every Prisoner, not being intitled to partake of the Poor's Box, to pay to the porter and Gaoler, now called Turnkey's, on his Commitment	0	2	0
Every Prisoner on a Commitment upon a Surrender at a Judge's Chamber, to pay to the Tipstaff	0	6	8
Every Prisoner on a Commitment upon a Habeas corpus, at a Judge's Chamber, to pay to the Tipstaff	0	4	2
Every Prisoner on a Commitment in Court, to pay to the Tipstaff	0	7	6

No other Fees for any Prisoner for the Use of Chamber, Bed, Bedding, or Sheets, or upon Commitment or Discharge of any Prisoner in any Civil Action, nor any Commitment Fee to be taken of any Prisoner entitled to partake of the Poor's Box, nor any Chamber Rent to be taken of any Prisoner on the Common Side.

Ed. Bellany,   *R. Raymond,*
John Thompson,   *R. Eyre,*
Rob. Alsop,   *Thos Pengelly,*
John Barnard.

A TABLE of the FEES appointed to be taken by the Clerk of the Papers of *The Fleet Prison,* under and by virtue of a Rule or Order of the Court of Common Pleas, made in Easter Term, 13 Geo. I. 1727.

	£	s	d
Paid by the Prisoner			
There is due and ought to be paid to the Clerk of the Papers, for every Discharge of every Action	0	2	6
Paid by the Person applying for them			
And for the Copy of every Cause, not exceeding Three	0	1	0
And for each and every Cause, exceeding Three Causes, besides the Shilling a piece for each of the said first Three Causes	0	0	4
These Certificates being considered useless to the Prisoner, are never taken for			
There is also due, and ought to be paid to the Clerk of the Papers, for his Certificate of the Prisoner's Discharge, delivered to the Prisoner himself, without any regard to the Number of Actions he stood charged with	0	2	6
And for his Certificate to the Warden of such discharge	0	2	6
Paid by Persons suing out such Writs			
There is also due to the Clerk of the Papers, for the Allowance of every Writ			

of *Habeas Corpus*, a Fee of	0	5	4
And for the Return of the first Cause	0	4	0
And for every other Cause	0	2	0

Appendix 7:
The Rules regarding Chummages
[from the 1818 Report, pp 82-3]

COPY of an Order to regulate the distribution of Rooms and Chummages.

Fleet Prison, 10th January 1793.

THE warden, having heard complaints that the distribution of rooms and management respecting the chummage, in this prison, have been frequently irregular, thinks it expedient to make the following Regulations, which are to commence and take place on the first day of Hilary Term next; viz.

That every prisoner, on paying the commitment fee, shall (if there be no rooms empty) within twenty-four hours after, be chummed on the first room in rotation (beginning at No. I in the hall gallery) without fee, gratuity, or reward: and if such prisoner refuses to accept such chummage within that time, he shall not be entitled to any other chummage in the prison, until every prisoner at the time junior to such prisoner so refusing, shall have been chummed.

No prisoner shall carry on any trade or calling in such room without the consent and approbation of his chum, as well as of the warden.

All the rooms on the master's side shall receive chums in rotation (except the rooms in lower floor called Bartholomew Fair, and those called the Slip Rooms:) but no room whatsoever shall receive a second chum until every room, except the said rooms in Bartholomew Fair and the Slip Rooms, and every room (except as before excepted) shall continue in the same progressive manner to receive any such and every additional chum.

Every prisoner shall in like rotation succeed to a room, and if any prisoner refuses such room as shall fall to his or her turn by rotation, he or she shall not be permitted to hold any room, but lose his or her seniority, and from that time become a junior prisoner.

Any prisoner, after having duly succeeded to a room, being desirous to exchange it for another, if there are more than one vacant, shall be allowed to exchange once only for the room that has been vacant the longest time, but if he or she refuses to accept such room, he or she shall not be permitted to claim any other; and if there happens to be more than one prisoner desirous (and having the right) to exchange, the eldest prisoner shall have the prior right; but no prisoner can be admitted to claim who has not paid all arrears due on account of any former room which he or she has possessed.

If any prisoner shall receive any fee, gratuity or reward or the promise of any fee, gratuity or reward, for resigning his claim in favour of any other prisoner, such prisoner so resigning, shall lose his room and be considered disqualified for possessing another.

The succession to the Slip Rooms shall be subject to the same rotation and regulations as other rooms on the master's side, except that they shall not receive a chum.

Women, being prisoners, must be chummed on such rooms in the possession of women prisoners as are nearest in rotation, notwithstanding the interruption of the general rotation, or of any right or claim to the contrary.

COPY of an Order for regulating the Price to be received by Prisoners choosing to be paid out of their respective chummages, or letting their rooms on hire.

Fleet Prison, 16th Dec 1796.

THE Warden having heard various complaints respecting the unreasonable demands made by prisoners, for chamber rent and chummage, and the mischievous consequences arising therefrom, as also from the hiring of rooms to let again, has thought proper to order that from and after Saturday the 24th day of December instant, no person shall demand to receive for the use of any chamber which he or she may let unfurnished to a fellow prisoner, any greater rent than eight shillings and three-pence per week.

Also, that every or any prisoner choosing to let his or her room furnished, shall not take on demand a larger sum than fifteen shillings and three-pence per week for such furnished room.

And further, that no prisoner shall possess or hold in his or her own name, or in that of any other person, more than one chamber.

That any person proved to the satisfaction of the warden or his deputy to have the possession of, or the profits arising from the letting out to hire any other room than the one that has fallen to him or her by regular rotation or allowed claim, after the said day, shall be deprived or his or her room or chummage.

And that any person subject by rotation to receive a chum in the room such prisoner is in possession of, and being desirous of enjoying the sole and entire possession of the same, shall not give, pay or offer a greater sum than four shillings per week for such forbearance to enter into the joint possession of such room.

And in like manner, no chum of such room shall receive or demand any larger sum than four shillings per week for such forbearance to enter into the joint possession of the said room.

And any person receiving any larger sum, either directly or indirectly, than mentioned in this order, shall in like manner be deprived or his or her room or chummage.

Appendix 8:
The Report of John Howard on the Fleet Prison, 1777

[from John Howard, *State of the Prisons* ... (Warrington 1777). pp 156-64]

LONDON

HIS MAJESTY'S PRISON

THE FLEET, for debtors

Warden: *John Eyles,* Esq.

Deputy Warden and Clerk of the Papers, *Daniel Hopkins*

Salary

Fees   £1.   6.   8   }on entrance, per account

    0.   2.   0   Turnkey   } from the prisoners

   Licence, for Beer and Wine to *John Cartwright,* who holds of the Warden on lease the Tap &c. *(see Remarks.)*

PRISONERS,

Allowance, none   Garnish, 0 : 2 : 0

Number	In the House	In the Rules
1774, April 26.	171	71
1776, April 2,	241	78

CHAPLAIN, Rev. Mr *Horner*
    Duty - Sunday twice; Wednesday prayers
    Salary
SURGEON, none

REMARKS,

To this Prison were committed formerly those who incurred the displeasure of the Star-Chamber. In the 16th of Charles I when that Court was abolished, it became a Prison for Debtors; and for persons charged with contempt of the Courts of Chancery, Exchequer, and Common Pleas.

In 1728 many abuses practised by the Warden were the subject of parliamentary inquiry.

The Prison was rebuilt a few years since. At the front is a narrow court-yard. At each end of the building, there is a small projection, or wing. There are four floors, they call them *Galleries*, besides the cellar-floor, called *Bartholomew-Fair*. Each gallery consists of a passage in the middle, the whole length of the Prison, i.e. sixty-six yards; and rooms on each side of it about fourteen feet and a half by twelve and a half, and nine and a half high. A chimney and window in every room. The passages are narrow (not seven feet wide) and darkish, having only a window at each end.

On the first floor, the *Hall-Gallery*, to which you ascend eight steps, are, a Chapel, a Tap-room, a Coffee-room (lately made out of two rooms for Debtors), a room for the Turnkey, another for the Watchman, and eighteen rooms for Prisoners.

Besides the Coffee-room and Tap-room, two of those eighteen rooms and all the cellar-floor, except a lock-up room to confine the disorderly, and another room for the Turnkey, are held by the Tapster, John Cartwright, who bought the remainder of the lease at public auction in 1775. The cellar-floor is sixteen steps below the hall-gallery. It consists of the two rooms just now mentioned, the

Tapster's kitchen, his four large beer and wine cellars, and fifteen rooms for Prisoners. These fifteen and the two before mentioned on the hall-gallery, the Tapster lets to Prisoners for four to eight shillings a week. [footnote states: An imposition of the same kind is noted in the Report of the Gaol-Committee 1728.]

On the *first Gallery* (that next above the hall-gallery) are twenty five rooms for Prisoners. On the *second Gallery* twenty-seven rooms. One of them, fronting the staircase, is their Committee-room. A room at one end is an Infirmary. At the other end in a large room over the Chapel is a dirty Billiard-table; kept by the Prisoner who sleeps in that room. On the highest story are twenty-seven rooms. Some of these upper rooms, viz. those in the wings, are larger than the rest; being over the Chapel, the Tap-room, &c.

All the rooms I have mentioned are for Master's-side Debtors. the weekly rent of those not held by the Tapster is one shilling and three-pence unfurnished. They fall to the Prisoners in succession, thus: when a room becomes vacant, the first Prisoner upon the list of such as have paid their entrance-fees, takes possession of it. When the Prison was built, the Warden gave each Prisoner his choice of a room according to his seniority as Prisoner. If all the rooms be occupied, a new comer must hire of some tenant a part of his room, or shift as he can. Prisoners are excluded from right of succession to the rooms held by the Tapster, and let at the high rents aforesaid.

The apartments for Common-side Debtors are only part of the right wing of the Prison. Besides the cellar (which was intended for their kitchen but is occupied with lumber, and shut up) there are four floors. On each floor is a room about twenty-four or twenty-five feet square with a fire-place; and on the sides seven closets or cabins to sleep in. Such of these prisoners as swear in Court of before a Commissioner that they are not worth five pounds, and cannot subsist without charity, have the donations which are sent to the Prison, and the begging-box, and grate. Of them there were at my last visit sixteen.

1 have in the Report of the Committee of the House of Commons 1728 a Table of some Charities: but I saw no such Table in the Prison.

There is plenty of water from the river and pumps: and a spacious yard behind the Prison.

I mentioned the billiard-table. They also play in the yard at skittles, Mississippi, fives, tennis, &c. And not only the Prisoners: I saw among them several butchers and others from the market; who are admitted here as at another public house. The same may be seen in many other Prisons where the Gaoler keeps or lets the tap. Besides the inconvenience of this to Prisoners; the frequenting of a Prison lessens the dread of being confined in one.

On Monday night there is a Wine-Club: on Thursday night a Beer-Club: each lasting usually till one or two in the morning. I need not say how much riot these occasion; and how the sober Prisoners are annoyed by them.

Seeing the Prison crowded with women and children, I procured an accurate list of them; and found that on (or about) the 5th of April 1776, when there were on the Master's side 213 Prisoners, on the Common side 30, total 243; their wives (including women of an appellation not so honourable) and children were 475.

I was surprised to see in this Prison a Table of Fees containing only those of the Clerks of the Papers and Inquiries: and that the date of it was 1727, i.e. before the Committee of the House of Commons made their inquiry. I did not doubt but another Table was settled after than inquiry; and that it contained the Warden's Fees also. But upon asking the Clerk of the Papers for a later Table, I was referred to that which hung up. It is as follows.

[The list is a modified version of that contained in Appendix 6]

There is in the Prison a Table of Rules or Orders. They were made at very distant times, from the reign of Queen Elizabeth, to the date they bear; and some of them partly coincide with others: those which do so I have put together to avoid repetition, and have presumed to abridge the whole.

[The list is printed in full in Appendix 3]

There is, moreover, a little Code of Laws, eighteen in number, enacted by the Master's-side Debtors, and printed by D. Jones 1774. it establishes a President, a Secretary, and a Committee, which is to be chosen every month, and to consist of three members from each Gallery. They are to meet in the Committee-room every Thursday: and at other times when summoned by the Cryer, at command of the President, or of a majority of their own number. They are to raise contributions by assessment: to hear complaints: determine disputes: levy fines; and seize goods for payment. Their sense to be deemed the sense of the whole House. The President or Secretary to hold the cash; the Committee to dispose of it. Their Scavenger to wash the galleries once a week; to water and sweep them every morning before eight; to sweep the yard twice every week; and to light the lamps all over the House. No person to throw out water &c. any where but at the sinks in the yard. The Cryer may take of a Stranger a penny for calling a Prisoner to him; and of a Complainant two-pence for summoning a special Committee. For blasphemy, swearing, riot, drunkenness, &c. the Committee to fine at discretion: for damaging a lamp, fine a shilling. They are to take from a New Comer, *on the first Sunday*, besides the two shillings Garnish to be spent in wine, one shilling and six-pence to be appropriated to the use of the House.

Common-side Prisoners *to be confined to their own apartments*, and not to associate with these Law-makers, nor to use the same conveniences.

Bibliography

MANUSCRIPT MATERIAL

The Public Record Office, London
    State, Treasury and Exchequer papers
    Records of the Court of Common Pleas
    The Fleet Prison books

British Library, London
    Additional, Egerton, Harleian and Hargrave manuscripts
    Fleet Prison Collection of Newspapers Cuttings and Broadsides etc [pm
        11633 h2)

Guildhall Library, London
    Surveyor Justice plans
    St Bride's vestry minutes
    Noble collection

Corporation of London Record Office
    Sessions papers
    Miscellaneous manuscripts

Bodleian Library, Oxford
    Tanner, Rawlinson and Ashmolean manuscripts

PRINTED WORKS

The location and press mark [pm] of the pamphlets are given.

Ashton, John: *The Fleet, its River, Prison, and Marriages* (London1888).

Babington, A: *The English Bastille* (London 1971).

Bambridge, Thomas: *Mr Bambridge's Case against the Bill now Depending* (London 1729) [GLL, broadside 7.27].

> *The Committee's Memorial against Mr Bambridge* (London 1729) [BL, pm 816 m15/31].

> *To the Honourable the Commons of Great Britain in Parliament now Assembled, the Case of Thomas Bambridge* (London 1729) [BL, pm 515 L5/27].

Bassett, Margery: "The Fleet Prison in the Middle Ages", *University of Toronto Law Journal*, V (1944) 383-402.

Berisford, John: *An Argument that it is Impossible for the Nation to be Rid of all the Grievances Occasioned by the Marshall of the King's Bench and the Warden of the Fleet without an Utter Extirpation of their Present Offices* (London 1699).

Bird, Lieutenant: *A Letter from the Shades to Thomas Bambridge in Newgate* (London 1729).

Blackstone, Thomas: *The Laws of England* (Kerr's edition, London 1857).

Brewer, J and Styles, J, *An Ungovernable People* (London 1980).

Brown, Ivor: *Dickens in his Time* (London 1963).

Brown, Roger L: "The Minters of Wapping", *East London Papers*, XIX (1972) 77-86.

> "The Rise and Fall of the Fleet Marriages", in R B Outhwaite, (ed), *Marriage and Society* (London 1981), pp 117-36.

Brown, William: *The Fleet: A Brief Account* (London 1843).

Burford, E J: *In the Clink* (London 1977).

Burn, J S: *The Star Chamber* (London 1870).

Buxton, Thomas Fowell: *An Inquiry whether Crime and Misery are Produced or Prevented by our Present System of Prison Discipline* (London 1818).

Bygrave: *The Case of Mr Bygrave, Late Clerk of the Papers of the Fleet* (London 1729) [BL, pm C116 14/104].

Calendar of State Papers Domestic.

Calendar of Treasury Books.

Calendar of Treasury Papers.

Case of Debtors now Confined, The [GL, pm broadise 18.20].

Case of the Mortagees of the Office of Marshall of the King's Bench, The [BL, pm BS fol Bills 359 d9-12/45].

Chandler's *Debates of the House of Commons* (London 1742).

Church, Leslie: *Oglethorpe* (London 1932).

Clay, C T: "The Keepership of the Old Palace of Westminster", *EHR*, LIX (1944) 1-21.

Clements, John: *The Case of John Clements* (London 1693) [BL, pm 816 m15/14f].

Coke, Edward: *The Institutes of the Laws of England* (London 1642).

Colvin, H M (ed): *The History of the King's Works* (London 1976).

Committee's Memorial against Bambridge, The (London 1729) [BL, pm 816 m15/31].

Considerations about the Regulating of the King's Bench and Fleet Prisons [GLL, pm broadside 8.124].

Considerations Humbly Offered in Relation to the Bill now Depending in Parliament for the Further Relief of Creditors in Cases of Escapes [BL, pm 1888 C11/15].

Considerations on the Laws between Debtors and Creditors (London 1779) [BL, pm 518 il5/4].

Considerations relating to the Bill for the Regulating of the Prisons of the King's Bench and the Fleet (London 1702) [BL, pm 816 m15/20].

Cranley, Thomas (ed by Frederic Ouvry), *Amanda, or the Reformed Whore* (London 1869).

Debtor and Creditor's Assistant: A Key to the King's Bench and Fleet Prisons, The (London 1793) [BL, pm 518, h17].

Debtor and Creditor's Guide, The (editions of 1813 and 1823).

Description of the King's Bench, Fleet and Marshalsea Prisons, A (London 1828).

Dickens, Charles, *Pickwick Papers*.

Dobb, Clifford: "London's Prisons", in *Shakespeare Survey*, XVII (1964) 87-100.
    Unpublished Oxford B.Litt thesis, 1952, *Life and Conditions in the London Prisons, 1553-1643, with special reference to Contemporary Literature*.

Driver, Cecil: *Tory Radical: the Life of Richard Oastler* (New York, 1949).

Duffin, P W and Lloyd, Thomas: *The Trial of P W Duffin and Thomas Lloyd for a Libel in the Fleet Prison* (London 1793).

Enquiry into the Nature and Effect of the Writ of Habeas Corpus, A (London 1758).

Entick, J: *History and Survey of London* (London 1766).

Fees of the London Prisons (London 1701) [BL, pm 816 m15/22].

Feltham, John: *The Picture of London* (London 1803).

General Considerations relating to a Bill for Regulating the Abuses of Prisons and Pretended Privileged Places (London *c* 1697) [BL, pm cup 645 b11/33].

George, M D: *London Life in the Eighteenth Century* (London 1951).

Gregg, P: *Free Born John* (London 1961).

Harris, Alexander: *The Oeconomy of the Fleete* (edited by Augustus Jessop for the Camden Society, NS XXV, 1879).

Hatton, Edward: *A New View of London* (2 volumes, London 1708).

Hibbert, C: *The Road to Tyburn* (London 1957).

Holdsworth, W: *A History of English Law* (9th edition , London 1966).

Honeybourne, Marjorie B: "The Fleet and its Neighbourhood in Early and Medieval Times", *London Topographical Record*, XIX (1947) 13-87.

Howard, John: *The State of the Prisons in England and Wales* (1st edn, 1777; 2nd edn, 1780; 3rd edn, 1784: all published at Warrington).
   An Account of the Present State of the Prisons in London and Westminster taken from a late Publication of John Howard, and Printed by Order of the Society lately Instituted for giving Effect to his Majesty's Proclamation against Vice and Immorality (London 1789).

Howell, T B: *A Complete Collection of State Trials* (London 1816).

Hughson, David: *Walks through London* (London 1817).

Humble Petition of Debtors in the Fleet Prison, The (London 1750)   [GL broadside 18.18].

Innes, Joanna: "The King's Bench Prison in the later Eighteenth Century", in J Brewer and J Styles, *An Ungovernable People* (London 1980), pp 250-98.

Jones, William: *Observations on the Insolvent Debtors' Acts* (London 1827).

Journal of the House of Commons.

Keble, Jos: *Reports in the Court of King's Bench* (London 1685).

Leigh, William: *New Picture of London* (London, editions of 1823 and 1834).

Lilburn, John: *Liberty Vindicated against Slavery* (London 1646).

Lillywhite, Bryant: *London Coffee Houses* (London 1963).

London Sessions Papers.

Lord Keeper: *The Present Lord Keeper ... His Report to Her Majesty upon the Petition of Mr Tilly and Mr Leighton* (London c 1705) [GLL, pm broadside 17.26].

McConville, Sean: *A history of English Prison Administration* (volume 1, London 1981).

Macdonald, Thomas: *A Treatise on Civil Imprisonment in England* (London 1791).

Mackay, John, senior: *A True State of the Proceedings of the Prisoners of the Fleet Prison, in order to the Redressing of their Grievances before the Court of Common Pleas* (London 1729).

Makower, SV: *Richard Savage* (London 1909).

Malcolm, J P, *Londinium Redivivum* (London 1802).

Microcosm of London, The (London 1904 edition).

Neale, Robert Dorset: *The Prisoners Guide, or every Debtor his own Lawyer* (London 1800).

Neild, James: *Account of the Persons Confined for Debt in England and Wales* (London 1800).
   State of the Prisons (London 1812).

Nightengale, Joseph: *London and Middlesex* (1815).

Notestein, Wallace: *Commons Debates, 1621* (New Haven, 1935).

Oastler, Richard: *The Fleet Papers* (London 1841-2).

Observations on the Law of Arrest for Debt (London 1827).

Oration on the Oppression of Jailers, Spoken in the Fleet Prison, A (London 1731).

Paget, William: *The Humours of the Fleet* (London 1749) [contained in BL, pm 116 h2].

Parliamentary Papers, 1833-42.

Pearce, Jones: *A Treatise on the Abuses of the Laws, particularly in Actions by Arrest* (London 1814).

Penrice, William: *The Extraordinary Case of William Penrice, late Deputy Marshall of the King's Bench Prison* (London 1768).

Pierce, Egan: *Life in London* (London, new edition of 1904).

Pitt, Moses: *The Cry of the Oppressed* (London 1691).

Plea for the City Orphans and Prisoners for Debt, A (London 1690) [GLL, pm A8.7(48)].

Powell, B R: *Eighteenth Century London Life* (London 1937).

Pugh, Ralph B: *Imprisonment in Medieval England* (Cambridge, 1970).

"The King's Prisons before 1250", *Transactions of the Royal Historical Society*, 5th series, V (1955) 1-22.

Reasons against the said Bill Suppose, for the Relief of Creditors, and Preventing Escapes (London 1698) [BL, pm Cup 645 bll/37].

Reasons regarding the Bill for the Future Relief of Creditors in Cases of Escapes (London c 1698) [BL, pm 816 m15/33].

Reasons why the Bill should Pass without the Clause Proposed by Edmund Boulter [BL, pm 816 m15/33].

Remarks upon the Bill for Preventing Escapes out of the Queen's Bench and Fleet Prisons (London 1702) [BL, pm Cup 645 b11/4].

Remembrancia of the City of London, Index, (London 1878).

Report of the Committee Appointed to Enquire into the State of the Gaols of this Kingdom, relating to the Fleet Prison, A (London 1729).

Report of the Committee Appointed to Enquire into the State of the Gaols of this Kingdom, relating to the King's Bench Prison, A (London 1729).

Report of the Committee Appointed to Enquire into the State of the Gaols of this Kingdom, relating to the Marshalsea Prison, and further relating to the Fleet Prison, A (London 1729).

Report of the Committee Appointed to Enquire into the Practice and Effects of Imprisonment for Debt, The, in *Journal of the House of Commons*, XLVII (1792) 640-71.

Report of the Committee Appointed to Enquire into the State of the King's Bench, Fleet and Marshalsea Prisons, in PP 1814-15 (152) IV 531.

Report of the Commissioners Appointed to Enquire into the State, Conduct and

Management of the Prison and Gaol of the Fleet, The, in PP 1819 (109) XI
  325.

*Report of the Sub-Committee respecting Prisons and Houses of Correction of the
  Society for Giving Effect to His Majesty's Proclamation against Vice and
  Immorality, The*, (London 1790) [GLL, pm Pam 3823].

Riley, H T: *Memorials of London and London Life* (London 1868).

Rowcroft, C: *Chronicles of the Fleet Prison* (3 vols, London 1847).

*Schedule or List of the Prisoners in the Fleet Remaining in Custody, May 23,
  1653, A* [BL, pm E698/13].

Several Considerations for Passing the Act relating to the Discharge of Prisoners
  [BL, pm 816 m15/184 (7)].

Short View of Some Complaints against the Warden of the Fleet, A (London
  1705) [GLL, pm Broadside 29.86].

Smith, William: *Mild Punishments Sound Policy* (London 1778).

        State of the Gaols in London, Westminster and Southwark (London
  1776).

Smollett, Tobias: *The Adventures of Peregrine Pickle*.

*Some Better Reasons for Passing the Act relating to the Discharge of Prisoners
  and the Regulation of Gaols and Gaolers* (BL, pm 816 m15/41).

Some Brief Reasons for Passing the Act relating to the Discharge of Prisoners
  [BL, pm 816. m15/184 (7)].

Some Considerations about the Regulating of the King's Bench and Fleet Prisons
  [BL, pm Cup 645, b11/40].

Some Considerations for Regulating the King's Bench Prison [GLL, broadside
  8.124].

*Some Considerations Humbly Offered in Relation to the Bill now Depending in
  Parliament for the Further Relief of Creditors in Cases of Escapes* (London
  1698) [BL, pm 1888 c11/15].

*Some Considerations relating to the Bill for Regulating the King's Bench and
  Fleet Prisons* (London 1701) [BL, pm Cup 645 b11/39].

Speech without Doors, on behalf of the Insolvent Debtors in the Fleet Prison, A
  (London 1729).

Speed, Samuel: *The Prisoners' Complaint, or the Cries of the King's Bench*
  (London 1673).

State of the King's Bench Prison, The (London 1765) [BL, pm 748 f12/8].

Stephen, James: *Considerations on Imprisonment for Debt* (London 1770).

Stockdale, Eric: *A Study of Bedford Prison* (London 1977).

Stow, John, *Survey of the Cities of London and Westminster* (edition of John
  Strype, London 1720).

Taylor, John: *The Case of John Taylor, Esq, Marshall of the King's Bench, in
  relation to a Clause added to the Bill, entitled "An Act for regulating the
  Abuses of Prisons and Pretended Privileged Places"* [BL, pm 1888 c11/17].

Warden of the Fleet's Case, in relation to Mr Baldwin Leighton's Petition to the

Honourable House of Commons, Wherein he Suggests the Forfeiture of the Office of Fleet to the King and the Grant thereof to Himself, The [BL, pm 1888, c11/61].

Webb, Sidney and Beatrice, *English Prisons under Local Government* (London, edn of 1963).

Wheatley, H B: *Hogarth's London* (London 1907).

Wheatley, H B and Cunningham, P: *London Past and Present* (London 1891).

Williams, Montagu: *Round London* (London 1893).

Wood, Simon: *Remarks on the Fleet Prison, or Lumber House for Men and Women* (London 1733).

World Displayed, or Mankind Painted in their Proper Colours to which is Added, a Description of a Prison, The (London 1742) [GLL, pm A7.3/60].

Index

STUDIES IN BRITISH HISTORY